FORSYTH LIBRARY - FHSU
072S524s 1966
main   Some forerun

2 1765 0006 7864 2

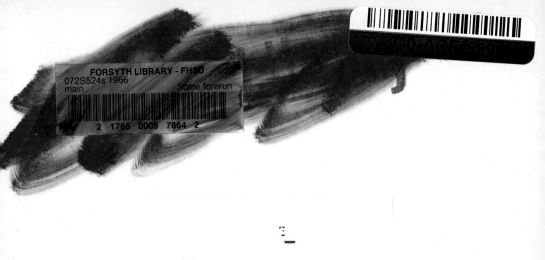

SOME FORERUNNERS
of the
NEWSPAPER IN ENGLAND

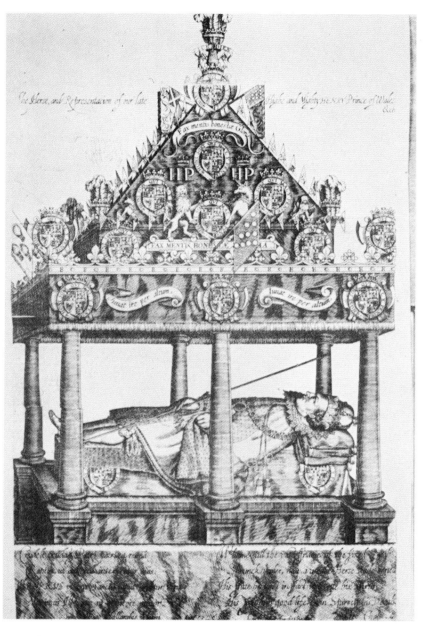

The Herse, and Representacion of our late Highe and Mighty
HENRY Prince of Wales &ct:

From *An epicede or Funerall Song: On the most disastrous Death, of the High-borne
Prince of Men, Henry Prince of Wales, &c.,*
by George Chapman (1612)

SOME FORERUNNERS
of the
NEWSPAPER IN ENGLAND

1476-1622

BY

M. A. SHAABER

1966

OCTAGON BOOKS, INC.

New York

072
S524 s
1966

Copyright 1929 University of Pennsylvania Press

Reprinted 1966
by special arrangement with M. A. Shaaber

OCTAGON BOOKS, INC.
175 FIFTH AVENUE
NEW YORK, N. Y. 10010

LIBRARY OF CONGRESS CATALOG CARD NUMBER: 66-17494

Printed in U.S.A. by
NOBLE OFFSET PRINTERS, INC.
NEW YORK 3, N. Y.

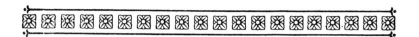

PREFACE

SOME forerunners of the newspaper" is almost a misnomer as the title of this treatise: in reality, it is almost exclusively concerned with but one—printed news. Many other departments of our daily journalism have their forerunners too, but I have made no attempt to give an account of them except in so far as they are inseparable from printed news. I have not even described all kinds of printed news: there is no mention in these pages (except a few times incidentally) of reports of travel and discovery, numerous as they were in the sixteenth and seventeenth centuries; but these have not been overlooked as most of the kinds of news treated here have been. For a comprehensive understanding of the beginnings of English journalism, we still want an examination of written news, of the tract, the ancestor of the editorial, of the "feature story," and of printed advertisements. Much, therefore, remains to be added to our knowledge of these beginnings, and I feel certain that most of it would be interesting and some of it important. Indeed, I hope I shall be able to make further explorations myself.

What these pages contain, then, is rather a first assault, tentative and incomplete, than an inclusive or definitive account of the news printed before the evolution of the newspaper in England. For, although the subject is extensive and the name of journalism has often been applied to the ephemeral writings of the sixteenth century, this treatise is, so far as I am aware, the first attempt to survey any part of the length and breadth of this journalism. On this account, I am all the more desirous of acknowledging the help I have had from the labors of two scholars who, with special reference to the broadside ballad, have done almost all that has been done to illuminate the subject of English journalism before the advent of the newspaper—Sir Charles Firth, who has written a "ballad history" almost coextensive with the period treated here, and Dr. Hyder E. Rollins, who, in various articles on the ballad and in the introductions to his collections of ballads, has again and again called attention to the rôle played by the ballad in the journalism of the time. Furthermore, from his *Analytical index to the ballad-entries* I have borrowed many identifications.

I should like also to acknowledge my indebtedness to the *Short-title catalogue of books printed in England . . . 1475–1640*, for there is no evidence of this debt in the ensuing pages. Without this invaluable list I should never have found nearly so many early books of news as I have found; besides, almost all my attributions of anonymously-printed books to their authors and publishers and most conjectural dates of publication have simply been lifted from the *S. T. C.*

I should like to return thanks to the libraries which have permitted me to examine books in their possession—specifically, the British Museum, the archiepiscopal library at Lambeth Palace, the Bodleian, the Cambridge University Library, and the Society of Antiquaries of London. Sir Leicester Harmsworth, Bt., has also been good enough to let me use books from his collection. The librarians of Queen's College, Oxford, St. John's College and Emmanuel College, Cambridge, the Shrewsbury School, and the Henry E. Huntington Library have helped me by furnishing copies. I am grateful to the British Museum and the Bodleian Library for permission to reproduce the illustrations included in this book.

I owe at least a word of thanks to my colleague, Mr. R. D. James, for the advice he gave me on points about which I consulted him.   I owe much more to my teacher, Dr. Felix E. Schelling, who has been the godfather of this treatise from the beginning, whose sympathetic encouragement and good judgement have both inspired and steadied it, and whose acceptance of it is its best recommendation.

To Mr. Alfred H. Gumaer, who has helped to read the proof, I am very grateful for his patient assistance.

CONTENTS

CONTENTS

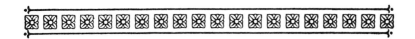

ILLUSTRATIONS

[xi]

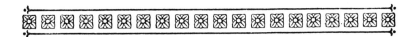

CHAPTER I

INTRODUCTION

THE word *news* is only a little more than four hundred years old; the *New English Dictionary* says that it was "in common use only after 1500," and the earliest example which it cites, from Scotland, is dated 1423. Of the several English synonyms, *tydings* seems to be the oldest. But the thing itself is almost as old as the hills. The child of chance and curiosity and simple wonder, it must have had its origin in the earliest awakenings of human intelligence. We are so used, nowadays, to associating it with the ink and paper by means of which it is recorded and disseminated that we may sometimes forget that it existed—was collected, exchanged, and admired—in all probability before ink and paper were first manufactured and certainly long before it was much circulated in written form. All through the records of history, we find evidence of an appetite for news which found means of gratifying itself with little or none of that elaborate organization by which it is fed today. We know, for example, that in early times the marketplace served as a kind of exchange where bits of news, important and trivial, were bruited about and discussed. We also hear, again and again, that travelers were eagerly pumped of the news they brought from the places they had visited, that, indeed, it was at least a point of good manners, if not a duty, for a traveler to relate the news he had picked up, often, it would seem, as a fair return for hospitality. Travelers meeting on the road would exchange bits of news in a spirit almost fraternal. A curious instance of the passing of news on the wing, so to speak,

[1]

occurs in an account written by Somerset-Herald (no idle gossip, we may be sure) of the Earl of Nottingham's embassy to Spain in 1605.[1] Just off the English coast, his lordship gave orders to hail a passing sail, apparently to ask news of the weather out at sea. She proved to be a barque from Barnstaple returning from Bayonne; how far she was able to satisfy his lordship's curiosity Somerset-Herald does not say, but he does record that she "declared for newes that there was a yongue Prince borne in Spayne."

The usefulness of private letters in circulating news is obvious too. The obligation to pass on to his correspondent whatever news he may have heard was rather well understood to devolve upon a letter writer; in Renaissance times and later, a literate traveler abroad was sure to write the news of the countries he visited to his friends at home, was even charged to do so. Back home, his letters would be passed round through many hands for the sake of the news in them. Important or curious persons—politicians, courtiers, great merchants—particularly anxious to know what was going on abroad established a regular correspondence with their friends or their agents in important cities and were thus kept *au courant* with events of the kind it was necessary for them to have knowledge of. In time, the writing of newsletters which anybody might buy became a trade, though there is no evidence of the public newsletter writer in England until the time of Charles I, when the printed newspaper had already been evolved. As for official intelligence—news of affairs of state and matters touching the public interest, imparted by the government itself—from very early times this seems to have been communicated by oral proclamation; furthermore, the ingenious

---

[1] *A relation of such things as were obserued . . . in the iourney of . . . Charles Earle of Nottingham, . . . to . . . Spaine: . . . for the maintenance of Peace betweene . . . Great Brittaine and Spaine . . .* By Rob[ert] Treswell, Esq. London: for Gregorie Seton, 1605.

Romans developed written proclamations and records in various ways anticipating the modern newspaper. Letters relating the progress of the campaign in France were written by King Henry V to various municipalities in England, but it would hardly appear that they were sent purely out of a benevolent desire to keep his subjects informed, for they alternated with letters demanding immediate supplies.

It is abundantly evident, then, that the newspaper did not create news, but that news (plus the printing press) created the newspaper. What is usually reckoned the first English newspaper appeared in the spring of 1622. The first number, as we learn from the Stationers' register,[2] was dated 14 May. The second, the earliest of which a copy still exists, was put out a week later, 23 May. This periodical had no regular name, but the date of the issue usually appeared first, and from the fact that the title of the issue of 23 May commences with the words "Weekely Newes," it is often alluded to under that name. Beginning in October, the issues were numbered; with a little irregularity, the periodical was continued until 1632. As a matter of fact, it was not, strictly speaking, a newspaper at all, and it most certainly was not so called. It was printed in the form of a book of about twenty pages, on the average, and was called a newsbook. In the seventeenth century, a "paper" meant a single sheet; the word *newspaper* and the custom of printing news-periodicals on a single sheet do not occur until after the Restoration.[3]

But nearly a hundred and fifty years intervened between 1622 and the introduction of printing into England, a hundred and fifty years of which the histories of journalism tell us nothing. Yet on *a priori* grounds, without a shred of evidence, one would suppose that news was surely put

---

[2] *A Currant of generall newes Dated the 14th of may last.* Entered 18 May 1622 by [Nicholas] Bourne and Thomas Archer (Arber, IV. 68).

[3] See Williams: *History of English journalism.*

in print before 14 May 1622, for an institution like the newspaper is not created overnight, nor does it spring full-armed from the forehead of Jupiter, or, more precisely, from that of Mercurius Britannicus. It is the aim of this dissertation to give an account of the printing of news in England during these hundred and fifty years, to trace out the antecedents of the newspaper, to show, indeed, that in 1622 it was in no way a novelty except in being issued in a continuous series. During this period a great deal of news was indeed printed; the following pages will attempt to describe it, to show whence it came, for whom and by whom it was written and printed, and how, summarized and published at brief intervals, it was shaped into the news-paper.

For present purposes, it is happily unnecessary to take into account those metaphysical aspects of the idea of news which trouble modern journalists and *censores morum.* They find this idea elusive and difficult to fix in words; though newspaper men write books on what is news, in the end they are obliged to rely chiefly on parables, such as the classic illustration of the reporter and the dog, to define the commodity they deal in. As far as this discussion is con-cerned, news is, in the words of the *New English Dictionary,* merely a "report or account of recent events or occurrences, brought or coming to one as new information" (or, by allow-ance, the events themselves). News is less than journal-ism, which is all writing for the public prints on matters of current interest; topical writing is news only when it is an account of recent events, a narrative; news is primarily matter of fact, data, particulars which tell a story, the story of to-day's intimate history.

The modern newspaper contains, of course, much besides news—advertisements, editorial or leading articles, fiction, "feature" articles, reviews, to say nothing of photographic illustrations, comic strips, and crossword puzzles. The newsbooks of Charles I's time, on the other hand, save for an occasional rude woodcut, were devoted exclusively to news, or to what passed for news in those days, and most of the early newsbooks and newspapers are exactly described by their name. Certain of these elements which go into the making of the modern newspaper—certainly the editorial and the "feature" article—can trace their ancestry back to the sixteenth century, when matter of the same sort was written for the same reasons as now and published separately, only to be caught up later in the ample drag-net of the public journal. But this discussion is concerned primarily with the element of news; it is concerned exclusively with news except in so far as the news published before 1622 cannot be entirely disentangled from other matter, from the moralizing, for example, with which it nearly always went arm in arm. In the sixteenth century, the news was not published in vast miscellaneous bundles such as our newspapers are (in which, however, the news is plainly distinguished from whatever accompanies it), but it was seldom published alone, without being tempered or seasoned with something else. According to the standards of modern journalism, events should be observed accurately and dispassionately, as if the reporter were an Olympian able to pierce the partiality of the actors in daily occurrences to the truth that lies behind their postures, and, unlike the Olympian deities, were above all partiality himself. If we apply this standard to what was printed in the sixteenth century, we shall find almost no news at all, for at that time news was almost invariably partial, without scruple or apology. Comment never lagged far behind it, and we shall sometimes find it in the company of other things as well, as will duly appear. It is quite true that comment on current events is often just as interesting as news itself, and certainly a London tradesman in the sixteenth century can scarcely have made a distinction between them in his own mind. To him, a new assault by a fire-eating reformer, a Bale or a Joye, on the Bishop of Winchester, let us say, or a tart reply by a Catholic apologist such as Sir Thomas More, was, as news, at least as interesting as a narrative record of a diet in Germany. But the present discussion, as a rule, takes into account only such publications as contain data and particulars, as offer a report of recent events. To find records of this sort it will often be necessary to tolerate the most tedious impertinences and we shall find the news masked by exhortation, lamentation, objurgation, and a dozen other concomitants. But we must look for it wherever it may be found.

In fact, it may even be doubted whether such a thing as a concept or definition of news existed in the sixteenth century. Without having a very nice idea of what news is, or thinking much about it, the average man to-day at least knows where to look for news when he wants it—in his newspaper, and there he does not expect to find it in the editorial columns, among the advertisements, or in the daily *feuilleton*. To him, news is at any rate something distinct from the other kinds of reading matter which his newspaper furnishes him. But in the sixteenth century, news of the sort we have to do with—printed news, public news—was a thing so new that the concept of it must have been only in the earliest stages of formation. News itself there had always been since events began to happen on this planet, but never before had an ordinary man been able to go to St. Paul's churchyard and, for a few pennies, buy news, news which thereby became his own. Surely this innovation revolutionized the concept of news, and equally surely time was required to make the intellectual adjustment. Is it, indeed, too much to say that making information public and common property was an epoch-making step?—though, to be sure, it belongs to the philoso-

[6]

pher or the historian rather than to the literary student to develop notions of that sort.

The point for us is that, if printed news was such a tremendous novelty, it is no wonder that the popular idea of it was ill-defined, that it was not easily distinguishable from other topical matter, and that it was commonly found in mixed company. When the idea of news was still unfixed, it is not surprising that men wrote and published news from many motives, of which the disinterested desire to serve the public interest that prompts the modern journalist is only one. Consequently much news was written by men who were moved by an ulterior purpose—the inculcation of godliness, for example, or the glorification of the English nation—and who studied this purpose at the same time as they reported news. Consequently, also, the ethical standards of the age, which as yet scarcely recognized news in print as something good in itself, and by which a homily inspiring the sluggish souls of men or a warning to the unrepentent of the doom to come was unquestionably rated higher than mere news, may have approved, even demanded, the mixture with news of something meet for edification. It is even possible that the suspicious attitude of the authorities of church and state, who were inclined to think of news as something dangerous and explosive except when they published it themselves, made it wise to justify the printing of news by drawing a moral from it or impressing it into the service of an irreproachable cause. The printers and booksellers themselves, who were interested in news because they could sell it, because it was popular with their clientele, but no more interested, with but few exceptions, than in any other matter for publication that was equally popular, seem to have had no very clear notion of what is news, as their publication of it in a great variety of guises and their indiscriminate use of the word *news* itself would indicate.

[7]

And least of all did the London tradesman, the typical reader of the news that was published in the sixteenth century, hold clearly-defined ideas on the subject. Curious, news-loving as he was, he very likely also admired the news-writer's holy zeal in interpreting the birth of a two-headed pig in Hampshire as a sign of God's wrath against the sinfulness of his people in England and was thrilled by the news-writer's exultation over the checkmating of the latest Jesuitical treason against the queen. Even if he had a conscious preference for unalloyed information, the idea of public news was still so delightfully novel to him that he was uncritically content to take his news as he found it. Indeed, in these lay sermons with which his news was tricked out, he may have found his justification for reading it, for all the professed satirists of the time (especially in the reign of King James and later, when they gave the subject a liberal share of their attention) assured him that his fondness for news was a paltry and shameful weakness sure to lead him into dotage, as, a century later, it led Addison's political upholsterer. At any rate, it is quite certain that he did not feel, as the modern newspaper-reader does, that he was entitled to his news; rather it was a boon for which he was humbly grateful, and which he took as it came.

But however ill-defined the sixteenth-century concept of news as matter for separate publication, once we extract the news of the time from the extraneous matter with which it was published, we find it very much like the news in this morning's paper. It is a record of affairs of state, of war and battle at sea and on land, of the conduct of the great magnates, the heroes, and the personalities of the age, of murders, deeds of violence, and acts of God. As far as the events which they furnish an account of are concerned, the most striking difference between the printed news of these earlier times and the contemporary newspaper is what the former omitted. Some reasons for these omissions will be suggested in a later chapter. Of all the many fields in which the modern newspaper gleans its news, there seems to be but one which was utterly neglected in the sixteenth century (as it was likewise neglected until the second quarter of the nineteenth), *viz.*, local news, news of the more ordinary daily occurrences in the life of the great mass of the citizenry. It is as if the quality of being extraordinary, sensational, prodigious was regarded as essential to news, or at least the most acceptable characteristic of it. News was not merely information: it was exciting information. Certainly news that stirred the greatest astonishment, the most profound wonder, the most unexpected surprise was the most copiously published; news must have been understood as something which excited the reader's feelings very strongly. The eager interest in the sensational which our stern Catos reprehend in the newspaper-readers of this day and age in no way exceeds that of their sixteenth-century ancestors. All in all, the journalists of these early times, in their own quaint way, and within the limits beyond which they dared not trespass, "covered" the news happening round about them with a fair degree of thoroughness.

One further point had better be made clear in advance. The printing of news on the continent grew up in substantially the same way as in England, but some years earlier. It might therefore be argued that English journalism was imitated from foreign example. In some ways, it may have been. There is no doubt whatever that foreign books were imported into England, and some of them may have been books of news. It seems especially likely that books of news in Latin, printed on the continent, were often circulated in England. Certainly these, when imported into England, could have been read by the educated classes just as easily as anywhere else, and there is every probability that they were imported and read. For instance, I have been able to find no trace of a contemporary account, printed in England, of the meeting of Henry VIII and Francis I at the Field of the Cloth of Gold in 1519. In the British Museum, however, there are several such narratives printed in France, one in Latin[4] and three in French. It is by no means impossible that these books were imported for English consumption, and, as far as the Latin book is concerned, it is even likely. Certainly an English bookseller ordering books from abroad or visiting the continental book markets to buy stock would have realized that he could find a sale at home for such a book as the *Campi, Convivii atque ludorum ordo* mentioned above and might very well have bought a supply. But, at that time, it could hardly have struck Englishmen as an innovation. From the middle of Henry VIII's reign to the accession of Elizabeth, a good many English books were printed abroad at the instance of the English reformers, but when circulated in England these tracts were no new departure; the same sort of thing, containing better approved doctrine and less invidious information, had long since been printed there. A great many foreign books of news were imported into England after about 1555 and published in translation, but they do not differ essentially from those produced at home at the same time and earlier.

In all this commerce between the English and the continental publishing trade, there is no evidence and little probability of any direct influence of continental trade practices upon the printing of news in England, and what happened in England can quite sufficiently be accounted for without crossing the channel for causes. It is much more likely that the publishing of news in England grew up through the same stages as abroad because the same conditions operated upon it in both places. The backwardness

[4] *Campi, Convivii atque ludorum agonisticorum ordo, modus atque descriptio* [Paris: 1520.]

of England is explained by the fact that there printing was newer and technically inferior to the practice of the mystery on the continent, and that the nation, isolated by nature, was firmly governed and free from the serious internal dissensions which have always acted as a strong incitement to the publishing of news. Not until the end of our period, the year 1620, does a really important direct foreign influence enter into the history of English journalism, as will duly appear.

The form in which news was printed throughout the period under discussion may as well as not be disposed of here, for is not a matter of great importance. News was printed in the form of either a book, usually so small that nowadays we should rather call it a pamphlet (as it was sometimes called at that time too), or a single sheet or broadside. The books of news, from the point of view of the printer's technique, differed in no wise from the books in which matter of other kinds was printed, except, perhaps, in that, like other popular books, they were even more badly printed than usual. The broadside was the standard form for proclamations and ballads; very rarely was any other kinds of news put in print on a single sheet.[5] Surely it is not difficult to account for this custom. Both the proclamation and the ballad were by no means new at the beginning of the era of printing, though, to be sure, the palmiest days of the latter were still before it. Furthermore, the proclamation certainly and the ballad very probably had previously been circulated in manuscript broadsides. That they should have been printed in the same form was, therefore, practically inevitable. Besides, this single-sheet form had decided advantages with regard to each. As official proclamations were commonly stuck up in public places, no other form is conceivably as suitable. As for the ballad, since it was intended to be sung, the single-

[5] But see p. 314 below.

sheet form was likewise the most convenient; and besides, a ballad is so short that there was no need of making a book of it, especially since the single sheet recommended itself to the printer because of its simplicity. In these forms news went on being printed until after the Restoration.

A word about the technical terms applied to reports of news is also in place here. A ballad was usually called by that name (spelled indiscriminately *ballad, ballade, balade, ballat,* or *ballet*), but also a *ditty, song, sonnet,* or even *psalm,* whether the subject-matter was news or something else. For a prose account there seems to have been no standard term, but the word *relation* occurs most frequently in titles and even more often in the accounts themselves. From the fact that early seventeenth-century German books of news were sometimes headed "*Aviso* [or *Avisa*], *Relation oder Zeitung,*" it would appear that the term had some international currency; furthermore, its Latin ancestor, *relatio,* was used with the same meaning. Sometimes the word *news* itself was used substantively in the sense of a piece of news, *e.g.,* in the title of a ballad of Elderton's:

> *A New merry newes,*
> *As merry as can bee,*
> *From Italy, Barbary,*
> *Turkie, and Candee.*[6]

But many other words were also used in titles—*discourse, report, declaration, description, narration,* as well as words indicative of the form in which the news was cast, such as *examination, dialog,* and *articles.* Indeed, even to-day we have no better name for a prose report of news than *news-story.*

---

[6] Hugh Iackson, 1606. But this was hardly the first printing. It was also frequently republished after 1606.

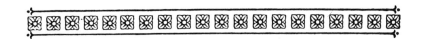

CHAPTER II

PERSONAL NEWS

PERSONAL news, as we may call it, is probably the oldest kind. It is a record or, more often, merely a celebration of the achievements of a personage of importance, from the sovereign himself to a prominent London merchant, written by one of his liegemen, retainers, or clients, or by an admirer whom his attainments have inspired at a distance. Sometimes encomia of this sort were written from motives little better than selfish, for the courtier who wrote a poem glorifying the virtues of his master might reasonably expect a reward, and indeed the court poet whom a royal or noble master kept, clothed, sheltered, and even pensioned customarily discharged his obligation by this kind of employment. Thomas Love Peacock's ironical outline of the business of the official poet is by no means altogether inaccurate and it furthermore points out the antiquity of his calling:

The natural desire of every man to engross to himself as much power and property as he can acquire by any of the means which might makes right, is accompanied by the no less natural desire of making known to as many people as possible the extent to which he has been a winner in this universal game. The successful warrior becomes a chief; the successful chief becomes a king; his next want is an organ to disseminate the fame of his achievements and the extent of his possessions; and this organ he finds in a bard, who is always ready to celebrate the strength of his arm, being first duly inspired by that of his liquor. This is the origin of poetry, which, like all other trades, takes its rise in the demand for the commodity, and flourishes in proportion to the extent of the market.

Poetry is thus in its origin panegyrical. The first rude songs of all nations appear to be a sort of brief historical notices, in a strain of tumid hyperbole, of the exploits and possessions of a few pre-eminent individuals. They tell us how many battles such an one has fought, how many helmets he has cleft, how many breastplates he has pierced, how many widows he has made, how much land he has appropriated, how many houses he has demolished for other people, what a large one he has built for himself, how much gold he has stowed away in it, and how liberally and plentifully he pays, feeds, and intoxicates the divine and immortal bards, the sons of Jupiter, but for whose everlasting songs the names of heroes would perish.[1]

Verses of this kind, then, were no novelty at all at the beginning of the era of printing, and they served to spread whatever news they contained merely by being printed. Examples of personal news written in England not long before our period can be found in the works of Laurence Minot in the fourteenth century and of John Lydgate in the fifteenth.

Laurence Minot was probably a minstrel, possibly a court minstrel, and certainly an enthusiastic admirer of his king, Edward III.[2] Each one of his eleven poems is the celebration of a battle of the king's against the Scots or the French, an account which, even if it is sometimes unhistorical, gives much information about what took place. "Political journalism in rhyme" Ker calls these pieces.[3] During the reign of Henry VI, or at least until the fortunes of the king began to decline, Lydgate wrote verses in celebration of nearly every important public occasion in the life of his master, no less than four pieces, for instance, at the time of his coronation in 1429. In discharge of this duty, he became, consciously or unconsciously, a writer of news, for it would be well-nigh impossible for any one to glorify the triumphs of his master without occasionally deviating into the particulars thereof. The best example of this kind of news from Lydgate's pen is the poem which he wrote in 1432, when the king returned to

[1] *The four ages of poetry.*
[2] See *C. H. E. L.*, I. 398 ff.
[3] *English literature medieval*, p. 151.

London from France, recounting in 544 lines full of exact detail the municipal reception offered him.[4] This is a genuine piece of reporting: Lydgate is even so accurate as to reproduce two addresses by the lord mayor in the prose in which they were spoken.

On the other hand, these verses were sometimes written and published out of mere literary vanity, especially after the Renaissance made poetry fashionable; the coronation of a king or the birth of an heir was an acceptable subject ready made to the hand of the poetical amateur. At the same time, the professional versifier, a man who had his living to make by the pen, rather than a dependent, a poetical pensioner, or a courtier with a taste for verse-making, would also seize upon the same sort of occasion to exercise his wits, for the sake of whatever he could get for his verses from a publisher (which was usually little enough) and for the sake of whatever honorarium he could flatter out of his subject or the worthy to whom he dedicated his piece. When such a writer wrote his topical verses with the expectation of profiting by their publication, he is indistinguishable from a journalist.

These verses, rarely inspired, sometimes easy and elegant, more often conventional and insipid, were compounded of eulogy and news in varying proportions, but the traces of the latter revealed by analysis are as a rule slight and sometimes negligible. Yet even those which impart no information at all are still to be considered journalistic, for they were called forth by a passing event—an anniversary, a battle, an edict or decree, a marriage. Even if the motives which moved their authors to compose them were not always journalistic, as soon as they were printed and offered for sale they took on a journalistic color, for it could seldom have been anything but their pertinence, their

[4] Reprinted by Halliwell: *Selections from the minor poems of Dan John Lydgate,* Percy Society, 1840, II. 1.

dependence upon an interesting recent event, which found buyers for them.

The chief subject of personal news would naturally be the reigning sovereign himself. He was not only the most important and the most conspicuous person in the realm, but one of the most liberal patrons of poetry as well. Furthermore, most of the Tudor rulers enjoyed a good deal of personal popularity, so that it was not always mere policy which produced verses of personal praise and records of their glory. The chief occasions for composing and publishing them were, again naturally, such epoch-making events as the coronation, the marriage, or the death of the sovereign. The earliest of these which I have found were occasioned by the death of Henry VII in 1509. Only a fragment of the elegy attributed to John Skelton and printed by Wynkyn de Worde has survived, but there are copies of two editions of Bishop Fisher's funeral sermon,[5] which was probably interesting in the same way as verses lamenting the same misfortune. Much more typical of the effusions of the official poet is Stephen Hawes's *Joyfull medytacyon of the coronacyon of Henry the eyght,*[6] which describes the author as "somtyme grome of ye chambre of our late souerayne lorde kynge Henry ye seuenth." As a matter of fact, if that practitioner and patron of poetry, King Henry VIII, inspired a great deal of this sort of eulogy, an unusually large proportion has been lost, for I have found only two panegyrics printed during his reign and one lamentation for his death. There is also a prose account of the coronation procession of Queen Anne

---

[5] *This sermon folowynge was compyled & sayd in the Cathedrall chyrche of saynt Poule . . ., the body beynge present of . . . Kynge Henry the .vij. the .x. daye of Maye, . . . m.ccccc.ix. . . .* Wynkyn de Worde, 1509. (All printed pieces mentioned in this treatise should be understood to have been printed at London, unless a different place is stated.)

[6] Wynkyn de Worde, [1509].

Boleyn,[7] but this is quite as much a description of a sumptuous municipal pageant as anything else, for all its doting on the graciousness of the lady.   No one in England dared speak a good word for the divorced Queen Katharine when she died in 1536, but far away, in Mainz, Bishop Nausea printed a tribute to her memory.[8]   Both Edward VI and Mary, however, did not lack admirers in print, the untimely death of the former in particular exciting the compassion of the poets, even though it became dangerous to express one's regard for the defender of the Protestant faith as soon as his sister had gained the throne.   This sentiment, however, persisted into the reign of Elizabeth, and during her early years the printing presses bore a fresh crop of epitaphs on the decease of the king.

It is in the time of Elizabeth and James I, however, that addresses in praise of the sovereign and reports of personal history become most numerous.   Several reasons suggest themselves: in the first place, there was more verse-making and more printing of all sorts; again, both monarchs had a weakness for flattery; and besides, Elizabeth's real popularity and King James's peculiar susceptibility to praise from the learned and the ingenious probably added to the tale.   But the most significant reason is that by this time versifiers of a humbler sort, the ballad-writers, had joined the chorus formerly raised by the court poets alone and considerably swelled its volume.   Now the meanest poetaster's artless verses might see the light just as well as the courtier's elegant encomium, and, if only they were fervent enough in praise of the queen, no doubt they were equally acceptable to her majesty's loyal subjects.   In consequence, though the courtier by no means ceased expressing

---

[7] *The noble tryumphaunt Coronation of Quene Anne, Wyfe vnto the most noble kynge Henry the viii.*   For Iohan Goughe, [1533].

[8] *Friderici Nauseæ . . . in diuam Catharinam . . . Funebris Oratio.* Moguntiæ: Ivo Scoeffer.

his duty to his queen in verse, his panegyrics were now out-numbered by those of the ballad-writer. The most curious and the best known of these is the ballad beginning, "Come ouer the born Bessy," by William Birche, "a dyologe sett furthe by twene the quenes maiestie and Englonde"[9] in terms of the most delightful intimacy.

During the reign of Elizabeth the custom also grew up of publishing laudatory ballads and verses for the anniversary of her coronation, 17 November, which was usually celebrated with tilting and pageantry. Though only a few of these pieces have been preserved, so many of them were entered in the Stationers' registers as to warrant the supposition that no anniversary after about the middle of the reign was left unmarked by simple and hearty tributes of this kind. Furthermore, the proportion of real news in them is often higher than in most of the productions of the class under consideration, for an account of the tournament held in honor of the day was sometimes made the substance of the whole piece. George Peele's *Polyhymnia*[10] (courtly in tone, of course) is a book of verses of this sort. Again, in 1588, a book of verses called *The blessednes of Brytaine*, by Maurice Kyffin, which had been printed for the coronation day of the preceding year, was reissued "with a new addition containing the late Accidents and Occurrents of this yeere 88. being the Thirtieth of hir Maiesties Raigne."[11]

When Queen Elizabeth died, all the grades of the poetical academy were heard from, beginning with the learned scholars of the University of Oxford and men like Bishop

[9] It is thus that the ballad was described in the Stationers' register when it was entered by William Coplande in 1558–9 (Arber, I. 96). The copy in the library of the Society of Antiquaries of London was printed by William Pickringe and is entitled *A songe betwene the Quenes maiestie and Englande*. Pickering entered the ballad again on 4 September 1564 (Arber, I. 262).

[10] Richard Ihones, 1590.

[11] The 1587 edition was printed by Iohn Windet; the second by Iohn VVolfe.

[18]

Hall and descending in the scale through ready and needy wits like Thomas Churchyard, Henry Chettle, and Samuel Rowlands to the anonymous ballad-writers. Here again we find, in the books by Chettle,[12] Richard Niccols,[13] and Henry Petowe,[14] indubitable news in the form of an appendix describing the queen's funeral. But in their pardonable preoccupation with the living rather than the dead, the poets saluted the accession of King James even more industriously. Frequently they handled both subjects at the same time and thereby produced books with titles ingeniously looking both ways, such as *Sorrowes Ioy*[15] and *Weepe with Ioy*.[16] These welcomes to King James are but the beginning of a steady shower of panegyric which rained upon that impressionable monarch as long as he sat on the throne of England.

In fact, the London journalists' interest in King James had begun long before he succeeded to the throne of England. In 1581 William Elderton's ballad beginning, "Iesus God what a griefe,is this," which tells the story of an attempt against the king's life and his rescue by an English serving-man, was entered in the Stationers' register.[17] There is no historical foundation for this legend, but it was very probably believed as news. A book concerning

[12] *Englandes Mourning Garment: Worne here by plaine Shepheardes; in memorie of their sacred Mistresse, Elizabeth . . . To which is added the true manner of her Emperiall Funerall . . .* For Thomas Millington, 1603 (2 issues).

[13] *Expicedium. A funeral Oration, vpon the death of . . . Elizabeth . . . Whereunto is added, the true order of her . . . Funerall.* By Infelice Academico Ignoto. For E[dward] VVhite, 1603 (2 edd.).

[14] *Elizabetha quasi viuens, Eliza's Funerall. . . . (The order and formall proceeding at the funerall of . . . Elizabeth . . .)* For Matthew Lawe, 1603 (2 edd.).

[15] Cambridge: Iohn Legat, 1603.

[16] Broadside. For Edmund Mutton, 1603.

[17] Arber, II. 393. It was printed for Yarathe Iames, presumably in the same year, as *A new Ballad, declaring the great Treason conspired against the young King of Scots, and how one Andrew Browne an Englishman, which was the Kings Chamberlaine, preuented the same.* There is an oral ballad, *King James and Brown*, apparently the work of a minstrel, on the same subject (Child: *English and Scottish Popular Ballads*, III. 442).

another attempt on the king's life was published in 1585,[18] and still another in 1593.[19]   At the time of his marriage in 1590, no less than four ballads on the subject were entered in the Stationers' register,[20] and in 1594 two pieces describing the baptism of his heir, a book[21] and a ballad,[22] were published.   Again in 1600, when the Earl of Gowrie attempted to assassinate the king, an account of the incident was published in London.[23]

After the death of Queen Elizabeth, the belauding of King James began the moment he left Edinburgh for London, and almost every stage in his journey was marked by the publication of a book or a ballad.   It reached its climax at the time of his coronation in midsummer, when scarcely a detail of the ceremonies could have gone unrecorded. These pieces are not mere panegyric; some of them describe the king's movements in considerable detail.   All told, the output of the London presses at this time includes ballads full of a holiday spirit of naïve delight, grave compliments from the universities, exultant outbursts from his patriotic countrymen pluming themselves on a Scotchman's ascending the throne of England, weighty discourses by the sober-minded on the advantages of the union of the two kingdoms, addresses of congratulation by major poets such as Drayton and Daniel, and fearful and wonderful concoctions in Latin

[18] *Treason Pretended against the king of Scots, by certaine Lordes and Gentlemen* . . . *With a declaration of the Kinges Maiesties intention to his last Acts of Parliament* . . . For Thomas Nelson.

[19] *A Discouerie of the vnnaturall and traiterous Conspiracie of Scottish Papists* . . . For Iohn Norton, 1593 (reprinted from the edition printed at Edinburgh by R[obert] Walde-graue).   Reprinted in 1603.

[20] Arber, II. 548–9.

[21] *A true reportarie of* . . . *the Baptisme of* . . . *Frederik Henry,* . . . *Prince of Scotland* . . . Edinburgh: R[obert] Walde-graue, [1594?].   Entered 24 October 1594 by Johane Butter (Arber, II. 662).   Reprinted in 1603.

[22] Arber, II. 663.

[23] *The Earle of Gowries conspiracie against the Kings Maiestie of Scotland.* . . . Valentine Simmes, 1600 (from the edition printed at Edinburgh by Robert Charteris).   Reprinted in 1603.

or Greek or both, probably designed to flatter his majesty's pretensions to learning. The eulogists, hackwriters, and booksellers expended their ingenuity liberally in devising novel ways of honoring the king. Several royal genealogies were printed, as indeed usually happened on an occasion of this kind; new editions of old books somehow relevant to the occasion, such as the account of the baptism of Prince Henry, that of the popish conspiracy of 1593, and that of the Earl of Gowrie's attempt mentioned above, and the description of Queen Elizabeth's progress to her coronation which Tottel had published in 1559,[24] were printed; and one "Britanno-Scotus," with exquisite tact, even composed a broadside *In effigiem Mariæ Reginæ, Iacob. Magni Britan. Reg. matris.*[25] Some of these pieces must certainly have been dictated by self-interest as much as by loyalty. One Robert Fletcher, for example, wrote *A briefe and familiar epistle shewing his maiesties . . . title to all his kingdomes; with an epitaph for the late maiestie; and lastly a prayer for his maiesties most happy succession, and for the queene and their children.*[26] This worthy subscribed himself "Yeoman purucyor of carriages for remooues of our sayde late soueraigne Lady the Queene," and thereby exposed himself to the charge of having his eye on the main chance. The somewhat miscellaneous nature of the contents of this book is not unusual: many of these effusions were made up of several pieces; some are in both verse and prose; some were written by several authors; and some were even padded with unrelated further specimens of the author's poetical vein.

Another occasion sure to be reflected in print was a visit by the sovereign, in progress through the country, for instance, or his passage in state through the city. Some of

[24] *The passage of . . . Quene Elyzabeth through the citie of London to westminster the daye before her Coronacion. Anno. 1558[/9].* (2 edd.) There are two issues of the reprint: 1) for Ione Millington, 1604; 2) for Iohn Busby, [n.d.].
[25] By Io. Gordonius. Typis Iohannis Norton, [1603].
[26] For Iohn Harrison, 1603.

the printed pieces thus called into being are mere bubblings-over of popular enthusiasm, but many of them are more or less exact descriptions of what actually took place. Some of the books describing the progresses of Queen Elizabeth were published by the authors of the entertainments in her honor and amount to nothing less than *scenari* or librettos. Such are *A Discourse Of the Queenes Maiesties entertainement in Suffolk and Norfolk: With a description of many things then presently seene. Deuised by Thomas Churchyarde Gent. With diuers shews of his own inuention sette out at Norwich: And some rehearsal of hir Highnesse retourne from Progresse*, printed by Henry Bynneman in [1578]; and *Certaine Deuises and shewes presented to her Majestie by the gentlemen of Grayes-Inne at her Highnesse Court in Greenwich*,[27] which consists chiefly of the text of Thomas Hughes's *Misfortunes of Arthur*, but includes also the ceremonious speeches introducing the play and notes on the manner of performance. The formal addresses made to the queen on her visits were sometimes printed too.[28] The best-known descriptions of royal visits are the famous letter of that mad wag, Robert Laneham, an humble member of the queen's suite, describing her entertainment at Kenilworth in 1575,[29] *The Princelye pleasures, at the Courte at Kenelwoorth*, on the same event,[30] and

---

[27] Robert Robinson, 1587.

[28] 1) *Carmen Gratulatorium Aedium Cecilianarum in aduentū . . . reginæ . . .* By William Cecil, Lord Burghley. Broadside. [Henry Bynneman? 1571?] 2) *Ad illus^m R. Elizabetham, L[aurence] H[umphrey] Vicecan. Oxon. oratio Woodstochiæ habita. . . .* Apud Iohannem Dayum, 1572; another edition in 1575. 3) *The Speeches and honorable Entertainment giuen to the Queenes Maiestie in Progresse, at Cowdrey . . ., by . . . the Lord Montacute. 1591.* Sold by William Wright, 1591. 4) *Speeches deliuered to her maiestie this last progresse, at . . . the Lady Russels, at Bissam, . . . the Lorde Chandos at Sudley, at . . . the Lord Norris, at Ricorte.* Oxford: Ioseph Barnes, 1592.

[29] *A Letter whearin part of the entertainment vntoo the Queenz Maiesty at Killingwoorth Castle . . . in this Somerz Progress 1575 is signified . . .* [1575.]

[30] [By George Gascoigne and others.] Richard Ihones, 1576.

[22]

Thomas Deloney's lively ballad of *The Queenes visiting of the Campe at Tilsburie with her entertainment there*,[31] published during the summer of the Armada's coming, when the English army was encamped on Tilbury plain. King James's movements were followed by the press with the same persistence, his visit to Scotland in 1617 in particular producing a torrent of encomia from his excited countrymen.[32]

The popular interest in the sovereign extended to the other members of the royal family as well, and we also find printed records of their activities and verses in praise of their virtues. A very early example is the prose account written by Petrus Carmelianus, Henry VII's Latin secretary, of the marriage by proxy of Prince Charles of Castile (later the Emperor Charles V) and the Princess Mary, the king's daughter, in 1508. Richard Pynson printed two versions of this narrative, one in Latin,[33] the longer and more elaborate, and the other in English[34] in the same year. They are a detailed and particular account of the reception of the embassy from the Emperor Maximilian, Charles's grandfather, the agreements entered into, and the marriage by proxy. During Henry VIII's reign it was often a little uncertain whether his children belonged to the royal family or not, and during the next

---

[31] Broadside. For Edward White, 1588.

[32] The annual lord mayor's show in London was another occasion of pageantry somewhat resembling the entertainments given to royalty. A book containing all or part of the *scenario* was usually published. Copies of the following are extant: the pageants for 1585, 1588, and 1591 by George Peele; 1590 by Thomas Nelson; 1605, 1609, 1611, 1614–6, 1618 by Anthony Munday; 1612 by Thomas Dekker; 1613, 1617, 1619, 1621 by Thomas Middleton; 1620 by John Squire.

[33] *Hoc presenti libello . . . Cōtinentur . . . Solemnes cerimonie & triūphi nuper habiti In suscipie[n]da . . . Maximiliani Romanorum Imperatoris . . . et . . . sui filii Karoli Principis castelle Archiducis austrie Legatione . . . pro sponsalibus et matrimonio inter . . . principem Karolum et . . . Dominam Mariam . . .*

[34] *The solempnities and triumphes doon at the spousells of the kyngs doughter.*

three reigns there was no royal family. King Philip of Spain, however, was greeted with exquisite courtly flattery in print when he came over to marry Queen Mary, and there is a curious ballad which was printed on the queen's persuading herself, on insufficient grounds, that she had conceived an heir in 1554.[35] But the children of King James were favorite subjects for the ballad-writers and courtly poets, and Prince Henry and Princess Elizabeth must certainly have attracted a genuine popularity. Prince Henry was sometimes included in the congratulations offered the king on his accession. In 1610 two reports of the celebration of his creation as prince of Wales were printed.[36] But it was his premature death in 1612 that provoked the loudest and most prolonged outburst of sentiment. Before the end of the year, seven weeks after his death, eighteen laments had been entered in the Stationers' register,[37] and there are at least eight more bearing the date of that year which do not appear to have been entered or were printed outside London.[38] And this

[35] *Nowe singe, now springe, oure care is exil'd*
Oure vertuous Quene is quickned with child. W[illiam] Ryddaell, [1554].

[36] 1) *The Order and Solemnitie of the Creation of . . . Prince Henrie . . . Prince of VVales, . . . Together with the Ceremonies of the Knights of the Bath . . . Whereunto is annexed the Royall Maske* [*i.e.,* Daniel's *Tethys Festival*]. For Iohn Budge. 2) *Londons loue, to the royall Prince Henrie, meeting him on the riuer of Thames . . . the last of May, 1610. With a breife reporte of the water Fight, and Fireworkes.* For Nathaniell Fosbrooke.

[37] Arber, III. 501–10.

[38] 1) *An Elegie on the Death of Prince Henrie.* By William Alexander, Earl of Stirling. Edinburgh: Andro Hart, 1612, 1613. 2) *Epicedium Cantabrigiense in Obitum . . . Henrici . . .* Cambridge: Ex officina Cantrelli Legge, 1612 (2 edd.). 3) *Iusta Oxoniensium.* Iohannes Bill, 1612. 4) *In Henricum Fridericum . . . lachrymæ.* By Alexander Julius. Edinburgh: Thomas Finlason, 1612. 5) *Memoriæ Sacra . . . Henrici . . . Laudatio Funebris.* By Sir Francis Nethersole. Cambridge: Cantrell Legge, 1612. 6) *Eidyllia in Obitum Fulgentissimi Henrici . . .* Oxford: Iosephus Barnesius, 1612. 7) *Luctus Posthumus: sive, . . . Magdalenensium officiosa Pietas.* Oxford: Iosephus Barnesius, 1612. 8) *Gloucesters myte for the remembrance of Prince Henrie.* By Thomas Rogers. For Ionas Man, 1612.

was not the end: the next year eight or more additional pieces were printed.[39] A list of the authors of these epicedia makes a very respectable poetical galaxy: it includes poets such as Chapman, Wither, the Earl of Stirling, Webster, Joshua Sylvester, John Davies of Hereford, Christopher Brooke, Thomas Heywood, and Cyril Tourneur, to say nothing of pedants like Alexander Julius or of John Taylor the water-poet and the ballad-writers. Conventional as these laments are in a sense, the spontaneity with which they were produced alone argues some sincerity. And now and then we find in them news as well as mourning sorrow, in the form of a history of his life or a description of his funeral. Even Chapman's *Epicede* was pieced out, more likely by the publisher than by the author, with an account of the funeral and a "Representation of of the Herse of the same . . . Prince."[40] Furthermore, with the enterprise and adaptability that we must expect of a journalistic publisher, Mrs. White entered in the Stationers' register on 12 January 1613 a ballad of *Great Brytaynes greatest comfort. or Brytaynes hope for the roiall prynce Charles prynce of great Brytayne and Ireland Duke of York and Albany.*[41]

By an unfortunate coincidence, the death of Prince Henry occurred just as preparations were going forward for the marriage of the Princess Elizabeth and the Count Frederick, Palsgrave of the Rhine. But it does not seem

[39] 1) *Two Elegies* . . . By C[hristopher] Brooke and W[illiam] B[rowne]. For Richard More, 1613. 2) *Mausoleum* . . . Edinburgh: Andro Hart, 1613. 3) *A funerall elegie upon the death of Henry* . . . By Thomas Heywood. For William Welbie, 1613. 4) *Illustrissimi Principis Henrici Iusta.* By David Hume. For Richard Boyle & William Iones, 1613. 5) *A monumental Columne* . . . By Iohn Webster. For William Welby, 1613. 6) *The Period of Mourning* . . . By Henry Peacham. For Iohn Helme, 1613. 7) *In Obitu summæ spei* . . . *Lessus.* By David Wedderburn. Edinburgh: Andreas Hart, 1613. 8) *Sundry Funeral Elegies* . . . Humphrey Lownes, 1613.
[40] For Iohn Budge, 1612, 1613.
[41] Arber, III. 511.

[25]

to have set back these preparations in any way, and it certainly did not diminish one whit the popular enthusiasm for this Protestant alliance or the expression thereof in print. The journalists of the day followed the ceremonies step by step—from the arrival of the Palsgrave, through the ceremony of betrothal in the chapel at Whitehall, the shows and pageants displayed in his honor, the marriage itself, celebrated with an ingenuous appropriateness on St. Valentine's Day, the tournament on 24 March, to the departure of the married pair and their arrival in their principality on the Rhine—and apparently missed nothing. Among many nuptial poems and verses of mere praise, we find a good deal of description of events, *i.e.*, a good deal of news.

Two other occasions later in the reign of King James brought forth more celebrations in print of the same order. The first of these was the creation of Prince Charles as prince of Wales in 1616: the program of the municipal water-pageant arranged by Thomas Middleton[42] and "a true Relation of the Solemnity held at Ludlow in the Countie of Salop, vpon the fourth of Nouember . . . Being the day of the Creation of . . . Charles, Prince of Wales, . . . in his Maiesties Palace of Whitehall"[43] were both promptly printed. The second was the death of Queen Anne in 1619, which seems to have produced nothing but memorial verses in the most conventional style.

Another occasion which sometimes produced laudatory verses by the courtly poets was the visit of a foreign potentate or the reception of an embassy. These occasions also produced books of news describing the entertainments offered the visitors, and again the two were sometimes

[42] *Ciuitatis amor. The Cities Loue. An entertainement by water, at Chelsey, and White-hall.* . . . For Thomas Archer, 1616.

[43] *The loue of VVales to their soueraigne Prince* . . . By Daniel Powell. Nicholas Okes, 1616.

praise too. The Shirley brothers, famous travelers and adventurers at the beginning of the seventeenth century, were frequently celebrated in print, chiefly by narratives of their exploits.[56] It is interesting to notice, as a sign of journalistic alertness, that on 7 June 1616, just when he was rising rapidly to the position of royal favorite, *The picture or portrature of Sir George Villiers* was entered in the Stationers' register.[57] An unusual sort of pamphlet, *The Charterhouse with the last vvill and Testament of Thomas Sutton*,[58] which was published in 1614, about three years after Sutton's death, is probably a testimonial of the esteem in which this philanthropist came to be held on account of his benefactions. It consists of a pious exordium on the virtue of charity, a brief history of the purchase of the Charterhouse property, a list of the endowments which Sutton settled upon his hospital, and a copy of his will, "taken out of the Prerogatiue Court."

Among the personal news of our period, the numerous epitaphs and elegies published on the death of a prominent personage must be mentioned. In these laments we shall not always find news and we shall almost never find a great deal of news, but it does sometimes appear in the form of a review of the life of the late worthy or a description of his funeral. For the most part they are simply poetical exer-

[56] 1) *A true report of Sir Anthony Shierlies iourney ouerland to Venice.* For Iohn Iaggard, 1600. 2) *A new and large discourse on the Trauels of sir Anthonie Sherley.* By William Parry. For Fletcher Norton, 1601. 3) *A true Journall of the late voyage made by . . . Sir Thomas Sherley the yonger . . . on the Coaste of Spaine &c.* Book. Entered 20 August 1602 by Thomas Pavyer (Arber, III. 214). 4) *The three English Brothers. . . .* By Anthony Nixon. Iohn Hodgets, 1607 (2 issues). 5) *Sir Robert Sherley, sent ambassadour in the name of the King of Persia, to Sigismond the third, King of Poland and Swecia . . . His Royall entertainement into Cracouia . . . , with his pretended Comming into England.* By Thomas Midleton. For Iohn Budge, 1609. 6) *Sir Antony Sherley his relation of his trauels into Persia.* For Nathaniel Butter & Iohn Bagfet, 1613.

[57] By Laurence Lisle (Arber, III. 590).

[58] For Thomas Thorp.

cises on a doleful theme, full of weeping and wailing and almost barren of information. Indeed, we are likely to find more solid fact in the elaborate titles prefixed to them than in the verses themselves. Consider, for example, an epitaph printed in 1578 on the death of the Countess of Lennox: *An Epitaphe on the death of the right noble and most vertuous Lady Margarit Duglasis good grace, Countisse of Liuinox (and Daughter to the renowmed and most excellent Lady Margarit Queene, Sister to the magnificent and most mighty Prince Henry the eight of England, Fraunce and Ireland, Kinge, and by Gods permission Queene of Scotland,) who diseased this life the ninth day of March. Anno. 1577. at hir mannoure in Hackny in the countye of Midelsex and lieth enterred the .3. day of April at Westminster in the Chaple of King Henry the seuenth, her worthie Grandfather of Englande, Fraunce and Ireland King. &c. The yeare of our Lorde God. 1578, and in the .20. yeare of our soueraigne Lady Queene Elizabeth by the grace of God of Englande, Fraunce and Irelande, Queene, defendour of the faith. &c.*[59] This alone is a fairly satisfactory obituary notice.

Many of these epitaphs are in the style of courtly compliment with which the great were honored while still alive. These are likewise the work of courtiers and scholars, written often in Latin, a labor of duty quite as often as of love, and sometimes mere poetical apprentice-work. Epitaphs of this kind were usually published in book form. The earliest I know of is *The Epitaffe of the moste noble & valyaunt Iasper late duke of Beddeforde*, a book of ten leaves printed by Richard Pynson in 1496. The verses are signed "Smerte, maister de ses ouzeaus," but they have sometimes been attributed to Skelton. The subject was Henry VII's uncle, who had died in the last month of the preceding year. It hardly seems possible that nothing else of this sort was published until 1542, but that is the date of

[59] By I[ohn] Phillips. Broadside. For Edward White, [1578].

the next epitaph I am able to cite. Much more likely, those which were published in the meantime have been lost, though doubtless the idea of honoring in print eminent personages outside the royal family took root only gradually. Sir Thomas Wyatt, the poet, is the subject of two memorial pieces published on his death in 1542, one in Latin by John Leland, the antiquary,[60] and another in English.[61] Many of these verses were written by genuine poets—Daniel, Chapman, John Ford, Joshua Sylvester, Cyril Tourneur, Thomas Watson, for instance; indeed, it is even possible to bring Spenser into the story of English journalism by citing his *Daphnaida*, published in 1591, a few months after the death of Lady Douglas Howard. Certain writers seem almost to have specialized in dirges of this kind: Thomas Churchyard was always ready to lament the death of a hero of the sort he admired, and George Whetstone, between 1577 and 1587, published verses on Gascoigne,[62] Sir Nicholas Bacon,[63] the Earl of Sussex,[64] Sir James Dyer,[65] the Earl of Bedford,[66] and Sir Philip Sidney.[67] The

[60] *Naeniæ in mortem Thomae Viati Equitis incomparabilis.* [Reginald Wolfe,] 1542.

[61] *An excellent Epitaffe of syr Thomas Wyat, with two other compendious dytties* . . . For Roberte Toye, [1542].

[62] *A remembraunce of the wel imployed life and godly end of George Gaskoigne Esquire, who deceased at Stalmford in Lincolne Shire, the 7 of October 1577. The reporte of Geor. Whetstone, Gent., an eye witnes* . . . For Edward Aggas, [1577].

[63] *A Remembraunce of the woorthie and well imployed life of* . . . *Sir Nicholas Bacon* . . . For Myles Iennyngs, [1579].

[64] *A Remembraunce of the Life, Death, and Vertues of* . . . *Thomas,* . . . *Erle of Sussex* . . . Iohn Wolfe & Richard Iones, 1583.

[65] *A Remembraunce of the precious vertues of* . . . *Sir Iames Dier,* . . . *Lord Cheefe Iustice of the Common Pleas* . . . Iohn Charlewood, [1583].

[66] *A Mirror of Treue Honnour and Christian Nobilitie:* . . . *Frauncis Earle of Bedford,* . . . *who deceased* . . . *the xxviii of Iune, 1585.* . . . *Whereunto is adioyned a Report of the Vertues of* . . . *S. Frauncis, Lord Russell, Sonne and Heire Apparent of the* . . . *Earle,* . . . *slaine* . . . *the 27 day of the said month of Iune.* Richard Iones, 1585.

[67] *Sir Phillip Sidney, his honorable Life, his valiant Death, and his true Vertues* . . . For Thomas Cadman, [1587].

universities of Oxford and Cambridge and their colleges individually were accustomed to publish corporate tributes to the heroes of the day and to their own members. Occasionally, even as early as 1551, books of epitaphs, made up of contributions by a group of writers, were published.

Even more numerous were epitaphs of a less pretentious kind, written in loping ballad measures by the humbler sort of versifiers, especially poetically-inclined clergymen and the semi-professional ballad-writers, and published in broadside form. In style and substance they are highly conventional, so that it is indeed difficult to distinguish one from another. Sometimes they bewail the death of persons of the same quality as the courtly epitaphs just mentioned: Bishop Jewel, Sir Nicholas Bacon, the Earl of Bedford, the Earl of Leicester, Sir Philip Sidney, and the Earl of Derby, in dying, elicited lamentations of both kinds. But the subject of the popular epitaphs is much more often a lord mayor, a great city merchant, a popular preacher, or some other personage a little closer to the popular admiration. Sir Philip Sidney's death, in 1586, seems to have excited greater compassion than any other, if the number of memorial pieces printed is a true index. It is said that two hundred elegies were written on this occasion, but of course most of these were never printed: no less than eleven books and broadsides, however, did appear soon after the news reached England.[68] The Earl of Pembroke's death

[68] 1) *The Epitaph of Sir Phillip Sidney* . . . By [Thomas] Churchyard. For Thomas Cadman, [1586]. 2) *A dolefull dytie of the death of Sir P. Sydney.* [Ballad.] Entered 22 February 1587 by Henry Carre (Arber, II. 464). 3) *Vpon the life and death of . . . Sir Phillip Sidney* . . . By A[ngel] D[ay]. Robert Walde-graue, [1586]. 4) *The Life and Death of Sir Phillip Sidney* . . . : *His funerals* . . . ; *with the whole order of the mournfull shewe, as they marched thorowe the citie of London* . . . By Iohn Philip. Robert Walde-graue, 1587. 5) *The buriall of Sir Phillip Sydney.* Ballad. Entered 27 February 1587 by William Bartlet (Arber, II. 464). 6) Whetstone's book mentioned above. 7) *The mourninge muses of Lod Bryskett vpon the Deathe of . . . Sir Phillip Sydney* . . . [Book.] Entered 22 August 1587 by John Woulfe (*ib.*, II. 474). 8) *Academiæ*

in 1570 called forth at least six,[69] and the Earl of Derby's in 1593 five.[70] The execution of the Earl of Essex in 1601, although the fact that he did not die a natural death made the event all the more exciting to popular interest, probably produced more regret than any of these, but at the moment it was dangerous to print a lament which showed any sympathy for the traitor. We hear from contemporary testimony that epitaphs were printed at the time, only to be suppressed at once, but none of them seems to have been preserved, at least in its original form. Within two months, however, of Queen Elizabeth's death, on 18 May 1603, Margaret Allde entered in the Stationers' register the ballad-epitaph beginning "Sweet Englands pride is gone,"[71] which she printed as *A lamentable Dittie composed vpon the death of Robert Lord Deuereux late Earle of Essex, who was beheaded in the Tower of London vpon Ashwednesday in the morning. 1601,* a ballad which was reissued several times during the seventeenth century. Many other memorials of Essex were subsequently printed as well.

Another reason for the popularity of broadside epitaphs is probably to be found in the pious custom of hanging them on tombs. Puttenham describes them as "large tables . . . hanged up in Churches and chauncells over the tombs of great men and others," and further complains that they were

---

Cantabrigiensis lacrymæ, tumulo . . . *Philippi Sidneii sacratæ per Alexandrum Neuillum.* Impensis Thomæ Chardi, 1587. 9) *Exequiæ* . . . *Phillippi Sidnaei* . . . Oxford: Joseph Barnes, 1587. 10) *Peplus* . . . *Philippi Sidnaei* . . . *honoribus dicatus.* Oxford: Joseph Barnes, 1587. 11) *Sequitur celebritas & pompa funeris* . . . Latin & English. By Tho[mas] Lant. Grauen in copper by Derick Theodor de Brij, 1587.

[69] Arber, I. 411-3.

[70] *Ib.,* II. 637,639,642,647. Also *Epicedium in obitum* . . . *Comitis Derbeiensis* . . . By M. G. Oxford: Joseph Barnes, 1593.

[71] Arber, III. 234.

so exceeding long as one must have halfe a dayes leasure to reade one of them, & must be called away before he halfe come to the end, or else be locked into the Church by the Sexten, as I my selfe was once served reading an Epitaph in a certain cathedrall Church of England.[72]

[72] *Arte of Poesie*, Lib. I, Chap. XXVIII.

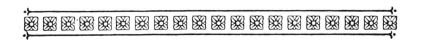

CHAPTER III

OFFICIAL NEWS

NEXT after personal news, the earliest kind that we meet is news of public affairs—the official acts and proceedings of the sovereign and the various departments of the state, the preservation of law and order and the defense of the realm, and the transactions of the crown with neighboring states and princes. News of this sort was perhaps the most eagerly sought after before the era of printing, and although it is not always the most entertaining kind, it is still the staple of the contemporary newspaper. During our period, it was published in many forms, from a variety of motives, and by many agents, but first of all, we are a little surprised to notice, by the government itself.

It is surprising to find that the government itself took the earliest steps in the printing of news of public affairs because, throughout the sixteenth and seventeeth centuries, the official attitude towards the meddling of printers and pamphleteers in matters of high state was severely intolerant. Some of the books which the authorities took the trouble to suppress seem to us today altogether harmless; those which plainly did not play the government's game were hunted down with savage persistence; and of those which were tolerated we can say that, practically without exception, their tenor and purport were such as the authorities themselves would have contrived had they been the authors and publishers. The most pointed official declaration on this subject is the opinion submitted to the king by the judges of the realm in 1680. "His Majesty," they said, "may by law prohibit the printing and publishing of all newsbooks and pamphlets of news whatsoever not licensed by his Majesty's authority as manifestly tending to the breach of the peace and disturbance of the kingdom." It is true that in Charles II's time the printing trade was fettered by an even more rigorous censorship than in Elizabeth's, but this opinion was stated to have been based on precedents extending back through the sixteenth century, and represents, if not the practice of the authorities during our period, the legal status of printed news of public affairs. In short, news existed only as the government saw fit to allow it. Yet even to an autocratic government it was indispensable. Merely as a means of scotching idle rumors and shallow gossip it was too useful to be neglected, and it could also be applied to subtler uses, such as preparing the public mind for the measures the government had determined upon or strengthening the loyalty of the nation. Consequently we shall see the government not only permitting the booksellers to give news-reports to the people, but actually preparing and sending them forth itself.

1. PROCLAMATIONS

It is possible almost to watch the government being drawn into the habit of publishing its own news of affairs of state step by step. First we see it adopting the printing press to multiply official, especially royal, proclamations. It was chiefly for the purpose of putting proclamations in print that the office of royal printer was created. These proclamations themselves were, of course, nothing new at all; for centuries, through the mouths of heralds and sheriffs and through written copies, they had been a medium of communication from the crown to the nation. Proclamations hardly belong to the history of journalism because they were not printed primarily for sale, but they undoubtedly served to impart news just the same. What

[36]

they divulged was sometimes nothing more interesting than that the king thinks it wise "to restraine excessive carriages in wagons" by forbidding the use of four-wheeled carts, that whale-fins must not be brought into the realm except by the Muscovy merchants, or that the people must not destroy the nests of the queen's swans, but, on the other hand, it was sometimes a declaration of war against a foreign power, an offer of pardon to rebellious subjects, or (as in Henry VIII's proclamation of 15 January 1534) the establishment of the succession to the throne. Unquestionably many an Englishman must have gleaned what he knew about such events from reading proclamations set up on walls, and no doubt their contents were disseminated still further by word of mouth. It is significant that a few proclamations were printed simultaneously in folio and in book form.[1] They are identical except in format; the books must have been printed because it was felt that they would command wider attention. Most of these are unusually long proclamations and of more than ordinary interest or importance. We do not know, of course, whether it was by the foresight of the government or of the royal printer that such books were issued, and to be sure there was conceivably an advantage to each, the printer's lying in having these proclamations in salable form.

It seems to be taken for granted that royal proclamations were printed only for official use, but is it not possible that the royal printer may have sold folio copies to persons who

---

[1] *Viz.:* 1) *By the Quene. A declaration of great troubles pretended against the Realme by . . . priests and Iesuits . . .* [18 October 1591.] Deputies of Christopher Barker, 1591. 2) *By the King. A Commission with Instructions, . . . for compounding for Wards, Ideots, and Lunaticks . . .* [23 February 1618.] Bonham Norton & John Bill, 1618. 3) *By the King. A Proclamation concerning Ale-houses.* [19 January 1619.] Norton & Bill, 1618 [o.s.]. 4) *By the King. A Proclamation declaring His Maiesties pleasure concerning the dissoluing . . . of Parliament.* [6 January 1622.] Norton & Bill, 1621 [o.s.] (2 issues of the 4° edition). The proclamation entitled *A Declaration of His Maiesties Royall Pleasure . . . in matter of Bountie* (R[obert] Barker, 1610 [o.s.]) was published in 4° only.

wanted them? It is certain that they found their way into private hands; a gentleman named Humphrey Dyson preserved a complete set of Elizabeth's proclamations. There is a curious passage on this subject in a book printed in 1549 called *A Copye of a Letter contayning certayne newes . . . of the Deuonshyre and Cornyshe rebelles*, which was presumably written by a country gentleman in the southwest, though, as we shall see later on, the writer may have been wearing a mask. After thanking his London correspondent for sending him a copy of the king's reply to the petition of the rebels, he says:

[I pray you,] yf any suche lyke thynges come fourth in printe, I may haue some sent me wyth the fyrst, & yf you wyll speake to the Kynges Prynter in my name, I dare say, he wyll not denye you.

Now this book was almost certainly printed by Grafton, "the Kynges Prynter," himself, and in view of his stout Protestantism it may even have been issued by his contrivance, or at least by his connivance. Consequently it seems unlikely that the book would mention a private gentleman's obtaining copies of a royal proclamation if the idea were quite fantastic. And surely if the royal printer would furnish copies of proclamations to private persons, he did not give them gratis, but for a charge. Perhaps it is to such a supplementary income from the sale of proclamations that Christopher Barker, printer to Queen Elizabeth, referred in a letter to Lord Burghley: "I loose oftentymes more by one Proclamation, than I gayne by sixe . . . and in many yeres there hapeneth not a proclamation of any benefit at all."[2] It is just possible that royal proclamations could be bought, at least by persons of some consequence, as well as any other kind of printed news.

2. DOCUMENTS AND STATE PAPERS

From the printing and scattering of royal proclamations

[2] December 1582. MS. Lansdowne 48. 189. Quoted in Lindsay: *Bibliography*, I. xxxv.

to the printing and scattering of other documents and state papers which the government wished to make known is but a short step, and there can be no doubt that the latter was suggested by the former. Possibly we can even trace the transition. The earliest known printed proclamation is that of 1486 in which King Henry VII published to his subjects the bull of Pope Innocent VIII confirming his title to the throne and his marriage to Elizabeth of York.[3] In 1494, after the accession of Pope Alexander VI, and perhaps because of Perkin Warbeck's denial of the king's title, it was thought advisable to obtain a confirmation of Pope Innocent's bull, and copies of this were likewise printed.[4] These copies, however, consist of nothing but the Latin text of the document promulgated by Pope Alexander, and they are therefore not royal proclamations, though they were unquestionably printed in England under the same auspices and for the same purpose as the proclamation of 1486. In 1486 the government issued a royal proclamation to accomplish its purpose; in 1494 it merely caused a state paper to be put in print, but from the same motive precisely. Copies of two similar documents, one in the form of a royal proclamation[5] and the other merely a transcript of the papal decree,[6] were subsequently printed when, as it would seem, they might have served to remind the nation that King Henry's hold on the crown was supported by the pope's authority.

Knowing as we do how eager King Henry was to satisfy all his subjects of the legality of his title and how often it was denied by other claimants, we see in these extraordinary measures to make known the pope's sanction that the crown was constrained in its own interest to give out and

[3] Broadside. [William de Machlinia.]

[4] Broadside. [Westminster: Wynkyn de Worde.]

[5] Folio. [Westminster: Wynkyn de Worde, 1495.] In Lindsay: *Bibliography* this is dated 1499.

[6] Broadside. [Richard Pynson, 1497?]

to circulate information regarding a matter of high state which may fairly be called news. In time to come, the crown was again and again constrained to do the same thing and thus became, unwittingly, even unwillingly, a publisher of news.

The attitude of the crown towards the disclosing of information about affairs of state is summed up by King James I in an apology which he published to justify his dissolution of Parliament early in 1622:

> Hauing of late . . . determined to dissolue the Assembly and Conuention of Parliament, . . . Wee were pleased by Our Procla-mation, giuen at Our Palace at *Westminster* the sixt day of this instant *Ianuary*, to declare, not onely Our pleasure and resolution there-in, but also to expresse some especiall passages and proceedings, moouing vs to that resolution . . . [Further,] that all men might discerne, that Wee, like Gods true Vicegerent, delight not so much in the greatnesse of Our place, as in the goodnesse & benignitie of our gouernment, We were content in that one Act to descend many degrees beneath Our Selfe: First, by communicating to all Our people the reasons of a resolution of State, which Princes vse to reserue, *inter arcana Imperij*, to themselues and their Priuie Councell: Secondly, by mollifying and mixing the peremptorie and binding qualitie of a Proclamation, with the indulgence of a milde and fatherly instruction: And lastly, leading them, and opening to them that forbidden Arke of Our absolute and indisputable Prerogatiue, concerning the calling, continuing, and dissoluing of Parliaments: which, though it were more then superabundant to make Our Subiects know the realitie of Our sincere intentions; yet Wee not satisfied therewith, but finding the bounds of a Proclamation too straight to conteine and expresse that boundlesse affection that Wee beare to Our good and louing people, are pleased hereby to inlarge Our Selfe, . . . by a more full and plaine expression of those Letters and Messages that passed from Vs to the Commons in Parliament.[7]

King James was, of course, the self-appointed exponent of this doctrine of the divine right of kings, but we may be sure that, in the sixteenth century, every sovereign and

[7] *His maiesties declaration, Touching his proceedings in the late Assemblie . . . of Parliament.* Bonham Norton & Iohn Bill, 1621 [o.s.].

every government was ready to insist upon the same prerogative as far as was convenient and possible. The same notion precisely is expressed in a manifesto of Queen Elizabeth's:

Although kings and princes soueraignes, owing their homage and seruice onely vnto the Almightie God the king of all kings, are in that respect not bounde to yeeld account or render the reasons of their actions to any others but to God their onely soueraigne lorde; . . . yet we are notwithstanding this our prerogatiue at this time specially mooued, for diuers reasons hereafter briefly remembered, to publish not onely to our owne naturall louing subiectes, but also to all others our neighbours, specially to such princes and states as are our confederates, . . . what our intention is at this time, and vpon what iust and reasonable groundes we are mooued to giue aid to our next neighbours the naturall people of the Low Countries.[8]

But none of them, least of all King James, could afford, on occasion, not to "descend many degrees" beneath himself; the loyalty and the complaisance of the people were too important to him and the publication of state papers was too efficacious a way of informing their minds and lulling their suspicions. Consequently we find that throughout the sixteenth century the crown resorted to this practice, for its own purposes, again and again.

Henry VIII, for example, made valiant use of the printing press in his widespread campaign to influence opinion in his own favor at the time he was seeking to have his first marriage annulled. These tracts, indeed, were aimed not only at the English nation but at the whole western world. In his efforts to maneuver the pope into granting an annulment, the king obtained opinions on the sinfulness of marrying one's brother's widow from learned bodies and jurisconsults all over Europe and spread them broadcast in printed copies. The most impressive of these is the opin-

[8] *A Declaration of the causes moouing the Queene . . . to giue aide to . . . the people afflicted and oppressed in the Lowe Countries.* Christopher Barker, 1585. Quoted from Somers' *Tracts,* I. 410.

ion given him by the universities of France and Italy.[9] The briefs of the king's counsel in the proceedings at Rome were also printed.[10] These opinions do not, of course, contain news, but, in a matter of such high interest, the mere delivering of them was news in itself. No account need be taken here of the vast quantity of controversial writing which this cause brought forth. Having determined, at length, to have his own way without the pope's consent, King Henry imparted his decision to the nation in a book entitled *Articles deuised by the holle consent of the kynges . . . counsayle, his gracis licence opteined therto, not only to exhorte, but also to enfourme his louynge subiectis of the trouthe.*[11] A few years later he used the same means to foment opinion against the pope's proposal of a general council to consider matters of religion.[12] Furthermore, in 1536, when rebellion broke out in the north, the somewhat

[9] 1) *Grauissimæ, atq3 exactissimæ . . . totius Italiæ, et Galliæ Academiarū censuræ . . . de ueritate illius propositionis, . . .* quod *ducere relictam fratris mortui sine liberis ita sit de iure diuino . . . prohibitum: ut nullus Pontifex . . . dispensare possit.* Thomas Berthelet, April 1530. 2) *The determinations of the . . . vniuersities of Italy and Fraunce, that it is so vnlefull for a man to marie his brothers wyfe, that the pope hath no power to dispence therwith.* Thomas Berthelet, 7 November [1531].

[10] *Diuino implorato præsidio. De licentia ac concessione Sanctissimi. D. N. et ad instantiam . . . Regis Angliæ, Nos . . . infrascriptas Conclusiones . . . defensare conabimur . . .* Tho[mas] Berthelet, [1532?].

[11] Thomas Berthelet, 1533, 1534.

[12] 1) *Illus[t]rissimi ac potentissimi regis, senatus populiq3 angliæ sententia de eo concilio quod Paulus episcopus Rom. Mantuae futurum simulauit.* Thomas Berthelet, 1537. 2) *A protestation made for the . . . kynge of Englande . . . and his hole counsell and clergie, . . . that neyther his hyghenes nor his prelates . . . is bounde to come . . . to the pretended councell, that Paule byshoppe of Rome, fyrst by a bul indicted at Mantua . . . & nowe & late . . . hath prolonged to a place no man can tell where.* Thomas Berthelet, 1537. 3) *Henrici octaui . . . ad Carolum Cesarem Augustum . . . epistola qua Rex facile causas ostendit, & cur is Vincentiam, ad concilium falso nomine generale appellatum, non sit venturus, & quam periculosum sit aliis . . .* Thomas Berthelet, 1538. 4) *An Epistle of . . . Henry the viii . . . to the Emperours maiestie, to all Christen Princes, and to all those that trewly and syncerely professe Christes Religion . . .* Thomas Berthelet, 1538.

testy replies which the king made to the grievances of the rebels, article by article, were put in print.[13]   These tracts were possibly intended for circulation among the disaffected, who are directly addressed, and we cannot feel any more certain that they were sold as news than that proclamations were sold as news.   But there is no doubt that to any subject who obtained copies, whether by purchase or otherwise, they were news of the highest interest.   The Protector Somerset, in the next reign, followed the same course at the time of the enclosure riots in the southwestern counties.[14]   Again, in 1542, when he despatched an army into Scotland, the king sent a printed manifesto ahead of it, "to notify vnto the world his [i.e., the Scottish king's] doinges and behauour in the prouocation of this warre, and lykewyse the meanes and wayes by vs vsed to exchue and aduoyde it, and the iuste and true occasions, wherby we be nowe prouoked to prosecute the same"[15]—a method of propaganda also imitated by Somerset in the same circumstances.[16]

On several occasions, Queen Elizabeth likewise published manifestoes to the whole world declaring her intentions and justifying her courses.   That the government intended they should have the widest possible circulation is shown by the fact that they were printed simultaneously in vari-

---

[13] 1) *Ansvvere made by the kynges hyghnes to the Petitions of the rebelles in Yorkeshire.* Thomas Berthelet, 1536.   2) *Ansvvere to the petitions of the Traytours and rebelles in Lyncolneshyre.* Thomas Berthelet, 1536.

[14] *A Message sent by the kynges Maiestie, to certain of his people, assembled in Deuonshire.* Richard Grafton, July 1549.

[15] *A declaration, conteyning the iust causes . . . of this present warre with the Scottis, wherin also appereth the . . . title, that the kingts . . . maiesty hath to the souerayntie of Scotlande.* Thomas Berthelet, 1542.

[16] 1) *Epistola exhortatoria ad pacem, Missa ab . . . Protectore Angliæ . . . ad Nobilitatem ac plebem, uniuersumq; populum Regni Scotiæ.* Reginald Wolf, 9 March 1548. 2) *An Epistle or exhortacion, to vnitie & peace, sent frõ the Lorde Protector . . . of England To the . . . inhabitaunts of . . . Scotlande.* Richard Grafton, 1548.

ous languages. For example, *A Declaration of the Causes moouing the Queenes Maiestie . . . to . . . send a Nauy to the Seas, for the defence of her Realmes against the King of Spaines forces* . . . was printed in English, Latin, Dutch, French, Italian, and Spanish.[17] Thus the war of propaganda was carried into the enemy's country and the good will of neutral opinion was solicited. Other similar books were printed in 1562, when an army was sent to help the Protestants in France,[18] in 1585, when it was decided to send an army abroad to help the Netherlands against the Spaniards,[19] and once more in 1589.[20] In 1560, in the course of diplomatic negotiations with France, the government published two pamphlets, one a statement by the French king's ambassador[21] and the other the queen's reply[22]—according to its own account, to correct the misleading impression given by the recent publication of the French case alone. Part of the government's assiduous campaign to justify the execution of the Queen of Scots was the publication of a letter sent by Queen Elizabeth to the officials of the city of London, together with a complaisant speech made by a municipal councillor

[17] Deputies of Christopher Barker, 1596.

[18] 1) *Expositio causarum, quibus Angliæ Regina commouebatur, vt quasdam . . . cohortes armis instrueret* . . . Reginald Wolfe, 1562. 2) *A declaration of the Quenes Maiestie: . . . Conteyning the causes which haue constrayned her to arme certaine of her Subiectes* . . . Rycharde Iugge & Iohn Cawood, [1562].

[19] As above, p. 41. Printed in English (2 issues), Latin, Dutch, French, and Italian.

[20] *A declaration of the causes, which mooued the chiefe commanders of the nauie of . . . England, in their voyage . . . for Portiugal, to take . . . certaine shippes of corne and other prouisions of warre . . . prepared for the seruices of the king of Spaine.* Printed in English and Latin (2 editions). Deputies of Christopher Barker, 1589.

[21] *Protestatio Christianissimi Regis Gallorum, . . . exhibita . . . reginæ Anglie, per Ordinarium . . . Regis, ad . . . Reginam Legatum.* Reginald Wolf, 1560.

[22] *Responsum ad Protestationem, quam orator Regis Gallorum . . . Angliæ reginæ obtulit xx. die Aprilis, . . . M.D.L.X.* Reginald Vuolf, [1560].

on its reception.[23] These pamphlets are partly narrative records of recent events, and besides they are news in precisely the same sense as the speeches and letters of public men which our present-day newspapers faithfully print.

King James, for all his insistence upon his prerogative, was the most prolific apologist of them all. He not only caused or allowed the text of important state papers to be printed, but, as we have already seen, with his own hand he drew up declarations of policy for the enlightenment of his subjects. Some of these, such as his argument for the divine right of kings or his admonition "concerning lawfull sports to be vsed," are better known than the example cited above. Still others reveal him in his favorite rôle of arbiter and mediator. He also made what was practically an innovation in sending to the press the text of treaties with foreign powers[24] and verbatim transcripts of several of his speeches to the Parliament.[25]

3. News Published by Authority

Besides state papers, royal speeches and pronunciamentos, and other documents given out by the government, which obviously spoke for the crown, as it were, in the

[23] *The true copie of a letter from the queenes maiestie, to the Lord Maior of London, and his brethren: . . . read openly . . . in the Guildhall . . . the 22. day of August. 1586. . . .* Christopher Barker, 1586.

[24] 1) *Articles of peace, entercourse and Commerce, Concluded in the names of . . . Iames . . . , king of great Britaine . . . And Philip the third, King of Spaine . . . In a Treatie at London the 18. day of August . . . 1604.* Robert Barker, 1605. 2) *Articles concluded at Paris the xxiiij. of February 1605* [o.s.] *. . . By . . . Iames . . . King of Great Britaine, . . . And Henrie the Fourth most Christian French King . . .* Robert Barker, 1606.

[25] 1) *The kings majesties Speach To . . . this present Parliament at Whitehall, . . . the xxj. of March . . . 1609.* Robert Barker, [1609]. 2) *His majesties speach in the Starre-Chamber, The xx. Of Iune. Anno 1616.* Robert Barker, 1616 (2 edd.). 3) *His Maiesties Speach in the Upper House of Parliament, . . . the 26. of March, 1621.* Bonham Norton & Iohn Bill, 1621.

[45]

first person, other news—reports of official transactions drawn up for publication—was also printed and circulated by authority. Some of it has to do with the same subjects as the publications mentioned in the preceding section and differs from them only in being news-reports rather than documents printed literatim. Such is *A particular declaration . . . of the . . . traiterous affection borne against her Maiesty by Edmund Campion, Iesuite, and other condemned Priestes, witnessed by their own Confessions,*[26] which plainly states:

> Some disloyal and unnatural Subjects . . . have published divers slanderous Pamphlets, and seditious Libels, as well in this Realm, as in Foreign Parts, in sundry strange languages, in excuse and justification of the said Traytors . . . H. M. Privy Council . . . have [therefore] found it very expedient that as well certain Confessions taken of the said Campion, and others, . . . as also certain Answers, lately made to certain Articles propounded . . . should be published truly and sincerely.[27]

Most of these pamphlets are not quite so frank in disclosing their origin; more usually they begin by premissing that "diuers false and corrupt Collections and Relations" have been spread abroad, and go on to conclude merely that "therefore it hath beene thought fit to publish to the world" a "true and perfect" account of the matter "for the satisfaction of those, who desire to be informed" and the making plain of the justice, liberality, and fatherly affection of the sovereign toward his erring and misguided subjects. But their tenor, the fact that they are frequently bolstered up by documentary evidence from the official archives, such as the confessions of offenders, which the government was not likely to make public except for its own purposes, and the further fact that they were published by the royal printer are sufficient evidence of their origin and purpose, as, indeed, must have been apparent to any-

26 Christopher Barker, 1582.
27 Quoted from *Phoenix Britannicus*, I. 481.

[46]

body from the first. When their authorship has been determined from extrinsic evidence, they are shown to have been prepared by officers of state or persons in the confidence of the government, such as Sir Francis Bacon, William Day, bishop of Winchester, or John Spotiswood, archbishop of Glasgow. It was doubtless nothing new for a government to put about information, opinions, even rumors such as would best serve its own interests; the novelty is the use of the printing press, a means of dissemination too useful to be overlooked. And thereby again the government published news.

Most of these pamphlets have to do with trials in the courts and their sequel and are based chiefly on court records, signed confessions, and the like. One of the most interesting is *The saying of Iohn late Duke of Northumberlande vppon the scaffolde, at the tyme of his execution. The .xxii. of Auguste. A[nno] 1553.*[28] This includes not only a confession of wrong-doing by Lady Jane Grey's father in his own words, but also a brief account by an anonymous reporter of his last acts. There is nothing to prove it was officially inspired but its evident usefulness to justify the government's executing him and the fact that it bears the imprint of the queen's printer, who would scarcely have published it without approval, if not inspiration. Another is a report of a conference of clerics called by the queen in the spring of 1559 to frame an agreement about matters of religion in controversy.[29] Its efforts were frustrated by the contumacy of the party with Catholic sympathies, and when it broke up the bishops of Winchester and Lincoln were committed to the Tower. This report follows the transactions of the conference from beginning to end, but,

[28] Iohn Cawood, [1553].

[29] *A declaracyon of the procedynge of a conference, begon at Westminster the laste of Marche, 1559, concerning certaine articles of religion and the breaking vp of the sayde conference* . . . Richarde Iugge & Iohn Cawood, [1559?].

in spite of some show of impartiality, its animus is evidently against the refractory bishops, so that it was probably issued by the royal printers at the instance of the Privy Council, which had tried to bring about a composition of differences, or of some one in the council's confidence. On one occasion, at least, the government saw fit to cause the publication of a pamphlet exposing the impostures of an alleged exorcist of demons, who had the misfortune to be a Jesuit as well.[30] This tract was written by Dr. Samuel Harsnet, a future archbishop of York, and printed by order of the Privy Council.[31] There are other books on the trials of Essex[32] and Raleigh[33] and of various Catholic offenders such as Campion, Blackwell,[34] and Ogilvie.[35]

A curious example of governmental supervision is found in the year 1556. We learn from the minutes of the Privy Council that, on 13 March, William Ryddall and William Coplande, printers, were haled before the Council and gave

[30] *A Declaration of egregious Popish Impostures,* . . . *vnder the pretence of casting out deuils. Practised by Edmunds, alias Weston a Iesuit* . . . Iames Robert, 1603. One of Shakespeare's "sources."

[31] *D. N. B.,* XXV. 53.

[32] *A declaration of the Practises & Treasons attempted and committed by Robert late earle of Essex and his Complices,* . . . *and of the proceedings as well at the Arraignments & Conuictions* . . . *as after: Together with the very Confessions and other parts of the Euidences themselues, word for word taken out of the Originals.* [By Sir Francis Bacon.] Robert Barker, 1601. Bacon is said to have received £1,200 for his services against Essex; see Abbott: *Bacon and Essex,* p. 251.

[33] *A declaration of the demeanor and cariage of Sir Walter Raleigh, as well in his Voyage as in, and sithence his returne; and of the true motiues and inducements which occasioned his Maiestie to proceed in doing iustice vpon him, as hath bene done.* Bonham Norton & Iohn Bill, 1618.

[34] 1) *Mr. George Blackwel* (. . . *Archpriest of England) his Answeres vpon sundry his Examinations: Together, with his Approbation and taking of the Oath of Allegeance* . . . Robert Barker, 1607. 2) *A large examination taken at Lambeth* . . . *of M. George Blakwell* . . . [and other documents]. Robert Barker, 1607.

[35] *A true relation of the proceedings against Iohn Ogiluie, a Iesuit, executed at Glasgow, the last of Februarie, anno 1615.* . . . [By Archbishop Spotiswood.] Edinburgh: Andro Hart, 1615.

recognizances of £40 each (a considerable sum) to deliver to John Cawood, the royal printer, "to be by the said Cawood brent," all the copies which they had printed of a book of the recantations of Archbishop Cranmer, who was burned eight days later. At the same time they were enjoined not to print any further books without official license. On the 16th Richard Lant and Owen ap Rogers, stationers, were treated in the same fashion.[36] There is, however, a book entitled *All the submyssyons and recantations of Thomas Cranmer* which bears Cawood's imprint and the significant statement, "Visum et examinatum per reuerendum patrem et dominum, Dominum Edmundum [Bonner] Episcopum London. Anno MDLVI." We must therefore infer that, after suppressing the book printed by Ryddall and Coplande, the government put out its own version of Cranmer's statements. The fact that Elias Newcomen, in the preface to *A Defence and true declaration of the thinges lately done in the lowe countrey*, a . translation which he published in 1571,[37] charges that "So dyd that honest man *Boner* immediately vppon the death of the excellent Martyr the Archebyshop of Caunterbury openly cause to be published in Print a report of the Archbyshops death and his woordes before hys death, directly contrarie to that which was spoken, and all in fauor of Papistrie," and that later historians have deemed this book of Cawood's doubtfully authentic are a confirmation of this inference.

There is a little evidence to show how some of these official news-reports were fabricated. In 1592 Henry Arthington, a simple-minded disciple of William Hacket, the fanatic who had been executed the year before on a charge of conspiring to murder the queen, made an abject submission which probably saved him from the same fate. His case was made public in a book entitled *The seduction*

[36] *Acts P. C.*, new series, V. 247–9.
[37] Iohn Daye.

[49]

of Arthington by Hacket especiallie, with some tokens of his vnfained repentance and Submission,[38] in which he explains:

> Christian Reader, I am to giue thee to vnderstand, that the Epistle before, and the booke following, were both perused and allowed by authoritie: and after sent mee agayne to examine, that I might see and testifie what vpright dealing I found therein. In verie trueth, I finde nothing in substance added to the originall, but certaine wordes and sentences changed for the better. The rest (I protest) is mine owne doinges, as I was directed by the spirite of God.

It is apparent from this testimony that the publication of the book was overseen and that the text was probably corrected for the press by some one in authority. It might very well be supposed that the original suggestion to issue such a book came from a high quarter too. At any rate, there is no doubt that the authorities took pains to see that, when published, it would create the right impression. And indeed, it is not very uncharitable to suspect that, if Arthington was instructed to testify explicitly that his MS. had not been tampered with, tampering of this sort was not altogether unknown.

In 1581 a certain John Nichols, a Welshman who had once been a minister of the Church of England, since turned Catholic abroad, and now recanted in the Tower, was given a taste of the notoriety so dear to him by the publication of two books, *A declaration of the recantation of Iohn Nichols,*[39] and *Iohn Niccols Pilgrimage, wh[e]rein is displaied the liues of the proude Popes, ambitious Cardinals, lecherous Bishops, fat bellied Monkes, and hypocriticall Iesuites.*[40] The former, issued by the royal printer, was undoubtedly published by authority. Two years later, languishing in jail in Rouen, Nichols remorsefully confessed in a letter to Dr.

---

[38] For Thomas Man, [1592].
[39] Christopher Barker, 14 February 1581.
[40] For Thomas Butter and Godfray Isaac, 1581.

Allen, the doyen of the English Catholic clergy, that these revelations of hierarchical iniquities were a tissue of lies and flimsy rumors. Nichols at no time can be regarded as a trustworthy witness, but this confession was voluntarily made and is in no way implausible, so that the picture it draws of the readiness of the government—or perhaps we should say, of an overzealous and unscrupulous officer—to foist upon the nation the paltriest fictions as true informa- tion is most interesting.

Nichols acknowledged that the discreditable secrets of the lives of the Catholic clergy which he had revealed were gossip he had heard "in Italie of peisantes and poore men." He protested that he would never have perpetrated either book had he not been deluded by "desire of vaine glorie," by threats of torment, and by promises of reward, and in what he wrote he was prompted by his captors.

Sir *Ovven Hopton* the Lieutenant of the Tovver [he said] commaunded me vvith threates, to vvrite mine examination according to his will & pleasure, & willed me (when I published the names of the Papists, many of vvhose names I neuer heard of before) not to be afraid to affirme them to be fautors of the Pope, of the Queene of Scots, to be mortal ennimies to the Queenes Maiestie, to her Counsellers, & to al those which were defendors of the religion vvhich is novv publickly taught in England. . . .
If thou vvilt do this (quoth he) the Queene vvill promote thee, and thou shalt find me most ready to helpe the[e]: al the nobilitie vvill loue thee excedingly, and thou shalt vvant nothing: I vvill send my man with thee to *Oxford*, and thou shalt be mainteined there: I vvill find the meanes that thou shalt haue one hundred Marks yerely: and vvithout all doubt, thou shalt haue a fat benefice. If thou vvilt not do this, thou shalt be tormented . . .
M. *Stubs* gaue me the matter of my booke in the Tovver, in- tituled: *The recantation of Iohn Nicols, &c.* M. *VVilkinson* did vvrite in the margent the notes: and also added to that vvhich I vvrote, and corrected the faults by me escaped.[41]

[41] *A true report of the late apprehension and imprisonnement of Iohn Nicols, Minister, at Roan* . . . Rhemes: Iohn Fogny, 1583. See also below, p. 94.

4. Officially-inspired News

Besides publishing information in the manner already mentioned, the government also put out further news surreptitiously, without acknowledging its part in the enterprise and with every effort to conceal it. We can only guess at the means by which these reports were written and published and how far they were formally ordained and authorized. Possibly they originated in the maneuvers of particular officers or departments of state, who sent them forth as part of their work in preserving order and due obedience in the realm. Lord Burghley, for instance, has been credited with several. At any rate, there is no doubt that they represent the official point of view and were calculated to spread the impression which the government wished to create, and the presumption is strong, from what evidence is available, that they were secretly inspired by the state itself.

First we shall have to deal with a few doubtful instances, for it is not always possible to decide infallibly that a printed book is not what it says it is. Some of these, even if they are deceptions, are relatively harmless. But, on one account or another, although we do not have evidence enough to convict them of duplicity, we suspect them of not being exactly what they seem. When, for example, we find an account of the last-minute reprieve granted Lord Cobham and others on the day appointed for their execution in 1603 which was published by the royal printer (but signed only with his initials) as *The copie of a letter written from Master T. M. neere Salisbury . . .*, and notice that in another issue of the pamphlet Master T. M. becomes Master C. S., we naturally suspect that this informant is a fictitious person, and the tone of the report suggests that it was officially-inspired. We also find several other reports, including royal speeches, in which the royal printer, in addressing the reader, asserts or implies that they were issued on his own responsibility.

Hauing receiued (gentle reader) [says Robert Barker in one of them] diuers and different copies of his Majesties Speech to this last Session of Parliament in Whitehall, . . . my labour hath bene to conferre all these copies together, and with the helpe of some gentlemen that were auditors thereof, to make such an extraction as I here present vnto thee. Which though I dare not maintaine to bee a true and full relation of all his Maiestie spake, as being farre short both of the life of his Majesties eloquent phrases, and fullnesse of the matter: yet seeing (as I hope) it conteines most of the substantiall reasons and arguments that therein were vttered, and that it is a thing desired by so many, though not rightly related by any, I haue taken the boldnesse to present it vnto thee, such as it is, being the rather at mine owne suite permitted to print it, for eschewing the wrong that might be done vnto thee, by the publishing of so many false copies that begin already to be spread thereof.[42]

And again:

To publish any thing of the late most barbarous and damnable Treason, and Conspiracie, of *Blowing vp the House of Parliament with Gunpowder*, . . . is necessary, and wil be very profitable . . . , Aswell for that there do passe from hand to hand diuers vncertaine, vntrue, and incoherent reports, and relations of such Euidence, as was publiquely giuen vpon the said seuerall Arraignments; As also for that it is necessary for men to vnderstand the birth & growth of the said abominable and detestable Conspiracy, and who were the principal Authors and Actors in the same.[43]

All this may be perfectly true, but it does not seem entirely plausible. It is quite certain that the state was much more likely than the royal printer to be the judge of what "it is necessary for men to vnderstand." It may even be doubted that the royal printer would often take it upon himself to suggest the publication of this or that bit of information to the authorities; it is more likely that the first

---

[42] *His majesties speech to both the Houses of Parliament . . . the last day of March 1607.*

[43] *A true and perfect relation of the whole proceedings against . . . Garnet . . . and his Confederats . . .* Robert Barker, 1606.

impulse came from the state itself. In short, it is possible, though we have not proved the case, that these books were intended to put before the nation news which the government thought expedient to be known without confessedly condescending to waive the prerogative so dear to the king. True, the government had already published precisely the same kind of reports without concealing its complicity, but it may have felt reluctant to follow such precedents too often.[44]

Against some others we can urge even less; the only grounds for suspecting them are that they look innocent on the surface and that they were published (sometimes unacknowledged) by the royal printer and were surely acceptable to the government. Take, for example, the pamphlet published in 1549 when riots broke out in Devonshire and Cornwall against the enclosing of common lands and the destruction of the practices of the old faith. It is entitled *A Copye of a Letter contayning certayne newes, & the Articles or requestes of the Deuonshyre and Cornyshe rebelles*; it bears no printer's name, but looks like the work of Grafton, the royal printer. It is apparently a letter from a loyal gentleman in the southwest to a friend in London, written under an arrangement to exchange news, and news it does contain, but it is news which is mostly damaging to the rebel cause, and this is embroidered with long exercises in objurgation and grim prophecies of what will happen when the king's forces go into action. It is remarkable that in a tract which, by whomever published, is obviously designed to discredit the aims of the rioters we should

[44] See 1) *A true and plaine declaration of the horrible Treasons, practised by William Parry* . . . C[hristopher] B[arker, 1585]. 2) *A true and Summarie reporte of the declaration of* . . . *the Earle of Northumberlands Treasons* . . . C[hristopher] Barker, [1585]. 3) *A Letter written out of England to an English Gentleman remaining at Padua* . . . Deputies of Christopher Barker, 1599. 4) *His maiesties speach in this last Session of Parliament* . . . Robert Barker, 1605. 5) *The copie of a late decree of the Sorbone at Paris* . . . R[obert] B[arker], 1610.

find their grievances fully set out, but as these would instantly repel any convinced Protestant, the writer possibly felt they were an effective proof of the waywardness of these disobedient subjects.[45]

Next we find several pamphlets published by official inspiration which are disingenuous merely in concealing all evidence of their origin so that the simple-minded might very well have been misled into thinking them much more impartial than they really were. They bear no evidence of authorship other than such statements as that the author was "a very honest gentleman, who I [the printer] knew to haue good and sufficient meanes to deliuer the trueth" or "a gentleman of good vnderstanding and learning," and the royal printer published them without any imprint or with only his initials. These well-informed and truth-loving gentlemen, however, turn out on examination to be such as Lord Burghley, lord high treasurer of England, and his notes are a justification of the government's policy.[46]

There are several presumptive private letters which are certainly intended to look like what they are not. One of these, *The copie of a Letter written by one in London to his frend, concernyng the credit of the late published detection of the doynges of the Lady Marie of Scotland*,[47] is a resumé of a tract in which George Buchanan, the Scottish humanist,

---

[45] See also 1) *A Packe of Spanish Lyes sent abroad in the world* . . . Deputies of Christopher Barker, 1588. 2) *Her maiesties most Princelie answere, deliuered by her selfe at the Court at VVhite-hall, on the last day of Nouember 1601* . . . [Robert Barker,] 1601.

[46] See 1) *A Declaration of the fauourable dealing of her Maiesties Commissioners appointed for the examination of certaine Traitours, and of Tortures vniustly reported to be done vpon them for matters of Religion.* [By Lord Burghley.] 1583. 2) *The Execution of Iustice in England for maintenance of publique and Christian peace, against certeine stirrers of sedition* . . . [By Lord Burghley. Christopher Barker,] 1583 (2 editions). Also printed in Latin and French by Thomas Vautroullier, 1584; in Dutch at Middelburg by Richard Schilders, 1584; in Italian by John Wolf, 1589.

[47] [John Day, 1572.]

had fallen foul of the Queen of Scots; according to the editor of Somers' *Tracts*, "to give its [*i.e.* Buchanan's *Detection's*] contents currency among the unlearned commons of England, this abridgement or review was carefully circulated."[48] *A discouerie of the treasons practised . . . by Francis Throckmorton*[49] also purports to be a letter written by "a gentleman of Lions Inne" to a doubting friend, but the "verie perfect declaration of the whole proceedings" which this gentleman had obtained "by the meanes of a secret friend "and which he encloses to convince his correspondent of the sufficiency of the evidence against the traitor is a solemn, official-sounding document which begins "Whereas there haue bene very lewde and slanderous bruites and reportes giuen out, of the due and orderly proceedings held with Francis Throckmorton, . . . it hath bene thought expedient . . . to deliuer vnto your view and consideration a true and perfect declaration of the treasons practised and attempted by the said Throckmorton against her Maiestie and the realme, by him confessed before his arraignment." The tract came from the press of the royal printer, but was not acknowledged.

In 1571, at the time of the second commitment of the Duke of Norfolk to the Tower, John Day, without putting his name to it, printed a pamphlet which was presumably the copy of a letter written by one R. G. to his brother-in-law. It explains its purpose and very ingeniously creates the impression of straightforwardness and credibility as follows:

Hearing that amongst the common sorts of men at thys time: it is not certainly knowne what is the cause that the Duke of Norffolke is newely commytted to the Towre, and sundrie others: And knowing that good men wil be wel satisfied to vnderstand the truth which euil men would couer and oppresse: I could not but in conscience to satisfie the good, and brydle or stop the lying and open slaunderous

48 I. 183.
49 [Christopher Barker,] 1584.

literally true or not, is interpreted in the light most favorable to the government. Much of the news published by the state, then, would seem to be distinctly Machiavellian.

5. SEMI-OFFICIAL NEWS

Finally, we must take account of what may be called semi-official news, *i.e.*, news published not by the initiative or connivance of the government but by persons in close sympathy with it who shared its views and aimed at an approved purpose. Some of these are merely patriotic enthusiasts and volunteer apologists, such as the authors of the two books proving that the king was by right entitled to the crown of Scotland which appeared just before the military expedition against the Scots in 1548.[53] Both were dedicated in admiring terms to the lord protector, and contain other matter besides news. John Heywood's *Breefe balet touching the traytorous takynge of Scarborow Castell*[54] is an example of news written out of loyal indignation. According to his biographer,[55] Francis Walsingham devoted a part of his apprenticeship in statecraft, under the tutelage of Secretary Cecil, to writing a tract against the marriage of the Queen of Scots and the Duke of Norfolk.[56] Walsingham was not yet in the service of the government, but there is no doubt that he expressed the point of view of a powerful official faction. There is, however, little news in his book.

Most of this semi-official news proceeded from those two

[53] 1) *An exhortacion to the Scottes to conforme themselues to the . . . vnion betwene . . . Englande & Scotland.* By James Harrison. Richard Grafton, 1547. 2) *An epitome of the title that the Kynges Maiestie of Englande, hath to the souereigntie of Scotlande . . .* By Nicholas Bodrugan, otherwise Adams. Richard Grafton, 1548.

[54] Tho[mas] Powell, [1557].

[55] Read: *Mr. Secretary Walsingham*, I. 63.

[56] *A discourse touching the pretended match betwene the Duke of Norfolke and the Queene of Scottes.* [John Day? 1569?]

powerful allies—instruments, if you like—of authority, the church and the bar. Just as is true today, men of law owed a certain duty directly to the state and were likely to identify its interests with their own. The connection between church and state was much closer than it is now; prelates occupied high positions in the councils of the government, and in the matter of enforcing conformity they were, of course, entrusted with a large part of the carrying out of the government's policy. It is not at all surprising to find that they shared the official point of view and that, when it seemed expedient to do so, they published their own versions of the events they took part in.

For example, the same R. C. who wrote the alleged letter to the Earl of Leicester mentioned above published, in 1587, *A short declaration of the ende of Traytors, and false Conspirators against the state . . . Wherein are also . . . touched sundry offences of the S[cottish] Queene, cōmitted against the crowne of this land, and the manner of the honorable procedings for her conuiction thereof.*[57] Except that I do not suspect it of trying to give the reader a false impression of its impartiality, it is no different in tenor from the earlier book, and I call it semi-official rather than officially inspired for no better reason than that it was not issued by the royal printer. It may plausibly be set down as an enterprise of Crompton's own, inspired by his veneration, as a lawyer, of the due and just execution of the statutes and his reprobation, as a loyal subject, of the enmity of foreign conspirators to the realm. Crompton is sincerely justifying and defending his own. There is no insincerity in his doing the same thing in his *Copie of a Letter to the . . . Earle of Leycester*; the insincerity there is in contriving the pamphlet to look like the report of a much more casual and disinterested eyewitness than he really was.

From the ecclesiastical arm, we have a report of a con-

[57] For Thomas Gubbins & Thomas Newman, 1587.

ference with Catholic prisoners, much like the report of the disputation with Campion published after his execution,[58] but, since it is not the work of the royal printer, probably the unprompted labor of the divine who represented the official church;[59] and several accounts of ecclesiastical assemblies, including Dean Barlow's report of the Hampton Court conference in 1604.[60] This he says he compiled from the notes of various divines present on the occasion, and he declares that he published it to give an unprejudiced account of the proceedings to the nation, in correction of unfounded reports circulated by the puritanical wing of the church. The most interesting exhibit is this same Dr. Barlow's *Sermon preached at Paules Crosse, on . . . Martij 1. 1600. With a short discourse of the late Earle of Essex his confession, and penitence, before and at the time of his death . . . Whereunto is annexed a true copie, in substance, of the behauiour, speache, and prayer of the said Earle at the time of his execution.*[61] The execution had taken place on 25 February; immediately, it would seem, the government appointed Dr. Barlow to preach on the subject at Paul's Cross the next Sunday. There was ample precedent for such a step: it was customary to hold public meetings at this place and the sermons preached there often touched on public questions and were arranged for by the highest authorities. Barlow was probably chosen on this occasion because he had been one of the two priests to attend Essex at his execution.

[58] *A true report of the disputation . . . had in the Tower of London, with Ed. Campion . . thought meete to be published in print by authoritie.* [By Alexander Nowell and William Day.] Christopher Barker, 1 January 1583.

[59] *A true reporte of a Conference had betwixt Doctour Fulke, and the Papists, being at VVisbiche Castle . . . the 4. of October 1580.* For Tobie Smith, 1581.

[60] *The Summe and Substance of the Conference which it pleased his . . . Maiestie to haue with . . . his Clergie . . . at Hampton Court, Ianuary 14, 1603 . . .* For Matthew Law, 1604, 1605.

[61] For Mathew Law, 1601.

From the time of this purpose for the Crosse [he says], but three dayes in all, till the Saboth for the sermon, I was not one day from the Court, still [= always] labouring to informe my selfe of euery thing which I doubted, that I might in these calumnious times, keep my selfe . . . from the controlment either of ill tongues, or mine owne conscience.

He knew what his work was. Essex had been very popular in London and there was a good deal of sympathy for him among the people; in his sermon Barlow labors to break down this popularity, even quoting statements by Essex in despite of the commons. He is at great pains to substantiate his account of Essex's treasonable acts: "I will deliuer nothing," he says, "vpon meere information and report, . . . but what these eares of mine haue heard from his owne mouth, in that two houres conference with him before his death, and these eyes of mine seene vnder his owne hand." His motive in printing the sermon was partly to justify himself, for he says,

Notwithstanding all this my care and paines, . . . it was giuen out that I was stroken, if not with madnesse, yet with a dreadfull sicknesse; or, as if I had spoken treason, that I was, the next day, committed close prisoner to the Tower; or at least, I had highly offended her maiestie, and receiued a great check from the Councell,

and partly to spread the light which his sermon contains farther abroad—"being . . . *by name*, appointed by the honourable Lordes to be present at the late Earle his execution, I thought my selfe bound . . . to declare vnto you, what my selfe in his case know, and what is fit for you to heare."

Thus we see that the government, in spite of its view of the prerogative of the crown, was practically forced, in its own interest, to publish news of its own transactions. It had little enough sympathy with the idea of confiding information about its courses to the vulgar, but at the same time it was by no means insensible of the fact that it was better to give out this information itself than to leave the task to somebody else, who might not see eye to eye with it, or to let the public form its opinion on common rumor. It was never entirely successful in suppressing printed news which it objected to, much less written reports and unfavorable rumors; it was constantly complaining of all three and justifying its own news as a corrective of false and malicious statements. Neither was it slow to see that in publishing news itself, with or without provocation, it had a useful means of instructing the nation in its duty. Consequently, although these official publications by no means form a complete running record of contemporary politics, and although they were not printed as news but as moves in the game of statecraft, they nevertheless comprise the most valuable collection of political news available to a student of affairs in their time. Interesting as are the reports from other sources which we shall examine next, and valuable as is their supplementary shading of the picture, they do not compare in copiousness and pertinence with the government's own news.

There remains one question which can hardly be answered definitely—was this official news sold in the booksellers' shops like other books of news or was it printed for the use of the officers and agents of the government rather than for the book-market? A little of it, we can feel quite sure, was not intended for sale, and a little more undoubtedly was; of the remainder we can only say that it probably was sold over the counter. There is every reason why it should have been. As news, it was certainly worth whatever it cost; better printed information on the same subjects could seldom be had. If men were willing to pay for the vague and insubstantial rumors sometimes offered them as news, it is hard to believe that they would not have paid for the very explicit information which their government printed for them. At the same time, we can hardly suppose that the government and the royal printer would have published free what they could make a charge for. Yet even if this officially-published news was distributed rather than sold, it is still important in the history of journalism because it fostered that "Sense of Liberty, which inspires us with a Curiosity to know the Affairs of our Superiors, in order to censure or applaud them as we see Cause," and because it incited professional journalists to publish the same sort of news as soon as they could get access to it and dared put it in print.

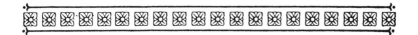

CHAPTER IV

NEWS PUBLISHED UNDER PARTISAN AUSPICES

JUST as the government published news in its own interest, various parties, sects, groups, and organizations in the realm made public such news as would benefit their cause and put in print their own versions and interpretations of passing events. They did not have as free a hand as the government, and many of them opposed the official doctrine on the subject in which they were interested, so that most of the news to be considered in this chapter was printed secretly or abroad and circulated surreptitiously in England. Their object, however, was precisely the same as the government's—to inform and direct the mind of the people, to justify their own courses, and to enlist popular sympathy on their side—and their methods were also the same.

We must understand, of course, that very little of all the news published in the sixteenth century was strictly impartial, written by witnesses who had not stake or no selfish interest in the events they related, and published merely for the information of the public. Respectable newspapers nowadays are wary of displaying bias in their news-reports even when they are sure their readers would approve the bias; they are careful to print biased and tendencious information within quotation marks and comment by the writer is excluded from the news columns. Not so in the sixteenth century; then almost every printed piece of news evinced a definite point of view and a sympathy for or against the tenor or consequence of the events narrated: this was usual; it was possibly even expected. But sympathy and bias which fall in with official and popular prejudices are so common that if we should classify as partisan all the news in which they appear, we should have almost nothing left over. News which reveals an animus against the pope, the Spaniards, or the enemies of the queen, unless published by the government, is not really propaganda; it is simply a reflection of the view endorsed by the state and the greater part of the nation. It is rather news which reveals some other animus, news published by partisans of unpopular, unapproved, or minority opinions, that we have to consider here.

1. PARTISAN POLITICAL NEWS

Of partisan political news we find little; it was highly dangerous, and it was not always inspired by that divine guidance which emboldened religious partisans to print dangerous matter. There was, besides, little organization of political opinion to produce it. We do find, for one thing, a number of printed petitions to the king and to Parliament—"of English Marchants, trading into Spaine and France" praying for relief from the excise levied upon the wines they imported,[1] "of the Owners and Masters of shipping trading to the Southwards, against the patent for Dungennesse lights,"[2] of "the Binders of Bookes in London" complaining of the goldbeaters' monopoly of the importation and sale of gold leaf.[3] The broadside entitled *An extract Translated out of the French Copie, and taken out of the Registers of the French Kings Priuie Councell*,[4] though not formally a petition, was undoubtedly published by English merchants trading in France as part of a plan to

[1] Broadside. [1612.]
[2] Broadside. [21 February 1621.]
[3] Broadside. [1621.]
[4] Simon Stafford, [1600?].

these political tracts may have been religious partisans; the author of *A Warnyng for Englande,* for example, may have learned to hate the king of Spain as he did because of the latter's Catholic principles, but in his tract he has almost nothing to say about religion. It is an account of "the horrible practises of the Kyng of Spayne / in the Kyngdome of Naples / and the miseries whereunto that noble Realme is brought. Whereby all Englishe men may vnderstand the plage that shall light vpō them / yf the Kyng of Spayn obteyne the Dominion in Englande," and it was published in 1555, at the time of his marriage to Queen Mary. It is a good example of the way in which news can be used as propaganda, for it is full of very particular information about the lot of the Neapolitans; although the author no more fancied himself a journalist than king of Spain, he was providing news for any reader of his book who wanted it.

Another tract written by a politician with an ax to grind from which a good deal of information can be gleaned— though here it is information of a very untrustworthy kind—is *The copie of a leter, vvryten by a master of arte of Cambridge, to his friend in London, . . . about the present state, and some procedinges of the Erle of Leycester and his friendes in England . . . published, vvyth most earnest protestation of al duetyful good vvyl and affection, tovvardes her . . . Ma[jesty] and the Realm, for vvhose good onely it is made common to many* (1583).[11] This is an account of certain political maneuvers libelously attributed by the author to the Earl of Leicester. It enjoyed a great deal of notoriety in its time and was commonly spoken of as the work of Father Parsons, the celebrated Jesuit political intriguer, but there is no evidence for connecting him with it. The letter which the Privy Council wrote to the lord mayor of London on 26 June 1585, at the queen's behest,

---

[11] Probably printed abroad.

expressing her indignation at libelous reports which were being circulated regarding Leicester and denying them on her own knowledge, probably refers to this book.[12] It came to be known, in the seventeenth century, as *Leicester's Commonwealth.*

In 1620, Thomas Scott, a pamphleteering Protestant divine, had the temerity to publish a book called *Vox Populi, or Newes from Spayne,*[13] in which he exposed the alleged schemes of Gondomar, the Spanish ambassador, to bring England into subjection to his master and to effect the marriage of the Prince of Wales and the Infanta. The book purports to be an account of Gondomar's report to the council of state in Madrid on his return thither in 1618. As a matter of fact, it is an arrant forgery, but there is no doubt that it was widely believed at the time or that its anti-Spanish tenor was very welcome to many Englishmen at a time when the traditional hatred of the Spaniards was protesting against King James's conciliatory attitude and the plans for bringing in a Spanish queen. It was suppressed by the government and Scott thought it advisable to betake himself abroad for a little while. The next year, however, he perpetrated another imposture in the form of a book purporting to be the text of a speech delivered in the House of Commons[14] appealing for funds in aid of the Palatinate, whose elector, King James's son-in-law, was at the moment seriously embroiled with the Roman emperor over his election to the throne of Bohemia. The burden of this tract was likewise very popular in England. Scott wrote many more political pamphlets before he was murdered at Utrecht in 1626.

Much more valuable as news than any of these, how-

---

[12] *C. S. P. D. 1581–90*, p. 248.

[13] Printed abroad, probably at Gorcum.

[14] *A Speech made in the Lower House of Parliament . . . by Sir Edward Cicill, Colonell.* Reptd. 1624.

ever, is the anonymous tract entitled *A record of some worthy proceedings: in the honourable, wise, and faithfull Howse of Commons in the late Parliament*, printed on the continent, possibly at Amsterdam, in 1611. This consists of a speech by an unnamed member on the failure of the house to arrive at an agreement with the king regarding the contract which had been proposed to settle the vexatious question of supplying the royal purse, and also of a copy of the terms of the contract and of two petitions and a list of grievances drawn up by the house. In a preface addressed to the nation, the sponsor of the pamphlet, an Englishman living abroad, explains that he has been moved by the king's proclamation dissolving Parliament on 31 December 1610 to come to the defense of the House of Commons. King James had been displeased by the obstinacy of the Commons in declining to meet his wishes, and in the proclamation he peevishly complained that they had sat too long and not done what was expected of them. Against this charge the sponsor of the pamphlet champions them. To clear himself of any imputation of disloyalty, he argues, on exceedingly shaky grounds, that, because the proclamation is written in the third person instead of the first, it does not express the king's opinion, but is the work of a secretary. The documents printed in the pamphlet are the proof he relies on to show that this same house, "covertly traduced" by the proclamation, is "the worthiest house of Commons that ever was."

The main service of this book is unmistakable: it is a declaration, in the form of news, of the platform of the popular party. The documents of which it is composed must have been obtained from members of the house themselves; it is hard to imagine any other source from which our exile could have got them. When we remember how many overbold printers were punished during the next two centuries for publishing accurate accounts of the proceed-

[73]

ings of Parliament and that it was hardly before the beginning of the nineteenth century that the right of the nation to know what its representatives in Parliament did in their sessions was acknowledged, this book becomes a notable publication. The fact that it was reprinted in 1641 suggests that it was regarded as a memorable document to the cause of liberty.[15]

2. NEWS IN THE FORM OF RELIGIOUS PROPAGANDA

It is a well-known fact that both parties to the religious controversies which began in England during the reign of Henry VIII, and went merrily on throughout all the remainder of our period, made free use of the printing press in carrying on the warfare. Most of what they published was polemical and dialectic, but they also published news. Anything that would serve the cause was grist to their mill, and when they possessed themselves of a piece of news favorable to their doctrines or purposes or bethought them of an interpretation of recent events which would tend to justify them to their countrymen, they rushed it into print. Consequently we find all kinds of news which owed its life in print to sectarian zeal.

In this miscellaneous collection of news, we find side by side reports of the proceedings of ecclesiastical conferences[16]

---

[15] This section could be extended considerably, for almost any discussion of public policy, unless carried on in the most general terms, was pretty sure, in its allusions to recent events, to contain news, or something very like news. For example, there is some news, *i.e.*, some recounting of recent events, in the unfortunate Stubbs's *Discouerie of a gaping gulf* (1579). See Albright: *Dramatic Publication*, p. 78, for an account of the offense given by a book on the art of war—Sir John Smythe's *Certain Discourses . . . concerning the formes and effects of diuers sorts of weapons* (Richard Iohnes, 1590)—because of its references to recent events.

[16] 1) *Of the auctorite of the word of god agaynst the bisshop of london/ wherein are conteyned certen disputacyons had in the parlament howse . . . abowt the nomber of the sacraments . . .* By Alexander Alesius. [Leipzig? 1537?] 2) *A faithfull report of proceedings anent the assemblie of ministers at Aberdeen vpon Tuesday 2 Iuly 1605.* [Middelburg: Richard Schilders,] 21 February 1606. 3) *A briefe*

[74]

and fanatical jeremiads on passing events,[17] narratives of miraculous manifestations supposed to declare God's will in time of doubt[18] and reports of the arguments of counsel in a hearing before the Ecclesiastical Court of High Commission,[19] petitions to the sovereign[20] and memorials of the martyrs—all of them published as salvos in the religious warfare rather than as news, though more or less news they divulge just the same. The address to "the Chrysten Reader" in *A trew report of the dysputacyon . . . in the conuocacyō hows at London*, which is attributed to the martyr Philpot,[21] puts the object of all these publications quite·plainly and shows how, in the minds of their fosterers, they were of the same rank and purport as doctrinal dissertations:

And to the intent that all men may knowe and see what reasons and answers were made on both partys / I haue thought good to publyssh so moch thereoff as came vnto my handis / trusting that no man wyll be more o̍ffe̍ded wyth the settyng furth thereof / to the inte̍t that such as were not present may reade such thingys as there were done and sayd / . . . than they were that all that were prese̍t shuld heare them. . . .

. . . *Narration of proceedings at an Assemsemblie* [sic] *in Glasco, 8. Iun. 1610* . . . [London?] 1610. 4) *Perth Assembly.* [By David Calderwood. Holland:] 1619.

[17] *The intended Treason, of Doctor Parrie . . . Against the Queenes . . . Maiestie. . . .* By Philip Stubbes. For Henry Car, [1584].

[18] *A miraculous work of late done at Court of Strete in Kent, published . . . by Edward Thwaytes, Gent.* John Skot, 1527. No extant copy is known.

[19] *The argument of Master Nicholas Fuller, in the case of Thomas Lad, and Richard Maunsell, his Clients.* [Printed abroad:] 1607. This book was apparently printed without Fuller's knowledge. Sir Francis Bacon seems to have suspected his colleague Sir Henry Yelverton of having had a hand in it; see Spedding: *The letters and the life of Francis Bacon*, IV. 95.

[20] 1) *The humble petition of the communaltie to their . . . Soueraigne, the Ladie Elizabeth . . .* [Middelburg: Richard Schilders, 1588?] 2) *An abridgment of that booke which the ministers of Lincoln diocess deliuered to his Maiestie . . . Being . . . an apologye for themselues and their brethren that refuse the subscription . . . 1605.*

[21] Basil [= Antwerp?]: Alexander Edmonds, [1554].

And as by readyng and weyng the reasōs and answers of thys dysputaciō I dowt not but thow shalt be suffyciētly confyrmed in the truth of the artycles thereī reasoned and debated / euyn so in a lytle treatyse of the trewe sacryfyce of a christē mā which by gods grace shall shortly also be set furth / thow shalt be instructed what to iudge off other artycles / as of the masse / of altarys / of the inuocatyon of sayntys / and such lyke.

During the reign of Mary, when the minions of Antichrist had the upper hand, the reformers laid down a barrage of printed matter by means of foreign presses and secret presses in England. In Rouen they printed a book called *The Communication betwene my lord Chauncelor and iudge Hales*,[22] a literal account, written in dialog form, of a colloquy between Bishop Gardiner and a judge suspected of Protestant leanings in which the former forbade the latter to take his oath of office. Somewhere on the continent they printed *The copie of certaine lettres sent to the Quene [and others] . . . by . . . Thomas Cranmer . . . from prison in Oxeforde . . .* (1556?) with a bitterly anti-papal preface to the reader. *The Lamētacion of England* (1558), a tract against the queen, the privy council, and the Spaniards, was written abroad and probably printed there too. It was possibly abroad that a remarkable document entitled *A supplicacyō to the quenes maiestie* was printed; at any rate, one edition of it has been assigned to a Zurich press. The other, however, bears the imprint of John Cawood, "Prynter tho the quenes Mayestie wyth here most gracyus lycence." Surely this imprint is a forgery; Cawood would never have dared to print a tract like this which speaks of high councillors like Bishops Gardiner and Bonner in terms for which "disrespectful" is a mild description. The matter of the book makes it certain that the royal printer's name was attached in the spirit of irony. A Latin version of *The trew report of the*

---

[22] [Rouen: Michael Wood, 1553.]

dysputacyon . . . *in the conuocacyō hows,*[23] and *The Copye of a letter sent by Iohn Bradforth to* . . . *the Erles of Arundel, Darbie, Shrewsburye and Penbroke, declaring the nature of Spaniardes* (1555) are tracts from the reform party, containing more or less news, which were probably printed under cover in England.

After the establishment of Protestantism under Queen Elizabeth, the presses of London, for several years, issued a series of mementos of the martyrs of the previous reign for which we are undoubtedly indebted to their closest sympathizers and confederates. These took the form of metrical epitaphs,[24] minutes of their examinations,[25] records of their last statements,[26] and memorials of their sufferings and imprisonment.[27] As news, they were not strictly fresh,

[23] *Vera expositio disputationis, institutæ in synodo ecclesiastica Londini* . . . Romæ: coram castro S. Angeli ad signum S. Petri, 1554.

[24] 1) *The Epythafe of Bradfordes.* Book. Entered 1561 by Thomas Marshe (Arber, I. 155). 2) A ballad of John Careless ("Some men for sodayne ioye do wepe") was printed in Coverdale's *Certaine most godly* . . . *letters* (possibly in print as early as 1560) and was very probably printed separately not later than the same time. The first record of its separate publication is its entry in the Stationers' register 1 August 1586 by Edward White (*ib.,* II. 451). 3) *An epytathe vpon ye Deathe of J Bradforde.* Ballad. Entered 4 September 1564 by William Pekerynge (*ib.,* I. 262). 4) *A Epytaphe of John Philpotte.* [Ballad.] Entered 1564–5 by Pekerynge (*ib.,* I. 268).

[25] 1) *The examinacion of* . . . *Iohn Philpot.* [Henry Sutton, 1559?] 2) *All the examinacions of* . . . *Iohn Bradforde, before the* . . . *cōmissioners* . . . William Griffith, 13 May 1561.

[26] 1) *The complaynt of Veritie, made by Iohn Bradford.· An exhortation of Mathewe Rogers* . . . *The complaynt of Raufe Allerton and others* . . . *A saieng of maister Houper* . . . [London? Owen Rogers?] 1559. 2) *The wordes of Maister Hooper at his death.* 1559. 3) *A frendly farewel, which* . . . *Doctor Ridley* . . . *did write beinge prisoner in Oxeforde* . . . *Newly set forth* . . . Ihon Day, 10 November 1559.

[27] 1) *Certain most godly* . . . *letters of such true Saintes and holy Martyrs* . . . *as in the late bloodye persecution* . . . *gaue their lyues* . . . [Collected by Miles Coverdale.] Entered November 1560 by Owen Rogers (Arber, I. 152). Iohn Day, 1564. 2) *A briefe Treatise concerning the burnynge of Bucer and Phagius at Cambrydge, in the tyme of Queen Mary with theyr restitution in the tyme of our* . . . *Souerayne Lady that nowe is.* Translated by Arthur Goldyng. Thomas Marshe, 1562.

but the most notable martyrs had been burned as lately as in 1555 and 1556, and without doubt the memory of those difficult times was still green. The Rev. Thomas Brice's metrical martyrology was printed in 1559[28] and Foxe's *Actes and Monuments*, which had been printed in Latin at Basle in the same year,[29] and which we will not call news if an objection is heard, followed it in 1563.[30]

During all of the reigns of Elizabeth and James I, the various dissenting Protestant sects, which were almost as repugnant to the authorities as the Papists themselves, kept up a campaign of ink and paper in which we occasionally find a book of news. The miracles claimed for Henrik Niclas, the founder of the Family of Love, for example, were set forth in a book, written in scriptural style, and published by one of his apostles about 1575,[31] when he was beginning to attract unfavorable notice from the official church. We hear further news of these quaint sectaries in two books published for their reproof.[32] It is, of course, not unusual to obtain information—not always of the most reliable kind—about a cause from its opponents; for instance, the three reports of church assemblies in Scotland mentioned above were published abroad by anti-episcopal agitators for the purpose of exposing the horrid papistical usages of the prelates. There are especially full records of the persecution of two of the most celebrated Protestant martyrs of Elizabeth's reign—John Penry, the

[28] *A compendious register in metre, conteinyng the names; and pacient suffryngs of the membres of Iesus Christ, and the tormented and cruelly burned within Englande; since the death of . . . Edwarde the sixte . . .* [For Richard Adams,] 1559.

[29] *Rerum in Ecclesia gestarum . . . commentarii. Pars prima . . . de rebus per Angliam et Scotiam gestis . . .*

[30] Iohn Day, 20 March 1563. Frequently reprinted.

[31] *Mirabilia opera Dei . . .* [1575?]

[32] 1) *The Displaying of an horrible secte of . . . Heretiques, naming themselues the Familie of Loue . . . Neuely set foorth by I* [ohn] *R* [ogers]. For George Bishop, [1578], 1579. 2) *A supplication of the Family of Loue . . . Examined, and found to be derogatorie . . . vnto the glorie of God . . .* [For] Iohn Legate, 1606.

reputed author of some of the Marprelate tracts, and the proto-Congregationalist Henry Barrow. Most of these were written by the prisoners themselves, smuggled out of jail, and printed abroad. A petition addressed by Penry to Parliament,[33] a farewell address to his coreligionists[34] and another to his wife,[35] Barrow's petition to the queen,[36] and three reports of examinations by the authorities[37] all contain news, some of them a great deal of news.

3. FOREIGN NEWS PRINTED AS RELIGIOUS PROPAGANDA

We must also recognize that the earliest considerable body of foreign news printed in English was due likewise to the zeal of religious reformers. The printing of it was a part of their activity for the propagation of their faith, just as was that of the domestic news mentioned in the preceding section. The earliest reformers, who derived comfort and inspiration from the progress of reformed doctrine on the continent, eagerly put this news before their compatriots at home in any shape in which it promised to be serviceable. They printed news of foreign events favorable to their tenets; they printed news of foreign events unfavorable to their opponents when that was available, such as the letter of the papal legate to Poland complaining

[33] *Th' appellation of Iohn Penri vnto . . . Parliament, from the . . . injurious dealing of th' Archb[ishop] of Canterb[ury] . . .* [Printed abroad:] 1589.

[34] [Begins:] *I Iohn Penry doo heare . . . set doune . . . the Whole truth . . . which I hold . . . in regard of my faith towards my God and Dread Soueraigne Queene Elizabeth. . . .* [1593.]

[35] *To my beloved wife Helener Penry.* [1593.]

[36] *A petition directed to her . . . Maiestie. . . .* [Middelburg: Richard Schilders? 1590] (3 edd.)

[37] 1) *A Collection Of certain Letters and conferences, Lately Passed Betwixt Certaine Preachers & Tvvo Prisoners In The Fleet.* [Dort?] 1590. 2) *A Collection of certaine sclaunderous articles gyuen out by the Bisshops against such faithful Christians as they now uniustly deteyne in their prisons . . .* [Dort?—Hanse?] 1590. 3) *The examinations of Henry Barrowe, Iohn Grenewood and Iohn Penrie* [Dort?—Hanse? 1593]; for W. Marshall, [1594?].

of his difficulties with the Lutherans there,[38] or the Emperor Charles V's rebuff to Pope Paul III's summons to the Council of Trent.[39] They chronicled the lives and acts of the leading proponents of the new faith;[40] they recorded the proceedings or conclusions arrived at by assemblies and councils met to deliberate on questions of faith;[41] and they made known the creeds, liturgies, and forms of worship adopted by foreign congregations.[42] They were, without

[38] *A Copye of a . . . letter sent from . . . Levves Lippomanus . . . late Legate in Polone. . . . .* Translated from the Italian by Michael Throckmerton. Curtigiane of Rome, 1556.

[39] *The answere of Carolus the fyfte vnto Paule the thyrd, concerninge a generall councell at Trident.* [1543?] Another edition by Richard Grafton, [1543?].

[40] 1) *The true hystorye of the Christen departynge of . . . Martyne Luther . . .* By Iustus Ionas; translated by Iohan Bale. [Wesel: Derik van der Straten, 1546?] 2) *The rekening and declaraciō of the faith and beleif of Huldrik Zwingly . . .* Zürich: March 1543; Züryk [=London]: Richard Wyer, 1548. 3) *The Epistle of . . . Philipp Melancton made vnto . . . Kynge Henry the Eyght, for the reuokinge . . . of the six Artycles . . .* Translated from the Latin by I. C. Weesell [=London? John Day?] 18 May 1547. 4) *The Tragical death of Dauid Beatō . . . : Whereunto is ioyned the martyrdom of maister George Wyseharte . . .* Iohn Day & William Seres, [1548?].

[41] 1) *The confessyon of the fayth of the Germaynes in the councell at Augusta . . . 153[0].* Robert Redman, 1536 (2 edd.) 2) *The actes of the disputaciō in the cowncell of the Empyre holden at Regenspurg . . .* Translated from the Latin by Mylys Couerdale. [Antwerp?] 1542. 3) *The Supplicacion . . . of Osteryke . . . vnto kyng Ferdinandus, in the cause of the Christen Religion. . . .* [1543?] 4) *A request presented to the King of Spayn . . . by the inhabitantes of the Lowe countreyes protesting that they will liue according to the reformation of the Gospell . . .* Edinburgh: Leighe Mannenby [=London: Henry Bynneman], 1578.

[42] 1) *The confescion of the fayth of the Sweserlādes.* Translated by George Vssher. [Thomas Raynalde, 1548?] 2) *Geneua. The forme of common praiers vsed in the churches of Geneua . . .* Edward Whitchurche, 7 June 1550. 3) *The order that the churche . . . in Denmark, and . . . Germany doth vse . . .* By Miles Coverdale. [John Day & William Seres, 1550?] 4) Another Geneva confession. [1556.] 5) *The Confession of the Faythe . . . professed by the Protestantes . . . of Scotlande . . .* Rouland Hall, 1561. 6) *A confession of Fayth, made by . . . diuers reformed Churches beyonde the Seas . . .* For Lucas Harrison, [1568?], 1571. 7) *A short and generall confession of the true Christian Faith . . . according to Gods Word, and Acts of our [Scotch] Parliament . . .* Broadside. For Ionas Man, [1581]. 8) *The Confession of the . . . christian Fayth according to Gods word, and Actes of Parliament . . .* Robert Waldegraue,

knowing it, or intending to be, the first publishers of foreign news.

4. NEWS PUBLISHED IN THE INTEREST OF FOREIGN POWERS

A quite different kind of propaganda which occasionally found it serviceable to print news is that by which a foreign nation, or an important faction in a foreign nation, or an active partisan of a foreign cause seeks justification in English eyes, usually for the purpose of gaining English good will, if not active aid. We do not find much of it, but there are a few pieces of printed news which can be traced back to such an origin.

In 1483, as it would seem, William Caxton printed a quarto consisting of six letters recently exchanged by Pope Sixtus IV, the College of Cardinals, and John Mocenigo, doge of Venice.[43] Their subject is the treaty of peace recently concluded between the Supreme Pontiff and the Duke of Ferrara and his allies; their purpose was to persuade the Venetians, the pope's allies, to ratify this treaty, which the Holy Father had arranged without their knowledge and at which they were therefore inclined to balk, feeling that he had rather sold them out. According to the colophon, the book was edited by Petrus Carmelianus, *poeta laureatus*, an Italian-born ecclesiastic living, and prospering, in England, and a Venetian partisan. Consequently, the most likely explanation of this book is that Carmelianus procured the publication of it, out of his zeal for the Vene-

---

[1581]. 9) *The confession of fayth of certayne English people, living in exile, in the Low Countreyes.* 1602, 1607. 10) *A full declaration of the faith . . . professed in the dominions of . . . Fredericke, . . . Elector Palatine.* Translated from the German by Iohn Rolte. For William Welby, 1614.

[43] *Sex qჳ elegantissime epistole / quarum tris a . . . Sixto Quarto et Sacro Cardinalium Collegio ad . . . Venetiarum ducem . . . totidemqჳ ab ipso Duce . . . ob Ferrariense bellum susceptum / conscripte sunt.* Westminster: Willelmus Caxton.

tian point of view, in order to work up sympathy for it in distant England. It is a question how useful English sympathy might have been to the Venetians in a spiteful little quarrel such as this; but thus to air the Venetians' grievances in his adopted country could at least have given Carmelianus a sense of self-satisfaction.

We find an extraordinary instance of a foreigner's addressing himself to the English people and attempting to convert them to his way of thinking in a book called *The copy of a letter lately vvritten by a Spanishe gentleman to his friend in England: in refutation of sundry calumnies, there falsely bruited, and spred amonge the people* (1589).[44] This gentleman, who had spent some time in England as a prisoner after the defeat of the Armada, begins as follows:

> Good Sir, and courteous freinde, since the tyme of my late deliuery from captiuitie, I haue often called to mynde, hovv desirous I founde you, to vnderstand the truthe of our intentiõ, thoughe litle doubtfull of the iustnesse of our cause. . . .
>
> Well, seing it hathe since pleased God, to lend me . . . meanes to send vnto you (which in so dangerous and vvatchfull a vvorld is moste difficill to be founde) I could not omitt to vvrite at this present, vvhereby yourself, and such others, as to vvhome you may with safty communicate it, may be the better satisfied.

His first wish, he says, is the conversion of England to "the one only Catholique & Apostolique faith," as it is that of "those of your nation that now liue in exile, retayning the true loue, and affection, that Christians oughte to cary to their country, preferring the soule before the body." "Nexte, the auncient tranquilitie, and quyet accorde thereof, with other Christian countries." The greater part of the letter is a discussion of recent events, interpreted, of course, from the Spanish and Catholic point of view, which our gentleman concludes by "wishing vnto all your countrymen, the due consideration of their case." The hardihood of this self-appointed mentor is astonishing: he is not

44 Signed I. B. Printed abroad.

only quite ready to believe the worst about the English, but to tell it to them as gospel truth. Unless he was an incurable optimist, he could not really have expected to make headway with "all your countrymen" by methods such as his; the book was more likely intended for English Catholics whose allegiance was already wavering.

We also find a few tracts apparently printed as pleas for assistance by distressed allies abroad. We might expect a good deal of this sort of propaganda from the Netherlands during the wars with Spain, but as a matter of fact I have found nothing which can be traced to the Netherlanders themselves or to any important faction of them. Some of their English sympathizers did exert themselves on behalf of the unfortunate Dutchmen, but that is another matter. Most of the news of the struggle against the Spaniards which was published in England was plainly sympathetic to the Netherlanders, but it was published by English booksellers, who were no more devoted to the Dutch cause than the average Englishman, and much less than to making a living for themselves; the Dutch had no hand in the printing of this news in England. The explanation is probably that there was no urgent need for the Dutch to plead their cause with the English people: their sympathy went out to their coreligionists and the enemies of Spain quite freely.

For others, it was more difficult to enlist English cooperation. The classic instance is Bohemia in 1619 and 1620, when King James's son-in-law, the Elector Palatine, having been elected king, was promptly ejected from his new kingdom and from the rest of his possessions as well by the emperor, who claimed Bohemia as his own. There was much sympathy in England for the Bohemian cause, and some sentiment for armed intervention, but King James chose to play the peacemaker rather than the helpful father. We have already seen an example of agitation for the elector's cause of domestic origin.[45] Much news from Bohemia was printed at the time, some of it plainly polemical and inspired, and probably put forth by the elector's party on the continent. Most of this was printed on continental presses—at Dort, Middelburg, Amsterdam, Flushing, the Hague, and Prague. If it had originated in England, there would have been little reason for carrying most of it abroad to be printed; other news equally favorable to the elector's interests was openly published there. Consequently we are obliged to suspect that this agitation in print was kept up by the elector's friends on the continent. That part of it which is merely argumentative and concerned with proving on juridical or even moral grounds[46] that the emperor's claim was invalid, we need not consider, but much of it contains news—acts of the Estates of Bohemia, edicts of the king-elect, the proceedings of the emperor, *etc.*[47] Its purpose is pretty plainly indicated by such statements as:

Thus now (curteous Reader) hast thou here a short Answere to the proposed Question; Consider the same well, and desire God to assist the right.[48]

[45] See above, p. 72.

[46] One fanatical tract, for example, *A plaine demonstration of the vnlawful succession of . . . Ferdinand the Second, because of the incestuous Marriage of his parents* (The Hage: 1620), argues that he has no rights of any kind whatsoever because his parents married within the forbidden degrees. True, the pope granted them a dispensation, but the pope is a false-hearted usurper whose dispensations have no authority in the face of the clear commands of the Scriptures.

[47] See 1) *The most illustrious Prince Fredericke, . . . King of Bohemia . . . , And . . . his Queene.* A broadside celebrating his election. Dort: George Waters, 1619. 2) *A declaration of the causes, for the which, wee Frederick . . . haue accepted of the crowne of Bohemia . . .* Middleburg: Abraham Schilders, 1620. 3) *A proclamation made by . . . Fredericke . . . of Bohemia, &c. Commanding all those his Subjects which are now in the Seruice of his Majesties Enemies, to repaire Home . . .* Prague: 1620. 4) *A Briefe Description of the reasons that make the . . . Ban made against the King of Bohemia . . . of no value . . .* The Hayf [*sic*]: Arnold Meuris, 1621.

[48] *An answere to the question: Whether the Emperour . . . can bee Iudge in the Bohemian Controuersie or no? . . .* 1620.

And the same States [of Bohemia] rest in good expectation, and full assurance that Christian Princes which professe the Gospell, will be watchfull with all their might to maintaine this most iust and honest Quarrell, which is the cause of Christ and his Church, and will defend the Kingdome of Bohemia.⁴⁹

The only part of this news which can be certainly traced to its origin is a few books attributed to John Harrison, an English divine who had gone to the Palatinate in the suite of the Princess Elizabeth after her marriage and who was still there at least until the end of 1619.   He composed a narrative of the departure of the elector from Heidelberg for Prague and of his coronation

to giue satisfaction to the world, as touching . . . his Maᵗⁱᵉˢ proceedings . . . As also to encourage all other noble & heroicall spirits (especially our owne nation, whom in honour it first and chieffe-lie concerneth by prerogative of that high, and soveraigne Title, haere-ditarie to our Kings & Princes: defendees of the faith) to the lyke Christian resolution, against Antichrist and his Adhærents.⁵⁰

Possibly he was the translator of a defense of the rejection of the emperor as king by the Estates of Bohemia which was printed at Dort.⁵¹   A certain I. H., who is probably the same person, also translated a Latin tract of like tenor, fortified by official documents, which was published, without any printer's name, at London.⁵²

About the same time we find two other foreign causes seeking the good will of England.   One of these was that of Poland, then threatened with invasion by the Turks. The Polish ambassador made an appeal in Latin to the king on 11 March 1621 which was promptly issued with an English translation, "commanded by his Maiestie to be pub-

---

⁴⁹ *A cleare Demonstration that Ferdinand is by his owne demerits fallen from the Kingdome of Bohemia* . . . Dort: George Waters, [1619].

⁵⁰ *A short relation of The departure of* . . . *Frederick King Elect of Bohemia* . . . *from Heydelberg towards Prague* . . . Dort: George Waters, 1619.

⁵¹ *The reasons which compelled the States of Bohemia to reiect the Archiduke Ferdinand* . . . Translated from the French. Dort: George Waters, [1619].

⁵² *Bohemica Iura Defensa.* [William Jones,] 1620.

[85]

lished in Print."[53]   But it was not printed by the royal printer and it was licensed for publication by the king's principal secretary, so that his majesty's command probably amounted to no more than permission to print.   At the same time, the ambassador was given permission to raise eight hundred volunteers, so that perhaps we should say it served as a recruiting pamphlet.[54]   The French Protestants also put their case before the English people.   In 1621 they printed at Rochelle a long tale of their recent afflictions, buttressed with two official documents, which they addressed to the English in the following terms:

Seeing then that all other remedies at this present are taken from vs, let vs fill our eyes with teares, the Ayre with our sighes, and this Paper with the true recitall of the miseries that we endure; And so at the least we shall reape that contentment to make our griefe knowne to our bretheren, & letting them vnderstand our troubles, we shall moue them to compassion with vs, it being a iust thing, that as we are vnited togither by one selfe-same Religion, and hated for one cause, we should be touched with one selfe-same and the like feeling. .

  And you Brethren, that by one selfe same band of Faith, and Religion are vnited, and strictly bound vnto vs: Behold in this sorowfull spectacle what hath bin done . . . : Consider our calamities therein . . . : Make your selues sensible of our miseries, helpe vs to find some remedies, either by your most humble prayers vnto God . . . , or else by your supplications to our good King, . . . or by your good assistance against those, that doe nothing else but labour vtterly to root out and destroy vs.[55]

Another pamphlet, the copy of a document issued by the Assembly, was printed at Rochelle on 12 July of the same year.[56]   On 26 June 1621 Nathaniel Newbery entered in the Stationers' register a *Declaration des Eglises Reformees*,

[53] *A true copy of the Latine oration of the . . . Lord George Ossolinsky . . .* For William Lee, 1621.

[54] *C. S. P. D. 1619–23*, p. 249.

[55] *A declaration set forth by the Protestants in France . . .* Rochell: 1621.

[56] *A letter vvritten by those of the Assembly in Rochell: To Monsieur le Duc de les Diguieres. . . .*

de France et soueraineté de Bearne. De l'iniuste persecution qui leur est faicte par les ennemis de l'Estat et de leur Religion. Et de leur legitime et necessaire defense. to be printed in English. if the translacon shalbe approued of.[57] Newbery, who was an active news-monger, may not have regarded it as propaganda, but evidently the authorities considered it dangerous matter, for the Stationers' clerk appended a note that the book was not to be printed "by expresse order" of the Archbishop of Canterbury's chaplain. Nevertheless it was printed, possibly abroad, for two issues, dated 1621, with the same text and different title-pages, are known.[58] To flout authority in this way is a risk a zealot rather than a journalistic publisher is likely to take. At all events, these books probably point to a campaign of propaganda directed upon the English nation by the Protestants of Rochelle.[59]

5. News Published in the Catholic Interest

During the last sixty years of our period, a certain amount of printed news was published by Catholic apologists. Discountenanced and, latterly, persecuted in England, they never gave up hope of bringing the errant English church into the fold, and, among many means, they used the printing press industriously in their efforts to do so. This work was chiefly in the hands of English Catholics, with the King of Spain as their chief secular ally, and they carried it on with unsparing devotion. They plied their pens indefatigably, and they disseminated their writings,

[57] Arber, IV. 56.

[58] 1) *The declaration of the Reformed Churches of France and the soveraigntie of Bearn.* . . . . 2) *A declaration made by the reformed churches of France and the principalitie of Bearn.* . . .

[59] The book entitled *The last summons, or an oration sent to the Inhabitants of* . . . *Rochell, To mooue them to yeild the Towne vnto his Maiestie, and to obay his Commandements,* dated 1621, but without imprint and therefore possibly printed abroad, may be a reply to these appeals for sympathy, for there is nothing in it to minister comfort to the Protestant mind.

[87]

printed abroad or on secret presses in England,[60] only at grave risks to themselves. Much of what they wrote is devotional and doctrinal, but some of it is news, for the religious disputes of the time were, of course, closely bound up with political policy.

These Catholic news-reports divide themselves roughly into two classes. First, there is the aggressive sort, those which triumphantly relate the successes of the old faith or other news which might help to win over the reader to toleration and belief. Early in the reign of Elizabeth, for example, an English Catholic printer living in the Low Countries, John Fowler by name, out of the goodness of his heart, issued a series of English books for the purpose of leading his countrymen into the way of light, among them a few containing news. One of these is *An oration Against the Vnlawfull Insurrections of the Protestantes of our time*,[61] which he translated from the Latin, he says, "to warne my deer Contremen of those mens [*i.e.*, the Protestants'] malice and cruelty." Another is a copy of a proclamation by Charles IX of France forbidding the practice of the Protestant faith.[62] Fowler also printed a defense of the Queen of Scots against the wickednesses imputed to her by her subjects,[63] and a reply to R. G.'s letter mentioned above.[64] There are two accounts of visits by the royalty of Spain to the English college at Valladolid, one printed in

[60] On the subject of Catholic presses in England, see Simpson: *Edmund Campion*, pp. 184–212; Law: *Collected Essays and Reviews*, pt. 6; Hawkes: "The Birchley Hall secret press" (*Library*, 4th series, VII. 137).

[61] Antwerp: 1566 (2 edd.).

[62] *An edict or ordonnance of the French King conteining a prohibition . . . of al . . . exercise of any other religion then of the catholique . . .* Lovan: 1568.

[63] *The copie of a Letter writen out of Scotland, by an English Gentlemā . . . vnto a frind . . . of his, that desired to be informed of the truth . . . of the slaunderous . . . reportes made of the Q̃uene of Scotland . . .* [Antwerp: 1572?]

[64] *A treatise of treasons against Queen Elizabeth . . .* [Translated from *L'innocence de . . . Marie, Royne d'Escosse*, by François de Belleforest. Antwerp:] January 1572.

1592[65] and the other in 1601,[66] designed to show how these seminaries were flourishing and how they were favored by the king. The first is in the form of a letter written by an English priest at the college to an English Catholic gentleman and his wife living in exile in Flanders. But it was intended for wider circulation, for the author says:

This [narrative] . . . no doubt will be verie grateful vnto this [English] nation, for that thereby they shall not onelie see, what passed in this acte of the Kings coming hither, but also further vnderstand manie things of the present state of Ingland, which they desyre to do, as hath appeared by their greedie acceptaunce of diuers bookes published in this language of late yeares, touching the affaires and present persecution of Ingland.

The book is aggressively anti-Protestant and it sets forth the exercises held at the college during the king's visit at fatiguing length, but it also provides some of the valuable information which it promises. The second book, which purports to have been written by a Spaniard, includes "An aduertisement to the Catholikes of England, of the present state of their children brought vp in this Colledge of Valladolid." The English translator dedicated the book to Lord Hunsdon, the lord chamberlain, in the following ingenuous terms:

Right honorable, I was drawen with no little curiosety and desire, to reade this booke when it came to my hands in the Spanish tongue, therby to gather the trewe causes, why the Spaniards fauor so much our Inglish Catholique fugetiues, and what hartes they cary to their country, euen these which for Religion, leaue it . . . And for as much as the relacion of these solemnityes written by a straunger, and published in print, to be read by so many graue persons as had bene present, must nedes be written with all truthe and sinceritie, I could not choose . . . but discouer vnto vs the secret affects, of both

[65] *A relation of the King of Spaines receiuing in Valliodolid, and in the Inglish College* . . . 1592.

[66] *A relation of the solemnetie wherewith* . . . *K. Phillip the III. and Quene Margaret were receyued in the Inglish Colledge of Valladolid the 22. of August. 1600.* By Ant[onio] Ortiz; translated from the Spanish by Frauncis Riuers. At N.: 1601.

[89]

parts. And therfore hauing seene it with attention, I was drawen with no lesse desire to put it in English, that it might be read by your honor and the rest of my good lords of her M[ajesty's] Councel. For yf the good will of the King of Spaine . . . to our countrymen, . . . be founded in these honorable respects of conformity in Religion on the one side, and of . . . gratitude on the other, . . . me thinke the assurance of good meaninge, and knowen continuance of good will in them that were wont to be our best frends, though of late prouoked to be our enemyes, should encorage vs much to Peace, . . . with those in whom yet . . . wee fynde far better harts and more true affection to our Country and Countrymen, (as in this occasion may be sene) then in others, whom . . . we labor (I feare in vayne) to make of old enemyes, new frends.

How effective propaganda like this, peppered with allusions to the late King Philip II's love for the English Catholics, may have been in inclining impressionable minds towards the Catholic faith we need not inquire. It is quite possible that the Spanish author of this tract is simply the *alter ego* of the English translator.[67]

The second class is more numerous. It is defensive; these books were written in justification of the ways and works of the English Catholic party and in reply to or in correction of the news published in England about it. Charges of malicious misrepresentation were freely hurled back and forth in this warfare; we cannot believe that there was a truthful publicist on either side as we read the reports of the other. One of the stoutest Catholic champions was Father Robert Parsons, an active and capable Jesuit with

[67] See also 1) *An extracte of the determinacion . . . of the Doctours of the vniuersities of Salamanca and Valledolid touching the vvarres of Ireland . . .* Broadside. [1603?] 2) *A Petition Apologeticall presented to the Kings . . . Maiesty, by the Lay Catholikes of England . . .* Doway: J. Mogar, 1604. 3) *Miracles lately vvrought by the intercession of the . . . Virgin Marie, at Mont-aigu . . .* [By Philips Numan;] translated from the French by Robert Chambers. Antwarp: Arnold Conings, 1606. 4) *A Briefe Relation of the Persecution lately made against the Catholike Christians in . . . Japonia . . .* Translated from the Spanish by W[illiam] W[right, S. J.] Gent. [St. Omer: press of the English College,] 1619. 5) *An oration made . . . in the Chamber of the Third Estate . . . vpon the Oath (pretended Of Allegiance) . . .* [Translated from the French by Antoine Estiene. St. Omer: press of the English College,] 1616.

an incurable taste both for political intrigue and for pamphleteering. In many of his tracts we can read the Catholic interpretation of recent events. One of them, *De Persecutione Anglicana, Epistola*, printed in various editions at several places on the continent in 1581 and 1582,[68] seems to have been trenchant enough to draw as return fire the two apologies by Lord Burghley already mentioned.[69] The latter's *Declaration of the fauourable dealing* advertises the fact that it was written "against those most slaunderous reportes . . . spread abroad by Runnagate Iesuites and Seminary men, in their seditious Bookes, Letters, and Libels." When the reformed seminarian John Nichols capitalized his conversion by publishing a somewhat imaginative description of the life of the English seminaries abroad,[70] Parsons wrote, and printed on his press near London, a scornful refutation of these revelations of Nichols,[71] who, to tell the truth, reflected very little credit on any cause he favored with his adherence. As Andreas Philopater, Parsons is supposed to have written a Latin tract in reply to the queen's proclamation against Jesuits and priests of 18 October 1591.[72] To circulate this tract in English, a Catholic pamphleteer—the British Museum catalog suggests either Joseph Cresswell or Parsons himself—hit upon an ingenious scheme. Posing as an English government intelligencer, or spy, he wrote a report to his "louing good frind" and superior officer, "N. secre-

---

[68] First printed in 1581. Reprinted, with varying titles, and sometimes with additional matter, at Strassburg (twice), Rome, and Paris in 1582.

[69] *A Declaration of the fauourable dealing of her Maiesties Commissioners* (1583) and *The Execution of Iustice in England* (1583). See above, p. 55.

[70] See above, p. 50.

[71] *A Discouerie of I. Nicols minister, misreported a Iesuite, latelye recanted in the Tower of London*. . . . [1582.]

[72] *Elizabethæ . . '. sæuissimum in Catholicos sui Regni edictum . . . Cum responsione ad singula capita* . . . Augsburg: Ioannes Fabrus, October 1592. Variously reprinted.

[91]

tary to . . . the L[ord] Treasurer" of England, as follows:

From Midleburg [and other cities] . . . I wrote vnto you . . . of
the great variety of bookes both in Inglishe and Latyn, and other
languages already come forth, or in makinge . . . against the laste
proclamation of her Maiestie published in Nouember [sic] for searching out . . . and punishing of Seminarie priestes, and Iesuites . . .
  But now comming to Augusta [= Augsburg], I haue learned of an
other booke also written in Latin, and lately sent hither to be printed
againe, & is now in hande, . . . though I can neyther hynder the
printinge thereof, (for I haue assayed) nor yet get any whole copy
into my handes to sende vnto you . . . yet . . . I gat for mony
the sighte of the booke, and in some few nightes I took out all the
summe, and chiefe effecte thereof, & doe sende it herewith vnto you.

Thereupon ensues a summary in English of Parsons's
counterattack. The whole was entitled *An aduertisement
written to a secretarie of my L. Treasurers of Ingland, by an
Inglishe Intelligencer as he passed throughe Germanie . . .
Concerninge An other booke newly written in Latin, and
published in diuerse languages . . ., against her Maiesties
late proclamation, for . . . apprehension of Seminary
priestes.*[73] Here is a match for the disingenuous maneuvers
of the government in this warfare of pot and kettle. Parsons's last essay in apologetics in which we find information
about current events is part of a controversy which started
in France and had heavy repercussions in England, early
in the reign of King James.[74]

Another Catholic tract, entitled *A declaration of the true causes of the great
troubles, presupposed to be intended against* . . . *England,* printed abroad in 1592,
I take to be another reply to this proclamation, though the author, who is said to
be Richard Verstegen, refers to the document he is striving to annihilate as a
proclamation of November 1592. His title is a parody of that of the proclamation
of 18 October 1591, for which see above, p. 37. This *Declaration* is a very intem-
perate polemic.

[73] Probably printed abroad: 1592.

[74] *A Relation of the Triall made before the King of France* . . . *betweene the
Bishop of Eureux and the L. Plessis Mornay* . . . By N. D. [St. Omer: Francis
Bellet? 1604.]

Cardinal Allen, though a less active pamphleteer than Father Parsons, also employed his pen in the cause. In 1584 he answered Lord Burghley's *Execution of Iustice in England* with a book called *A true sincere and modest defence of English Catholiques that suffer for their faith.*[75] In the year 1588 he wrote, or at least he suffered his name to put to, a manifesto entitled *An admonition to . . . England . . . concerninge the present vvarres made for the execution of his Holines Sentence, by the . . . Kinge . . . of Spaine*, a furious attack upon the queen's title to her throne, full of astounding information about her public policy and her private life. This is doubtless the book which is said to have been loaded in numbers in the Armada to be used for the purposes of propaganda when a landing was made on the island. An abridgement in broadside form, *A Declaration of the Sentence and deposition of Elizabeth, the vsurper and pretensed Quene of Englande*, was also prepared. If these two editions were embarked in the Armada along with the King of Spain's big battalions, it is a question how many copies were actually dispersed.

Another Catholic disquisition on English politics is *Newes from Spayne and Holland conteyning. An information of Inglish affayres in Spayne*, published in 1593. It is a letter "vvritten by a Gentleman trauelour borne in the lovv countryes, and brought vp from a child in Ingland, vnto a Gentleman his frend and Oste in London." There is a great deal of political animadversion in this tract, with special reference to Lord Burghley's policy and the succession to the throne, but it also contains much indubitable news—of ninety English sailors converted to Catholicism in Spain, of the flourishing of the English seminary at St.

---

[75] [Ingolstadt.] A Latin translation was published the same year [at Douai]: *Ad persecutores Anglos . . . vera, sincera, & modesta responsio.* Another Catholic reply to *The Execution of Iustice in England* is *De Iustitia Britannica . . . , quæ contra Christi Martyres continenter exercetur* (Ingolstadt: D. Sartorius, 1584).

Lúcar, of the celebration of the feast of St. Thomas of Canterbury in Seville, of the attempt of Queen Elizabeth to set the Great Turk against the King of Spain, *etc.* There is a note on this book in Lord Burghley's papers which mentions the means by which it was smuggled into England.[76]

The scholars in the English seminaries at Douai, Rheims, and St. Omer were also active in the work of propaganda, the latter two working their own presses. Many of the English books issued by the Catholics in the eighties came from Rheims and Douai, a number of which have already been mentioned. One more is worth noticing. In 1583, upon the apprehension in Rouen of John Nichols, the mercurial notoriety-seeker who never seemed to know himself which faith he wanted to belong to, the seminarians at Rheims published a tract declaring to the world his confession of the impostures he had practised at the time of his recantation in England. We have already heard something of this document in connection with the publicity given his last previous change of heart.[77] It consists almost entirely of the pitiable letters which the wretch addressed to Dr. Allen begging for help to get out of jail and offering his confession as a token of the sincerity of his repentance. It also contains retractions signed by four priests who had temporarily strayed from the fold in England. The press of the college at St. Omer was established about 1606, but it was the most prolific of all. The most important news-reports which came from this source are those which succeeded on the murder of Henry IV, in 1610, which aroused a bitter controvery over the responsibility of the Jesuits and their doctrine for the crime. It was an international free-for-all; the society was assailed on all sides and was hard put to it to keep up with its detrac-

[76] H. M. Commission: *MSS. of the Marquis of Salisbury*, IV. 498.
[77] See above, p. 51.

tors. As the translator of *The apologies of the . . .
Kinges of France and Nauar . . . for . . . the Society
of Iesus*[78] put it,

there commeth forth almost daily Libels against the *Society* of *Iesus*,
concerning the killing of Tyrants; and namely of the death of . . .
King *Henry* the fourth, as if that murder had taken occasion of that
so mischeiuous attempt from the *Iesuits* Doctrine. And what one
nameles Makebate of *France* writeth in French . . . the same
they translate into Dutch, Italian, Latin and English, to the end that
the lies therin conteined should not infect only the French, but the
Dutch, Italians, English, and as many others as vnderstand the Latin
tongue.

This book is made up of testimonials given the Jesuits by
Henry IV, Louis XIII, and the bishop of Paris, as well as a
record of the sentence meted out in Paris to one Joalin for
circulating copies of the *Anti-Coton*, a notorious French
tract against Father Cotton, a Jesuit apologist, which had
also been printed in England. There is some news in other
tracts in this controversy, such as *A Letter of a Catholike
man*[79] and *The copie of a letter sent from Paris to the . . .
Fathers of the Society of Iesus . . . in England.*[80]

The Catholics also contrived to put about their own versions of the execution of their priests in England as a
countercheck to the reports, often abusive, printed in
England. Two such narratives record the martyrdom of
Father Campion and his associates in 1581. The first[81]
purports to be the testimony of a priest who witnessed
the execution of Campion, Sherwin, and Bryan, and who is
said to be Stephen Vallenger.[82] The book is amplified
with tributes in verse. It also takes occasion to utter

[78] Translated from the Latin [by Anthony Hoskins, S. J. St. Omer:] 1611.
[79] By T. A. [= Thomas Owen, S. J. St. Omer:] 1610.
[80] By F. G. [= Thomas Owen, S. J. St. Omer:] 1611.
[81] *A true reporte of the death and martyrdome of M. Campion Iesuite and preiste,
& M. Sherwin & M. Bryan preistes* . . . [Douai: 1582.]
[82] See Allen: *A briefe historie of the glorious martyrdom of twelve reverend priests*
ed. J. H. Pollen, 1908.

"a caueat to the reader touching A, M his discouery."
A. M.—Anthony Munday—as self-appointed censor of
Campion's treason, already had one controversy on his
hands as a result of his first pamphlet on the capture of
Campion,[83] and now his second, *A Discouerie of Edmund
Campion and his Confederates . . . practises*,[84] was challenged. Nothing daunted, however, he attacked both the
new adversary and still another Catholic apologist[85] with
one onslaught in his *Breefe Aunswer made vnto two seditious
Pamphlets*.[86] In this book he mocks the memorial verses
printed in the *True reporte of the death and martyrdome*,
hurling them back at the traitors in line-for-line parodies.
He also replies to the caveat against his *Discouerie*, but with
little force. To refute the charge that he had been an idle
and turbulent apprentice, he prints a testimonial of good
behavior signed by his master, John Allde the printer, and
he corrects some statements of his adversary's about his
conduct in Rome, but he ignores the most serious charges
brought against him.

The second account of Campion's martyrdom is found in
*A Briefe Historie of the Glorious Martyrdom of xij Reuerend
Priests* (1582) by Cardinal Allen. As far as Campion is
concerned, this narrative is chiefly a reprint of the *True
reporte*, but it includes as well eleven other biographies of
recent martyrs. It is probably as authentic as it pretends
to be, and it is certainly a most interesting testimony of the
fervor which upheld these victims of the desperate policy
of the government. At the time of the execution of Edward
Squire for conspiring to assassinate the queen, the Catholics circulated two defensive tracts containing news.[87]

[83] *A Breefe discourse of the taking of Edmund Campion.* See below, p. 102.
[84] For Edwarde VVhite, 29 January 1582.
[85] The author of *L'Histoire de la mort que le R. P. Edmund Campion . . . et
autres ont souffert . . .* (Paris: 1582).
[86] Iohn Charlewood, 1582; another issue, for Edward White, 1582.
[87] 1) *The discouerie and confutation of the tragicall fiction deuysed by Edward*

We can say without hesitation that these Catholic books were not openly sold in the booksellers' shops; whether they were sold at all is a question. Some copies were not; we have records of their being mysteriously thrust upon those who would be most annoyed by them, such as Recorder Fleetwood, a celebrated persecutor of heretics, who woke up one morning to find on his doorstep a copy of a tract that was a hanging matter. Whether they were sold or presented to the English Catholics, who would have treated such as have been mentioned as something more than fuel for indignation, *i.e.*, as news, it is not easy to say, but surely they would have been glad to buy such news when they could. Again we must remark that even if they were never sold, they are worth mentioning in a history of journalism because they had a part in satisfying the appetite for news, an appetite which grows by what it feeds on, and is a necessary condition to the organization of a supply of printed news.

6. News Published in Self-justification

One more kind of special pleading to the public occasionally brought news into being—the efforts of aggrieved private persons to make known their grievances, of the wrongly-accused to clear themselves of the slanders uttered against them, and of the erring to do penance by confessing their sins. In these public attempts at self-justification we sometimes find a great deal of news because of the natural likelihood that the deponent will rehearse the events involved in his case, and sometimes it is news of a very rare kind—news of the daily lives of ordinary people.

Most common are the retractions and confessions of converts and reformed heretics. Having suddenly seen the

---

Squyer. By M. A., Preest. 1599. 2) *A defence of the Catholyke cause* . . . *Written by T[homas] F[itzherbert]. With an apology* . . . *of his innocency in a fayned conspiracy against her Maiesties person* . . . 1602.

light themselves, they often appear to have been very eager to make clear their motives to others, so that they made a public confession of their errors not only at Paul's Cross, as was the custom, but in print as well. Some of them were unquestionably sincere,[88] but most of the converts from Catholicism who rushed into print with an account of their turning coat, such as Nichols, as aforesaid, Munday,[89] Tedder, Tyrrell,[90] Musgrave,[91] and Nicholas, the reformed Spaniard,[92] have the look of being adventurers a little too eager to bathe in the light of publicity, a little too groveling in their submission to the true gospel of Jesus Christ, a little too glib with their revelations of popish impostures and scandals. It is possible that the books they published were intended to reap the benefits of conversion in terms of cash. And the fickle Archbishop of Spalatro, the fat bishop of *A Game at Chesse*, isn't much better.[93]

Another gaudy penitential exercise performed in full view of all who cared to read, not by a religious convert but by a reformed evil-doer, is the curious tract called *The life, confession, and heartie repentance of Francis Cartwright, Gentle-*

[88] 1) *The declaraciõ made at Poules Crosse . . . by Alexander Seyton / and mayster Willyam Tolwyn . . .* Rychard Lant, 1541. 2) *The submission of Nic[holas] Shaxton late bishop of Salisbury to the Kinges Maiestie . . .* For Rob[ert] Toye, [1546]. 3) *A godly and Faythfull Retractation made . . . at Paules Crosse . . . by Mayster Richard Smyth . . .* Reynolde Wolfe, 1547. 4) *A playne declaration made at Oxforde . . .* By Richard Smith. Reynolde Wolfe, 1547.

[89] *The English Romayne Lyfe.* For Nicholas Ling, 1582.

[90] *The Recantations . . . by VVylliam Tedder and Anthony Tyrrell . . . at Paules Crosse . . .* Iohn Charlewood & VVilliam Brome, 1588.

[91] *Musgraves Motives and reasons for his secession . . . from the Church of Rome . . .* For Richard Moore, 1621.

[92] 1) *Hispanus Reformatus . . .* Gualterus Burre, 1621. 2) *The reformed Spaniard . . .* Walter Burre, 1621. 3) *The Reformed Spaniard in French.* Entered 11 May 1622 by Philemon Stephens (Arber, IV. 67).

[93] 1) *M. A. de Dominis . . . suæ profectionis consilium exponit.* Ioannes Billius, 1616. 2) *A manifestation of the motives, whereupon . . . M. A. de Dominis, Archbishop of Spalatro, undertooke his departure thence.* Translated from the preceding. Iohn Bill, 1616.

[98]

*man: For his bloudie Sinne in killing of one Master Storr,
. . . Minister of Market Rason . . . Written with his
his owne hand.*[94] This detailed and romantic *peccavi* har-
rows the reader with two murders, a period of miserable
exile, a year's imprisonment, an escape from the Turks, and
the loss of a son (to say nothing of endless law suits and a
marriage) before our hero finds pardon and peace in religion. Then comes this book—"so may, perhaps, my
printed Contrition redeeme my reputation from those oblo-
quies it is almost buried in." It may be that Cartwright
was perfectly sincere in his public self-abasement, but there
can be no doubt at least that his publisher was well aware
of the market value of such a splendid triumph of virtue
over vice.

The murder of the Rev. Mr. Storre had a career of eighteen years in the public press. It was committed 30
August 1602, and the next year an account of it was printed
at Oxford.[95] This is certainly the work of one of Storre's
friends, probably a fellow-clergyman. At that time, Cartwright was still at large; justice was being cheated by the
influence of his friends, who were also defaming the
character of the victim. This book was written as a brief
in Storre's defense; it even includes testimonials of good
character from his parishioners, certain gentlemen of the
neighborhood, the preachers of his diocese, and the learned
doctors of Oxford University. In 1613 this book was reprinted along with reports of two current murders; the
reasons for this repetition were better examined elsewhere.[96]
Finally, in 1621, the printed history of the crime was wound
up by Cartwright's public penance.

Another scoundrel who appears to have capitalized his

[94] For Nathaniell Butter, 1621.
[95] *The manner of the cruell outragious murther of William Storre* . . . .Oxford:
Ioseph Barnes, 1603.
[96] *Three Bloodie Murders* . . . See below, p. 290 f.

notoriety is the conjurer Cox. On 25 June 1561, having been convicted of the use of "sinistral and diuelysh artes," he made a public retraction, which was printed in broadside form two weeks later.[97] Not long thereafter, as he had announced that he would in the broadside, he published *A short treatise declaringe the detestable wickednesse of magicall sciences, as Necromancie, Coniurations of spirites, Curious Astrologie and such lyke. I haue my selfe ben an offender in these moste detestable sciences.*[98] It is just possible that, having been deprived of his livelihood of sorcerer he decided to save what he could out of the shattering of his fortunes by setting up as exposer of wizardry.

Much more important as news are the apologies published by men in public life patiently explaining the probity of their motives and defending themselves against the slanders of their enemies. We have such communications from Sir Francis Bacon,[99] who was accused, with some justice, by the friends of the Earl of Essex of having played him false, and from Sir Lewis Stucley,[100] whose conduct towards Raleigh, servile, perhaps, but technically correct, was bitterly resented by the latter's friends. Partisans of the Earl of Leicester and of the Earl of Essex attempted to clear their names by printing accounts of their behavior after they were dead. The *Apologie of the Earle of Essex, against those which iealously and maliciously tax him to be the hindrer of the peace and quiet of his country. Penned by himself* is said to have been circulated, whether in print

[97] *The vnfained retractation of Fraunces Cox / which he vttered at the Pillery in Chepesyde* . . . Iohn Awdely, 7 July.

[98] Ihon Alde, [1561].

[99] *Sir Francis Bacon his apologie, in certaine imputations concerning the late Earle of Essex.* For Felix Norton, 1604.

[100] *To the kings . . . maieste, The humble Petition and information of sir Lewis Stucley . . . touching his own behaviour in the . . . bringing up Sir Walter Raleigh, and the scandalous aspersions cast upon him for the same.* Bonham Norton & Iohn Bill, 1618.

is not clear, as early as 1598;[101] the earliest known printed copy is dated 1603,[102] and is doubtless one of the series of books about Essex which the death of Queen Elizabeth permitted to come into the open. The apology for Leicester[103] speaks frankly as follows:

> If it bee tollerable for priuate men to deliuer in print, *Apologies* of their owne doings while they are aliue: mutch more reasonable I think it for the trothe of such matters to be published, as being concealed or misconceaued, may anie way touch the honor of so Publique a person as the Earle of *Leycester*, . . . now deceased, and not aliue to answere for himselfe. . . . Finding yet in my hands a briefe and true relation of his *Excellencies* honorable endeuours vpon her *Maiesties* . . . charges to relieue that Towne [of Sluys] (by me euen at that time committed to writing, when these matters were in Action, and my self present both at the *Consultations* and *Executions*:) I haue thought it my duetie likewise herewith to Print and publish the same, that neither the Honourable *Patron* of this Treatise now dead, . . . be vniustlie wronged, nor . . . the world seduced.

In the *Letter sent by F. A. touchyng . . . a priuate quarell and vnkindnesse, betweene Arthur Hall and Melchisedek Mallorie Gentlemen* (1579),[104] we have an instance of an aggrieved person's publishing on his own behalf the kind of news that nowadays is usually printed under the heading "Police Courts." It is interesting to notice that according to the testimony of the printer in the House of Commons, the few copies of this book which were delivered to Hall seem to have been distributed by him among his friends. Hall paid the printer a good round sum for his work. It would seem, then, that this book was not printed for sale, and, if so, it would be more exact to call it an advertisement than a book of news.

---

[101] *D. N. B.*, XIV. 431.

[102] Richard Bradocke.

[103] *A Breife and true report of the Proceedings of the Earle of Leycester for the reliefe of the Towne of Sluce . . . VVhereby it shall plainelie appeare his Excellencie was not in anie fault for the losse of that Towne.* [For Andrew Maunsell,] 1590.

[104] [Henry Bynneman, 1579.]

A few more examples will show that persons of a much humbler sort would also, on occasion, air their wrongs in print. Two days after Father Campion was lodged in the Tower in 1581, Anthony Munday's *Breefe discourse of the taking of Edmund Campion . . . and diuers other Papistes, in Barkeshire*[105] was entered at Stationers' Hall,[106] and we may suppose that it was soon for sale in the booksellers' shops. Munday's account of the capture was, however, greatly displeasing to George Elliot, the captor, and in consequence the latter immediately put forth his own authentic version of the exploit, entitled *A very true report of the apprehension and taking of that Arche Papist Edmond Campion the Pope his right hand . . . Conteining also a controulment of a most vntrue former booke set out by one A. M. alias Anthonie Munday, concerning the same, as is to be proued and iustified by George Ellyot one of the ordinary yeomen of her Maiesties Chamber. Authour of this booke and chiefest cause of the finding of the sayd lewde and seditious people.*[107] From the fact that Munday makes no mention at all of Elliot in his report, it would seem that the latter's real grievance was being robbed of the glory that was his due. It is likely that the publication of his book was due quite as much to eagerness to reap as much notoriety (and perhaps money) from his coup as he possibly could as to an anxious regard for truth. Having showed himself something of an opportunist as a pursuivant, he may be suspected of being an opportunist in newswriting as well. His quarrel with Munday was either assumed for literary purposes or soon healed, for in Munday's *Breefe Aunswer* we see Munday receiving Elliot in his lodgings, showing his guest the slanders printed about him in *L'Histoire de la mort que . . . Edmund Campion . . . et autres ont souffert*, and publishing his solemn and "vnreprooueable" denial in the *Breefe Aunswer*.

[105] For VVilliam Wright, 1581.
[106] Arber, II. 397.
[107] Thomas Dawson, 1581.

This was, alas, not the first time that the enterprising Munday had been "controlled," if we may believe the Catholic author of *A true reporte of the death and martyrdome of M. Campion*. According to him, Munday had written a pamphlet on the trial of another Catholic "traitor," Everard Haunce, executed 31 July 1581, which was immediately challenged "and disproued by one of his owne hatch." As a matter of fact, there are two books which answer to this description. The first is called *The Araignement, and Execution, of a wilfull and obstinate Traitour, named Eueralde Ducket, alias Hauns*, "gathered by M. S.,"[108] and the corrective to it is *A true report, of the Araignement and execution of the late Popish Traitour, Euerard Haunce, . . . with reformation of the errors of a former vntrue booke published cōcerning the same*,[109] which disposes of M. S.'s efforts in the following terms:

It is not well, that men of more needinesse than discretiō or vnderstanding, being not instructed in the truth of matters, do take vppon them, for a smal rewarde at a Printers hande, to sette downe matters of fact in writing, and the Printers likewise for gaine do publish the same being not true: whereby, bothe the state is in many things offended, religion and the proceedings thereof layd open to some infamie among ill affected persons, the orders of her Maiesties Iniunctions and commandementes broken, some priuate persons slandered, and other faultes committed, to the peril of greater inconuenience. Of this sort of vntrue reportes is a pamphlet lately published, as gathered by *M. S.* and printed by *Charlewoode* and *White*, touching the arainement and execution of a wilfull and obstinat traitor, named *Euerard Ducket alias Haunce*, &c. By cause the moste of the same Booke is vntrue, and manye partes thereof, do lay open the honor of iustice to slaunder, and the cause of religion to some disaduātage of cauillous speaches: it hath bin thought good, that the trueth bee more certainely deliuered, by some y^t haue better meane to knowe it, and better cause to be credited, and the Readers required to impute the errours of the former booke, to the audacitie of some one needy man, and not to any publique defacement of authoritie.

[108] Iohn Charlewood & Edward VVhite, [1581].
[109] Henrie Bynneman, 1581.

[103]

Who it was that took offense at the inaccuracy of M. S.'s book does not appear, but from the fact that the *True report* smells just a bit of the courts of law and that it is very careful to bestow high praise upon Recorder Fleetwood, who conducted the trial, I suspect that it was composed by one of Fleetwood's friends, or by some one in the confidence of the municipal authorities. If we accept the authority of *A true reporte of the death and martyrdome*, here is another title to add to the Munday canon.

It would also seem, on the strength of two late sixteenth-century broadsides, that persons with no claim whatsoever to a public character would sometimes appear before the tribunal of the public in print. One of these, known only from a copy which looks like a press proof, is entitled *A spectacle for Periurers*.[110] The circumstances leading up to its publication are not fully known, but its import is clear. The sponsors, whose names are Fulwood and Doughtie, had, according to their own account, been unjustly condemned in the Star Chamber on the false testimony of two witnesses named John Jones and "Bolton the Cutpurse." Thereupon they had this handbill printed to proclaim Jones and Bolton perjurers to all the world; "Flye Falshood" is its conclusion. The account which it gives of the transactions between the parties to the suit is by no means sufficient to convince an unprejudiced arbiter; it is at pains to show only that Jones did give the testimony on which Fulwood and Doughtie were convicted, not that his testimony was false. But there is no question that the broadside was intended to set its authors right in the reader's eyes.

The second is entitled *A true Copie of a writing Testimonial by aucthority deuised and commaunded, to satisfie the world, and to cleere Zachary Dow, of London Draper and his Children, from the reproach of a hand wryting, falsely compacted and maliciously published in Blackwell Hall and*

[110] 27 November 1589.

[104]

else where against him, and also from that most iniurious Clayme of 238. li. vpon the same wryting made by one . . . Sara Gough the wife of Iohn Gough as appeareth. This notice to the public also grew out of litigation, in which Dow eventually emerged victor. Having previously been placarded by the Goughs as faithless and dishonest, he felt called upon to clear his name in similar fashion. The broadside consists entirely of a signed statement by the Goughs exonerating Dow from the charges they had formerly made against him and acquitting him of the alleged debt.

It seems impossible that either of these broadsides was printed for sale, and doubtless they were not even intended for general circulation, but only for those circles in which the aggrieved were known. But it is interesting to see that a need was clearly felt for a means of making public correct information in controversies such as these, a need which is now supplied, in one way or another, by our newspapers.

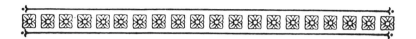

CHAPTER V
FURTHER NEWS OF AFFAIRS OF STATE

TURNING now from news published by the government and by other interests to further their own causes, we come, at last, to the nearest counterpart of modern journalism—news published for its own sake alone, by enterprisers who had no ax to grind and, beyond earning a living, no selfish interest to serve. As has already been observed, we must not expect even this kind of news to be impartial, colorless, and indifferent to what it relates, as the news in modern newspapers tends to be; it is, on the contrary, very partial, highly colored, and makes no effort to conceal its feelings about what it has to relate. But this partiality is dictated not by considerations of state policy, as in the news given out by the government, or by the interested motives of partisans and sectaries, as in the news they published, but merely by the patriotic, religious, and moral sentiments held by the great mass of the nation. Furthermore, this partiality belongs to the author rather than the publisher, for while we cannot suppose that the latter hated the pope and loved the queen any less than the next man, it is very plain that what interested him most in the news he published was its attraction for buyers, and he was willing to publish it in whatever guise they were most likely to fancy. These publishers, therefore, are journalists in the full sense of the term, as the sponsors of inspired news are not; they are men who turned to the publishing of news for a livelihood. It is to them that we are chiefly indebted for the most important developments of the journalistic trade, for the first English newspaper and for most of its descendants. It was their business instinct which brought about the printing of a more and more copious and dependable supply of news, the organization of the rudiments of a news-gathering system, and a part of the growth of a taste for news *qua* news, news unalloyed with moralizing and commentary, news which merely presents facts and allows the reader to draw his own conclusion. For the last we must also give credit to the development of a popular demand for unadulterated news, a quickening of men's curiosity about the busy world around them, and especially the rise of a desire for a vicarious experience of statecraft (the democratic spirit, if you will). The earliest publishers of news, then, the pioneers of English journalism, were preëminently men who, unlike such as Caxton and Ponsonby with their taste for literature, or Grafton and Waldegrave with their religious partisanship, were ready to publish whatever the public would buy, and such most journalists have been down to our own day.[1]

1. OFFICIAL TRANSACTIONS

Of news of the workings of the government, besides what has already been mentioned, of news, that is, gathered from the outside, there is next to nothing. The principal reason, the fact that the government was not disposed to tolerate the revelation of its acts and motives except as it saw fit to do so itself, has already been sufficiently made clear. It is

[1] As far as subsequent journalistic history is concerned, it should be borne in mind that the word *newspaper* has been used to mean both a journal of information and a journal of opinion. Most present-day newspapers are both rolled in one, but newspapers have not always been double-headed. Addison speaks of the newspapers of his day as of two distinct kinds—those one read for news, and those one read for political comment. Combining both in one publication did not become general until after his time. There have always been journalists who are primarily vendors of information, such as Northcliffe and Bennett, and others who are primarily preachers, such as Cobbett and Greeley. It is in the former that the instinct for business is likely to be strong and to them that we owe most new developments of the newspaper as a journal of information.

also true, however, that this kind of news was very readily passed round by common rumor and might often have reached a large number of interested persons, especially if these included chiefly the upper classes, without the help of the printing press. Just as is true in our own day, the common people were, as a rule, only mildly interested in the common run of news of public affairs; their attention could be captured only by an edict or tax, let us say, which affected their personal interests or by an event of unusual magnitude and importance, such as Leicester's expedition to the Low Countries or the Essex conspiracy. But the courtiers and great merchants, the nobility and gentry to whom news of this kind was interesting and valuable must have formed, at least in London, fairly compact groups which did not have to depend on the press for information. Men of position had private means of keeping informed which exempted them from all need of printed news. Chiefly by means of correspondence, either with well-posted friends or with agents and secretaries stationed where things happened, they kept in touch almost daily with the progress of events.

What we do find can be described briefly. There is a book published in 1555 in the form of a letter from one John Elder in London to a friend in Scotland[2] which is full of valuable news. Indeed, because it is so pious in its sentiments and because it contains some official documents, one would almost suspect it of being officially inspired, but I known of nothing to connect Elder with the state. The peace arranged between the emperor, Henry II of France, and Philip II of Spain in 1556 was also published in a broad-

---

[2] *The Copie of a letter sent in to Scotlande, of the . . . marryage of . . . Philippe, Prynce of Spaine, to the . . . Princes Marye Quene of England . . . Wherunto is added a brefe ouerture . . . of the legacion of . . . Cardinall Poole . . . With the very copye also of the Supplycaciō . . . by . . . the parlamente. Wherin they . . . haue submitted thēselues to the Popes Holynesse.* Iohn Waylande, [1555].

side in England, as one of the dominions of the last-named.[3] We do not know by whom this broadside was printed, but from the fact that it begins with seven lines of artless verse and ends with a prose description of the proclamation of the truce in Rouen, it does not seem to be an official publication. *The copie of his maiesties letter, sent on Tuesday the 26. of Iune 1604: signifying his Highnes pleasure to the Commons House of Parliament, in the matter of Subsidie* was printed anonymously at that time, "to be sold in Pauls Churchyard, at the signe of the Swan," Cuthbert Burby's shop. Since the royal printer seems, strangely enough, to have had nothing to do with this book, we must put it down as journalistic work. There are also reports of speeches by the two great legal lights of King James's reign—Coke and Bacon. Bacon's was probably published as an essay in jurisprudence,[4] but the other is genuine journalism. The author, a soldier out of work named Robert Pricket, was present at the Norwich assizes when Sir Edward delivered this charge and either took it down or reproduced it from memory—"if my Memorie hath giuen a true instruction to my pen" is his only allusion on this point—because, he says, it was "a charge so exelent as that it vvorthyly deserues to be continued in perpetuall memorie." Pricket also has the one further qualification needed to make a full-fledged reporter, want of ready money; he dedicated his book to the Earl of Exeter with a poignant complaint of being "vnseperably *yoakt* vvith leane-fac't pouertie."[5] The yoke, alas, must have contin-

---

[3] *The copie of the P[u]blication of the trewse made betwene . . . Kynge Henry second . . . [,] Themperour: and the Kyng of England his sonne published at roan on thursday the xx. daye of February.* Translated from the French. [1556.]

[4] *The Charge of Sir Francis Bacon . . . Attourney generall, touching Duells, vpon an information in the Star-chamber against Priest and Wright. With The Decree of the Star-chamber . . .* For Robert Wilson, 1614.

[5] *The Lord Coke his speech and Charge. (at the Norwich Assizes) . . .* For Christopher Pursett, 1607; another edition for Nathaniell Butter, 1607.

[109]

ued to gall, for Pricket's book was suppressed the day after publication.[6]

Further than these, we have only a few records of diplomatic transactions abroad. One of them, if it is allowed to be journalistic at all, is the earliest piece of journalistic printing struck off in England. It is the *Propositio Clarissimi Oratoris, Magistri Iohannis Russell*, printed by Caxton in 1476–8, a Latin oration delivered by the English ambassador on the occasion of the investiture of Charles the Bold, duke of Burgundy, with the Order of the Garter at Ghent in 1470.[7] *The Landgraue of Hessen his princelie receiuing of her Maiesties Embassador*,[8] a narrative chiefly concerned with the pomp and circumstance of diplomacy, was written by Edward Monings, a member of the ambassador's suite, in 1596. Two accounts were published of the Earl of Nottingham's embassy to Spain in 1605 to ratify a treaty of peace, the second[9] as a corrective of the first.[10] The second was written by Somerset-Herald, a member of the

[6] According to John Chamberlain in a letter to Sir Dudley Carleton dated 13 February 1607. *C. S. P. D. 1603–10*, p. 348.

[7] It is uncertain why Caxton printed this oration seven or eight years after it was delivered, and we cannot, therefore, describe it as a piece of journalism with much confidence. Various conjectures have been put forward to account for Caxton's putting it in print in 1476–7 (Duff: *William Caxton*, p. 44) or 1478 (de Ricci: *Census of Caxtons*, p. 91): he may have printed it as a compliment to Russell or merely as an experiment in printing; Russell may have procured the printing of it as a pardonable vanity; &c. But unless one may assume what I doubt, that there was an audience for uninspired literary exercises of this kind, is it not more than a coincidence that Russell was created bishop of Rochester on 22 September 1476 and that Charles the Bold, a turbulent prince constantly in the public eye and brother-in-law to the late King Edward IV, was killed in battle early in 1477? Perhaps, at the time the *Propositio* was published, there was sufficient public interest in both or either of the two persons principally concerned to make almost any memorial of them acceptable. If so, it was published as a bit of journalistic enterprise, though hardly of news.

[8] Robert Robinson, 1596.

[9] *A relation of such things as were obserued*, as above, p. 2.

[10] *The Royal entertainement of . . . the Earle of Nottingham . . . Ambassador . . . to the King of Spaine.* For William Ferbrand, 1605.

embassy, and was licensed for publication by the earl himself.[11] The next is the text of certain representations made by the king's ambassador to the king of France in 1615,[12] and the next two have to do with the Synod of Dort. The first of them, a speech made by Sir Dudley Carleton, the king's ambassador, to the States General of the Netherlands,[13] was much admired at the time; the second is a speech made by another Carleton, the bishop of Llandaff, one of the English commissioners sent to the synod.[14] Both the remonstrance of the ambassador to France and Sir Dudley Carleton's speech were translated from French copies. Mention might also be made of *A copie of the submission which those of the reformed religion in France requested the Viscount of Doncaster, ambassadour from his Maiestie of Great Britain, to present in their behalf to the King their soveraigne*, 1621.

It will be noticed that nearly every one of these books of news is merely a printed copy of a document rather than a narrative of events, and we should observe that, from the point of view of the publishers, the printing of a document literatim is the simplest kind of journalistic enterprise. To publish a narrative account of a recent occurrence must surely have cost much more effort; at worst, it required the publisher to go out and collect the requisite information and then reduce it to writing, or, as he was more likely to do, to arrange with one or more persons to do these things. Less troublesome, but still involving a distinct effort on his

[11] Arber, III. 296.

[12] *Remonstrances made by the Kings Maiesties ambassadour, vnto the French King . . . , Iune last past, 1615 . . .* For Nathaniel Butter, 1615.

[13] *The speech of sir Dudley Carlton lord ambassadour for the king of Great Britaine, made in the Assembly of . . . the Estates generall of the United Provinces . . . the 6, of October, 1617.* For Nathaniel Browne, 1618.

[14] *An oration made at the Hage, before the Prince of Orenge, and . . . the States Generall . . . : By . . . the Lord Bishop of Landaff . . .* For Ralph Rounthwait, 1619.

part, was the procuring of a narrative already written down —for example, a letter from a soldier in the army in the Netherlands to a friend in London. Even when his copy was brought to him by somebody willing or perhaps eager to have it appear in print, the trouble of preparing it for the press must sometimes have been considerable, except to the most careless publishers. Simpler than all these, and perhaps, as a rule, less likely to invite the disapproval of the censorship, was the printing of a document—an address, a manifesto, and edict, or an ordinance—which already existed in a form suitable for the press, which was often public or semi-public by nature and obtainable with the least effort, and which involved the publisher with no bothersome author, meddling in the preparation of his effusion for the reading public and expecting remuneration of some sort for his labor. Consequently, as we shall see, documents appear as one of the earliest forms of news to be published, and the supply of them available to whoever wished to buy increased rather than diminished during our period.

2. Rebellions and Trials for Treason

If we have found the news of the inner workings of the government, except what it chose to publish itself, somewhat meagre, when we get out into the open where occurrences cannot be concealed from view, we find much more news. The deliberations of the Privy Council, the proceedings of government departments, even the workings of the judicial machinery could be kept dark, but when subjects rose in rebellion against the crown, when riots broke out in the streets of London, when traitors were publicly hung at Tyburn, it was impossible to hide the fact from the nation. There was, indeed, no purpose in trying to hide such facts from the nation, in so far as preventing the publishing of news about them would do so, if that news were loyal to the government, as it almost always was. Yet it remains true that the news about rebellions and treasons which the government itself published, with all its shortcomings, is far and away the most explicit and the most comprehensive put in print. Outsiders had no means of access to any but the obvious facts of the matter, and they were doubtless deterred by due regard for the safety of their own necks from dealing with any but its most superficial and pious aspects. Consequently, we find that most of the news of rebellions and treasons published from the outside is news in a very weak solution, watered down with stern reproof of the rebels, unchivalrous crows of triumph over the execution of traitors, and fulsome praise of the queen. Nevertheless, unsatisfactory as news of this insipid kind must have been to those who wanted exact information, and in spite of several painful incidents in which certain brethren of the craft severely burned their fingers by presuming a little too far in publishing it, the printers and booksellers continuously provided a supply, throughout the reigns of Elizabeth and James I, as often as corruptions broke out on the body politic. We can scarcely doubt that if they could have got hold of it and if they had dared to print it, they would have published real news too.

Consequently, we have to do here chiefly with ballads and other pieces in verse which do not so much tell us what has happened as they comment upon it. Incidentally, of course, they frequently impart more or less information, but never as much information as sound patriotic doctrine. They frequently promise more than they perform, too: one might very well expect news of *A proper newe Ballad, declaring the substaunce of all the late pretended Treasons against the Queenes Maiestie, and Estates of this Realme, by sundry Traytors: who were executed in Lincolnes-Inne fielde on the 20. and 21. daies of September. 1586*,[15] but one

---

[15] For Edward White, [1586].

would find it only in modest proportions. The most that can be said for these pieces is that they are topical, they strike the note of the hour; as news they are lean fare. Yet numbers of them were printed when the provocation was sufficient, so that we must conclude either that the news secreted in them was sufficient for their readers, or that, unable to buy better news (except as the government published it), they were content with what they could get. Here is a list of all the pieces printed at the time of the rebellion in the north in 1569–70 which I have been able to trace; it will illustrate both the nature and the profusion of news of this sort.

1) *A godly ditty or prayer to be song vnto God for the preseruation of his Church, our Queene and Realme, against all Traytours, Rebels, and papisticall enemies.* By Ioh[n] Awdely. Broadside. Iohn Awdely, [1569?].

2) *To the Quenes Maiesties poore deceyued Subiectes of the north countrey, drawen into rebellion by the Earles of Northumberland and Westmerland.* By Thomas Norton. For Lucas Harrison, 1569 (3 edd.).

3) *A Discourse of Rebellion, drawne forth to warne the wanton wittes how to keepe their heads on their shoulders.* Verses by Thomas Churchyard. Wylliam Griffith, 1 May 1570.

4) *A ballat intituled Northomberland newes,*
   Wherein you maye see what Rebelles do vse. By W[illiam] E[lderton]. Broadside. Thomas Purfoote, [1570].

5) *The Rebelles.* Ballad. Entered 1569–70 by John Arnolde (Arber, I. 404).

6) *Newes from Northumberland.* By William Elderton. Ballad. Thomas Colwell, 1570.

7) *A Neweyeres gift to the Rebellious persons in the North partes of England.* By Edmond Eluiden. Richarde VVatkyns, 1570.

8) *An Aunswere to the Proclamation of the Rebels in the North.* By W[illiam] S[eres]. Willyam Seres, 1569.

9) *Ye welcom to London agaynste the Rebelles come into Northumberlande and those yat of his syde hath bene.* Ballad. Entered 1569–70 by Wylliam Greffeth (Arber, I. 405).

10) *Ioyfull Newes for true Subiectes, to God and the Crowne,*
The Rebelles are cooled, their Bragges be put downe.
By W. Kyrkh[am]. Ballad. For Richard Iohnes, [1570].

11) *A Lamentation from Rome how the Pope, doth bewayle,*
That the Rebelles in England can not preuayle. By Thomas
Preston. Ballad. Wylliam Gryffith, [1570].

12) *A letter with spede sent to the pope Declarynge the Rebelles.*
[Ballad.] Entered 1569–70 by Wylliam Greffeth (Arber, I. 405).

13) *The marchyng mates of Rebelles stoute.* Ballad. Entered
1569–70 by John Alde (*ib.*).

14) *The confusion of ye Rebelles with a songe of thankes for the same.*
Ballad. Entered 1569–70 by John Alde (*ib.*).

15) *The advertisment to the Rebelles in the north parties.* Book.
Entered 1569–70 by Lucas Haryson (*ib.*).

16) *Ye tryomphaunt churche Doth prayse the lordes name that he
hath confounded the enyme of the same.* Ballad. Entered 1569–70 by
Wylliam Greffeth (Arber, I. 406).

17) *Rebelles not fearynge God oughte therfore to fele the Rodde.*
Ballad. Entered 1569–70 by John Fayreberne (*ib.*).

18) *A Ballad intituled, A newe Well a daye,*
As playne, maister papist, as Donstable waye. By W[illiam]
E[lderton]. Thomas Colwell, [1570].

19) *The Dysordered Rebbelles in the north.* Ballad. Entered
1569–70 by Henry Kyrham (Arber, I. 407).

20) *ij shorte speaches agaynste Rebellion.* Entered 1569–70 by
John Alde (Arber, I. 408).

21) *A Ballad reioysinge the sodaine fall,*
Of Rebels that thought to deuower vs all. For Henry Kirkham,
[1570].

22) *The Plagues of Northomberland.* By John Barker. Ballad.
Thomas Colwell, [1570].

23) *A discription of Nortons falcehod of Yorke shyre, and of his fatall
farewel.* By William Gibson. Ballad. For Henrie Kyrkeham,
[1570].

24) *The Seuerall Confessions, of Thomas Norton, and Christopher
Norton: two of the Northern Rebels, vvho suffred at Tiburne, and were
drawen, hanged, and quartered, for Treason, May. xxvii. 1570.* For
Richard Iohnes, [1570].

25) *A Ballad intituled, A cold Pye for the Papistes* . . . By Iohn Phillip. For Richard Iohnes, [1570].

26) *A Friendly Larum, or faythfull warnynge to the true harted Subiectes of England. Discoueryng the Actes, and malicious myndes of those obstinate and rebellious Papists that hope (as they terme it) to haue theyr Golden day.* By I[ohn] Phil[lip]. For Rycharde Iohnes, [1570].

27) *The Confession and ende of Thomas Norton and Christopher Norton Rebelles in Yorkeshyre which Dyed xxvij of may 1570.* Verses by Sampson Dauie. William How [for William Pickering?] 1570.

In prose news-reports we are likely to find much more concrete information, but then very few prose news-reports were published. There is Proctor's *Historie of Wyates rebellion,*[16] the informing work of an amateur historiographer, but even that includes "an earnest conference with the degenerate and sedicious rebelles for the serche of the cause of their daily disorder." *The Seuerall Confessions, of Thomas Norton, and Christopher Norton* (no. 24 above) has, as a matter of fact, little to tell of confessions, but it is a narrative account of their execution. *The ende and Confession of Iohn Felton, the rank Traytour, that set vp the Traiterous Bull on the Bysshop of London his Gate*[17] is genuinely a piece of reporting. The poet Thomas Norton (a zealous Protestant, not to be confused with the namesake drawn, hanged, and quartered just above) wrote two tracts at the time of Felton's exploit in which he printed the bull which Felton had nailed on the bishop's gate and another bull conferring absolution on English converts, for the purpose, of course, of annihilating them.[18] Nevertheless we cannot deny that these documents were important news, and Norton's tracts include a few other scraps of information as well.

---

[16] Robert Caly, 22 December 1554.

[17] Richard Iohnes & Thomas Colwell, 1570, 1571 (3 edd.)

[18] 1) *A Bull graunted by the Pope to Doctor Harding & other, by reconcilement and assoyling of English Papistes, to vndermyne faith and allegeance to the Quene.* . . . 2) *An addition declaratorie to the Bulles, with a searching of the Maze.* Iohn Daye, [1570].

Two tracts written at the time of the execution of Dr. Story, the notorious Catholic heresy-hunter, both severe arraignments of this zealous persecutor, assay a considerable proportion of news;[19] they contain much information about the charges brought against him, extracts from his confession, and a report of his protestation on the scaffold.

As far as their giving a complete picture of the rebellions and treasons of the time is concerned, these publications cover most of the more notable, but not all. They begin with the uprising in Devonshire and Cornwall in 1548—a fragment of a ballad on this subject has survived—and run through Wyatt's rebellion, the trial of Lord Wentworth for the surrender of Calais, the Northern Rebellion, the trial of Felton, the capture of Story, the execution of the Duke of Norfolk, a riot of apprentices in 1581, the conspiracy of Dr. Parry, the suicide of the Earl of Northumberland in the Tower, the conspiracy for which the Queen of Scots and several others were executed in 1586 and 1587, the trial of Hacket, another apprentices' riot in 1595, the trial of Raleigh, Cobham, and others in 1603, a disturbance in Herefordshire in 1605 over certain recusants, the Gunpowder Plot, and the beheading of Raleigh. For a rudimentary news-publishing organization, under the heavy shadow of the censorship, this is not bad; most of what is omitted was too dangerous to handle. The Gunpowder Plot probably elicited the loudest outburst from the press, but, unless the record of the Stationers' register is very incomplete, as it quite possibly is, this incident did not touch the popular imagination nearly as much as the rebellion of 1570, for I have found mention of only four con-

---

[19] 1) *A copie of a letter lately sent by a Gentleman, student in the lawes of the Realme, to a frende of his concernyng D[r]. Storie.* [1571]. 2) *A declaration of the lyfe and Death of Iohn Story, Late a Romish Canonicall Doctor, by professyon.* Thomas Colwell, 1571.

temporary ballads on the subject.[20]   If, however, popular effusions were lacking, the balance was redressed somewhat by the extraordinary industry of the learned in producing Latin verses congratulating the king on his deliverance. This scholar with a *carmen* ἐπιχαρτικόν, that with a *descriptio*, another with an *adumbratio poetica* fairly bombarded his majesty with their felicitations, the conspirators with reproach, and the public, or such of it as could read in the learned tongue, with a very small residuum of information.   Dr. Francis Herring's *Pietas pontificia*, a versified history of the conspiracy, became a kind of classic: two Latin editions[21] and two English translations[22] were published, not to mention later reprints.   One ready publisher even put to the press a poem composed by a schoolboy of sixteen.[23]   The only known unofficial prose account of the matter, *The araignement and execution of the late traytors* . . . ,[24] contains very little news.

The news published about the Queen of Scots extends over a period of almost twenty years and emanates from so many different sources that it may be convenient to bring it all together here, to see what information, steeped in controversy as it was, found its way into print, in England or in English—much more was printed in other tongues—, about one of the most celebrated figures of the century.   Most of the dealings of the English government with her were, of course, carried on with the nation completely in the dark.

1) A Latin poem on the marriage of Mary and Lord Darnley, by Sir Thomas Craig, was printed in 1565, but where is not known.

[20] Entered 31 January, 1 February, 3 February, 14 April 1606 (Arber, III. 312, 319).

[21] 1) For Ric[hard] Boyle, 1606.   2) John Windet, 1609.

[22] 1) *Popish piety*. Translated by A. P. For William Jones, 1610.   2) *Mischeefes mysterie* . . . Translated and "dilated" by John Vicars. Edward Griffin, 1617.

[23] *Trayterous Percyes and Catesbyes Prosopopeia. Written by Edward Hawes, Scholler at Westminster.* Simon Stafford, 1606.

[24] For Ieffrey Chorlton, 1606.

2) *A Dolefull Ditty, or sorowfull Sonet of the Lord Darly* . . . , a ballad on his murder, signed H. C., was printed in 1579 by Thomas Gosson, and entered again 15 August 1586 by Henry Carre (Arber, II. 454). It is just possible that it was first circulated soon after the event.

3) *A discourse touching the pretended match betwene the Duke of Norfolke and the Queene of Scottes,* [1569?]. See above, p. 59.

4) *A defence of the honour of Marie Quene of Scotlande.* [By Bishop Leslie, the Scots ambassador at London.] London: E. Dicæophile [= printed abroad?] 1569. Other editions, with variant titles, were printed abroad in 1571 and 1584. Also published by the author in Latin (1580), French (1587), and Spanish (1587?). This is a reply to the preceding.

5) *De Maria Scotorum Regina . . . Historia.* 6) *Ane detectioun of the duinges of Marie Quene of Scottes, touchand the murder of hir husband, and hir conspiracie, adulterie, and pretensed mariage . . . And ane defence of the trew Lordis . . .* The Latin and English versions of George Buchanan's celebrated assault, composed at the instance of the Privy Council of Scotland. Both were printed, unacknowledged, at London by John Day in 1571, but chiefly, it would seem, for circulation in Scotland.

7) *The copie of a letter written by one in London . . . concernyng the credit of the late published detection . . .* See above, p. 55. A summary of the preceding.

8) *Salutem in Christo.* See above, p. 56.

9) *A treatise of treasons against Queen Elizabeth . . .* See above, p. 88. A reply to the preceding.

10) *The copie of a Letter writen out of Scotland . . .* See above, p. 88. Another reply to 8).

11) *The true copie of a letter from the queenes maiestie, to the Lord Maior of London . . .* See above, p. 44.

12) *The Copie of a Letter to . . . the Earle of Leycester . . .* See above, p. 57.

13) *A dutiful inuectiue, Against the . . . Treasons of Ballard and Babington . . . with the horrible attempts and actions of the Q. of Scottes . . .* In verse. By W[illiam] Kempe [a Plymouth schoolmaster, not the actor]. Richard Iones, 1587.

14) *The Censure of a loyall Subiect . . .* By G[eorge] W[hetstone]. Richard Iones, 1587. This book was entered in the Stationers' register 4 January (Arber, II. 462) and copies exist, with a different title-page, which speak of the Scottish queen as still alive.

[119]

In this edition, the last two pages are reset and the reference to the queen is replaced by a longer sentence recording her death.

15) *An excellent dyttye made as a generall reioycinge for the cuttinge of the Scottishe queene.* Ballad. Entered 27 February 1587 by Edward Whyte (Arber, II. 464).

16) *A defence of the honorable sentence and execution of the Quene of Scots* . . . Iohn Windet, 1587.

17) *A short declaration of the ende of Traytors, and false Conspirators against the state* . . . See above, p. 60.

18) *Maria Scotorum regina epitaphium.* By I[oannes] H[ercusanus,] D[anus]. For Robert VVallie, [1587?].

19) *The Scottish queens Burial at Peterborough, vpon Tuesday, being Lammas Day 1587.* For Edward Venge, [1587].

3. WAR NEWS

When we come to the news of military operations, we find, as we should expect, rather more of it than of affairs connected with political policy. The sixteenth century and the reign of King James were a comparatively quiet period in the annals of English arms, barring only the defeat of the Armada and possibly the almost continuous rebellion in Ireland, but throughout the greater part of Queen Elizabeth's reign, Englishmen were fighting somewhere on the continent, even if usually in small numbers. Furthermore, this news is, on the whole, more valuable, more largely compounded of information, than any other kind we have met with so far. Ballads of adieu to departing armies, prayers for the prosperous success of the queen's majesty's forces, and shouts of triumph over battles won are not lacking, but they do not bulk so large as the books which really satisfy the craving for facts. Once a book of war news was put in print, it could usually be depended upon, apart from a few conventional references to mythological and Roman parallels, to apply itself to supplying news, without so much of the digressive editorializing which infects much other news.

[120]

War news is one of the first kinds to appear at the beginning of the sixteenth century: there are contemporary pieces describing the Battle of Flodden Field. One of these is Skelton's *Ballade of the scottysshe kynge*,[25] a wild war-whoop of exultation quite as much as a narrative of occurrences, and another is a prose account, *Hereafter ensue the trewe encountre or Batayle lately don betwene Englāde and Scotlande*,[26] with lists of names and full particulars. Several books describing the Scottish campaign of 1544 were printed. Some of them are known only from a proclamation launched against them on 18 May, in which they are described as "certaine bookes printed of Newes of the Prosperous successe of the Kings Maiesties Armie in Scotland." As the English fleet did not sail from Tynemouth until 1 May and on the eighteenth the campaign was just coming to a close, the appearance of these books in London was remarkably prompt. Another is *The late expedicion in Scotlande, made by the Kynges hyghnys armye, vnder the conduit of the . . . Erle of Hertforde*,[27] an eye-witness's story sent from the north to the Lord Privy Seal. Except that most soldier-reporters did not forward their narratives to officers of state as highly placed as the Lord Privy Seal, this is quite typical of the greater part of all the military news published to the end of our period. From the campaign of 1547–8, we have the well-known "diary" of William Patten, another eye-witness, *The Expedicion into Scotlāde of . . . Edward, Duke of Soomerset . . . : made in the first yere of his Maiesties most prosperous reign*.[28] Next, after a lull of about thirty years diversified by nothing but a few accounts of forays into Scotland, we come to the beginning of a series of narratives of the feats of English

[25] [Richard Fawkes, 1513.]
[26] Richarde Faques, [1513].
[27] Reynolde Wolfe, 1544.
[28] Richard Grafton, 30 June 1548.

arms abroad, in the Netherlands, in France, and in Spain, which continues as a steady trickle until the Caledonian peacemaker, settled on the throne of England, stills the drum and sheathes the sword.[29] And yet, though a good deal of military news was undoubtedly published, there does not seem to be enough of it, especially during the reign of Queen Elizabeth. There are some puzzling gaps in this series of books of news,

[29] See 1) *A plaine or moste true report of a daungerous seruice . . . by English men, Scottes men, Wallons & other . . . for the takyng of Macklin . . . in Flaunders . . .* By Thomas Churchyard. [For] Ihon Perin, 1580. 2) *A true Relation of all suche Englishe Captaines and Lieuetenants, as haue beene slaine in the lowe Countries . . . , together with those now liuing, as also of such as are fled to the Enimie.* By Iohn Lingham. Roger Warde, 1584. 3) *A True Discourse of the late Battaile fought betweene our En[g]lishmen, and the Prince of Parma, . . . the 15. of Nouember 1585.* By W. M. Roger Ward, 1585. 4) *Newes out of the Coast of Spaine . . . of the . . . seruice . . . by Sir Frauncis Drake . . . vpon Cales; and . . . in the Cape S. Vincent and Cape Saker . . .* [By Henry Haslop.] Sold by Edward White, 1587. 5) *The true . . . Newes of the . . . exploytes . . . by . . . Syr Frauncis Drake: . . . at Sancto Domingo, and Carthagena, . . . at Cales, and vppon the Coast of Spayne.* Verses by Thomas Greepe. For Thomas Hackett, [1587]. 6) *A briefe report of the militarie seruices done in the Low Countries, by the Erle of Leicester. . .* By T. D. For Gregorie Seton, 1587. 7) *A Summarie and true Discourse of Sir Francis Drakes West Indian Voyage.* By Walter Bigges. Richard Field, 1589. Another edition by Roger Ward, 1589. 8) *A true Coppie of a Discourse written by a Gentleman, employed in the late Voyage of Spaine and Portingale.* For Thomas Woodcock, 1589. 9) *Ephemeris expeditionis Norreysij et Draki in Lusitaniam.* For Thomas Woodcocke, 1589. 10) *The true Reporte of the seruice . . . Performed lately by . . . Sir Iohn Norreys and other . . . souldiers before Guingand. . . .* Iohn VVolfe, 1591. 11) *True newes From one of Sir Fraunces Veres Companie. . . .* For Thomas Nelson, 1591. 12) *Newes from Brest. A Diurnal of al that Sir Iohn Norreis hath doone . . .* For Thomas Millington, 1594. 13) *A true report . . . of the taking of . . . St. Maries, by a shippe of Amsterdam and foure English pinnasses, 1599.* Translated from the Dutch. Iohn Wolfe, 1600. 14) *Extremities Vrging . . . Sir Fra. Veare to offer the late Anti-parle with the Arch-duke Albertus. . . .* For Thomas Pauyer, 1602 (2 edd.). 15) *The copie of a letter . . . from the campe before Graue . . . wherein is described the good successe . . . of her maiesties forces . . .* Simon Stafford, 1602. 16) *A true report of the seruice done vpon certaine Gallies passing through the Narrow Seas.* By Admiral Sir Robert Mansel. Sold by Iohn Newbery, 1602. 17) *Algiers voyage in a iournall . . .* By I. B[utton]. 1621.

and, in proportion to all the fighting in which English companies took part, the total sum of news seems rather small. What could the reasons be? News of this kind, coming from a distant source, was relatively hard to obtain, but on the other hand letters from soldiers at the front must have come to London every week and some of them, we know, found their way into the publishers' hands. Neither can we blame the scarcity entirely on the censorship, for surely there could be no objection to making known the successes of the English commanders and their allies or to celebrating the valor of English fighting-men. But perhaps, while it was possible to print news of English successes, it was dangerous to print news of English checks and reverses. There is, for example, very little news of Leicester's rather pretentious expedition to the Low Counties in 1585–6: in fact, I know of only one book.[30] Considering the popularity of this project, we must surely be right in thinking that the publishers would have found much more news to print if there had been better news. It must have been axiomatic that, as far as matters touching the credit of the state were concerned, the only kind of news fit to print was good news.

In many places, we can detect signs of a hunger for news of the Englishmen fighting abroad which, even if we make a generous allowance for books of news printed contemporaneously and since lost without a trace, the supply could hardly have satisfied. The prefaces almost universally allude to the desire of those at home for word of what was taking place at the front and to the importance of acquainting them with the gallantry of their countrymen in action. Sometimes the meagrest and most insignificant news was printed, as if that were better than nothing at all. Such is *The copie of a letter sent from sea by a gentleman, who*

---

[30] No. 6 in the preceding note.

was employed in discouerie on the coast of Spaine.[31]   This
is the report of a soldier who had apparently taken part in
a scouting expedition in March 1589, preparatory to the
descent of Norris and Drake on the coast of Portugal the
next month.   It consists of nothing but a few vague rumors
and surmises.   There is a curious instance of the vigilance
of a publisher in affording his readers the kind of war news
which most appealed to their patriotic sentiments in a
book called *Nevves from Sir Roger Williams* (1591).[32]   This
celebrated soldier was then serving with the king of France
in his war with the Catholic League.   What probably
happened is this: the publisher got hold of a French book
of news, or several books, containing an assortment of recent news—an account of a battle won by the Prince of
Conti, a letter from the king to the prince, an order of the
Parlement at Caen, and a somewhat bumptious letter from
Sir Roger Williams to the citizens of Paris, denying certain
false rumors about himself which he charges them with
having circulated and offering to defend his denial with his
good right arm.   This last is almost, if not quite, the least
important, but beyond question it comes home closest to
the English people.   Consequently, in the English translation, it is very properly put first, the whole book is christened *Newes from Sir Roger Williams*, and the rest of this
information becomes a mere appendix to the valorous deed
of our brave countryman.

In another book of news there is probably a further instance of the same kind of adaptation.[33]   It is an account of
the French king's military operations during the latter part
of the year 1589; it was translated from a French pamphlet,
for the entry in the Stationers' register was made from the

[31] By T. F.   Richard Field, 1589.
[32] Sold by Andrew White.
[33] *A Recitall of that which hath happened in the Kings Armie, since the taking of the Suburbes of Paris, vntill the taking of the Towne of Humflet.*   For Tobie Cooke, 1590.

[124]

latter.[34] Apparently the French text made no mention of the English troops serving with the king's army, but at signature C3, in the margin opposite a paragraph describing the siege of Alencon by the Marshal Biron, the following note appears:

> Here the English entred a bulwarke or rauelin, wel inuironed and defended with water, by pulling downe a draw bridg with a hooke, and wold haue assaied to[o] to enter the towne. but the marshal Byron forbad them expreslie.

Again, at the end, this statement is added in larger type:

> After the siege of *Falese*, the King gaue the English men leaue to depart; and he himselfe with his Armie, to weete, the French men and switzers, Rutters & Lants-knights went vnto *Lizeux*, which within ten days after he tooke: and from thence his Maiestie went vnto *Humflet*, which he did batter vpon Fridaie the xvi. of Ianuarie. At which time, part of our English Forces were shipped at *Dines* in *Normandie*, and the rest, the morrow after.

What probably happened is that the French book was brought over by the English contingent just mentioned, from whom the publisher somehow obtained it, along with the scraps of additional information quoted, which, knowing what his market demanded, he added in the way we have seen.

As a matter of fact, a number of books of news of the wars on the continent, published in England in translation, contained more or less information about the English forces. As a rule, they were translated literally without being edited for the greater glory of England as were the two just described, but the information is in them just the same. From the point of view of the authors of these books, the English were merely a small band of auxiliaries to be mentioned incidentally as their part in the operations dictated, but even this meagre record was doubtless very welcome to the patriots at home. The fact that the fighting

---

[34] Arber, II. 538.

in France and the Netherlands was done by forces which were either the past, present, or future comrades-in-arms of English soldiers accounts in part for the very large number of reports of this fighting which were published in England.[35]

The most important military operation during our period was, of course, the meeting of the Spanish Armada, and its importance is testified by the amount of news published about it. It is just a little curious that all this news was published only after the actual fighting was over, for as a rule the ballad-writers were accustomed to send up shouts of defiance and exhortations to the nation to stand fast well in advance of an event as grave as this. Two pieces have been preserved, a "prayer"[36] and an exhortation,[37] which may have been printed before the fight in the channel commenced, and possibly the *Praier Dayly vsed in Stepney parishe* which was entered in the Stationers' register 1 June[38] refers to the threat of invasion; otherwise we have nothing which can certainly be assigned to a date earlier than the end of the engagement, as if the publishers

[35] The following contain a good deal of news of the English forces: 1) *The true reporte of the Skirmish fought betwene the States of Flaunders, and Don Ioan . . . the first day of August . . . 1578.* By W. C. William Bartlet, [1578]. 2) *A True Discourse of the . . . victories obtayned by the French King, against the Rebels . . .* I[ohn] Wolfe & E[dward] White, 1589. 3) *A Particuler, of the yeelding vppe of . . . Zutphen, and the beleagering of Deuenter. . . .* Sold by William Wright, 1591. 4) *A true discourse historicall, of the succeeding gouernours in the Netherlands, and the Ciuill warres there . . . with the memorable seruices of our . . . English . . . Souldiers . . . there . . . and afterwards in Portugale, France, Britaine and Ireland . . .* Translated and collected by T[homas] C[hurchyard] and Ric[hard] Ro[binson]. For Matthew Lownes, 1602. 5) *A most true relation of the affaires of Cleve and Gulick . . .* By Henry Peacham jr. For John Helme, 1615. 6) *A relation of the passages of our English companies . . . , since their first departure from England, to the parts of Germanie, and the vnited Prouinces.* By A. M. For Henry Gosson, 1621.

[36] By Rob. H[arrison?]. For Henry Car, 1588.

[37] *An Exhortacion to all English Subiects, to ioine for the defence of Queene Elziabeth [sic], and their natiue country.* In verse. Richard Iohnes, [1588].

[38] By John Wolf (Arber, II. 491).

were reluctant to handle the subject while the outcome was doubtful. The first two entries in the Stationers' register after the Spaniards' retreat (which began 29 July), *A godlie prayer, for the perservation of the quenes maiestie* and *A Joyfull sonnet of the Redines of the shires and nobilitie of England to her maiesties service*, entered on 31 July[39] and 3 August,[40] show no knowledge of the outcome of the battle, and as late as 18 August a ballad of *The Englishe preparacon of the Spaniardes navigacon* was entered.[41]

Assuming that the order in which these pieces of news were entered in the Stationers' register is the order in which they were published and that the date of entry is approximately the date of publication, we find the first account of hostilities on August 10—Deloney's *Ioyful nevv Ballad, declaring the happie obtaining of the great Galleazzo*,[42] an account of an isolated incident in the engagement between the two fleets. Next comes *A true Discourse of the Armie which the King of Spaine caused to bee assembled . . . against England*, entered 30 August,[43] a collection of statistical information translated from the French. The following day Deloney's *New Ballet of the straunge and most cruell Whippes which the Spanyards had prepared to whippe and torment English men and women*, which is hardly news if news must be true, was entered.[44] In September and October news began to come in from Ireland and the Netherlands in the form of reports gathered from captured sailors.[45] It was probably in October or November that

[39] By Thomas Woodcock (Arber, II. 495).
[40] By J[ohn] Wolf (*ib.*).
[41] By John Wolf (Arber, II. 496).
[42] For Edward White, 1588. See Arber, II. 495.
[43] Translated by Daniel Archdeacon. Iohn Wolfe, 1588. See Arber, II. 498.
[44] Thomas Orwin & Thomas Gubbin, 1588. See Arber, II. 498.
[45] 1) *The late wonderfull dystres whiche the Spanishe Navye sustayned yn the late fighte in the Sea, and vpon the west coaste of Ireland in this moneth of September.* Ballad. Entered 28 September 1588 by John Woulfe (Arber, II. 501). 2) *The*

The Holy Bull, And Crusado of Rome . . .[46] appeared: this is a copy of the indulgences offered by Gregory XIII and Sixtus V to the Spaniards for fighting against the enemies of the faith and of an "arrogant" Catholic description of the Armada printed at Cologne, both said to have been found in captured ships of the Armada and here published in the spirit of mockery, fitted with sarcastic glosses. It was translated from a Dutch book printed at Middelburg 12 September. Before the end of the year the *Orders set downe by the Duke of Medina, Lord General of the Kings Fleet, to be obserued in the voyage toward England*[47] was published. *An answer to the vntruthes . . . printed in Spaine, in glorie of their supposed victorie atchieued against our English nauie* was entered 1 February 1589 and printed in both English and Spanish.[48] It purports to be the work of a disillusioned Spaniard. And this is all, as far as I have found, that was published by way of reports of the fleet and the fighting. There is no first-hand account of an English eyewitness, no report of some of the most brilliant individual exploits of the English fleet, such as the sailing of the fireships into the roads of Calais, and no account of the action as a whole except an unsatisfactory passage in a book of verses[49] and an illustrated summary, translated from the

---

valiant deedes of Mac Cab an Irishe man. Ballad. Entered 30 September 1588 by John Wolf (*ib.*). 3) *Certaine aduertisements out of Ireland, concerning the losses . . . to the Spanish Nauie . . .* For Richard Field, 1588. 4) *The Deposition of Don Diego Piementellj . . . before . . . the chiefest Lords of the Counsaile of the Haghe in Holland.* Iohn VVoolfe, 1588. 5) *A Dytty of thexploit of Therle of Cumberland on the Sea in October 1588. and of thouerthrowe of 1600 Spaniardes in Irland.* Entered 14 November 1588 by John Wolf (Arber, II. 506).

[46] Iohn Wolfe, 1588.

[47] Translated from the Spanish by T. Perez. For Thomas Gilbert, 1588.

[48] By D. F. R. de M. Translated by I. L[ea]. For Thomas Cadman, 1589. The Spanish edition is entitled *Respueta y desengano contra las falsedades . . . impresas en España . . .*

[49] *Elizabetha triumphans.* By I[ames] A[ske]. For Thomas Gubbin & Thomas Newman, 1588.

Italian of the historian Ubaldini, which was printed late in 1590.[50]

Of news from England concerning the preparations for meeting the invasion and the celebration of the repulse there is much more. We find accounts of the great camp at Tilbury,[51] of reviews of the troops in London,[52] and of the solemn thanksgiving in St. Paul's,[53] as well as ballads of defiance and jubilation in which there was doubtless little news indeed.[54] If it should seem, then, that the London

[50] *A Discourse concerninge the Spanishe fleete inuadinge Englande in the yeare 1588* . . . Translated [by R. Adams]. For A. Ryther, 1590.

[51] 1) *The Queenes visiting of the Campe at Tilsburie with her entertainment there.* By T[homas] D[eloney]. Broadside. For Edward White, 1588. 2) *A Ioyful Song of the Royall receiuing of the Queenes . . . Maiestie . . . at Tilsburie . . .* By T. I. Broadside. For Richard Iones, 1588. 3) *An excellen songe of the breaking vp of the campe.* Entered 23 August 1588 by J[ohn] Wolf (Arber, II. 497).

[52] 1) *A propper newe balled briefely shewinge the . . . Cumpanyes of horsmen and footemen . . . brought before her maiestie.* Entered 28 August 1588 by John Wolf (Arber, II. 497). 2) *The martiall shewes of horsemen before her maiestie at Sainct James.* [Book?] Entered 7 September 1588 by John Wolf (Arber, II. 499).

[53] 1) *A Joyfull ballad of the Roiall entrance of Quene Elizabeth into . . . London the   Day of november 1588 . . .* Entered 14 November 1588 by John Wolf (Arber, II. 506). 2) *A Joyefull Songe or Sonnett of the royall receavinge of the queenes maiestye into . . . London on Sondaye the 24th of November . . .* Entered 25 November 1588 by Thomas Orwyn (Arber, II. 508). 3) *An excellent dyttie of the Queenes comminge to Paules Crosse the 24th . . . of November 1588.* Entered 26 November 1588 by Thomas Nelson (*ib.*).

[54] 1) *A Ballad of thankes gyvinge vnto God, for his mercy toward hir maiestie.* Entered 7 October 1588 by Henry Kirkham (Arber, II. 502). 2) *A new ballad of the glorious victory of Christ Jesus, as was late seene by thouerthrowe of the Spanyardes.* Entered 3 November 1588 by H[enry] Carre (Arber, II. 505). 3) *A ballad of the . . . Victory obtained ouer the Spaniardes and yeir ouerthrowe in July last 1588.* Entered 3 November 1588 by H[enry] Carre & Thomas Orwyn (*ib.*).

4) *A newe ballad of Englandes Joy and delight In the back Rebound of the Spanyardes spyght.* Entered 21 November 1588 by Ric[hard] Jones (Arber, II. 507). 5) *The ioyfull Tryumphes performed by dyuerse christian princes beyond the Seas for . . . the ouerthrowe of the Spanishe Navye, shewing also the Justinge at Westminster on the Coronacon Daie . . .* Ballad. Entered 27 November 1588 by John Wolf (Arber, II. 508). 6) *A songe to be printed in Duch. French or English of thouerthrowe of the Spanysh navie.* Entered 4 March 1589 by John Wolf (Arber, II. 517). 7)

press failed to do justice to this glorious subject and satisfied only meagrely the voracious demand for news which
surely existed, we must put down its partial failure to the
difficulty of ensuring a supply of news from a distant place
and the publishers' dependence upon what chance would
bring them from foreign parts, to the nature of the engagement, scattered over more than a week's time and many
leagues of sea, and possibly to a certain diffidence about
handling news of this kind.[55]

As nearly all the news from Ireland concerns the military
operations against the cantankerous rebels in that island—
everything except an account of a fire in 1577[56] and several
reports of a marvelous battle of birds[57]—we may as well as
not consider it here. It is a somewhat monotonous series of
narratives of battles fought and rebels beheaded,[58] inter-

Triumphalia de Victoriis Elisabethæ . . . contra classem . . . Philippi . . .
Greek and Latin verses by N. Eleutherius (pseudonym) and others. [London?
1589.]

[55] One is sometimes tempted to suppose that the subject was hedged about with
a kind of taboo. "It is certainly curious . . . that (with the exception of an
allusion in Lyly's _Midas,_ and the treatment of the subject, such as it is, in Heywood's _If you know not me_) the references to the Armada in the Elizabethan drama
should be so few and slight."—_C. H. E. L.,_ V. 345, n.

[56] _A true declaracon of the lamentable burninge . . . of the market towne of the
Naas . . . the .3. of marche 1577._ Book. Entered 31 August 1577 by Richard
Jones (Arber, II. 318).

[57] 1) _A battell of Birds Most strangly fought in Ireland, vpon the eight day of
September last, 1621_ . . . . Broadside. W. I., [1622?]. 2) _The lamentable
Burning of the City of Corke . . . by Lightning: which happened the Last of
May, 1622. After the prodigious Battell of the Stares_ . . . Broadside. E[dward]
A[llde, 1622]. 3) _The Wonderfull Battell of Starelings: Fought at . . . Corke . . .
the 12. and 14. of October_ . . . _1621._ For N[icholas] B[ourne], 1622. 4) _A
Relation Of The Most lamentable Burning of . . . Corke . . . by Thunder and
Lightning . . . the last of May 1622 after the prodigious battell of the birds called
Stares_ . . . For Nicholas Bourne & Thomas Archer, 20 June 1622.

[58] 1) _A ballat of Fitzmorris._ Entered 4 September 1579 by Ric[hard] Jones
(Arber, II. 359). 2) _Newe newes contayning A shorte rehersall of the late enterprise
of certaine Rebelles: . . . Captaine Stukeley, and . . . MacMorice . . ._
I[ohn] C[harlewood], 1579. 3) _Brief discours de l'entreprise faicte sur Irlande par
aucuns rebelles . . ._ Londres: 1579. This seems to be either a free translation

spersed with ballads of encouragement to new companies of troops sent over[59] and rabid anti-Catholic deriding of the obstinate Irishmen.[60]   It paints a very black picture of this

of 2) or of the original thereof. 4) *A Moste true Reporte of Iames Fitz Morrice Death* . . . By Thomas Churchyard. [For] Edward White, [1579?]. 5) *Newes out of Irelande.* [Broadside.] Entered 10 December 1580 by John Aldee (Arber, II. 383). 6) *The true reporte of the prosperous successe which God gaue vnto our English Souldiours against* . . . *our Romaine enemies* . . . *in Ireland, in the year. 1580.* By A. M. For Edward White, [1581] (2 issues). 7) *The Copie of a letter sente out of Irelande.* [Book.] Entered 20 December 1580 by John Perin (Arber, II. 385). 8) *The Image of Irelande, with a discouerie of Wood karne* . . . In verse. By Ihon Derricke. Ihon Daie, 1581. 9) *A Scourge for Rebels: Wherin are many notable seruices truly set out* . . . By Thomas Churchyard. For Thomas Cadman, 1584. 10) *The Coppie of a Letter sent from M. Rider, Deane of Saint Patricks, concerning the Newes out of Ireland* . . . For Thomas Man, 1601. 11) *Englands Ioy.* In verse. By R. V. [= Richard Rowlands. London? 1601?] 12) *A letter from a Souldier of good place in Ireland* . . . *touching the notable Victorie of her Maiesties Forces* . . . Signed I. E. For Symon Waterson, 1602. 13) *A ioyful new Ballad of the late victorye obtained by my Lord Mount Ioy* . . . *in Ireland* . . . [1602.] 14) *All the newes out of Ireland with the yeildinge vp of Chinsale &c.* [Book?] Entered 22 January 1602 by Thomas Pavier & John Hardie (Arber, III. 200). 15) *A Discourse occasioned vpon the late defeat, giuen to the Arch-rebels, Tyrone and Odonnell* . . . In verse. By Ralph Birchensha. For M[atthew] L[ownes], 1602. 16) *The Ouer-throw of an Irish rebell, in a late battaile: Or The death of Sir Carey Adoughertie* . . . Dublin: Iohn Franckton; London: for I[ohn] Wright, 1608. 17) *The bloody Warres of Ireland.* Ballad. Entered 12 August 1608 by John Wright & Henry Gosson (Arber, III. 387). 18) *Newes From Lough-foyle in Ireland.* . . . For Nathaniell Butter, 1608. 19) *Newes From Ireland.* . . . *Newly imprinted and inlarged* . . . For Nathaniell Butter, 1608. 20) *The true exemplary, and remarkable history of the Earle of Tirone* . . . By T[homas] G[ainsford], Esquire. For Ralph Rownthwaite, 1619.

[59] 1) *A warninge to the Romishe Rebells to beware the Graye.* Entered 14 December 1580 by Richard Jones (Arber, II. 384). 2) *Londons Loathe to departe to the noble Erle of Essex* . . . Entered 31 March 1599 by Thomas Purfoote Sr. & Jr. (Arber, III. 141). 3) *The Fortunate Farewel to the* . . . *Earle of Essex* . . . In verse. By Thomas Churchyard. Book. For William Wood, 1599. 4) *A prayer for the* . . . *good successe of the Earle of Essex* . . . *in Ireland* . . . By Iohn Norden. Book. Edward Allde, 1599. 5) *A new ballade of the tryumpes kept in Ireland vppon Saint Georg's day last, by the* . . . *Earle of Essex* . . . [1599.] *Shirburn Ballads*, no. LXXVIII.

[60] 1) *A Solemne songe of the Rebelles State, To whome the Popes blessinge Camme somewhat to late.* Entered 20 December 1580 by Henry Carre (Arber, II. 385). 2) *A brief admonicion to the seduced sort of Irishe Rebelles.* [Book.] Entered 26 April 1599 by Ric[hard] Jones (Arber, III. 144).

willful race of ingrates, utterly lacking in an appreciation of the benefits of English mastery, in terms likewise familiar much more recently, and of course it has nothing but reviling for their allies, the Spaniards. It is not a complete picture by any means; it does not follow these many years of dreary campaigning with any thoroughness or consistency, but only gives us a glimpse of what was going on now and then, as a bit of news of its own accord got into the hands of a publisher or the sending out of a new commander drew a fresh encomium from a ballad-writer. Very possibly the tacit interdict against bad news kept down the total. The most interesting piece is the earliest—a broadside printed in 1542 reciting the terms on which the first earl of Tyrone submitted to King Henry VIII.[61]

About 1585 we begin to meet a new kind of military news which is possibly the most interesting of all—news of fights on the seas against the Spaniards and the Turks. These narratives, as a rule, relate small engagements by privateers and merchantmen rather than battles fought by ships of the royal navy, though we must mention, as an exception to the rule and as almost the only piece we have to describe which possesses high literary merit, Raleigh's *Report of the Truth of a fight about the Isles of Acores, this last Sommer. Betwixt the Reuenge . . . and an Armada of the king of Spaine,*[62] published a few months after the foolhardy and glorious battle it describes. If none of the other accounts of naval engagements are as well written, they are at least equally patriotic. These valiant English seamen always fought against tremendous odds—"a Ship of 220 Tun hauing in her but 36. men and 2. Boyes who were . . . set vpon by 6 Men of Warre of the Turkes, hauing at the

---

[61] *The copye of the Submissyon of Oneyll / which he made to the Kynges Maiestie at Grenewych the .xxiiii. daye of September.* For Johñ Gough, 1542.
[62] For William Ponsonbie, 1591.

least 1500. Men in them;"[63] "two great and well appointed
Spanish ships or Men of Warre. And A small and not very
well prouided English Ship;"[64] "fyue shippes of London
against xj galleis and ij fregates the strongest in christian-
dom"[65]—but they always came out on top, at least eluding
their assailants and often beating them. Their opponents,
the Spaniards, cut a sorry figure in these stories; in those
days it took as many Spaniards as tailors to make a man,
or at least to make a match for an English sailor, and in
these news-reports we see the same condescending attitude
as a later British sailor, Dick Dauntless's captain, took
toward the naval rivals of his day:

> "But to fight a French fal-lal—it's like hittin' of a gal—
>   It's a lubberly thing for to do;
>   For we, with all our faults,
>   Why we're sturdy British salts,
>   While she's only a Parley-voo,
>   D'ye see?
> While she's only a Parley-voo!"

There can be no questioning the popularity of this kind of
news in its own time, and it remains to-day an extremely
picturesque souvenir of one of the most important and one
of the most dashing episodes of the period, the rise of the
English navy.[66]

[63] *The Dolphins Danger and Deliuerance.* For Henry Gosson, 1617. As printed
in Taylor's *Workes*, 1630.
[64] *A true relation of a wonderfull Sea Fight* . . . For N[athaniel] B[utter],
1621.
[65] *A true report of the Late woorthie fight performed in the voiage from Turke* . . .
By Thomas Ellis. Entered 10 November 1586 by Humfrey Baett (Arber, II.
459).
[66] See also 1) *The Primrose of London with her valiant aduenture on the Spanish
coast* . . . By Humphrey Mote. For Thomas Nelson, 1585. 2) *The honorable
actions of* . . . *Edward Gleinham* . . . *latelie obtained against the Spaniards*
. . . *in foure sundrie fightes.* . . . For VVilliam Barley, 1591. 3) *The Valiant*
. . . *fight performed* . . . *by the Centurion of London, against fiue Spanish
Gallies* . . . [For Andrew White, 1591.] 4) *The sea-mans Triumph.* . . . For
William Barley, 1592. 5) *Newes from the Leuane Seas.* . . . By H[enry]
R[oberts]. William Wright, 1594. 6) *A true credible report of a great fight at sea*

4. RELIGIOUS AFFAIRS

Besides what has already been mentioned, the only important news of religious affairs which we have to take account of is reports of the trial and execution of heretics. Otherwise we find little, except the vindictive jubilations published on the death of Bishop Bonner, who was hated with unparalleled fervor because of his severity in Queen Mary's time,[67] a few accounts of conversions and recantations, and Barnaby Rich's *True report of a late practise enterprised by a Papist, with a yong Maiden in Wales* . . ., the story of the public confession of a girl who had been taught by a Catholic priest to feign inspired visions.[68]

The martyrology is an interesting record, if only because of the picture it draws of fanatical devotion, amounting almost to a selfish seeking after martyrdom, on one side, and on the other a bewildered grim determination, frequently mixed with callous savagery and, when responsible officials were involved, an unattractive hypocritical demeanor. The records themselves exhibit little variety: each martyr was accused of the same offense, which was, of course,

---

. . . For Walter Burre, [1600]. 7) *A True Relation of a . . . Fight . . . by . . . the Vineyard and the Vnicorne . . . against Sixe great Galles of Tunes.* By Henry Roberts. [1616.] 8) *A Fight at Sea, Famously fought by the Dolphin of London against fiue of the Turkes Men of Warre, and a Satty . . .* For Henry Gosson, 1617. 9) *A notable . . . sea-fight, Betweene Two great and vvel-mounted Spanish shipps, And a Small and not very well provyded English shipp. . . .* Amsterdam: George Veseler, 1621. 10) *A relation Strange and true, of a ship of Bristol named the Jacob . . .* For Nathaniel Butter, 1622. 11) *The famous and wonderful recouerie of a ship of Bristoll, called the Exchange, from the Turkish pirates of Argier.* By John Rawlins. For Nathaniel Butter, 1622.

[67] 1) *An Epitaph, or rather a short discourse made vpon the life & death of D. Boner . . .* In verse. By Thomas Knell Jr. Iohn Allde, 1569. 2) *A Commemoration or Dirige of Bastarde Edmonde Boner . . .* Prose & verse. By Lemeke Auale P. O. [= John Kingston], 1569. 3) *An Epitaphe declaryng the lyfe and end of D. Edmund Boner &c.* Broadside. By T[homas] Bro[ke] Jr. Iohn Daye, 1570. 4) *An Epitaphe declaring the life and end of D. Edm. Bonner. &c. . . .* By Tho[mas] Bro[ke] Jr. Iohn Daye, [1570]. 5) *A recantation of famous Pasquin of Rome.* In verse. Signed R. W. Iohn Daye, 1570.

[68] Robert Walley, 1582.

treason, not heresy; each was condemned on almost the same flimsy grounds; each was tormented with delegations of doctors of the true church sent to show him the error of his ways by quoting Scripture to him; each was drawn to Tyburn, heckled on the scaffold, hanged, and quartered in almost precisely the same way. The news-reports of these brave proceedings invariably describe the martyr's execution, usually through an eye-witness, and often his trial as well. Most of them include more or less sad repining of the blind obstinacy of such traitors and, of course, much stern reproof of their blasphemous, idolatrous, and superstitious tenets. Dissident Protestants received the same medicine as Catholics: the earliest memorial of a martyrdom which I know of is a broadside, apparently printed in 1540, on the burning of Robert Barnes, a contumacious Lutheran—a set of verses deriding his doctrinal errors and personal habits, but imparting little news.[69] The execution of Campion in 1581 undoubtedly created the greatest stir. Besides the accounts of his end which have already been mentioned, we find several ballads[70] and a book called *An aduertisement and defence for Trueth against her Backbiters, and specially against the whispring Fauourers, and Colourers of Campions . . . treasons*, a dreary polemic which, according to Cardinal Allen's *Briefe Historie*, was read on the scaffold by a schoolmaster named Hearne.[71] No one without a school-

---

[69] *This lytle treatyse declareth the study and frutes of Barnes borned . . . the xxx daye of Iuly . . .* For Richard Bankes.

[70] 1) *Master Campion the seditious Jesuit is welcome to London.* Entered 24 July 1581 by Richard Jones (Arber, II. 397). 2) *Nowe we goe, of the papistes newe ouerthrowe.* Entered 11 August 1581 by Edward White (*ib.*, II. 400). 3) *A Triumph for true Subiects, and a Terrour vnto al Traitours . . .* [By William Elderton?] Richarde Iones, 1581.

[71] Cardinal Allen describes it merely as "an aduertisement" and the *D. N. B.* (XXXIX. 292) states that the book read on the scaffold was Munday's *Discouerie*. But as the latter is dated 29 January 1582 and includes an account of the execution, it could hardly have been read on 1 December unless in MS. The *Aduertisement*, if piety is a recommendation, was the more suitable, so that the cardinal's statement seems more likely to be correct.

master's capacity for sustained vocalization could have read it, for it contains a sentence four pages long. In this case Anthony Munday covered himself with unenviable glory, not only by writing it up in four several books, but also, it seems, by testifying against Campion and the priests tried with him. Munday's books on this subject, with their constant emphasizing of his recent "faithfull seruice to her Maiestie," their parading of his inner knowledge of the popish arts ("sometime the Popes Scholler, allowed in the Seminarie at Roome amongst them"), and their blatant advertising of his *English Romayne Lyfe*, just about to appear, do him no credit.[72]

[72] See also 1) *The seuerall Executions & confessions, of Iohn Slade & Iohn Bodye* . . . By R. B. [Richard Iohnes? 1583.] 2) *The Lamentation of Englande: For the late Treasons conspired* . . . *by Fraunces Throgmorton* . . . Broadside. Richard Ihones, [1584]. 3) *The Life and end of Thomas Awfeeld* . . . *and Thomas Webley* . . . For Thomas Nelson, [1585]. 4) *A briefe Treatise. Discouering* . . . *the offences* . . . *of the late 14. Traitors* . . . For Henrie Carre, 1588. 5) *A true report of the inditement* . . . *and Execution of Iohn VVeldon, William Hartley, and Robert Sutton* . . . Richard Iones, 1588. 6) *A True Recitall touching the cause of the death of Thomas Bales* . . . For William Wright, 1590. 7) *Actio in Henricum Garnetum* . . . *Omnia ex Anglico a Guilielmo Camdeno Latine versa.* Iohn Norton, 1607. 8) *A True Report of the Araignment* . . . *and condemnation, of* . . . *Robert Drewrie* . . . For Iefferie Chorlton, 1607.

[136]

people were unquestionably interested in what went on at court, even though this interest could not often be catered to in print. At a very early date, 1501, we find a book which seems to have been designed to gratify this curiosity. It is entitled *The traduction & mariage of the princesse. A rēmembraūce for the traduction of the Princesse kateryne . . . as here in articles it dothe ensue.*[1] The contents seem to be official memoranda regarding the reception and entertainment of Katharine of Aragon and the ceremonies attending her marriage to the Prince of Wales. The memoranda were drawn up by various officials of the court and by the queen herself; they are very comprehensive, beginning with the arrival of the princess at Southampton and covering all the ceremonies planned until the arrival of the wedding party at Westminister Palace after the marriage; but they are quite evidently only tentative suggestions which have not yet received the king's approval. If they described the arrangement of the ceremonies, one would imagine that they were intended as a *scenario* for the guidance of the many persons concerned, but as they are merely provisional, it seems necessary to suppose that they were printed for public consumption, to satisfy popular curiosity, before the arrival of the princess, about the details of the many splendid ceremonies contemplated. This view is confirmed by the fact that the pamphlet was obviously printed to be sold and is even adorned by a woodcut. It would be interesting to know by whose initiative the book was issued. It does not seem to have been inspired, although Pynson was the royal printer; the official style of a report of state pomps is much handsomer. Consequently, it would seem that here is an example of genuine publishing enterprise, that Pynson, or a bookseller who hired him to print the book, realizing how great was the popular interest in the impending ceremonies, obtained a

[1] Richard Pynson, [1501].

copy of the memoranda and printed them to gratify this interest.

Another early example of news of courtly pleasures is a book of verses, apparently printed in 1507, describing two tournaments recently held.[2] It was, however, composed as a literary effort; its elegant courtly tone is apparent, and the poet's attention is frequently diverted from the jousting by the "sovereign lady" who presides over the tournament. Nevertheless, amidst a great deal that is purely encomiastic, we find some account of what did take place in the lists, and it may have served as news.   It seems likely that the printed copies of masques performed at court or at entertainments given by the nobility appealed to popular interest in courtly manners.   They were interesting also as specimens of poetical and musical composition, but to readers not amateurs of belles-lettres they may have had some interest as descriptions of courtly ways.   In the printed titles the name of the author is obscure by comparison with those of the persons of quality who witnessed or performed in the masking, and the title which the publisher gave to a pirated edition of Daniel's *Vision of the Twelve Goddesses*, namely, *The true description of a Royall Masque. Presented at Hampton Court . . . And Personated by the Queenes . . . Maiestie, attended by Eleuen Ladies of Honour*,[3] strongly suggests that it was chosen to catch the eye of such as would welcome the drawing aside of the curtains which concealed the pleasures of the court from the common view.   The printer of *The Princelye pleasures, at the Courte at Kenelwoorth* (1576) confided to the reader that an account of this entertainment had "been sundry times

[2] *Here Begynneth The Iustes of the Moneth of Maye, Parfurnysshed & Done by Charles brandon.   Thomas knyuet. [and others] . . . The .xxii. yere of the reygne . . . Kynge Henry the seuenth. . . .   Here Begynneth The Iustes and tourney of ye Moneth of Iune, Parfurnysshed and Done By Rychard Gray, erle of Kent, By Charles brandon, wt theyr two Aydes agaynst All Comers.*
[3] Edward Allde, 1604.

6) *Mistris Turners Teares, for the Murder of Sir Thomas Overbury* Ballad. Entered 29 November 1615 by John Trundle (Arber, III. 579).

7) *Mistris Turners Farewell to all women.* Broadside. For Iohn Trundle, [1615].

8) *Iames Franklin A Kentishman of Maidstone, his ovvne Arraignment, Confession, Condemnation, and Iudgement of Himselfe, whilst hee lay Prisoner in the Kings Bench for the Poisoning of Sir Thomas Ouerbury.* Broadside. For I[ohn] T[rundle, 1615].

9) *Franklins Farewell to the World. With his Christian Contrition in Prison, before his Death.* Broadside. For Henry Gosson, [1615?].

10) *The picture of the vnfortunate gentleman, Sir Geruis Eluies knight, late leiftenant of his Maiesties Tower of London.* With verses. Broadside. Paul Boulenger, 1615.

11) *The Lieutenant of the Tower his speech and repentance, at the time of his death, Who was executed vpon Tower Hill, on the 20. day of Nouember. 1615. . . .* For Na[thaniel] Butter, [1615] (2 edd.).

12) An unnamed ballad on Sir Jervis Elwes. Entered 19 December 1615 by John Trundle (Arber, III. 580).

13) *The Iust Downfall of*
Ambition,	*Where-vnto*	*Weston*
Adultery,	*are added 3.*	*M. Turner*
and Murder	*notorious sin-*	*and Franklin.*
	ners	

In verse. Book. I[ohn] T[rundle, 1616?].

14) *The portrature of Sir Thomas Overbury.* Entered 20 January 1616 by Laurence Lisle (Arber, III. 581).

15) *Sir Thomas Ouerburies Vision. With the ghoasts of Weston, M*ris *Turner, the late Lieftenant of the Tower, and Franklin.* Verses by R[ichard] N[iccols]. Book. For R[ichard] M[eighen] & T[homas] I[ones], 1616.

Some of these ballads contain little enough news: they are compounded chiefly of lamentation, repentance, and exhortation to the reader to avoid evil courses. As poetry they are contemptible, but then they were neither written nor read as poetry, but as a reflection of passing events. They are all very much alike, so that they might almost have been written by the same hand; ballads of this sort were reduced almost to a formula, which the hacks who

[143]

wrote them never deviated from. Their most curious feature is the fact that nearly all of those embodying the last-minute confession and repentance of the criminal are written in the first person and purport to be his own inspired work. They are vouched for by such statements as "which he wrote the day before his death," "made with his owne hand in the Marshalsye, after his condemnation," "written by the said Cosby in the time of his imprisonment," as if the gift of song were imposed upon the condemned along with the sentence of death. The tune of "Fortune my foe," because "the metrical lamentations of extraordinary criminals have been usually chanted to it for upwards of these two hundred years,"[7] came to be known as the hanging tune. Books describing murders were the basis of some of the murder plays on the popular stage.

3. MIRACLES, PRODIGIES, AND WONDERS

The credulity and innocence of the sixteenth century are quaintly illustrated in the contemporary accounts of miracles and wonders. The age was never weary of reading signs and portents in natural happenings of all sorts or of explaining miraculously what it was difficult to account for otherwise. This disposition is the counterpart of our sublime modern faith in "science," which appears in newspaper stories of perpetual motion machines and of pseudo-scientific marvels illustrated with prodigiously enlarged photographs of the common house fly, in the man in the street's notion that psychology is a kind of black art by which one can subject others to one's will, or in the belief that beauty of face and figure can be obtained or preserved by artificial means. The sixteenth-century variety is perhaps the more picturesque.

At that time, even thunder, lightning, and the appear-

[7] Chappell: *Popular Music*, I. 163.

ANTHONY PAINTI

THE

Blaspheming Caryar.

Who sunke into the ground up to the neck, and there stood two day
two nights, and not to bee drawne out by the strength of Hor
or digged out by the help of man: and there dyed the
3. *of Nouember.* 1613.
Also the punishment of *Nicholas Mesle* a most wicked blasphemer.

Reade and tremble.

Published by Authoritie.

At London printed for *Iohn Trundle* : and are to be sold at
Christ Church Gate. 1614,

ance of comets were accounted miraculous and excited the utmost awe. The comets seen in London in October 1580 and early in 1583 inspired both books and ballads describing them and unfolding their significance. In the latter year the learned even fell out about the interpretation of the prodigy and carried on a pamphlet war on the subject. Miraculous apparitions in the air were also not uncommon. From contemporary accounts we learn that three suns were seen in Cornwall in 1621,[8] that two angels "came before" the city of Droppa in Silesia in 1593,[9] that two dragons were seen fighting over Ghent in 1609,[10] that in 1605, at Carlstadt in Croatia, "the Sunne did shine like Bloude nine dayes together, and . . . two Armies were seene in the Ayre, the one encountring the other . . . also a Woman was deliuered of three prodigious sonnes, which Prophisied many strange & fearefull thinges, which should shortly come to passe,"[11] that in 1597 "the cytie [of] Strale Sonet" was deluged by a rain of blood and brimstone,[12] that in 1577, in the parish church at Bungay, "in a great tempest of violente raine, lightning, and thunder, . . . an horrible shaped thing [was] sensibly perceiued of the people then and there assembled," which in the twinkling of an eye, mortally wrung the necks of

[8] *Somewhat: written by occasion of three sunnes seene at Tregnie in Cornewall*· [By John Everard, D.D. For Thomas Walkley,] 1622.

[9] *A booke of newes of Twoo angels that came before the Cytie of Droppa in S[i]lesia.* Entered 22 November 1593 by John Wolf (Arber, II. 640). A ballad on the same subject was entered at the same time.

[10] *The worldes warninge of an Alarum from sinne by the vision of 2 Dragons seene fightinge in the ayre neere Gaunte.* Ballad. Entered 6 February 1609 by Henry Gosson (Arber, III. 401).

[11] *Strange fearful & true newes, which hapned at Carlstadt, in the kingdome of Croatia. . . .* [Translated by Ed. Gresham.] For George Vincent & William Blackwall, [1606].

[12] *Trewe and Dreadfull newe tydinges of bloode and Brymston which God hathe caused to Rayne from heaven within and without the cytie Strale Sonet . . .* [Book.] Entered 26 September 1597 by John Oxenbridge (Arber, III. 91). A ballad on this subject was entered by George Shaw on 30 September (*ib.*).

[146]

several worshipers.[13] From the persistence of news of this sort, we may judge that it was greatly admired, for one of the popular tracts printed by John of Doesborch, which contains a letter dated 1517 and was probably printed soon after that time, is a fairy tale describing, as sober truth, the miraculous appearance of two splendid armies out of a wood "in the land of Bergame," a battle between them, and their equally miraculous disappearance.[14] Many of the miracles reported happened in foreign countries, but there is nothing to suggest that they were not as terrifying as home-grown marvels.

Another recurrent kind of miracle was a prolonged fast. Young maidens were the heroines of these miracles: some of them lived for as long as sixteen years without taking food or drink or, like Eve Fliegen, a woman living in Holland, by the simple plan of inhaling the perfume of roses.[15] This maiden, like condemned murderers, was endowed with the gift of poetry, for the ballad describing her strange power recites that "this song was made by the maide her self." Other miraculous preservations, especially of persons wrongly convicted of crime and hanged, for as long as five days, are also recorded.[16]

[13] *A Straunge and terrible Wunder wrought very late in the parish Church of Bongay* . . . By Abraham Fleming. Frauncis Godly, [1577].

[14] *The Copye of the letter folowynge whiche specifyeth of ye greatest* . . . *batayle that euer was sene or herde of.* Andwarpe: Johñ of Dousborowe.

[15] 1) *The Protestants and Iesuites vp in Armes in Gulicke-land. Also, A true and wonderfull relation of a Dutch maiden (called Eue Fliegen of Meurs* . . . *) who* . . . *hath fasted for the space of 14 yeares* . . . Translated from the Dutch by Thomas Wood. For Nicholas Bourne, 1611. 2) *Of a maide nowe dwelling at the towne of meurs in dutchland, that hath not taken any foode this 16 yeares, and is not yet neither hungry nor thirsty; the which maide hath lately beene presented to the lady elizabeth, the king's daughter of england.* A ballad in the Shirburn MS.; see *Shirburn Ballads,* no. X. 3) *The Pourtrayture of Eua Fliegen* . . . Broadside. Sold by Georg[e] Humble, [1615?].

[16] 1) *A True relation of Gods wonderfull mercies, in preseruing one aliue, which hanged fiue days who was falsely accused.* Edward Allde, [1605?]. 2) *A most miraculous, strange, and trewe Ballad, of a younge man of the age of 19 yeares, who was wrongfully hangd at* . . . *Bon* . . . *since christmas last* . . .*; and how*

[147]

All of these miracles were exhibited in print as signs of God's mercy or wrath, as warnings of the Day of Judgment, or as summons to repentance. A lugubriously moral tone or an interpretation of the miracle in terms of approved Christian morality is seldom lacking; indeed, the moral often swallows up the news. According to one observer, the "blazyng starre" of 1580 was "set on fire by Gods prouidence, to call all sinners to earnest & speedie repentance;"[17] one of the ballads on the same subject is entitled *An exhortacon to amendemente of life by . . . the laste Blasinge Starre*;[18] another ballad is described as *An exhortation to London to turne in tyme vnto ye Lord by thexample of fier seen ouer the same 2° Septembris 1583.*[19] Indeed, this evidence leaves little doubt that the queen's subjects, or their ghostly spokesmen, had a very satisfactory Calvinistic consciousness of sin. Many other miracles designed to drive home a pious moral were published from time to time. Everything testified to the handiwork of God—in Holdt, a city in Germany, in 1616, three dead bodies arose from their graves "admonishing the people of Iudgements to come;"[20] a prophecy of the Day of Judgment was found in the church of St. Denis wrapped in lead in the form of a heart;[21] at Orford and Aldeburgh in Suffolk "Godes mercye [was] showed to the poore" by "the soden growth of peaze vppon the Sea Rock;"[22] in Germany "a poore Countrey

---

god *preserued him aliue, and brought his false accuser to deserued destruction.* See *Shirburn Ballads,* no. XXXVIII.

[17] *A blazyng Starre or burnyng Beacon, seene the 10. of October laste (and yet continewyng)* . . . By Francis Shakelton. For Henry Kirkham, 1580.

[18] Entered 5 November 1580 by John Charlewood & Edwarde White (Arber, II. 381).

[19] Entered 6 April 1584 by Edward White (Arber, II. 431).

[20] *Miraculous Newes, From the Cittie of Holdt . . . the twentieth of September . . . 1616* . . . Translated from the Dutch [by T. F.] For Iohn Barnes, 1616.

[21] *A Prophesie of the Iudgment Day.* . . . Broadside. For I. W., [c. 1620].

[22] *Godes mercye showed to the poore at Orford* . . . Ballad. Entered 21 July 1596 by John Danter (Arber, III. 67).

[148]

Maide, . . . being dead . . . 24. houres, reuiued
againe, and lay fiue dayes weeping, and continued proph-
esying of strange euents to come, and so died the 5. day following."[23]

The *censores morum* of King James's time took especial
delight in an incident which happened at Lyons in 1607,
when the performance of a play by members of the Society
of Jesus was interrupted by a severe thunderstorm and the
players representing God the Father, God the Son, the
Virgin Mary, and Lucifer were stunned by lightning. As
the Jesuits and play-acting were about equally repugnant
to right-thinking moralists at that time, they seized upon
this news as a sign of God's wrath against both. No less
than two ballads[24] and three books[25] on the subject were
printed. Indeed, even occurrences which there need have
been no difficulty in explaining were sometimes attributed
to miraculous causes, if it flattered English moral and religious prejudices to do so. The book called *Most strange
newes from Lishbourne*[26] relates that "two of the cheefe of
the Holy-house" were struck dumb "as they were pro-
nouncing the sentence of death against two English Mari-
ners, vnto whom they had offered great promotions, to
haue them to serue against the King of France, and their
owne Countrie," and that six days later two ships of corn
"brought out of France to releeue the King his enimies"
were consumed by fire upon the direct intervention of the
Almighty. The *Strange Newes from Antwarpe, which happened the 12. of August . . . 1612,*[27] published as an awful

[23] *A Miracle, of Miracles.* For Iohn Trundle, 1614.

[24] Arber, III. 361–2.

[25] 1) *The Iesuites comedie, acted at Lyons.* For Arthur Iohnson, 1607. 2) *The
Iesuites play at Lyons in France . . .* Signed R. S. For Nathaniel Butter, 1607.
3) *Recit touchant la comedie iouee par les Jesuites . . . en la ville de Lyons . . .*
1607. 4) Possibly *A bloody tragedye or Romishe masque Acted by fyve Jesuytes and
16 yonge Germayne froes,* a book entered 7 November 1607 by John Trundell
(Arber, III. 364), refers to this subject.

[26] For William Barley, 1591.

[27] Ralph Blower, 1612.

[149]

judgment upon idolatry, is the damaging of the church and steeple of St. Michael by lightning—or, as the narrator preferred to put it, by Satan in person. Here the author's theology seems to have gone awry: in English books, as a rule, Satan was found on the side of idolatry. Possibly the most pleasant of all these exemplary miracles is the story of the rich woman who mocked at a poor sister who had borne twins (a common belief of the time being that twins were begotten by two different fathers) and was straightway punished by being delivered of three hundred and sixty-five children, one for each day of the year, at a single birth.[28] Many more similar marvels could be mentioned—judgments upon perjurers,[29] blasphemers,[30] drunkards,[31] and hoarders of grain,[32] miraculous sinkings and movings of ground,[33] rainfalls of wheat,[34] miraculous disclosures of

[25] *The Lamenting Lady* . . . Broadside. For Henry Gosson, [c. 1620].

[29] 1) *A wonderfull example againste Periurie late happeninge in Jermanye.* [Ballad.] Entered 3 November 1580 by Henry Carre (Arber, II. 381). 2) *A Fearefull Example, Shewed vpon a periured Person.* For Thomas Nelson, [1591]. This is really nothing but an account of the perjurer's suicide, but the book characteristically represents it as an "example."

[30] 1) *Two wunderfull and rare Examples* . . . *the one vpon a wicked and pernitious blasphemer* . . . By Phillip Stubbes. For William Wright, [1581]. 2) *A fearefull and terrible Example of Gods iuste iudgement executed vpon a lewde Fellow, who vsually accustomed to sweare by Gods Blood* . . . By Philip Stubbes. Broadside. For William Wright, [1581?]. 3) *Anthony Painter the Blaspheming Caryar.* . . . *Also the punishment of Nicholas Mesle a most wicked blasphemer.* For Iohn Trundle, 1614.

[31] 1) *A ballad of vij dronkardes whome the evill spirit procured to Death at Ravenspurgh in Swaben.* Entered 26 June 1579 by Jhon Charlwood (Arber, II. 354). 2) *The wrath of God in the punishmente of Twoo Drunckardes at Nekers Hofen in Almayne.* [Ballad.] Entered 22 August 1581 by John Charlewood (Arber, II. 400). 3) *A dolefull dittye of fiue vnfortunat persons that were drowned in their drunknes in crossing ouer the Thames neare Iuy Bridge,* . . . *the 15 of October last, 1616* . . . See *Shirburn Ballads,* no. XIV.

[32] *The poores lamentacon for the price of corne with Godes Justice shewed vppon a cruell horder of corne.* Ballad. Entered 16 October 1594 by Edward White (Arber, II. 662).

[33] 1) *The tru Reporte of the newes in Heryfordshyre.* [Book.] Entered 1570–1 by Thomas Colwell (Arber, I. 443). 2) *A most true report of the myraculous mouing and sinking of a plot of ground* . . . *at Westram in Kent* . . . By John Chap-

murder[35]—, but the examples already cited should be sufficient.

4. MONSTERS

One of the most curious fancies of the sixteenth-century taste for the marvelous was its interest in monsters, both animal and human. The report of a misshapen creature of almost any kind was received with awe and trembling and perpended as a visible manifestation of divine power. Numerous broadsides picturing, describing, and moralizing upon prodigies of this sort attest to this susceptibility. The taste was common to the whole of Europe; news of monsters born on the continent was published in England and was apparently received with the same delight as that of domestic origin. In fact, the earliest broadside of this kind which I have met with, printed in 1531, describes a monstrous pig born in Prussia.[36] It consists of two large, well-drawn, and shockingly realistic representations, front and rear elevations, of two shoats partly joined at birth,

---

man. Thomas Creede, 1596. 3) *A Caveat for England by the Example of Cockham hill in Kent* . . . Ballad. Entered 23 January 1597 by Thomas Millington (Arber, III. 78).

[34] *A wonderfull and strange newes which happened in* . . . *Suffolk and Essex the firste of februarie* . . . *where yt rained wheate the space of Sixe or seauen miles compasse.* [Book.] Entered 22 February 1583 by Edwarde White (Arber, II. 420).

[35] 1) *A man or a monster discoueringe the most inhumane Conspiracye of one Paule Rawlins a Butcher in Whitechappell agaynst the lyfe of his apprentice reuealed by a miraculous accident.* Book. Enterea 10 September 1613 by [George] Elde (Arber, III. 532). 2) *A murder in Lancashire revealed by A Calfe.* Ballad. Entered 12 March 1615 by John Trundle (Arber, III. 564). 3) *Newes out of Lancashire or the* . . . *miraculous revelacon of a murther by a ghost a Calf a pigeon &c.* Book. Entered provisionally 12 September 1615 by John Trundle (Arber, III. 572).

[36] *This horryble monster is cast of a Sowe in Eestlande in Pruse* . . . *in a vyllage which is called lebēhayn* . . . According to Mr. Pollard (*Transactions Bibliographical Society*, IX. 98), this broadside was printed in Germany and imported in quantity by Wynkyn de Worde; he then cut off the German text at the top and printed his own in the vacant space between the figures.

with a few specifications in prose between the drawings. Swine, it would seem, were most likely to be brought forth in unnatural shapes, but we hear also of "Foules, having the Fethers about their heads, like to the Frysled Fore-tops, Lockes, and great Ruffes, now in use amongst men and women,"[37] and of a herring "hauing on the one side the picture of two armed men fighting, and on the other most strange Characters, as in the Picture is here expressed."[38] Even sea-creatures in no way unnatural or misshapen, but infrequently seen—sharks,[39] cuttlefish,[40] and whales[41]—, were likewise regarded as marvelous. Mermaids are suggested by the terms of several entries in the Stationers' registers.[42] The most famous supernatural beast discovered during our period was the Sussex dragon which, in 1614, according to the testimony of witnesses whose names were printed in the book on the subject,[43] slaughtered "both

[37] *A most wonderfull and true report, the like never heard of before, of divers unknowne Foules . . . Lately taken at Crowley in . . . Lyncolne.* Book. Robert Robinson, 1586. Entered 21 November 1586 (Arber, II. 459). This description is quoted from Hazlitt: *Handbook*, p. 335; I have not been able to find the book myself.

[38] *A most strange and wonderfull Herring, taken on the 26. day of Nouember 1597. neere vnto Drenton . . . Norway.* Translated from the Dutch. Iohn Wolfe, 1598.

[39] *The true discription of this marueilous straunge fishe whiche was taken . . . the xvj. day of Iune . . . M.D.lxix.* By C. R. Broadside. Thomas Colwell, 1569.

[40] *The discription of a rare or rather most monstrous fishe taken on the East cost of Holland the .xvii. of Nouember, Anno 1566.* Broadside. Thomas Purfoote, [1566].

[41] *A true report and exact description of a mighty sea-monster, or whale, cast upon Langar-shore ouer against Harwich . . . Februarie 1617.* For Henry Holland, 1617.

[42] 1) *The most true and strange report of A monstruous fishe that appeared in forme of A woman from the wast vpward Seene in the Sea.* Book. Entered 2 April 1604 by William White (Arber, III. 258). 2) *A true and faithfull relation of a wonderfull seamonster, A sea-man lately taken at sea, betweene Denmark and Norway.* [Book.] Entered 18 May 1621 by Joseph Browne (Arber, IV. 54).

[43] *True and wonderfull. A discourse relating a strange and monstrous serpent (or dragon) Lately discouered, and yet liuing . . . In Sussex, two Miles from Horsam, in . . . St. Leonards Forrest, and thirtie Miles from London, this present Month of August, 1614. . . .* For John Trundle, 1614.

[152]

Gods Handy-vvorke in VVONDERS.

Miraculously shewen vpon two Women, lately deliuered of two
Monsters : with a most strange and terrible Earth-quake, by
which, Fields and other grounds, were quite
remoued to other places :

The prodigious births, being at a place called *Perre-farme*, within a
quarter of a mile of Feuersham *in* Kent, *the* 25. *of* Iuly
last, being S. *Iames* his day. 1615.

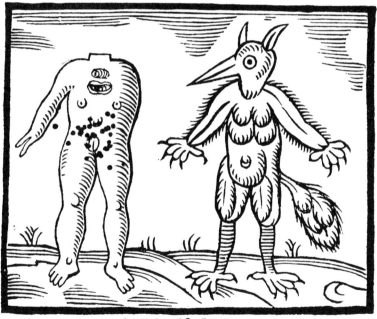

London, Printed for I. W. 1615.

[153]

. . . Men and Cattell, by his strong and violent Poyson."
This monster was too much even for the credulity of a
credulous age and was laughed out of existence.

Reports of monsters of the human species were even com-
moner. Most of these were *lusus naturæ* who happily died
as soon as they were born, or such as we nowadays call
Siamese twins.[44] But we also hear of a child born with a
cluster of grapes[45] or of long hair about the navel,[46] of two
children with ruffs,[47] and sundry other marvelous deformi-
ties.

These news-reports are almost invariably illustrated and
the broadsides among them are unusual in sometimes consisting of a prose account or adding a prose appendix to the
customary ballad. These prose notes give interesting particulars of the shape of the monster or curious information
anatomical—*e.g.*, that the child had "neyther hande,
foote, legge, nor arme . . . [and] it hath a codde and
stones, but no yearde"[48]—or genital—*e.g.*, that the parents
had natural children before and the mother "went with this
her full tyme"[49]—or social—*e.g.*, that the child was "begot
out of matrimony, but borne in matrimonye,"[48] or that

[44] The earliest I know of is a broadside which begins, *Thou shalte vnderstande,
Chrysten Reader, that the thyrde daye of August . . . M.CCCCC . . . in a towne
called Myddleton stonye . . . at the In, called the Sygne of the Egle, there the good
wyfe of the same, was deliuered of thys double Chylde, begotten of her late housbande
Iohn Kenner . . .* [1550.]

[45] Arber, I. 266.

[46] *The true description of a monsterous Chylde, borne in the Ile of Wight, . . . M
D lxiiij. the month of October . . .* By Iohn Barkar. Broadside. Wylliam
Gryffith, 8 November [1564].

[47] 1) *The true Discripcion of a Childe with Ruffes, borne in . . . Micheham,
. . . Surrey, . . . MDLXVI.* By H. B. Broadside. Iohn Allde & Richarde
Iohnes, 20 August 1566. 2) *An admonition to all women to see the iust Judgement
of God for the punishment of pride purtraied in a wonderfull child.* [Book.] Entered 17 May 1587 by Henry Carr (Arber, II. 470).

[48] *The true reporte of the forme and shape of a monstrous Childe borne at Muche
Horkesleye, . . . Essex, the xxi daye of Apryll . . . 1562.* Broadside. Thomas
Marshe, [1562].

[49] *A discription of a monstrous Chylde, borne at Chychester in Sussex, the xxiiii.*

the mother, "being vnmaryed, played the naughty packe."[50] Sometimes we meet with a list of witnesses,[51] and several broadsides inform the reader where the monster is on exhibition and therefore must have partaken of the nature of advertisements.[52]

The text of these news-reports, especially the ballads, was nearly always given a moral turn. "These straunge and monstrous thinges," says an account of a monstrous pig, "Almighty God sendeth amongest vs, that we shuld not be forgetfull of his almighty power, nor vnthankeful for his great mercies so plentifully powred vpon vs."[53] The lesson to be drawn from a fowl or a child with ruffs, or from a female child having on her forehead "a peece of flesh of two fingers thicke round about, the flesh being wonderfully curled like Gentlewomens attire: being of a very blew coullour like a turcke Locke,"[54] is obvious to any moralist who reprehends excessive display in dress. The author of a book about a deformed child born in Herefordshire in 1600, "begotten by incestuous copulation betweene the Brothers sonne and the Sisters daughter, being both vnmar-

---

daye of May . . . MCCCCCLXII. By Ihon D. Broadside. For Fraunces Godlyf, 1562.

[50] *The forme and shape of a monstrous Child, borne at Maydstone in Kent, the xxiiij. of October, 1568.* Broadside. Iohn Awdeley, 23 December [1568].

[51] 1) *The forme and shape of a monstrous Child, borne at Maydstone,* as above. 2) *A most strange and trew ballad of a monst[r]ous child borne in Southampton . . . the 16. day of March last, 1602, as it is verified by the maiestr[a]ts and officers of the same towne . . . Shirburn Ballads,* no. LXXII.

[52] 1) "To be seene in Glene Alley, in Suthwark, beeing aliue and x. weeks old and iiij. dayes, not vnlikly to liue long." *The true Discripcion of a Childe with Ruffes,* as above. 2) "At this present to be seene at London." *A right strange and vvoonderful example of the handie vvorke of a mightie God, . . . three children, borne in . . . Paskewet, . . . Monmouth, . . . the third of February last. 1585.* Richard Iones, 1585. 3) "To bee seene in London, at the Red Lyon in Fletestreete." *The true discription of this marueilous straunge fishe,* as above, p. 152.

[53] *The description of a monstrous pig, the which was farrowed at Hamsted . . . the xvi day of October, . . . M.D. lxii.* Broadside. For Garat Dewes, [1562].

[54] *A wonder woorth the reading . . .* William Iones, 1617.

[155]

ried persons," deplored it as "a notable and most terrible example against Incest and Whoredom."[55] This kind of news, indeed, served both God and Mammon in providing the godly with apt texts for their homilies and in regaling the vulgar with information highly palatable to their appetite for the marvelous.

5. WITCHCRAFT

Another staple article in the stock-in-trade of the popular publishers was a narrative of the practices of witches. This kind of news seems to have had a large audience, and the supply of it was quite steady, most of it being taken from the trials and confessions of witches at country assizes. With a good deal of similarity, they were adjudged guilty of conversing with familiar spirits and of casting spells which brought cattle and humankind to an untimely end. Thus Elizabeth Stile, a witch executed at Abingdon in 1579, confessed that she kept a familiar in the form of a rat, which she had christened Philip and fed with her own blood. She and her confederates cast a fatal spell upon their enemies by the familiar method of making a wax image to represent the intended victim and piercing its heart with a hawthorn prick.[56] Sometimes the practice of witchcraft was added to the burden of sins which the Catholics were obliged to bear in England. John Walsh confessed at Exeter in 1566 that he had been seduced into the practice of witchcraft by a Catholic friar, and the book describing his examination before the bishop of Exeter's commissary gives also an account of the diabolical arts practised by several popes.[57] In 1603 certain persons who

[55] *A Most straunge, and true Discourse . . . Of a Monstrous, deformed Infant . . . borne at Colwall, . . . Hereford, vpon the sixt day of Ianuary . . . 1599.* By I. R. Richard Iones, 1600.
[56] *A Rehearsall both straung and true, of hainous and horrible actes committed by . . . Fower notorious Witches . . .* E[dward] White, [1579].
[57] *The Examination of Iohn Walsh . . .* Iohn Awdely, 23 December 1566.

had formerly been persuaded that they were possessed by demons confessed that they had been exorcised by Catholic priests,[58] and so, it was alleged, was a boy named William Perry at Bilson, Staffordshire, in 1621.[59]

Much more astonishing are the accounts of the sufferings of persons possessed or otherwise tormented by demons. An unclean spirit which entered the body of Alexander Nyndge, at Herringswell in Suffolk in 1573, wrestled so powerfully for possession of him that six men, clinging to the body in midair, were barely able to prevent the spirit from making away with it. This demon was at length exorcised by prayer and reading of the Scriptures, and fled through the window crying "bawe wawe, bawe wawe."[60] A devil which visited Mrs. Margaret Cooper, at Dichet, Somersetshire, in 1584, in the likeness of a headless bear "did thrust the womans he[a]d betwixt her legges, and so roulled her in a rounde compasse like an Hoope" "thorow three Chambers, and doune a high paire of staiers."[61] There are also a few accounts of bargains with the devil. Lewes Gaufrydey, "a scholler of Fraunce," made a Faust-like contract to give his soul and body to the devil in exchange for the enjoyment of the pleasures of the world, but he was found out and burned in June 1612.[62] One Stubbe Peeter, living near Cologne, obtained from the devil a magic girdle by which he was enabled to change himself into the likeness of a wolf. In this form he devoured many men, women, and children in the course of a career of crime lasting twenty-five years. "That this thing is true," asserts the

[58] *A Declaration of egregious Popish Impostures* . . . See above p. 48.
[59] *The boy of Bilson* . . . By Richard Baddeley. For William Barret, 1622.
[60] *A Booke Declaringe the Fearfull Vexasion, of one Alexander Nyndge.* . . . Thomas Colwell, [1574?].
[61] *A true and most Dreadfull discourse of a women possessed with the Deuill* . . . For Thomas Nelson, [1584].
[62] 1) *The life and death of Lewis Gaufredi* . . . For Richard Redmer, 1612. 2) See Arber, III. 493.

book which tells his story, "Maister Tice Artine a Brewer dwelling at Puddle-wharfe, in London, . . . is able to iustifie."[63]

The belief in witchcraft and sorcery was so common that the church was impelled to take measures to stop some of the abuses which it gave rise to. In 1599 the Rev. John Darrell, a highly celebrated exorcist, was investigated by the bishop of London and examined by the ecclesiastical commissioners. Up to this time Darrell had very fully reported his own successes in print[64] and had attained such a celebrity that he was called in from afar to deal with obstinate cases. His method of exorcism was fervent prayer and other godly exercises. The commissioners at Lambeth, however, pronounced him a fraud, and Dr. Samuel Harsnet, the bishop's secretary and a member of the commission sitting on the case, published a tract exposing his impostures.[65] Darrell was clapped into the Gatehouse, whence he sent forth *A detection of that sinnful, shamful, lying, and ridiculous Discours of Samuel Harshnet . . .*[66] steadfastly contending that it was impious to deny the doctrine of possession and dispossession by evil spirits because the word of God is authority for it. His disciples rushed

[63] *A true Discourse. Declaring the damnable life and death of one Stubbe Peeter* . . . Translated from the German. For Edward Venge, [1590].

[64] 1) *The most wonderfull and true storie, of a certaine Witch, named Alse Goode-rige* . . . For I[ohn] O[xenbridge], 1597. The preface is signed I. D., and the book, if it was not written by Darrell, was certainly published by him. 2) *A true Narration of the . . . Vexation by the Deuil, of 7. persons in Lancashire, and William Somers of Nottingham.* Entered 29 August 1597 by Raffe Jackson (Arber, III. 89). The earliest existing copy, which may have been printed abroad, is dated 1600. 3) *A Breife Narration of the possession, dispossession, and, repossession of William Sommers: and of some proceedings against Mr. Iohn Dorrell* . . . 1598. 4) *An Apologie, or defence of the possession of William Sommers* . . . [1599.] One of Darrell's books was ordered burned by the Stationers 29 October 1600: see *Transactions Bibliographical Society*, new series, VIII. 415.

[65] *A discouery of the Fraudulent practises of Iohn Darrel* . . . Iohn Wolfe, 1599.

[66] [London?] 1600.

into print to aid him.[67]   In 1602 he was still battling over the old ground with his armory of scriptural citations against two new adversaries.[68]   Another book published under the auspices of the church to put a damper on this form of superstition is *A true discourse, vpon the matter of Martha Brossier of Romorantin* . . . ,[69] an account of the deceptions practised by a pretended demoniac in France.   It was translated by Abraham Hartwell, secretary to the archbishop of Canterbury.

6. THE PLAGUE

When the plague broke out in London, it overawed the minds of the people more completely than any other subject.   But little news came of it.   There was no urgent need of printed news; the plague was too close at hand to need announcement, too familiar to need description.   A good deal of printing came of it: the popular publishers drove a steady trade in propitiatory ballads, prayers for deliverance, prophylactic treatises by the professors of physic, and spiritual nostrums concocted by the curators of souls, who, as usual, ascribed the pest to the sinfulness of God's chosen people and confidently recommended repentance and retribution as a cure.   But these are not news.

Possibly there was news in the piece (very likely a ballad)

[67] 1) *A Brief apologie prouing the possession of William Sommers. Written by Iohn Dorrell,* . . . *but published without his knowledge* . . . 1599. 2) *The Triall of Maist. Dorrell, or, a Collection of Defences* . . . 1599. 3) *A true Discourse concerning the certaine possession and dispossessiō of 7 persons* . . . *in Lancashire* . . . By George More. 1600. Nothing seems to be known at the present time of a ballad on the dispossession of Somers from which Dr. Harsnet quotes a few lines in his *Discouery.*

[68] The Rev. John Deacon and John Walker.   See their *Dialogicall Discourses of Spirits and Diuels* (for George Bishop, 1601) and *A Summarie Answere to al the material points in any of Master Darel his bookes* (for George Bishop, 1601).   Darrell's replies are *A suruey of certain dialogical discourses* ([London?] 1602) and *The Replie of Iohn Darrell to the Answer of Iohn Deacon and Iohn Walker* ([London?] 1602).

[69] Iohn Wolfe, 1599.

[159]

which Richard Jones entered for publication on 24 March 1579 entitled *The progresse of the plag*,[70] but all copies of it apparently have perished. It seems possible that, in 1603, that untiring purveyor of popular wares, John Trundle, made an attempt to provide news of the course of the plague. At any rate, on 27 July he entered a book (now lost) called *A Relation of many visitations of the plague*,[71] which was doubtless edifying as well as informing, and in October he published a pirated copy of the official bill of mortality.[72] These two swallows do not make a summer, but it may be more than a coincidence that, among the very few pieces of evidence that we have of news about the plague, two so close together should be due to the same publisher.

There is information aplenty in Dekker's *VVonderfull yeare* and other tracts of the same sort, but, for all their graphic description of the horrors of the scourge, they were hardly written to disseminate information, and resemble the modern "feature story" rather than a report of news.

All that we can fairly call news is the orders and directions which the authorities issued to prevent the spread of the infection and to insure the proper care of the infected and the bills of mortality from time to time published. Orders for combating the plague were drawn up and published by the officers of the city of London, where it was, of course, most severe, for use within the limits of their authority, and by the Privy Council for the rest of the country. The London orders, according to Mr. Wilson,[73] are the older and in their earliest form were drawn up in 1518; they were amplified from time to time and first printed not later than 1574. The general orders were probably printed as early as 1578; the oldest surviving copy Mr. Wilson as-

---

[70] Arber, II. 349.
[71] *Ib.*, III. 243.
[72] See Wilson: *The Plague in Shakespeare's London*, p. 192.
[73] *Op. cit.*, p. 15.

signs to 1592.[74]   These orders were primarily intended for the guidance of the officers charged with their execution, but sometimes, if not always, they were published to the populace, *e.g.*, by being set up on posts.   Whether they were sold is a question; we can regard them as news only in the sense that proclamations and printed ordinances required to be observed are news.

Bills of mortality were compiled since almost the beginning of the sixteenth century, but there is no record of their having been printed before 1593.[75]   On 14 July of that year John Wolf was granted the privilege of printing "the billes, briefes, notes and larges gyven out for the sicknes weekely or otherwise."[76]   This monopoly fell to Wolf's lot as city printer, an office to which he had just been appointed.   According to Tom Nash, his self-appointed biographer, Gabriel Harvey edited the bills which Wolf printed:

He [Harvey] did for him [Wolf] that eloquent *post-script* for the Plague Bills, where he talkes of the series, the classes, & the premisses, & presenting them with an exacter methode hereafter, if it please God the Plague continue.   By the style I tooke it napping, and smelt it to be a pig of his *Sus Mineruam*, . . . and since the Printer hath confest it to mee.   The vermilion *Wrinckle* de *crinkledum* hop'd (belike) that the Plague would proceed, that he might haue an occupation of it.[77]

None of Wolf's bills has been preserved.   He was succeeded as city printer and official publisher of these morbid statistics by John Windet in 1603.[78]   The bill which Windet printed

[74] *Op. cit.*, p. 14.

[75] Except the statistics for the year ending 27 December 1582.   These, however, seem to have been printed in a book, which is known only from a fragment containing the mortality figures; they were merely quoted.   It is uncertain when this book was printed.   See Wilson: *op. cit.*, p. 200.

[76] Arber, II. 634.

[77] *Haue with you to Saffron-Walden*; quoted from *Works*, ed. McKerrow, III. 89.

[78] "Entred for his copie . . .   The billes of suche as Dye and are buried this yere of the plague and other sicknesses provided that he shall print London and the Liberties thereof by them selues in one sheete.   And the places in Middlesex and Surrey by them selues in Another sheete."   Arber, III. 243.

[161]

for the week from 13 to 20 October 1603 is the oldest printed bill of mortality known;[79] it includes "a true Relation" of all the deaths since the beginning of the plague on 17 December 1602. In 1611 William Stansby succeeded to Windet's privilege,[80] though not to his office: in 1625, at the same time as he printed the bill for that year, he also issued broadsides containing the current bill and that for 1603 by way of comparison.[81] No other printed bills falling within our period are known. It is probable that they were printed and sold only at such times as the plague was acute, but when they did appear, we may be sure they were seized with avidity as the most unwelcome, yet the most fascinating news of the week.

7. ACTS OF GOD; THE WEATHER

The news-record of calamities by flood, fire, *etc.* describes only the more destructive and more extraordinary occurrences of these kinds. There is little variety in it; each new burning of a village or a church-steeple and each new overflowing of waters was described, bewailed, and abjectly attributed to a jealous God much as the last had been. Sometimes the bewailing and the cringing before the Almighty are much more prominent than the describing. The first fire we meet is probably the most important—the burning of the steeple of St. Paul's by lightning on 4 June 1561. Six days later William Seres printed *The true report of the burnyng of the steple and churche of Poules in London*, an official account of the calamity by my lord of Durham. For several years this subject kept recurring in the output of the press. One ballad on the subject, "Lament eche one the blazing fire," has been preserved; several others, at

---

[79] *The true copie of all the burials and c[hristenings] as well within the City of London as the Liberties thereof . . . From the 13. of October, 1603. to [the 20th of the] same . . .*

[80] Arber, III. 467.

[81] *A true Report of all the Burials and Christnings within the Citie of London and the Liberties thereof, from the 23. of December, 1602. to the 22. of December, 1603. . . .*

least, were published.[82] The bishop of Durham, in 1563, was moved to publish another book,[83] but it is almost entirely given up to settling the causes of the disaster on theological grounds. The last entry on this subject in the Stationers' register, in 1564, is very significant—*The incorragen all kynde of men to ye Reedyfinge and buyldynge Powles steple agayne.*[84] Other notable fires are that which burned down the Globe Theater in Southwark on 29 June 1613 (two ballads on the subject were entered the very next day[85]) and the conflagrations which destroyed the Devonshire village of Tiverton in 1598 and again in 1612, each recorded in a book and a ballad.[86] Floods are described in the printed news in 1580, 1607, and 1613, but the disastrous floods in many parts of England in the late winter of 1607 seem to have excited the greatest interest; I have found four books and two ballads on this subject in the month of February alone.[87]

[82] 1) *A Diolige of the Rufull burr[n]ynge of Powles.* Entered 1562-3 by John Cherlewood (Arber, I. 202). 2) *Whan yonge Powlis steple olde Powlies steples chylde.* Entered 1562-3 by John Cherlwood (*ib.*, I. 210).

[83] *The burnynge of Paules church in London . . . by lyghtnynge . . .* Willyam Seres, 10 March 1563.

[84] Entered by William Greffeth (Arber, I. 263).

[85] 1) *A Sonnet vpon the Pitiful Burning of the Globe Playhouse in London.* Simon Stafford, 1613. 2) *A dolefull ballad of the generall ouerthrowe of the famous theater on the Banksyde, called the Globe.* By William Parrat. Entered 30 June 1613 by Edward White (Arber, III. 528).

[86] 1) *The True lamentable discourse of the burning of Teuerton . . .* For Thomas Millington, 1598. 2) *The burninge of the Towne of Tiverton.* Ballad. Entered 28 April 1598 by Thomas Purfoot Sr. & Jr. (Arber, III. 113). 3) *Woofull newes from the west partes of England being A discours of the burninge of Tyverton . . .* Book. Entered 14 August 1612 by [Thomas] Pavier (*ib.*, III. 492). 4) *A ballad of the burning of Tyverton. the. 5 of August 1612.* Entered simultaneously.

[87] 1) *A true report of certaine wonderfull ouerflowings of Waters, now lately in Summersetshire, Norfolke, and other places of England.* For Edward White, [1607]. 2) *More strange Newes: Of . . . late ouerflowings of Waters. Ibid.* 3) *A lamentable Dyttie of Diuers overflowinge of Waters in Sumersett Sheire Norfoulke Northwales, and other partes in England.* Ballad. Entered 11 February 1607 by John Hardie (Arber, III. 340). 4) *Lamentable newes out of Monmouthshire in Wales. . . .* For W[illiam] W[elby, 1607]. 5) *Gods warning to his people of*

But unquestionably the most awful calamity visited upon England during our period was the earthquake of 6 April 1580. It seems to have taken but two lives and done little real damage to property, but it made a profound impression upon the popular mind, as the output of the printing presses at the time witnesses. Within two days, three books and two ballads were entered in the Stationers' register, and they were by no means the end.[88] In all this printing there is, however, very little news—for one thing, I imagine, because there was very little news to print. It is nevertheless voluble and copious on the subject of historical parallels, of the signs by which this stroke was portended, and of what punishment might next be expected,

England. . . . For W[illiam] Barley & Io[hn] Bayly, 1607. Another edition has a somewhat different title-page. 6) *Gods warninge to the people of England.* Ballad. Entered 23 February 1607 by Raffe Blore (Arber, III. 341).

[88] 1) *A godly newe ballat moving us to repent by ye example of ye erthquake* . . . Entered 7 April 1580 by William Barteley (Arber, II. 367). 2) *A true report of this earthquake in London.* [Book.] Entered 8 April by John Aldee (*ib.*, II. 368). 3) *A warning to the wise* . . . *Written of the late earthquake* . . . Verse & prose. By Thomas Churchyard. For John Allde & Nicholas Lyng, 8 April 1580. 4) *A fatherly admonycon and lovinge warnynge to England* . . . [Book.] Entered 8 April by H[enry] Kyrkham (Arber, II. 368). 5) *A shorte and pithie Discourse, concerning* . . . *Earthquakes* . . . By T[homas] T[wyne]. Richarde Iohnes, 1580. 6) *Thearthquake.* "A thinge in verse." Entered 11 April by John Kingston (Arber, II. 368). 7) *Alarm for London and Londoners settinge forthe the thunderinge peales of Gods mercye* . . . [Book.] Entered 10[20?] April by J[ohn] Aldee (*ib.*, II. 369.) 8) *Quake. quake. yt is tyme to quake.*

When towers and townes and all Doo shake. Ballad.

By [William] Elderton. Entered 25 April by Ric[hard] Jones (*ib.*). 9) *A true and terrible example of Gods wrathe shewed by ye generall earthquake* . . . [Ballad.] Entered 3 May by H[enry] Kyrkham (*ib.*, II. 370). 10) *A discourse vpon the Earthquake* . . . By Arthur Golding. Henry Binneman, 1580. 11) *The second earthquake in Kent.* [Book.] Entered 16 May 1580 by E[dward] White (Arber, II. 370). 12) *A praier gathered vpon thoccasion of thearthquake.* [Book.] Entered 6 June by H[enry] Denham (*ib.*, II. 371). 13) *A bright Burning Beacon* . . . Translated & collected by Abraham Fleming. Henrie Denham, 1580. 14) *An admonycon concerninge thearthquake.* [Book.] Entered 27 June by H[enry] Bynneman (Arber, II. 372). 15) *Three proper and wittie lettres passed betwene twoo vniuersitie men touchinge the earthequake.* [Book.] Entered 30 June by H[enry] Bynneman (*ib.*, II. 373).

and it uniformly raises a loud cry for repentance and turning from sin. One ballad is directed specifically against plays.[89] By the end of June the excitement seems to have subsided—until the next awful warning from heaven stirred the moralists, meteorologists, and ballad-writers to another outburst.

Without doubt, the weather was just as grave and familiar a topic in the sixteenth century as it is now, and just because of its familiarity we do not expect it ordinarily to make news worth printing. Only a few times in three-quarters of a century did the weather run to extremes warranting the printing of a book or ballad. Thus we learn that the winter of 1578–9 brought forth a memorable blizzard[90] and that those of 1608[91] and 1614[92] were extraordinarily cold. Much more excitement was produced by "the windy year," the winter of 1612–3, during which storms took a heavy toll of life by land and sea.[93]

8. Sporting News

Sporting news, as we understand the term to-day, is really a modern innovation; early in the nineteenth century,

[89] *Comme from the plaie. comme from the playe:*
  The house will fall so people saye:
  The earth quakes lett vs hast awaye. Entered 8 April by Henry Carre (Arber, II. 368).

[90] 1) *Tarltons Devise vpon this vnlooked for great snowe.* [Ballad.] Entered 7 February 1579 by Jhon Aldee (Arber, II. 346). 2) *A ballat of a northerne mans reporte of the wonderfull greate snowe* . . . Entered 14 February 1579 by Richard Jones (*ib.*, II. 347).

[91] 1) *The Late great frost.* Ballad. Entered 7 March 1608 by Thomas Pavier (Arber, III. 371). 2) *The Great Frost.* . . . For Henry Gosson, 1608.

[92] *The Cold Yeare, 1614.* . . . For Thomas Langley, 1615.

[93] 1) *The VVindie Yeare.* . . . For Arthur Iohnson, 1612. 2) *Lamentable Newes, Shewing the wonderfull deliuerance of Maister Edmond Pet Sayler* . . . For William Barley, 1613. 3) *The Wonderfull deliuerance of master Pett sayler* . . . Ballad. Entered 12 January 1613 by William Barley (Arber, III. 511). 4) *The VVonders of this windie winter.* . . . For Iohn Wright, 1613. 5) *The last terrible Tempestious windes and weather.* . . . Sold by Iohn Wright, 1613. 6) *Losses by these tempestes.* Ballad. Entered 7 January 1613 by Joseph Hunt & Henry Gosson (Arber, III. 511).

most newspaper editors felt they would be soiling their hands if they mentioned prize fights and horse races in their papers. There are few signs of any such fastidiousness in the attitude of sixteenth-century publishers towards the news of their day, but on the other hand there was very little sporting news, and almost no organized competitive sport, to report. It is therefore interesting to notice a few dim foreshadowings of this very important branch of contemporary journalism.

There are just two kinds of "sporting event" reflected in the printed news of the time which can be mentioned. One of these is a hazardous journey made on a wager. William Kemp's morris-dance from London to Norwich is easily the best-known of these.[94] John Taylor, the water-poet, was another such madman: in 1618 he made a trip afoot from London to Edinburgh "not carrying any money to or fro, neither Begging, Borrowing, or Asking Meate, drinke or Lodging,"[95] and in 1620 he and one Roger Bird made a voyage on the Thames from London to Queenborough in Kent in a paper-bottomed boat rowed with oars which consisted of a stockfish tied to a stick.[96] More dangerous and possibly even more famous in its day was the adventure of Richard Ferris and two other Thames watermen who, in 1590, paddled themselves in a wherry from London to Bristol by sea.[97] All these redoubtable sportsmen wrote their own stories.

The other is a contest of archery. Ballads on this sub-

[94] *Kemps nine daies Wonder.* . . . For Nicholas Ling, 1600.

[95] *The Pennyles Pilgrimage, or The Money-lesse perambulation, of Iohn Taylor* . . . Verse & prose. At the charges of the Author, 1618.

[96] *The Praise of Hemp-seed.* . . . For Henry Gosson, 1620.

[97] 1) *The most dangerous and memorable aduenture of Richard Ferris* . . . For Edward White, 1590. 2) *A new Sonnet Made vppon the arriuall and braue entertainement of Richard Ferris* . . . By James Sargent. Entered 7 August 1590 by Edward White (Arber, II. 557). Printed in the preceding. 3) *The ioyfull entertainement of the wherry and iij wherrymen* . . . Ballad. Entered 10 August 1590 by Henrye Carre (*ib.*, II. 558).

ject are recorded in 1577, 1579, 1581, 1582, and 1589,[98] but only one of these, Elderton's *New Yorkshyre song*,[99] which is an account of a match at York, is now known. Archery contests seem to have been held annually in London and were even encouraged by the government. King Henry VIII facetiously created a champion archer duke of Shoreditch and this title appears to have been borne by succeeding champions as well. Prince Arthur is another *nom de guerre* borne by master-bowmen and perhaps the name of the Black Prince of Portugal, found in the title of one of the ballads mentioned, is another sobriquet, assumed in the same whimsical spirit as our own pugilists call themselves Battling This and Kayo That.

[98] 1) *A merye reioisinge historie of the . . . feastes of Archerye of the . . . Duke of Shordiche.* Entered 23 August 1577 by Richard Jones (Arber, II. 318). 2) *Ye Renovacon of Archery. by. prince Arthure and his companions.* Entered 19 August 1579 by Edward White (*ib.*, II. 358). 3) *A Joyfull Songe of the worthie Shootinge in London . . .* Entered 25 September 1581 by Richard Jones (*ib.*, II. 401). 4) *The vallure of our Englishe Archers and shott that accompanied the Blacke Prince of Portugall their governor into the feildes . . . the 12 of August . . .* Entered 13 August 1589 by William Jones (*ib.*, II. 528).

[99] Richard Iones, 1584.

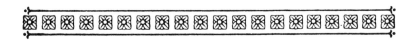

CHAPTER VII

TRANSLATED NEWS

THE sixteenth-century English reader was more liberally supplied with news of neighboring states than any other kind. Even when he was in the dark about the policy and measures of his own government, he was rather fully informed about the posture of affairs, let us say, in France by means of documents, narratives, and polemical treatises translated from French sources. This state of affairs may be attributed to two chief causes. In some ways, foreign political news was safer than news touching the state of England. It is true that the English government was quick to punish any reflection on the *amour propre* of a friendly prince and very attentive to the complaints of ambassadors against affronts to their royal masters, but just the same it did not look upon inoffensive news from abroad with the same jealousy that it looked upon all domestic news of affairs of state. In the second place, foreign news was easy to obtain. Practically all of it was merely translated from books of news which somebody else had already had the labor of publishing. These books could be picked up from returned travelers or they could be arranged for with foreign booksellers and friends or agents residing abroad, so that the English publisher was put to almost no trouble at all up to the moment they arrived by the foreign post. Then all that was necessary was to have them translated, a trifling task compared with undertaking an original work. Besides, news of this sort was surely very popular. For Englishmen it was a vicarious experience of war and battle, of the trial of the security of the state and the citizen, and of the struggle for liberty of conscience, or, as the phrase of the day put it, for the true Christian faith. Such stirring events as the French and the Hollanders lived through in those days must have imparted a thrill to the Englishman who read of them in his books of news, though he doubtless preferred the security and quiet of merry England. In the bitter religious wars of France and the Netherlands, he saw a lifelike picture of the fate which England, by her greater good fortune, had escaped.

It was also from France and the Netherlands that most of this news came, three-fourths of it, at least. These nations not only lay nearest to England, but they acted out the most spectacular scenes in the current religio-political drama. English sympathies were allied to the Protestant cause in both countries in many ways, most enthusiastically at those times when, as we have seen, Englishmen were actually fighting in the Protestant armies. Except for a few German cities, these two countries produced nearly all the Protestant news that was being published abroad, and of course it was only Protestant news that was fit to print in England. During the capital episodes in the current history of these two nations, what can be called only a great profusion of news was published in England. The siege of Ostend, the assassination of Henry IV, and other outstanding developments were rehearsed in many books published almost simultaneously, as if anything relevant which the publishers could lay hands on would help to slake the popular thirst for news about them. Perhaps better than anything else could, the following list of nearly forty pieces published or entered during 1590—the year of Henry IV's greatest successes against the league, and the most abundantly reported, by a safe margin, of all the years in our period—will show how Englishmen were informed of the affairs of their neighbors:

1) *The Letters Pattents of the Kings Declaration for the referring of the generall assemblie . . . vnto the 15. day of March next . . .* For Augustine Lawton, [1590].

2) *A Recitall of that which hath happened in the Kings Armie, since the taking of the Suburbes of Paris . . .* For Tobie Cooke, 1590.

3) *Discours au vray. de ce qui s'est passee en l'armee. Conduitte par sa maieste Depuis son advenement a la courone iusques a prinse de faux. bourges de Paris.* [Book.] Entered 12 February 1590 by John Wolf (Arber, II. 539).

4) *An excellent Ditty made vpon the great victory, which the French king obtayned against . . . the Romish Rebels in his kingdome, . . . the fourth day of March . . . 1590.* [For William Wright?]

5) *The Copie of a Letter, sent by an English Gentleman out of France . . . , concerning the great victorie which the French King obtained against . . . the Romish rebels in his Kingdome, vpon the fourth daie of March . . . 1589* [o.s.] *. . .* For William Wright, 1590.

6) *Deploration De La mort Du foy. Henry Troisiesme, et Du scandale qu'en a L'eglise.* Book. Entered 13 March 1590 by Augustine Laughton (Arber, II. 540).

7) *The coppie of the Anti-Spaniard made at Paris by a Frenchman a Catholique. Wherein is directly proued how the Spanish King is the onely cause of all the troubles in France.* Iohn Wolfe, 1590.

8) *A Triumphant Ditty shewinge the victories of the Frenche kinge . . . and the seightes in the ayre.* Ballad. Entered 2 April 1590 by William Wright (Arber, II. 543).

9) *A discourse and true recitall of euerie particular of the victorie obtained by the French King on . . . March 4 . . .* Thomas Orwin, 1590. Another edition for Richard Oliffe, 1591.

10) *Le vray discours De la victoire merueilleuse obtenue par le Roy . . . Henry 4. . . . pres le bourg d'Yury . . . le 14. de Mars l'an 1590.* Pour Thomas Man, [1590].

11) *The true discourse of the wonderfull victorie, obteined by Henrie the fourth . . . neere the town of Yurie . . . the fourteenth day of March . . . 1590 . . .* For Thomas Man, 1590.

12) *News from Rome, Spain, Palermo, Geneuae, and France. With the miserable state of the Citty of Paris, and the late yeelding vppe of sundrie Towns . . .* Sold by William Wright, 1590.

13) *The Frenche kinges lettre to mounsieur de Vernue touchinge the vyctorye againste the rebelles and leagers the 14 of marche 1590. / Item the decree of the courte of parliment of Normandie for the seasinge of ye rebelles goodes.* Books. Entered 15 April 1590 by John Wolfe (Arber, II. 545).

14) *A canticle of the victorie obteined by Henrie the Fourth, at Iury.* By Guillaume de Saluste du Bartas; translated by Joshua Sylvester. Richard Yardley, 1590.

15) *A dolorouse dittye and most sweet sonett made vppon the lamentable end of a godlie and virtuous Ladie lately famished in Parris.* Entered 29 April 1590 by Thomas Nelson (Arber, II. 546).

16) *A songe of the Frenche kinges vyctorie the 14 of marche 1590.* [Ballad.] Entered 19 May 1590 by John Wolf (*ib.*, II. 547).

17) *Credible reports from France and Flanders . . .* Sold by William Wright, 1590.

18) *La Manifeste De la France.* [Book.] Entered 23 June 1590 by Edward Aggas (Arber, II. 551).

19) *A Briefe Declaration of the yeelding vp of Saint Denis to the French king the 29. of Iune, 1590. . . .* Sold by W[illiam] Wright, 1590.

20) *Le procez criminel Des Parisiens Ligueurs, autheurs de tous les troubles, guerres et calamitez de la France: Et a present qu'ils se sentent pressez, pris et subiuguez, demandans Composition.* [Book.] Entered 23 July 1590 by John Wolfe (Arber, II. 555).

21 *A sonnett made vppon the good successe, which mounser De La Nouee lately obteigned in Pikerdye in the Frenche Kinges behalfe . . .* [Ballad.] Entered 29 July 1590 by William Wrighte (*ib.*, II. 556).

22) *A lettre from the Colledge of Sorbonee in Parris, to the Pope / Together with the generall confession of the pillers of the holly vnion / and certen Epigramms.* [Book.] Entered 29 July 1590 by John Wolfe, (*ib.*)

23) *The oration and declaration of Henrie IV., the 8. day of August, 1590.* Sold by Humphrey Lownes, 1590.

24) *The miserable estate of Paris with strange visions lately seen in the ayre vpon the coasts of Brittayne.* For Thomas Nelson, 1590.

25) *The Parlé betwene the French kinge and the Parisians the 6 of Auguste 1590, together with what happened in his Campe aboute the same tyme.* [Book.] Entered 24 August 1590 by Edward White (Arber, II. 560).

26) *A Dolorous sonnet made by their Inhabitantes of Paris vppon their grevous famyne and miserable estate . . .* Ballad. Entered 31 August 1590 by Thomas Scarlet (*ib.*, II. 561).

27) *The coppie of a letter sent into England . . . from . . . Saint Denis . . . Wherein is truely set forth the good successe of the Kings Maiesties forces against the Leaguers and the Prince of Parmas power. . . .* For Thomas Nelson, 1590.

[171]

28) *True news concerning the winning of the town of Corbeyll by the French King.* E[dward] A[llde], 1590.

29) *Sommaire discours au vray de ce qui est aduenu en l'armee du Roy . . . depuis que le Duc de Parme s'est ioint a celle des ennemis, iusques au 15. de Septembre.* . . . Thomas Scarlet, 1590.

30) *A discourse of all such fights . . . and other politike attempts which haue happened in France since the ariuall of the duke of Parma* . . . Thomas Scarlet, [1590].

31) *Discours veritable des horribles meurtres et massacres . . . perpetrez de sang froid, par les troupes de Duc De Savoy . . . sur les paures paisans Du Bailliage De Gep.* [Book.] Entered 26 September 1590 by John Wolfe (Arber, II. 563).

32) *A true and perfecte description of a straunge monstar borne in . . . Rome . . . in . . . 1585 . . .* By I. L. [Sold by William Wright,] 1590.

33) *The things which happened vpon the Prince of Parmas retire . .* For Andrew White, 1590.

34) *Les Lauriers Du Roy, Contre les foudres pratiques par l'Espagnol.* [Book.] Entered 9 December 1590 by John Wolf (Arber, II. 569).

35) *The successe which fell out in the pursute of the Prince of Parma, together with a lettre of the Kinges to the marshall of Byron.* [Book.] Entered 17 December 1590 by John Wolfe (*ib.*)

36) *An abstract of the proceedings of the French King.* . . . W[illiam] Wright, 1590.

37) *The discouerer of France to the Parisians.* Translated by E[dward] A[ggas]. 1590.

38) *A treatise concerning the extreme famine of the citie of Paris* . . . Thomas Scarlet, 1590.

This foreign news may be divided roughly into three kinds—edicts, proclamations, and manifestoes published literatim; narratives of battles, campaigns, and other developments; and polemical treatises.

Edicts, proclamations, and decrees were published in great numbers. We must include under this heading treaties, articles of surrender, petitions, such as those of religious minorities appealing for toleration, and public letters written by political personages and officers of state. One reason why they were so numerous is certainly the fact that they were easy to procure. They were thrust upon the world full-blown; the official agencies which prepared them invited the fullest publicity for them and when they bore the seal of a friendly prince, there could seldom be an objection to printing them in England. Possibly they even attracted readers by their very weight and portentousness. Usually they were translated literally and allowed to speak for themselves, though an explanatory or editorial preface was sometimes added by the translator, sponsor, or publisher, and sometimes the title-page, as in *A iustification or cleering of the Prince of Orendge agaynst the false sclaunders, wherwith his ilwillers goe about to charge him wrongfully*,[1] a collection of official papers, shows which way English sympathies leaned. Still more of these documents were appended to narrative and polemical tracts: English readers were thus kept well informed of the acts and decrees of foreign governments—of those of France and the Netherlands, at least—in their own official pronouncements. These pronouncements, published in the tedious jargon of official communications, could hardly have made lively reading, but at least they partook of the authenticity which we attribute to original sources. Indeed, it is possible to say that the sixteenth-century reader was oftener informed of foreign political news in the original texts of official declarations than we are to-day, news of this kind usually coming to us in condensed and predigested form. These proclamations divulge the official will on every kind of subject, from the form òf religion his majesty's subjects are to embrace[2] to the clothing they shall wear,[3] though to be sure there are more on such subjects as the former than

---

[1] Translated from the French by Arthur Goldyng. Iohn Day, 24 February 1575.

[2] *The [French] Kinges edict, for the Reunityng of his Subiectes in the Catholique, Apostolique and Romish Churche.* Richard Ihones, 1585.

[3] *Edict du Roy portant reglement Des habits* . . . Book. Entered 29 April 1613 by William Wright (Arber, III. 522).

the latter. In general, they are exactly like the royal proclamations promulgated in England, but, exemplifying as they do the troubles and schisms which rent France and the Netherlands in the latter half of the sixteenth century, while England remained comparatively calm and orderly, they are often of a graver import.[4]

The wide dissemination of these foreign proclamations in printed copies makes us suspect all the more strongly that English royal proclamations, as mentioned above,[5] must have had some value as news in England, that copies of them must have been printed for other than official uses, and that they probably could be bought like any other printed news. Important English proclamations were published in translation abroad, just as important French proclamations were published in England: if we cannot suppose that they were translated from copies purchased in England, we are obliged to assume that they were stolen from the public places where they were set up or copied by hand from walls and hoardings. If so many copies of foreign proclamations made their way into the hands of English publishers, it seems a fair inference that these documents were everywhere rather widely disseminated and acted as bearers of news.

Except for the fact that they are preponderantly concerned with battles and campaigns, the narratives of news translated from foreign copies are very much like those which were composed in England, both in subject-matter and in style. The news which interested readers on the continent was essentially the same as that which interested

---

[4] *E. g.,* 1) *The Declarations as well of the French king, as of the king of Nauarre. Concerning the Truce agreed vpon betwene their Maiesties* . . . Richard Field, 1589. 2) *A true Coppie of the transportation of the Lowe Countries, Burgundie, and the Countie of Charrolois: Doone by the King of Spayne, for the Dowrie of his eldest Daughter.* . . . For Paule Linley, 1598. 3) *An Edict or Proclamation published by the States General* . . . *how all Jesuits, priests and monkes of the Popish or Romish religion* . . . *shall behave themselves* . . . For Thomas Archer, 1612.

[5] See p. 37 f.

Englishmen: news of royalties and of heroes and personalities, descriptions of state pomps and ceremonials, state trials, political developments, natural calamities, miracles (as we have seen already), and even a few murders—all these were translated for consumption in England. King Henry IV of France and Prince Maurice of Orange were heroes in England by adoption; the personal fortunes of such celebrities as the Duc de Guise, the Cardinal de Lorraine, the Maréchal d'Ancre, and Jan van Oldenbarneveld were fully related to English readers. A coronation, a royal marriage, or such a book as *A true Discourse of the whole occurrences in the Queenes voyage from her departure from Florence, vntil her arriuall at . . . Marseilles . . .*[6] was always of interest to English readers. The trials of offenders against the state were not as regularly related as the proceedings against traitors at home; they were interesting only when an exceptional malefactor, such as Serac,[7] Ravaillac,[8] Biron,[9] or Barnevelt,[10] was on trial. There are also few narratives of political developments, but of course much information on this subject could be gleaned from official edicts and polemical tracts. Earthquakes, floods, and fires made an impression on the English mind even when they happened far off and tidings of them were frequently borne to England in books of news. One

[6] For Cuthbert Burby, 1601.

[7] *The true report of the lamentable death, of VVilliam of Nassawe* . . . By G. P. Middleborowgh: Derick van Respeawe, 1584.

[8] 1) *The terrible and deserued death of Francis Rauilliack* . . . Translated from the French by R. E. For William Barley & Iohn Baylie, 1610. 2) *The Copie of a Letter . . . from Paris . . . , Declaring the manner of the execution of Francis Rauaillart* . . . At Britaine Burse, 1610.

[9] *A true and perfect discourse of the practises and treasons of Marshall Biron . . .* P[eter] S[hort], 1602.

[10] 1) *Newes out of Holland: Concerning Barnevelt and his fellow Prisoners their Conspiracy* . . . For Nathanael Newbery, 1619. A new edition, enlarged by an account of Barnevelt's execution, *The true description of the execution of iustice . . . vpon Sir Iohn van Olden Barneuelt . . .* , was issued about a month later. 2) *The Arraignment of Iohn van Olden Barnevelt . . .* For Ralph Rounthwait, 1619

[175]

kind of news was developed in this translated matter to proportions exceeding those of its domestic counterpart— accounts of conversions from the Catholic church. During the last thirty years of our period, scarcely a year failed to bring forth its crop of these triumphs of the true Christian faith. Most of them came from France, where converts were sometimes reported in batches of eight or ten, but others came from the Netherlands and even from Italy as well.

The battle-pieces from abroad, plentiful as they are, do not make a complete record: they are nearly always silent about checks and reverses of the Protestant armies. When the Hollanders beat the Spaniards or the King of Navarre's forces beat those of the league, books appeared in profusion, emitting loud crows of triumph over the minions of Antichrist, but when the wrong side, from the English point of view, came out on top, the news-publishers either kept silent or turned to werewolf stories or accounts of the sufferings of demoniacs. The reports of fighting that were published are quite like those of native growth. They came chiefly from soldiers at the front, usually in the form of letters; they give partial and enthusiastic rather than comprehensive and considered pictures of the action. They were, however, written of battles which were fought much closer to the readers for whom they were composed than most of the war news furnished England, and they consequently lack a certain remoteness, even detachment, perceptible in the latter. The distance between England and the theater of operations obliged the London publishers to issue maps and descriptions of the geography and topography of the towns where fighting took place.[11] They

---

[11] 1) *The mappe or discription of Sutfen* . . . Entered 5 December 1586 by Thomas Purfoote (Arber, II. 461). 2) *The discription or explanacon of the plott of Cadiz.* Entered 15 December 1596 by Thomas Purfoote Sr. & Jr. and licensed by the Earl of Essex (*ib.*, III. 77). 3) *A mapp and true situacion of . . . Graue.* Middleborough, [1591?]

are all properly serious and decorous, as befits a profession separated from the chivalry of the middle ages by only a hundred years. In all the pieces which I have examined, only one was lighted up by the faintest trace of what has since been christened human interest. This is a book called *A iournall or daily register of . . . the Siege of Ber-ghen-vp-Zoome . . .: with some particular accidents of warre, which were occasions of mirth to the beholders.*[12] These particular accidents occupy about five pages at the end of the book under the heading of "Tragedies and Commedies of Bergen." If the very trivial incidents there recorded actually moved the beholders to mirth, they must have been unnaturally disposed to laughter, for these accidents are nothing but the most ordinary mis-chances of city life, with or without a siege—a soldier's untimely ripping of his breeches, a *femme de chambre's* discharging a slop-pail upon a passer-by, and other trage-dies and comedies of that order. But this is the only relief from the uniform tone of high seriousness which I have so far met in reading these stories of battles long ago.

The relatively small number of polemical treatises which were translated for English readers appeal directly to their religious and political prejudices. These pieces belong to the same order as Buchanan's *Detectioun* or *Vox Populi* or *A Warnyng for Englande:*[13] they are broadsides in the war of opinion in the countries from which they were borrowed. *A Summe of the Guisian Ambassage to the bishop of Rome, founde lately amongst the writinges of one Dauid an Aduocate of Paris* (1579), for example, is a covert attack on the Duc de Guise's party and an exposure of their alleged conspiracy with the pope; it was published under cover of anonymity in England, doubtless by a Protestant bitter-ender. All that the Duc de Guise and his adherents stood for was

---

[12] For Nathaniel Bourne, Bartholomew Downes, & Thomas Archer, 1622.
[13] See above, pp. 55, 71, 72, 119.

[177]

utterly repugnant to right-thinking Englishmen; again
and again his faction acts the villain's part in the French
drama of state as it was pictured in English books of
news.[14] *The Hellish and horribble Councell, practised . . .
by the Iesuites . . . when they would haue a man to murther
a King According to those damnable instructions, giuen (by
them) to . . . Francis Rauilliacke, who murdered Henry the
fourth . . .*[15] is one of the many bitter polemics which
sprang from the complicity of which the Jesuits were
accused in this assassination. Obviously this tract was
extremely appetizing to English Protestants, and besides,
in that it pretends to reveal the secret machinations of the
Society to bring about the crime, it was news in the full
sense of the word. Some of these treatises are compilations of gratuitous advice, prescriptions for the cure of
diseases in the body politic.[16] Others are counterblasts
to aggressive tracts published by the adversary, *i.e.*, the
Catholic party.[17] A number of them revolve about per-

[14] 1) *Ho Guyse the chefe of that gredy garyson.* Ballad. Entered 1562–3 by
Owen Rogers (Arber, I. 202).

2) *A Warnynge to Englonde herein to aduaunce
by the Cruell tyranny of the Guyse late of Fraunce.* Ballad. Entered 1562–3
by Francis Godlif (*ib.*, I. 208). 3) *A necessary Discourse concerning the right which
the house of Guyze pretendeth to the Crowne of France.* For Edward Aggas, 1586.
4) *The Contre-Guyse* . . . Iohn Woolfe, 1589.

[15] Sold by Iohn Wright, 1610.

[16] 1) *A briefe and necessary discourse concerning the meanes to preserue both the
Religion and estate of the lowe Countries.* For Thomas Charde, 1584. 2) *A
Caueat for France, vpon the present euils that it now suffereth. Together with the
remedies necessarie for the same.* Translated by E[dward] Aggas. Iohn Wolfe,
1588. 3) *A Discourse vpon the present state of France.* [By Michel Hurault. John
Wolf,] 1588. Another edition, a different translation by Edward Aggas, was also
published. 4) *The Restorer of the French Estate, discouering the true causes of these
warres in France & other countries.* Richard Field, 1589.

[17] 1) *An ansvver* . . . *to a certain Letter lately sent by the Duke of Alba* . . .
to those of Amsterdam . . . Henry Middleton, [1573]. 2) *An Aduertisement from
a French Gentleman, touching the intention* . . . *of the house of Guise* . . .
Written as an answere to a certaine Declaration . . . *of the Cardinal of Burbon.*
[Christopher Barker,] 1585. 3) *The Contre-League and answere to certaine letters*

[178]

sonalities: there are panegyrics and defenses of figures such as Admiral Coligny,[18] King Henry IV,[19] William the Silent,[20] and even, strangely enough, Marie de Médicis,[21] as well as assaults upon the Duc de Guise, the Cardinal de Lorraine, and others of their party,[22] Catherine de Médicis,[23] and Barnevelt.[24] Occasionally tendencious ideas

---

sent to the maisters of Renes . . . Translated by E[dward] A[ggas]. Iohn Wolfe, 1589. 4) *An answere to the last tempest and villanie of the league.* . . Translated by T. H. For Cuthbert Burby, 1593.

[18] 1) *De furoribus Gallicis,* . . . *Amirallij Castillionei caede* . . . *narratio.* By Ernestus Varamundus Frisius [= François Hotman]. Henry Bynneman, 1573. An English translation, *A true and plaine report of the Furious outrages of Fraunce* . . . , was published at Stirling. 2) *The Lyfe of* . . . *Iasper Colignie Shatilion.* . . . Translated from the Latin by Arthur Golding. Thomas Vautrollier, 1576.

[19] 1) *The Brutish Thunderbolt: or rather feeble Fier-Flash of Pope Sixtus the fift, against Henrie* . . . *King of Nauarre.* . . . Translated from the Latin by Chr. Fetherstone. For G[eorge] B[ishop] & R[alph] Newberry, 1586. 2) *A Lamentable Discourse, vpon the paricide* . . . *of Henry the Fourth.* . . . By Pierre Pelletier. For Edward Blount & William Barret, 1610. 3) *The lamentab[l]e complaint of Fraunce, for the death of the late King Henry the 4.* . . . Broadside. For William Barley, 1610. 4) *The sighes of Fraunce for the death of their late King* . . . For Iohn Budge, 1610. 5) *The Heroyk Life and Deplorable Death of* . . . *king Henry the fourth.* . . . By Pierre Matthieu; translated by Ed[ward] Grimeston & Ios[hua] Syl[vester]. George Eld, 1612. 6) *Three precious teares of blood, flowing* . . . *in memory of* . . . *Henry the Great.* [Translated by Richard Niccols.] For Iohn Budge, 1611.

[20] 1) *A iustification or cleering of the Prince of Orendge,* as above, p. 173. 2) *The apologie or defence of the most noble Prince William.* . . . Translated from the French of Hubert Languet. Delft: 1581 (two edd.), 1582. Entered 8 February 1582 by Thomas Marshe, but "neuer printed by him" (Arber, II. 406).

[21] *A congratulation to France, vpon the happy alliance with Spaine.* . . . By F[rançois] de Menantel S. Denis. Sold by W[alter] Burre, 1612.

[22] 1) *A short discourse of the meanes that the Cardinal of Loraine vseth, to hinder the stablishing of peace.* . . . For Lucas Haryson, 1568. 2) *A legendarie, conteining* . . . *the life and behauiour of Charles Cardinal of Lorraine, and* . . . *of the house of Guise.* By Francis de L'isle [= Louis Regnier de la Planche. Geneva?] 1577.

[23] *A meruaylous discourse vpon the lyfe* . . . *of Katherine de Medicis.* . . . [By Henri Estienne.] Heydelberge [= London: Henry Middleton?] 1575.

[24] 1) *Barnevels Apology.* . . . For Thomas Thorp, 1618. 2) *Barnevelt displayed.* . . . For Nathanael Butter, 1619. 3) *Murther vnmasked, or Barneuiles base Conspiracie.* . . . Broadside. W. I[ones? 1619].

were insinuated allegorically. In a book called *A vision or dreame contayning the whole State of the Netherland warres* . . . ,[25] "a louer of the Netherlands lying in his bed" sees "a fayre comely Horse well brideled and sadled" but riderless. A discussion of who shall ride him naturally follows. In another book published about the same time, *A description of the prosperitie, strength and wise gouernment of the Vnited Prouinces* . . . ,[25] this agreeable prospect is "signified by the Batauian virgin in her seat of vnitie." The elation of the Hollanders and their sympathizers over the siege of Ostend in 1602 is fancifully expressed in a book called *A dialogue and complaint made vpon the siedge of Ostend, made by the king of Spaine, the archduke, the infanta, the pope, the prince Morrice, and the eldest son of Sauoye* . . .[26] In general, it may be said that, because of his greater unfamiliarity with the posture of affairs abroad, an Englishman could gather more new information from these treatises than those for whom they were originally written. We cannot deny them the estate of news.

News from other countries than France and the Netherlands is sparse. Apparently Englishmen had little interest in political developments in Germany, Italy, and Spain; if they had, their purveyors of news left them in the lurch. There is no sign of a wide-ranging interest in news for its intrinsic importance; what was published was selected according to English prejudices. Germany, for instance, was a prolific source of miraculous wonders, but of little else: the emperor and the German princes are shadowy figures in this pageant of history which our news-reports furnish. This obscurity was not due to any great difficulty in obtaining news from Germany, for when England became interested in the Palatinate through the elector's mar-

[25] For Edward Marchant, 1615.
[26] For Matthew Law, 1602.

riage to the Princess Elizabeth, news in abundance, comparatively speaking, arrived from that quarter. Even in what little news we do find from central and southern Europe, earthquakes, floods, and old wives' tales bulk disproportionately large. Russia, the Scandinavian countries, and Poland are represented by a few pieces each; Portugal fares a little better solely because the marvelous history of Dom Sebastien set the whole world agog; Barbary does better still because of the romantic halo surrounding so strange and different a people and because of the violence of its dynastic changes. There is even only a little news from Scotland before the union, and that, except for a few accounts of the articles of faith adopted by the national church, is almost entirely dynastic and concerned only with the tempestuous history of the royal family.

Although the Italians were pioneer publishers of news, little information from their country made its way to England. Most of what was published, aside from the usual accounts of earthquakes and monstrous children, concerns the pope: the death of a pope and the election of his successor was often reported in England, sometimes even respectfully, and an occasional falling out with one of his neighbors was sometimes related in a spirit not altogether complimentary. Englishmen were not well informed of what happened in Spain, as if they carried their enmity to the unwise length of preferring ignorance of Spanish affairs. Such news as was offered them either concerns English interests there or is distinctly uncomplimentary to the Spaniards.

More news was printed about the Turks than about any other people except the French and the Dutch. It is nearly all news of fighting; only once in a great while does something else, such as a description of their outlandish infidel manners, turn up. The Turks were regarded as

[181]

a menace to all Christendom throughout our period and the report of a battle won against them was always good news in England. One of the earliest pieces of news printed in England is an account of their unsuccessful siege of the city of Rhodes in 1481.[27] It was written in Latin by Gulielmus Caorsin, vice-chancellor of the Order of St. John of Jerusalem, which had defended the city, and is therefore practically an eye-witness's story; it was translated into English by Johan Kay, who describes himself as King Edward's "humble poete lawreate." In all this news the Turks make a bizarre appearance, often, it is to be feared, at the expense of truth. In a book called *Newes from Rome*, published in 1606,[28] for example, we hear of "an Hebrew people . . . comming from the Mountaines of Caspij, who pretend their warre [is to] recouer the Land of Promise, & expell the Turks out of Christendome." It is from this book, by the way, that Shakespeare is supposed to have borrowed the name of Shylock. These glimpses of the Turks lend a romantic touch to the foreign news of our period.

Almost all of this foreign news can be traced to a characteristic bent of the English mind; little of it was published merely because it appealed to intelligent curiosity. It stirred in English readers the same feelings of sympathy or displeasure as their home-grown news; it interested them as the counterpart of what happened in Englànd, as a familiar theme doubled. Monstrous births, miraculous portents, earthquakes, and floods were occurrences which terrified Englishmen regardless of their local habitation: they were warnings to all God's people everywhere. In the wars of France and the Low Countries the English saw the religious conflicts of their own country reënacted

[27] [Begins:] *To the moste excellent . . . kyng Edward the fourth.* [William de Machlinia or John Lettou.]
[28] For Henry Gosson, 1606 (2 issues).

by a new cast of characters. Some of the foreign news published in England deals directly with English affairs abroad. Besides the books reporting English diplomatic transactions and military actions, which have already been mentioned,[29] others concerned themselves with the affairs of other Englishmen and other English interests. In such as *The copie of a double letter sent by an Englishe gentilman from beyond the seas, . . . containing the true aduises . . . of the death of one Richard Atkins, executed by fire in Rome, the seconde of August, 1581; The strange and cruel martyrdome of an English man in the Towne of Dunkerke . . .;*[30] *A true Report of the general Imbarrement of all the English Shippes, vnder the dominion of the Kinge of Spaine . . .;*[31] *The Coppy of a Letter and Commission, of the King of Spain . . . Wherein the dealings and trade of ships & marchandize is forbidden with the subiectes of Holland . . . and England . . .;*[32] *An act of the court of Parliament at Paris against a book intituled, Francisci Suares Defensio fidei catholicæ aduersus Anglicanæ sectæ errores;*[33] *A decree of the Court of Parliament at Paris . . . against the pernicious Doctrine of Attempting against the sacred persons of Kings,*[34] it is evident that they were translated and published in England because they touched English loyalties, interests, and prejudices; less obviously, most of the remainder of all this foreign news was translated and published for the same reason.

There is no better evidence of the fact that foreign news was an echo of the trend of English opinion with regard to home affairs than the scarcity of news from abroad which does not flatter English hopes, coincide with English prej-

---

[29] See above, pp. 110 f., 125 f.
[30] For VVilliam VVright, 1591.
[31] Signed R. D.   For Thomas Butter, 1585.
[32] For Thomas Pauier, 1602.
[33] For John Barnes, 1614.
[34] For Nicholas Bourne, 1615.

udices, and confirm English notions. For example, popular as was King Henry IV of France and eagerly as Englishmen followed his movements both before and after his accession to the throne, there is no overt mention anywhere in the news of 1593 of his embracing the Catholic faith. Though this fact was surely startling news to England, and certainly was not unknown in London, it was not published in print, partly, no doubt, because the English government would have frowned on proclaiming the conversion of the great Protestant hero to idolatry, and partly because bad news was unpopular. Books containing unwelcome news are very few. What bad news we do find was almost always published as an illustration of the cruelty of the enemies of England and the Protestant faith or as the butt of English scorn. A good example is the book printed about 1585 entitled *An Aduertisement to the king of Nauarre, to vnite him selfe with the king and the Catholique Faithe. Beeing in trueth a very slaunderous, false, and seditious Libell, against the said King of Nauarre, and other Christian Princes . . . But this beeing subtilly conuayed, vnder pretence of winning him to the Romish Religion, is therfore the rather set downe in the same nature as it is written: to showe a wicked minde against God, the King, and the sinceritie of true Religion.* Unfavorable military news likewise appeared, if at all, as an instance of the cruelty of the leaguers or the Spaniards, as in such a book as *A briefe relation, of what is hapned since the last of August 1598. by comming of the Spanish campe into the Dukedom of Cleue and the bordering free Countries, which with most odious and barbarous crueltie they take as enemies, for the seruice of God, and the King of Spaine (as they say.). . .*[35]

There are, however, a few signs, most of them late in our period, of a more tolerant attitude than that suggested

[35] Iohn Wolfe, 1599.

by the facts just mentioned, in a few pieces of news published to inform Englishmen of what had befallen certain of their inveterate enemies, but with little or nothing in them to pander to English prejudices in the manner of so many other books. In 1599 William Aspley published an account of the death of Philip II of Spain in which, perhaps on the principle of *nihil nisi bonum* or perhaps out of common fairness, there is none of the baiting of the Spaniards which almost invariably accompanied all references to them in print.[36] Later Aspley entered a more sensational sequel, *The secret Last Instructions that king Philip the Second . . . Left to his son Kinge Philip the Third . . . conteining howe to governe him self after his fathers Death . . .*,[37] now lost. In 1600 John Wolfe published *The Ceremonies . . . vsed at the opening . . . of foure Churches, within . . . Rome, in the yere of Iubile*, a literal description free from the virulent antipopery indispensable to nearly all English news in which the Roman church and its head were mentioned. This piece, published at a time when, if "the Nationall Synod of Gap, in the prouince of Dolphine in France" by a solemn decree pronounced the pope of Rome to be the great and proper Antichrist, this news was triumphantly printed in London,[38] is exceptionally fair to its subject. We also find a more tolerant attitude in several books about the Holy Roman Empire, which, as a great Catholic power, was liable to be treated with scorn and contempt, as if they were inspired by a desire to inform their readers of what was taking place rather than to aggravate English prejudices. One of them, published in 1612, describes the election of

[36] *A briefe and true Declaration of the sicknesse, last wordes, and death of the King of Spaine . . .*
[37] Arber, III. 149.
[38] *A solemne decree of the Nationall Synod of Gap . . .* Broadside. English & Latin. Edward Allde & A. I., 1607.

the Emperor Matthias.[39]   The second is even more curious. It was published about May of the year 1619, just before the meeting of the states of the empire to elect the last emperor's successor; it is what the newspaper world nowadays calls an "advance story."[40]   It explains the constitution of the empire, the method of electing an emperor, and the qualifications of the electors, and it must have been designed to meet the needs of persons who were looking forward to the coming election with a curiosity more intelligent than the conventional contempt for all popish princes.   It is still more remarkable that, the next year, after the election of the Archduke Ferdinand, at a time when he was an arch-villain in English eyes because of his quarrel with the Elector Palatine over the crown of Bohemia and when he was the object of unrestrained vituperation in many contemporary tracts, Robert Mylbourne published a description of his election and coronation which is unembittered by English prejudice against him.[41]   These examples, however, though they undoubtedly point to a growing interest in news for its own sake alone, free from the tutelage of narrow partisanship and insular patriotism, are nevertheless exceptional; the foreign news printed in England, like the domestic news, was chiefly biased, in its sins of both omission and commission, by native loyalties and hatreds.

Most of these books of foreign news are translations, more or less complete, of books previously printed abroad. There seems to be little doubt that the foreign books themselves were imported into England and translated in London; many entries in the Stationers' registers were

[39] *Newes from Francfort* . . . For Henry Holland, 1612.

[40] *The Golden Bull: or the Fundamentall Lawes and Constitutions of the Empire* . . . For Nathaniel Newbery, 1619.

[41] *A relation Containing the manner of the Solemnities at the Election and Coronation of Ferdinand* . . . *With Other Occurrences* . . .

[186]

made from the foreign copies. Occasionally we meet with a book which was translated by an enthusiastic amateur, who then placed his translation in the hands of a publisher in the same way that an author placed his MS.,[42] but most translations were made at the publisher's behest. The greater part of these translations were made from Dutch and French; many books first issued in another language were turned into English by way of one or the other of these. For example, *The strangest aduenture that euer happened* . . .[43] was written in Spanish, turned into French, and thence translated into English by Anthony Munday. *Good newes from Florence* . . .[44] was translated from the Italian into French and from the French into English. A book published in 1589 describing a prolonged fast[45] was written in German, done into French, and thence translated into English. There is even a book which passed from French into Dutch before being Englished.[46] Probably the most remarkable vicissitudes are those of a book called *Letters from the great Turke* . . ,[47] "translated out of the Hebrue tongue into Italian, and out of the Italian into French and now into English out of the French coppie." Even a book of British news was occasionally translated from another language, such as *Newe newes contayning A shorte rehersall of the late enterprise of certaine*

---

[42] 1) *The Brutish Thunderbolt*, as above, p. 179. 2) *Newes from France: containing two declarations of two new converts* . . . Translated by E. M. of Christ-Church in Oxford. For Nathaniel Butter, 1616.

[43] [By José Teixeira.] For Frances Henson, 1601.

[44] For Nathaniel Butter, 1614.

[45] *A notable and prodigious Historie of a Mayden who . . . neither eateth, drinketh, nor sleepeth, neyther auoydeth any excrements, and yet liueth* . . . Iohn Wolfe, 1589.

[46] *A true Copy Of a Letter sent by the Prince of Parma to the generall States* . . . Richard Ihones, [1579?].

[47] Iohn Windet, 1606.

fugytiue [*Irish*] *Rebelles* . . .,[48] which was translated from the Dutch.

There are only a few pieces of foreign news which were not translated from books in foreign languages but written by Englishmen. Nearly all of these were Englishmen living abroad at the scene of the occurrences they described, such as George Gascoigne, who chanced to be present at the sack of Antwerp and wrote a report of it because he thought it would "serue for profitable example vnto all estates."[49] All of the comparatively small number of ballads on foreign events were, of course, written in London, on the strength of information derived from current books of news in prose. In one way they are quite instructive: almost infallibly they mark those events abroad which made a great impression in England. These native-born tributes to the friends of England on the continent were reserved to occurrences of the first magnitude, such as the assassination of Henry IV or a battle as decisive as Ivry or Nieuport; just as surely as we find a ballad on such an event, we may be sure that the news created a genuine furore in England, that, for a fleeting moment, it dominated the imagination of the commonalty of the realm.

[48] I[ohn] C[harlwood], 1579.
[49] *The Spoyle of Antwerpe, Faithfully reported by a true Englishman who was present at the same.* Richard Iones, [1577?].

CHAPTER VIII

BALLAD NEWS

BEFORE we examine the broadside ballad of the sixteenth century as a vehicle of news, we had better recall exactly what sort of song this variety is. The word *ballad* is used to mean so many different things, from *Barbara Allen* to *The Face on the Barroom Floor*, that it is easy to become confused. The broadside ballad is not a popular ballad, a specimen of the art of the people, in spite of the fact that several broadside ballads crept into Bishop Percy's collection and may be found in Professor Child's corpus of the popular balladry. It belongs, of course, to the era of printing, but its origin is to be found in the sort of narrative ballad—as opposed to the dramatic popular ballad—which also grew up in the middle ages. These ballads existed, were composed and sung, for many years before the invention of printing, and there is good reason to believe they were sometimes circulated in manuscript broadsides. It was an old habit, this agreeable custom of making songs on passing events—battles, feuds, raids, murders, domestic tragedies—and remembering them, perhaps even passing the word round, thereby. Some of the ancient popular ballads which have been preserved were also based on occurrences of this kind. But such of these popular ballads as do commemorate actual events are much more than historical and probably only secondarily historical at that; it is more likely that they were prized for their emotional than for their documentary interest by those who sang them and listened to them and by the immediate successors of these primitive ballad

[189]

connoisseurs, just as they are by us. It is rather the minstrel's song that is the legitimate ancestor of the printed narrative ballad of the sixteenth century. Gummere speaks of the once exclusively choral ballad's becoming "a convenient form for narrative of every sort which drifted into the ways of tradition. This traditional process has been mainly epic . . . [i.e.] towards the chronicle, the story, the romance."[1] In this way a second class of ballads is accounted for, "the historical ballad, recited rather than sung, epic in all its purposes and details, and far removed from the choral ballad of dramatic situation."[2] "Instead of a short singing piece," he says, "steeped in repetition, almost borne down by its refrain, plunging abruptly into a situation, describing no characters and often not naming them, telling no long story and giving no details, here is a deliberate narrative, long and easy of pace, free of repetitions, bare of refrain, abounding in details, and covering considerable stretches of time."[3] These ballads were a part of the minstrel's repertory and most of them were probably composed by minstrels; at any rate, they are the products of conscious art, or (let us say) industry. Gummere says that they were felt by the singer "to be his property, a kind of enclosed common."[3] Now it is not difficult to see how such a ballad, "abounding in details," would, if it were recited soon after the event it commemorates, have a kind of news-interest and serve as a report of the incidents it describes, especially when there was seldom any other kind of report available to those who heard it. There is pretty good evidence to show that many of these ballads were composed immediately after the event and a strong presumption for the remainder; certainly there was much more reason

[1] *C. H. E. L.*, II. 413.
[2] *Ibid.*, II. 414.
[3] *Ibid.*, II. 402.

[190]

why they should have been composed promptly than at some later time.

In the sixteenth century, or possibly even earlier, the popularity of these narrative ballads (from the artistic point of view, now debased far below *The Hunting of the Cheviot* and the best medieval examples) caused them to be printed and sold. It is practically certain that they were produced in very large quantities, not only by minstrels but by doggerel poets and amateurs of all kinds, though comparatively few broadsides earlier than 1600 have been preserved. Hundreds otherwise unknown are entered on the registers of the Stationers' Company. Allusions to them abound in contemporary literature, and we are all familiar with the figure of the ballad-seller, in the person of Autolycus or Nightingale in *Bartholomew Fair*. Furthermore, besides narratives based on actual events, the kind with which we are alone concerned, stories of many other kinds—from romances and classical myths to old wives' tales and altercations between a 'prentice and an innocent country maid—and even sentimental fancies, such as we are regaled with in the popular songs of our own day, were cast in the ballad mold. In the reign of Queen Elizabeth, everybody knew ballads, almost everybody sang ballads, and ore is tempted almost to believe everybody wrote ballads.[4]

Furthermore, the ballad was certainly as popular with the publishers as it was with such admirers as Mopsa, the type of all ballad-lovers. Though it was disdained by the richer and more fastidious members of the trade, to many poorer brother it was the staff of life. Part of the copiousness of sixteenth- and seventeenth-century ballad

---

[4] "Such is the folly of this age . . . that there are scarce so manye pedlers brag themselues to be printers because they haue a bundel of ballads in their packe, as there be idiots that think themselues artists because they can English an obligation, or write a true staffe to the tune of fortune."—Chettle: *Kind-Harts Dreame*, dedication.

literature is surely due to the ease with which a publisher could put a ballad on the market, the small outlay of capital required, and the large number of potential buyers. The ballad was the lowest form of printing; it required a minimum of equipment and of forethought and editorial judgment on the part of the publisher, and it was sold to the least critical class of readers. At a time when most of the books in the greatest request were the property of a few monopolists and the commonalty of the trade were starved for copy to print and publish, sure-fire popular wares such as the ballad were a godsend to the unprivileged.

The broadside ballad, consequently, became highly conventionalized and was written to a formula as unvarying as the inevitability of rimes like "love" and "above," "moon" and "spoon" in modern popular songs. Picking first an appropriate tune—stirring, jovial, lugubrious, or sentimental—from the repertory of popular airs which everybody knew, the ballad-maker, in Queen Elizabeth's time and later, composed a song much like a hundred others of the same class that had gone before it—a song trundling along at the same jog-trot gait, long-winded, full of *clichés*, and, as Professor Rollins says, "telling a curiously attenuated story with no climax."[5] His opening was conventional—either the "come and give ear" formula or "Al English hearts reioyce and sing"[6] or "For mercy, Lorde, with one accorde:"[7] to wind up, he could seldom think of something better than an appeal to his readers to believe his tale or an underscoring of his already tedious moral. Indeed, the broadside ballad, as poetry, is such poor stuff that we need the help of other reasons to explain

---

[5] "The Black-letter Broadside Ballad," *P. M. L. A.*, XXXIV: 2: 258.

[6] *A godlie Dittie to be song for the preseruation of the Queenes . . . raigne.* By R. Thacker. Abell Ieffes, 1586.

[7] *The true description of a monsterous Chylde, borne in the Ile of Wight . . .* By Iohn Barkar. Wylliam Gryffith, [1564].

its popularity—the fact that it could be sung, the pre-posterous woodcuts with which it was invariably tricked out, its very close dependence on the event or the senti-ment of the hour.

To speak of the broadside ballad as a vehicle of news is perhaps misleading, and yet there are some ballads which are quite valuable for the information they impart and which must have served as news-reports when first pub-lished. Three of Thomas Deloney's ballads are so graphic and circumstantial as to have led his commentators to conclude that he must have witnessed the events he describes.[8] Elderton's *New Yorkshyre song*,[9] *A newe Ballade, declaryng the daungerous shootyng of the Gunne at the Courte*,[10] *A true discourse of the winning of the towne of Berke by Grave Maurice*,[11] for example, are all sufficiently full and particular to do reasonably well as news. Many of the metrical *adieux* of condemned criminals give us particulars of the wrongdoings which have brought them to the gallows. Besides, many ballads, including those which are disappointingly vague and general in substance, appeared under copious titles which in themselves are brief summaries of the events the ballads are founded on.

Ballads which tell their story well are, however, the exception rather than the rule. Normally, a news-ballad

---

[8] Apropos of *A proper new Ballad breefely declaring the Death and Execution of fourteen . . . Traitors* (1586): "Offenbar haben wir es hier mit einem Augenzeu-genbericht zu tun."—Sievers: *Thomas Deloney*, p. 28. Apropos of *The Queenes visiting of the Campe at Tilsburie* (1588): "Aus dem Umstande, dasz die Vorgänge so überaus genau geschildert werden, ist fast zu entnehmen, dasz der Autor dem Zuge beigewohnt hat."—*ibid.*, p. 21. Apropos of *The Winning of Cales* (1596): "From the graphic detail and the use of the first person in this ballad, it may be hazarded that Deloney himself may have taken part in the Spanish expedition."—Mann: *Works*, p. 581. Bishop Percy also inferred that this ballad had been written by some one connected with the expedition (Hales & Furnivall, III. 453).

[9] Richard Iones, 1584.

[10] For Edward VVhite, [1579].

[11] *Shirburn Ballads*, no. LXVII.

[193]

is not so much a record of events as a commentary upon them; it is not a harbinger of news but a follower in its wake, expressing the opinion of the mass of the people about it. That it served to some extent, nevertheless, to give currency to the news is not to be doubted, but its own substance is chiefly emotional rather than literal. A ballad on the queen's opening of Parliament is likely to be not so much a description of what took place as an enthusiastic huzza for the most famous, gracious, wise, and splendid of sovereigns and a sincere testimonal of loyalty; a ballad on the French king's defeat of the league will probably have little to say about military operations, but it will be sure to emit a crow of triumph over the discomfiture of the pope and to warn England against Catholic machinations; a ballad on a flood in the north may very well omit all but the meagrest particulars, but it will not fail to expatiate plentifully on this evidence of God's mercy in chastening the sinful or to exhort his people to repentance. The ballad, then, tends to distil the essence of a recent event rather than to disperse itself among the details; unlike a true report of news, it is derived not from the circumstances of outward occurrences, but from the impression they make on the popular mind. As contemporary historical documents these ballads are highly unsatisfactory, but as revelations of the majority opinion on passing events they are perfect.

The ballads, then, are to be regarded as accompaniments of the news, but not, of course, of all the news that was published—at least, they did not follow all the varieties of news with the same persistence. It is occurrences which in some way stirred the ballad-writer's patriotism or moral sense that were most often taken as the subject of ballads. They very rarely reflect anything whatsoever of grave matters of state; but let the queen visit the city in state or celebrate her coronation day with jousting and shows and

[194]

a crop of perfervid ballad-celebrations will spring up over-night. The ballad-writers unerringly picked out from what was happening round about them the news that could most readily be turned into a vociferous demonstration of loyalty and patriotic enthusiasm, and wrote their verses around it. Such is Skeleton's *Ballade of the scottysshe kynge*,[12] which has been called the oldest English printed ballad, though it was issued as a book, not as a broadside. It is too Skeltonic to be typical of broadside balladry in form, but its substance is representative. It was published very soon after the battle of Flodden Field to which it refers, and while it imparts a certain amount of information, it is chiefly a frenzied war-dance celebrating, in terms not at all chivalrous, the crushing of the Scots. Thus the public acts of the sovereign, the military successes of the English armies, and the discomfiture of the enemies of the realm are fully rehearsed in a long series of ballads running through our period as far back as the earliest time from which ballads have been preserved.

The writing of epitaphs, after the middle of the sixteenth century, grew into a large department of the ballad-making industry. These have already been referred to.[13] It remains only to say that, while the mere appearance of such a broadside setting forth in its title the late worthy's quality and attainments probably served as an obituary notice of a sort and may properly be called a report of news, the ballads themselves are excessively conventional and devoid of information. They are rather pious contemplations of the inescapable fact of death and commentaries on the vanity of worldly wishes. Bancroft, bishop of London, wrote to Sir Robert Cecil on 27 February 1601 (two days after the execution) that an epitaph on the Earl of Essex then being hawked in the streets

---

[12] [Richard Fawkes, 1513.]

[13] See above, p. 29 ff.

"was made half a year since, upon some other occasion."[14] It may well have been; almost any ballad-epitaph would have done equally well for any other subject of approximately the same rank in life.

Another distinct class of ballads are the "good-nights"[15] or *adieux* to the world of criminals condemned to death. It has already been remarked that they were usually written in the first person and offered to the gaping public as the work of the criminals themselves, probably in imitation of an older custom of writing farewell verses from prison. Although in some degree they were also written in a conventional style, they are one of the most piquant varieties and they were enormously popular in their day. The amount of news divulged in them varies: in some, it is considerable, and takes the form of a history of the criminal's misspent life; others are merely confessions of sin in general terms, petitions for pardon, and warnings to the hearer to avoid the same pitfalls. It seems probable that some of them were written as sincere exhortations based on the criminal's folly and punishment, but others are merely gaudy reveling in wickedness under the guise of morality.

A great many of the ballads dealing with passing events were written on the basis of printed books of news. Of that there is no manner of doubt: time and again, book and ballad were entered simultaneously, or a few days apart (the book almost invariably coming first), as a rule, though not quite always, by the same publisher. The publisher had a kind of proprietary right to the news he set forth which entitled him to exploit it in verse as well as prose, and most publishers safeguarded their title by

[14] H. M. C.: *Calendar of the MSS. of the Marquis of Salisbury*, XI. 88; Charlotte C. Stopes: *The Life of Henry, Third Earl of Southampton* (1922), p. 221; Rollins: *Index*, p. 122.
[15] The name is Mr. Rollins's.

[196]

of numbers. What, then, was the motive which persuaded them to put their thoughts into verse? Sometimes it was merely an impulse to imitate a popular fashion; but often it must have been an urgent inner necessity which these amateur ballad-writers could satisfy only by giving their thoughts deliberate expression, just as some people nowadays give vent to their feelings by writing letters to the editor of their favorite newspaper. If a ballad composed in this way was not hopelessly obscure in expression and if its sentiments were acceptable to a part of the ballad-buying public, a publisher would have found the printing of it worth his while. Or, to look at the same phenomenon from another point of view, suppose a public-spirited citizen, looking about him at the state of the commonwealth, espies an opinion, a discontentment among some of his fellow-citizens which his judgment heartily disapproves of. Suppose, for example, that, during the reign of Queen Elizabeth, when Protestant refugees in large numbers were emigrating to England from the continent and some Englishmen objected to offering asylum to so many strangers, our public-spirited citizen, feeling that it was admirable of England to receive these foreigners who had suffered for their faith, and quite in obedience to the injunctions of the Scriptures, was strongly displeased by this inhospitable attitude and was moved to express his reprobation to his fellow-countrymen. How could he do so? He would, of course, discourse on this topic to all his friends and in every company in which he found himself, but he could thereby reach only a minute fraction of the population. If he was eager to read a lecture to a larger audience, the ballad was the most accessible and the most promising means. It was popular; many people would welcome a ballad simply because it was a ballad. It was attractive; in a ballad the author's message was cloaked in a guise which brought it a larger audience than

[199]

it could have otherwise commanded. It was also cheap; a publisher risked less on a ballad than on a book handling the same subject, and therefore the effusion of our public-spirited citizen was more likely to see the light in the form of a broadside. Consequently, it seems probable that some ballads were written by persons quite like the writers of letters to our newspapers, and for the same reasons. It is certain that the ballad is the only vehicle of expression which, in the sixteenth century, could have served as a forum where the laity could express their individual and peculiar opinions.

As a matter of fact, there is a ballad on the subject mentioned above as an illustration. It is known only from a MS. copy,[20] but there is no reason why it could not have been printed. It is not incompetently written, though the author betrays a certain amateurishness in his careless use of pronouns. A reading of it leaves a distinct impression that the author was no poet writing because the divine afflatus had descended upon him, much less a journalist catering to the public taste, but a sincere and pious patriot who was moved by a righteous desire to reprove the uncharitable opinion of those who murmured against the influx of foreigners. Another ballad, which laments the death of a martyr burned during the reign of Queen Mary, was confessedly written by a private person, a friend of the martyr's and the godfather of his son.[21] This is likewise known only from a MS. copy, but it calls itself a ballad, it has some of the incidental earmarks of the printed ballad, it is much like other ballads on martyrdoms which were printed, and it was possibly kept out of print,

---

[20] *God doth blesse this realme for the receyving of straungers being persecuted for the gospell, although some do repine therat.* Sloane MS. 1896, ff. 56ᵛ–58. See Rollins: *Old English Ballads*, p. 180.

[21] *A ballad concernynge the death of mr. Robart glover, wrytone to maystrys marye glover, his wyf, of a frend of heres.* By Robart Bott. Stowe MS. 958, ff. 8ᵛ–17. See Rollins: *op. cit.*, p. 33.

if it was never printed, only by the fact that its tenor made it dangerous matter at the time it was written. It is given up chiefly to eulogy of the martyr and consolation for his widow, but it also describes his trial and execution. It seems clearly a volunteer and private rather than a professional and popular effort, and it reminds us of the contributed eulogies on recently-deceased worthies which appear almost daily in a column of the London *Times*. Although we have no conclusive proof, it seems that the ballad was the readiest, almost the only, printed vehicle in which a private person, in the sixteenth century, could air his notions and his feelings.

One further use of the ballad remains to be mentioned— it was not always so quickly forgotten as is most news. In our own times, to-day's news is almost completely forgotten next week; only a few items useful to historians are likely to be preserved out of the enormous grist our newspapers print every day. But in the sixteenth century, we often find an old story, which probably started as news, or was at least founded on a real occurrence, turning up again years later, hale and hearty, as a tradition still remembered, as a kind of folklore. It is perhaps something of an exaggeration to use the word traditional of stories preserved in print, and it may be that their recurrence is due even more largely than we think to the industry of printers in periodically taking down old wares, dusting them off, and sending them out for another round of the market, but since the popularity of many of these resurrected stories is unquestionable, it is at least possible that they themselves retained a certain vitality which perpetuated them long after the evaporation of whatever interest as news they may once have had.

It is not surprising to find that a sentimental or gnomic or moral ballad has lasted a century or more, for its point might be just as well taken at one time as the other, but the persistence of a narrative ballad telling a story confined to a particular moment of time must argue its possessing something of permanent or universal interest. For example, there are no less than seven versions printed in the latter half of the seventeenth century of the ballad known as *A True Relation of the Life and Death of Sir Andrew Barton, a Pirate and Rover on the Seas*. Barton, a Scotchman, is an historical figure of the time of King Henry VIII; he was captured by the English in 1511. We do not know when this ballad was composed, but it may very well have been soon after 1511, when it would have been interesting as news; then, because it was an attractive story of English valor on the seas, it was preserved for two hundred years, both in the memory of succeeding generations, for there is an oral version of it, and in the archives of the ballad printers. There is another story almost as old about an apprentices' riot in 1517, *The Story of an ill May Day*, which turns up as a printed ballad in 1727. It seems unlikely that an incident as obscure as this should have stuck in the popular memory unless it had been written down and fitted with a tune soon after it happened. The famous ballad of Anne Askew, a religious martyr in the reign of Henry VIII, "I am poore lame and blind," was still sung through the seventeenth century; it was known in the sixteenth too, though we have no copy of it so early; it very likely began its career soon after the martyrdom. Stories of all sorts took on this kind of immortality: a ballad on the Gunpowder Plot, "True Protestants, I pray you, do draw near," which was reprinted *c.* 1670; other ballads of religious martyrs, such as John Careless or the child born while its mother was burning at the stake which was thrust into the flames to burn with her; the "good-nights" of famous criminals, such as Hutton; ballads of fights at sea and of famous pirates. Some of these perennials, while in their later

[202]

careers they pretend to be historical, may never have been news at all: the famous ballad of Sir Walter Raleigh, usually called *The Golden Vanity*, popular down to the nineteenth century, rests on no discoverable foundation of fact and was probably made up in the seventeenth century out of Raleigh's reputation. Some others, such as "It was a lady's daughter," the story of "a virtuous maid of Paris" who died rather than turn Catholic, if they are true stories at all, cannot be assigned to a particular time of origin.

This sort of news, then, was not so perishable a commodity as its modern counterpart; the taste for it seems to have kept its zest rather longer. On this account some of these ballads remained current as history long after they had served their turn as news; they passed into the traditional balladry, found there a place alongside the traditional ballads of popular origin, and were preserved and handed down by the affectionate memory of generation after generation.

CHAPTER IX
NEWS TO INFORM AND NEWS TO INSTRUCT

THE Rev. John Hilliard, "preacher of the word of life in Sopley," as he described himself, in 1613 wrote a tract entitled *Fire from Heauen. Burning the body of one Iohn Hittchell of Holne-hurst. . the 26. of Iune last 1613. who by the same was consumed to ashes, and no fire see-ne, lying therein smoaking and smothering three dayes and three nights, not to be quenched by water, nor the help of mans hand.*[1] Scanning this title, we might very naturally expect to find news of a deplorable fatality inside the book. This expectation, however, would be somewhat dashed by the reverend author's plain declaration:

My end in publishing this Pamphlet, is not popular ostentation . . . The only purpose I haue, is to rouse vp the sloathfull carelesse, and instruct the filthy forgetfull, to behold the wonderfull workes of the Lord.

And this statement is quickly borne out by a reading of the tract: the burning and smoking of the late John Hittchell, to the length of barely more than a page, is tucked away among twenty pages of unabashed homiletics full of fire and fumes of quite another kind. Another ghostly father, the Rev. John Field, celebrated as one of the authors of the Puritan *Admonition to the Parliament*, published in 1583 *A godly exhortation, by occasion of the late iudgement of God, shewed at Parris-garden, the thirteenth day of Ianuarie: where were assembled by estimation; aboue a thousand persons, whereof some were slaine; & of that number, at the least, as is crediblie reported, the thirde person maimed and*

[1] Iohn Trundle, 1613.

[204]

1 6 0 7

Lamentable newes out of Monmouth-shire in Wales.

CONTAYNING,

The wonderfull and most fearefull accidents of
the great ouerflowing of waters in the saide Countye,
drowning infinite numbers of Cattell of all kinds, as Sheepe,
Oxen, Kine and horses, with others: together
with the losse of many men, women and
Children, and the subuersion of xxvi
Parishes in Ianuary last
1 6 0 7.

LONDON
Printed for *W.W.* and are to be solde in Paules Church
yarde at the signe of the Grey hound.

[205]

hurt. Giuen to all estates for their instruction, concerning the keeping of the Sabboth day.[2] This pamphlet promises a little less than the other, and performs a little more. Its subject is the collapse of the scaffolding at a popular bear-garden on a Sunday afternoon, whereby, according to Stow, eight spectators were killed "and many others sore hurt, and bruised, to the shortning of their liues." We must, however, be very patient to find any such information as we should call news, and wade through scolding of the civic authorities for permitting the desecration of the Sabbath and arguments to prove that the accident was not due to the rotting of the timbers, but to "the finger euen of God himself," who, according to our author, had personally intervened to rebuke the Sabbath-breakers. Not until the thirtieth page do we find it.

These examples are extreme rather than typical, but the habit which they represent of moralizing upon the news, of cloaking it in the form of a sermon, and of triumphantly drawing salutary lessons from it is very common: it extends to all kinds of news and runs all through our period. More typical, perhaps, is the book called *Lamentable newes out of Monmouthshire in Wales. Contayning, The wonderfull . . . accidents of the great ouerflowing of waters in the saide Countye, drowning infinite numbers of Cattell of all kinds . . .: together with the losse of many men, women and Children, and the subuersion [sic] of xxvi Parishes in Ianuary last 1607.*[3] This is an even more tedious imposture, for it clearly promises us news. And news it does contain, more than five pages of it, but it is encompassed by a cloud of pious ejaculations which cannot by any license be admitted under that title. "Wofull newes from Wales" reads a subtitle on the first page of the fourth leaf, immediately after the preface, but there is not

[2] For Henry Carre, 1583.
[3] For W[illiam] W[elby, 1607].

a shred of news in it; that is postponed until the eighth leaf, where it appears in the form of a list of parishes flooded. On the next, the narrator begins, at last, to tell his story, but after he has got through only one paragraph, by an evil chance he lets fall the remark that "alas, a man wil giue all that he hath, so that his life may be preserued," and at once he is off at a tangent on this theme. It is not until the bottom of the reverse of the eleventh leaf that he pulls himself up with "But to return vnto our foresaid narration." Now he buckles down to his job in earnest and gives us five pages of news, rounding them off with a pious conclusion two pages long.

Another book of news that is typical of many more besides is *Newes from France. A true Relation of the great losses . . . by . . . fire in the Citie of Paris, the 24. day of October last past, 1621.*[4] It commences as follows:

> God, whose goodnesse and clemencie is incomprehensible, to our humane thoughts and imaginations, doth not alwayes discharge the arrowes of his wrath vpon miserable sinners; who by the innumerablenesse of their offences, haue stirred vp and prouoked his wrath against them, because he desireth not the death of a sinner, but rather that he should conuert and be saued: But when he seeth that they waxe worse, and are hardened in their sinnes, and lull themselues asleepe in humane delights: Then he rouzeth vp himselfe with the scourge of aduersitie, and dischargeth the furie of his wrath against them, to make them turne vnto him, who is the Soueraigne Ruler, of whome they hold their being, and all their power. Then (I say) he employeth the great forces of the heauens, and the Elements, thereby to heale the vlcer of their vices, that wallow and take pleasure in sinne, as a Sow delighteth to wallow in the mire.
>
> Which plainely appeareth by the deplorable accident happened of late in the Citie of Paris . . .

But having once made this acknowledgment to correct morality, it turns to a straightforward recounting of facts, to the length of more than twelve pages. This manner of introduction was sometimes varied as follows:

[4] R[alph] R[ounthwaite], 1621.

When *Menelaus* the gallant King of *Greece*, for the recouerie of faire *Hellena* his wife, beseeged for ten yeares space the noble town of *Troy*, there was nothing that did more comfort his hart in hope of victorie, then to think that he was accompaned with a sort of wise & hardie Captaines, whose pollicie and prowes assured him in the ende of a fortunate conquest. . . . But if euer *Greece* had cause to spred the praise of *Achilles* . . . , Then hath Englande triple cause to declare the exceeding courage of her faithfull Countrimen, who . . . hath fought in forrain countries for their cōscience sake.[5]

This book also gets down to business after the exordium from which this extract is quoted.

One more example must be given to complete the gallery:

At a Towne in *Norfolke*, called *Rockland*, dwelt one Master *Iames*, a Minister, and Preacher of the word, a man wel reckoned in the generall report of all, who hauing two Benefices and growing somewhat in yeares, to bee the more ease vnto his age, receiued into his house one *Lowe* (a man that profest himselfe a Scholler, and one that had before time been Imployed in like place) as a Reading Minister to supply his place at one of his Cures. This *Lowe*, thus intertained had together with an Annuall stipend his diet and lodging in the house of his said Master. And now marke the subtilty of Sathan, who spares not to sow the seeds of enuy, and emulation euer, in the bosomes of those that are (or at least wise should be) the trew seedesmen of the euerlasting Haruest, as in the sequell is plainely Apparant. This *Lowe* had no sooner with Esops Snake felt the warme heate of entertainement, and tasted the sweete Milke of preferment: but the mortall enemy of all mankind, Insinuates himselfe into his bosome, perswading him that he was borne to higher Fortunes, then to liue so base and stipendary a life, vnder so meane and so much vnworthy a Master, and withall instructed him, how and which way he might raise his estate, to the very height and toppe of his desires, viz. If hee could but inauger or graft himselfe into the loue of his Mistresse, A woman of good Parentage, vertuous education, and (to the outward eye) of ciuill and vnblemisht reputation. This womans chastity notwithstanding, he speedely attempts, and effectually, as it manifestly appeares, obtaines: the maner how? the times when? the places where, and the meanes and causes by whom, were too intricate and tedious to expresse. Had they yet pausd heare, and waded no deeper into the whirlepoole of damnation? but Sathan that loues to haue his bondslaues, sooted all ouer with the Coale of damnation, further

[5] *A true Relation of all suche Englishe Captaines* . . . , as above, p. 122.

suggests, that howsoeuer hee may seeme to embrace the shadow of his content, the substance is still inioyed, and rests at the command of Master *Iames* his Master, and that hee but like a slaue by stealth, and by Times allowance, sparingly and fearefully inioyes it: Yet so apparant were their gestures, so publick their meetings, and so familiar their speeches and outward behauiours, that most thereabouts suspectted, many priuately murmured, and some letted not openly to repeate, that Master *Lowe* dieted at Master *Iames* his board, and lodgde in his wiues bed: which words hee himselfe hearing, (without any checke either to his wife or reproofe to his seruant) after enquiry made, and found of the first Authors, hee not onely admonisht but very seriously threatened them, that if they persisted in any such ill kind of speaking, hee would vrge the seuerity of the Law against them, affirming that if any shewe of familiarity were betwixt *Lowe* and his wife, hee durst contest (such and so confident was his trust in both their loyalties) it was both honest, ciuill, and without the reach of any such scandalous suspition: This his strong confidence and fauourable construction of their faulty, and tainted behauiours might haue beene a meanes, though not of altogether desisting from[,] yet to haue staid their intents from pursuite of further mischiefe, had they not beene altogether diuorst from christian humanity, and absolutely markt and seald for vesselles of perdition: But leauing him in his good thoughts, labouring to lay and beate downe the windy tempest of discredit, which their lewde practises had deseruedly raisde, & follow[ing] them in the pursuite of their most damnable and diabolicall intent, namely how to make those stolne pleasures (which all this while they did but pilfer from their trew Master) their own; To effect this his learned counsell the Diuel[,] bribed with no lesse fee then his miserable soule, laid him downe many and seuerall courses, but in the end concluded it could not any way bee securely wrought, Master *Iames* suruiuing, and against his murther many strong diswasions presented themselues, as first his entertainement into his seruice, his kind vsage, strength of loue, and weakenesse of suspition, notwithstanding so often and apparantly thereunto vrged: against all these the Deuill vrges, that the breach of all the commandements is but death, and one is no lesse. Adultery is a sinne, and murther is no more, whithal, how much more better it was to liue like a Master then a slaue, to command then to be commanded, with a number of such worldly intising Syllogismes, as intangled his poore and vnarmd soule in the limetwigs and snares of perdition, In breife it is finally concluded betwixt his counsell learned: the Deuill and himselfe: that Master *Iames*, notwithstanding his entertaining, maintaining, in and from all manner of scandall abetting and him defending, must with his wife and liuing, giue vp, and to his most bloody hands surrender his deare and most innocent life. This resolution confirmed, the time when, the place where, the meanes how, are speedily and most laboriously to be determined: how oft and many times attempted? how strangely and almost myraculously preuented, we omit, and come to the ineuitable and fatall time (twelfe night last past) predestined to bee the sad Mother of so vntimely and abortiue a prodigie.[6]

In the foregoing there is considerable information, and the pamphlet as a whole is an informing account of the murder and its punishment, but the information is intermixed with a good deal of comment and many pious asides.

A large part of all the news published in our period— almost all of that printed before 1590, copies of documents excepted—was served up in the style of one or another of the examples just cited. This intermixture of pious and edifying comment or historical parallels in what represented itself to be information is common to every kind of news published. There was scarcely any subject or occurrence that would not yield a moral to the piety of the sixteenth-century commentator. "These swelings vp and ouerflowings of waters," says an account of floods in Somersetshire in 1607, ". . . are . . . the very diseases and monstrous byrthes of nature, sent into the world to terrifie it, and to put it in mind, y^t the great God . . . can as well now drowne all mankind as he did at the first."[7] This habit was so inveterate as to raise several questions.

In the first place, how did it come about? What was the reason for publishing news decorated with so much moral ornament, or, if these books were published as homilies rather than as information, why was a certain portion of undoubted news thrown in? This confusion may be due in part to that want of a well-defined concept

[6] *A true relation of the most Inhumane and bloody Murther, of Master Iames Minister . . . at Rockland in Norfolke. . . .* For R[ichard] Bonian & H[enry] Walley, 1609.

[7] *A true report of certaine wonderfull ouerflowings of Waters . . . in Summersetshire, Norfolke, and other places* . . . For Edward White, 1607.

[210]

of news which has already been mentioned and so may be set down to the comparative novelty of printed news. News was still published casually and haphazard; it had not yet worked out any regular channel through which it could flow to those who wanted it or any recognized form of presenting itself. Consequently it was very likely to appear in all sorts of odd shapes, bearing on its back any outlandish baggage which it had picked up in its travels. Besides, it is certain that the age rather fancied the moralizing and commentaries which seem to us so impertinent in the company of news. After all, they are natural companions; there is usually some inner significance in the news that is made known from day to day and there is nothing extraordinary in the sixteenth-century habit, on the one hand, of pointing it out and, on the other, of respectfully attending to it. The fact that the significance sometimes discovered by the more ingenious moralists seems to us thoroughly fantastic does not alter the matter, and our present-day preference for discovering significances ourselves is merely a change of taste. Besides, our own news-writers, while they by no means interpret the importance of the events they describe as sedulously as the writers cited above, do not, perhaps, refrain from comment as rigorously as we often think they do. There are hundreds of ways in which a subtle bias of interpretation can creep into what we suppose to be, into what may be intended as, an impartial record; in the face of great events of which the significance is unmistakable, it is very difficult even for a twentieth-century reporter to confine himself strictly to literal facts. The significance, indeed, may be the most important fact of all. We too like to have our heroes applauded as well as described, our successes praised, and our calamities deplored. Our newspapers are deterred from deliberately infusing their own verdict upon current events into their news-columns only

[211]

by the notion that their duty is to furnish accurate and impartial information and to allow their readers to form unaided opinions, and by the law of libel, neither of which is a complete check. English newspapers, as opposed to American, are the more likely still to take a stand with regard to the news they are relating, especially by approving what recommends itself to sound morality and by frowning upon what is not in good taste. The American reporter has probably achieved the acme of cold-blooded unconcern in the facts he writes down, but even so, comment by "sob-sisters," special correspondents writing under a by-line, and other privileged characters, such as the sporting editor, is still common, is perhaps becoming more common.

Furthermore, the origin of much of the news published in the sixteenth century accounts for its being dressed in moral guise. It was written chiefly by amateurs who, moreover, had few precedents in news-writing to guide them. Many of them were impressed temporarily into the work by their own habits, hobbies, aims, and purposes, and they were guided by familiar habits of thought in recording the news they set themselves to give to the world. Much of the news written by the holy men of the time was scarcely conceived as news at all: it was a slightly specialized branch of the science of homiletics which started from a recent occurrence instead of a scriptural text. "I haue thought it fit," says the Rev. Thomas Wilcox (another of the authors of the *Admonition to the Parliament*) in the dedication of his *Short yet a true . . . narration of the fearefull fire that fell in the towne of Wooburne*,[8] ". . . to publishe though a short, yet a true narration of that pitifull spectacle, and therewithall, some meditations of mine owne . . . I haue aimed at nothing but this, that . . . men might bee lead by the hande to make

[8] For Thomas Man, 1595.

[212]

some profitable vse of it." This is no understatement. The reverend gentleman's complete indifference to the business of the contemporary historian is illustrated by his statement that, though it is reported that the fire was started by an old woman's carelessly throwing some old straw on a bed of warm ashes in her fireplace, as for himself, the true cause was the wrathful descent of the hand of God. It is no wonder that the news written by such men smacks strongly of the pulpit, that it is elaborately furnished with biblical citations, and that its moral and theological bearings are fully expounded. That a certain amount of moralizing was even regarded as conventional seems to be indicated by the statement of the author or editor of *Lamentable newes out of Monmouthshire* that "these newes" were brought to him "& an importunitie vsed to me, that I would giue thē some forme, & bestow an exhortation on them." The habit of lugging in historical parallels is probably an imitation of the style of the standard historical works of the day, the nearest precedent familiar to the literary soldiers, lawyers, scholars, and gentlemen amateurs who wrote the news of wars, state ceremonies, and political developments. Being amateurs, they were all the more likely to seek a reed to lean upon.

Moreover, it is possible that, to a limited extent, this cloaking of the news in pious comment is a form of protective coloration instinctively or cunningly adopted to disarm official suspicions against news, or even to lure readers, or certain kinds of readers, to buy. It is just possible that an unvarnished account of a foul murder would have been objectionable to many influential persons, but tricked out as a sermon against impiety or lawbreaking, it could hardly have been reproved even by the godliest. It is probable that a narrative of a military action on the continent was less likely to be suppressed by the authorities if it lauded the English troops employed and if it showed a healthy hatred of the Spaniards, or an account of the execution of a traitor if it loudly deplored the perversity of such ungrateful subjects in refusing to recognize the clemency and beneficence of her majesty's government.

The next question that occurs to us is, did the sixteenth-century reader regard matter written in the style of the examples cited as news or as improving reading? As far as the last three examples go, there can be little doubt that they were read as news: they are compounded of seven parts news to one part exegesis. But the others are a different matter. Anybody who bought the Rev. Mr. Hilliard's pamphlet hoping to read therein a thrilling account of an unusual fatality must certainly have been disappointed. And there is no doubt that there must have been a large audience for works of divinity, as the innumerable volumes of sermons, scriptural commentary, and Christian instruction published during our period testify. The best evidence that we have on this point is afforded us by the publishers themselves. It is to them, I think, that we may attribute the title-pages of contemporary books, and these regularly emphasize the element of news. The proportion of news to piety on the title-pages of the first two examples mentioned and in the books themselves is not the same at all, and in the third example, although the book is three-fourths piety, the title-page suggests nothing but news. It is hard to think of any reason for such a discrepancy except that the publisher felt that the promise of news would attract more readers. Trundle, the publisher of *Fire from Heauen*, was a prolific purveyor of all sorts of popular and sensational matter, and Henry Carre dealt largely in ballads. It would seem that even the most illusory offer of news had a certain charm.

[214]

We find confirmation of this conclusion in the fact that, under the guise of news, publishers often issued all sorts of matter in which there is no record of current events whatsoever: the word frequently occurs in the titles of books and ballads which do not belong to our subject at all. *A sack full of newes*[9] is a collection of humorous anecdotes; *Ioyfull newes out of the newe founde worlde*[10] is a treatise on the medicinal properties of transatlantic herbs; Samuel Rowlands's *Good newes and bad newes*[11] is a collection of "epigrams;" *Newes come from Hell of loue vnto all her welbeloued frendes*[12] is a diatribe against usury; Elderton's *New merry newes*[13] is a *jeu d'esprit; Strange Newes out of Calabria*[14] is a prophecy of calamities to come based on a star seen in Calabria, in which the word is apparently understood to refer to the future. Even the godly invested their propædeutics with the same meretricious appeal: in Becon's *Newes out of heauen both pleasaunt and ioyfull*[15] the "news"-bearer is the angel Gabriel; Hurlstone's *Newes from Rome concerning the blasphemous sacrifice of the papisticall Masse*[16] is no more news than the last; Foxe mentions a song against the mass and the queen's misproceedings, sung at a wedding by "a prentice to a minstrel," called *Newes out of London;*[17] *Newes from Niniue to Englande brought by the Prophete Ionas*[18] is a translation of an edifying treatise by Johann Brentz, one of Luther's

[9] Entered 1557–8 by John Kynge (Arber, I. 75). The earliest known printed copy is dated 1640.

[10] For William Norton, 1577.

[11] For Henry Bell, 1622.

[12] William Copland, 1565.

[13] As above, p. 12.

[14] [For John Perin, 1586.] A book called *The Confutacon of the prognosticacon out of Calabria* was entered 5 December by Robert Waldegraue (Arber, II. 460).

[15] For Iohn Gough, [1541?].

[16] Cantorbury: for E. Campion, [1550?].

[17] *Actes and Monuments* (ed. Townsend), VIII. 578.

[18] Henrie Denham, 1570.

disciples; *Good newes from Canaan*[19] is "an Exposition of Davids Penitential Psalm after he had gone in unto Bathsheba," by Bishop Cowper. W. B., the translator of a book printed in 1552, thus explains its purpose:

It is wonderfull (good Reader) to see the sundry diuersities of wittes what meanes they inuente to declare & publishe suche thynges as they thinke necessary to be knowē, some vnder the colour of fayned histories, some vnder the persons of specheles beastes, and some vnder yᵉ shadow of dreames and visions, of which thou haste here a notable and worthy example. For some wittie man[,] . . . priuie of the laste Popes secretes . . . abhominable[,] . . . willinge to declare to the worlde, howe men were deceyued in him, whiche not onely called, but also beleued hym to be more than halfe a god, hath . . . writtē an Epistle . . . Wherin after that he hath truly declared the time of his death, he fayneth a poesie in manner of a vision, in which he seeth Paule Frenes [= Farnese], the Pope[,] receyued in hell.

This was published as *Wonderfull news of the death of Paule the .iii. last byshop of Rome,*[20] two or three years after his death. We cannot say that titles such as these practise much deception, but they do seem to indicate that *news* was a charmed word which could be depended upon to make the ordinary reader prick up his ears.

But the most curious piece of what promises to be news but turns out to be a snare and delusion is possibly the verse-tract by William Baldwin called *The Funèralles of King Edward the sixt*, which was published by Thomas Marshe in 1560. The author introduces his verses as follows:

Great hath been the doubt among many, euer since the death of our late vertuous souerayne Lorde King Edward the syxt, by what meane he dyed, and what were the causes of his death. This doubte is fully resolued in this booke, penned before his corse was buryed, & endeuoured since by many meanes to haue had been printed: but such was the time, that it could not be brought to passe. Wherefore now at length (good Reader) it is set furth, both to take away all

[19] For Iohn Budge, 1613.
[20] Thomas Gaultier, [1552].

doubt in this matter, and to exhort thee to leaue thy sinnes, and noughty liuing: Least, that as they wer in part the vndoubted cause of that moost godly prynces death, so they becum the destruction of our vertuous Queen his sister, and the vtter ruyne of this whole realme.

After whetting our appetite for information with this promising beginning, the author proceeds to give his original and most remarkable explanation, as follows:

The almighty mynde that rayneth thre in one,
Disposing all thinges from his stable throne,
Beheld the earth and man among the rest:
Moude by the crye of such as wer opprest.
And when he had the maynland throughly vewed,
With Mahometrie and Idol blud embrewed, . . .
He turne his iyes from that so fowle a sight,
And toward the Iles he cast his looke a right . . .
But when he sawe all vice most vile and naught
Most rifely swarme, where truth had most be taught,
In England chefe, which he of speciall grace
Had made his wurd and chosens resting place, . . .
All wo and wroth he flang away his face,
And to him selfe he thus bewayld the case. . . .
Sith then they passe for neyther threats, nor loue,
Nor easy plages wherby I do them proue,
What els remayns but to destroy them all,
The yong, the old, the myghty with the small.
    Chryst hearing this, and moued with the teares
Of vertuous folke . . .
For his elect on this sort gan intreat. . . .
Yet stay thy wrath, haue mercy on our nede,
And sith through fayth a mayny of them be mine
Graunt leaue this once to water thys thy vyne. . . .
He neyther graunted it, nor yet denayd
But fatherlike thus to his sonne he sayd:
To sewe for mercy I maruayle what ye meane,
For such a sort as haue reiect vs cleane.
Beholde the heades, what els do they deuise,
Saue in our name to cloke their couetise?
Thine herytage they haue thee whole bereft,
Except thy shurt, let see, what haue they left?
Thy golde, they plate, thy lodgyng, yea thy landes
That are the poores, are in the richest handes:
They waste, they spoyle, they spill vpon their pride

[217]

That which was geuen the nedy corse to hide: . . .
But for to trye them once at thy request
I will but touch their king, and warne the rest
To amend their liues, which if they do delay
I will take their king, their comfort life and stay:
And if they set his death to at their heele,
I will powre downe plages till euery one do feele.
   This sayd, he called to his seruaunt Crasy cold,
Whom the Isy king kept prisoner in his hold
Beneath the Poales, where vnder he doth dwell
In grysly darke like to the diepe of hell. . . .

At the mention of Crazy Cold, the poet's imagination
expands with a proto-Spenserian opulence:

Scarce was this errand throwly to him tolde,
But forth he came this shiuering crasy cold,
With Ysikles bebristled like a Bore,
About his head behind and eke before. . . .
He got him vpon blustring Boreas backe,
And forth he went: but his horse so heauy trode
That al the world might knowe which way he rode.
For in his way there grew no maner grene,
That could in thre dayes after wel be sene,
His breth and braying was so sharp and shryl,
That fluds for feare hard cluddered stoode full stil.
The seas did quake and tremble in such sort,
That neuer a ship durst venter out of port,
The holtes, the heathes, the hilles became al hore,
The trees did shrinke, al thinges were troubled sore.

The moral should now be sufficiently obvious: the people
of England utterly ignored the divine warning and King
Edward died of pneumonia as a chastisement for his subjects' sins.

   Finally, is there no relief from this moralizing upon the
news? As a matter of fact, it was long after the end of our
period that comment in newspapers was separated from
information and segregated in the editorial columns, as is
now the vogue. But we find signs of an increasing taste for
unadulterated news, especially after about 1590, in the
publication of more and more information which the

[218]

writer allows to stand on its own feet without interposing an interpretation or commentary between it and the reader. This is not to say that, much earlier, books containing a very high proportion of valuable fact had not been published. Here is an example from the year 1562, possibly a translation, the first paragraph of which is a triumph of painstaking literalness:

Saterdaye beynge the last day of Februarie, the duke of Guyse lay at Dāmartin le frank to the which it is two leagues from Iainuille, and from the said Dammartin to Vassy are other two leagues, both the which make foure leagues distaunce betwene the sayd Iainuille (wher is the sayde dukes house and restyng place) and the said Vassy.

Sondaye the fyrste of Marche the said duke departed from Dammartyn aforesayde, accompanied with .ii. hundred horse at the least, euery horseman of them, hauynge two or thre pistolets, and many of theim hauyng long harquebuses.

The sayd duke of Guyse fayned he wold the straight way to Esclaron, without commyng to Vassy: And thereof was made a greate bruite before he dissoged, he passed by Broussell, a village neere to the said Vassy, within one quarter of a league. And at that time thei rang to a sermon in the reformed church of the said Vassy. Wherevppon the duke and his companye tooke occasion to say and aske, what meaneth this ryngyng?

Wherevnto it was aunswered by many of the Dukes band and som others of the sayd towne of Vassy, it is to the sermō of the Hugenots. Wheryupon they could not possibly so colour and dissemble the mattier, but there escaped oute of the mouths of the most honorable and respected persons among them: yea and others of meaner degree, these woordes folowynge, By Goddes deathe we will Hugenote them by and by of an other fashion.[21]

The rest of this story is well known. It is, however, not until about 1590, as has been said, that a more matter-of-fact style of reporting, somewhat closer to that in vogue today, begins to be generally noticeable. The moralizing habit died hard, but it gradually gave way to something like this:

[21] *The Destruction and sacke cruelly committed by the Duke of Guyse . . . in the towne of Vassy, the fyrste of Marche . . . M.D.LXII.* For Edvvarde Sutton, 1 May [1562].

In the moneth of *Nouember* last past, there were sundry Shyps appertayning to seuerall Marchants of *London*, which were rigde and fraught forth with marchandize, some for *Spaine*, and some for sundry other places of traffique, who together hauing wind and wether, which oft-time fell out very vncertaine, arriued safely in short space, at such places as they desired, among whom was the *Centurion* of *London*, a very tall Shyppe of burden, yet but weakely manned, as appeareth by this Historie ensuing, wherein God shewed a most wonderfull accident of his mercifull loue and fauour towards them, giuing them the victory, and deliuering them from the hands of their Enemies, at such time as it was thought vnpossible for them to escape.

Thys aforesaid Shyp called the *Centurion*, safely arriued at *Marseelis*, where after they had deliuerid their goods, they staied about the space of fiue weekes, and better, and then tooke in lading, intending to returne to England.

Now when the *Centurion* was ready to come away frō *Marseelis*, there were sundry other shypps of smaller burden, entreated the Maister thereof, whose name is *Robert Bradshawe*, dwelling at the *Limehouse*, to stay a day or two for them, vntill they were in a readines to depart with them, thereby perswading them, that it would be farre better for them to stay and goe together in respect of their assistance, then to depart of themselues without company, and so happily [= haply] for want of ayde fall into the hands of theyr Enemies the Spanish Gallies. Vpon which reasonable perswasion, notwithstanding that thys Ship was of such sufficiencie as they might hazard her in the danger of the Sea, yet they stayed for those little Ships according to theyr request, who together did put to sea from *Marseelis*, and vowed in generall not to flie one from another, if so they should happen to meete with any Spanish Gallies, beeing resolute rather to fight it out, then once to be taken by the *Spaniards* to endure their accustomed crueltie.[22]

This is not rapid narration, but it is at least free from burdensome moral exposition. To conclude, we may take one example of the utterly colorless and drearily chronological style in which, by the end of our period, practically all foreign news was offered to the reader. It was introduced by the news-collectors of the Netherlands and Germany, from whose publications it was translated into English. This is precisely the style of the first English newspaper; the following example is early for England:

[22] *The Valiant . . . fight . . . by the Centurion*, as above, p. 133.

As for the Countrie of Prouence, the Lord of Vins holdeth for the Court of Parliament, and so for those for the League. The Lord de la Valette, who holdeth for the King, is verie strong, and hath the greatest part of the said Countrie and of the fortresses there. Hee caused an assemblie of the states to bee holden lately, where it was agreed, that they shoulde take armes, and warre against the said court of Parliament, & the Lord de Vins: and for that purpose they deliuered 10000. French crownes to the Lord de la Valette.

The Lord de Mont-brun confederate to the sayde Lorde de la Valette hath of late surprised two verie strong fortes in the said Countrie. Monsieur de Diguieres so soone as he shall haue confirmed the truce in this Countrie, shall bring downe the whole campe into Prouence.

My Ladie de Mont-morencie in the beginning of this moneth passed ouer the territories of this Citie to go to the Court, and Monsieur des Diguieres brought her two miles onward of her waie.

Of late we had here the Declaration in print that the towne of Lions hath made, how it reserueth and holdeth it selfe towards and against all, vnder the name & authoritie of the King.

My Lady the Princesse of Lorraine came downe this way vpon the riuer of Rosne, accompanied with fiftie Barges, and kept her Easter at Auignon, from whence she is departed this present daie to embarke her selfe at Marseille with foure galleies, which stay there waiting for her, to conduct her to the Duke of Florence with whom she shall now bee married. Monsieur de Montmorency staied for her 15. daies at Beauquaire, but was forced to depart before her cõming without seing her, for that he was sent for away to Narbona, whither he is gone frõ Orenge in al hast. This 24. of March, 1589.[23]

[23] *Newes sent to the Ladie Princesse of Orenge.* Translated from the French by I. E. Iohn VVolfe, 1589.

CHAPTER X

NEWS-WRITERS

MOST of the news published during our period appeared without an author's name, but from the exceptions to this rule and from the helpful custom of introducing books, both acknowledged and anonymous, with dedications and addresses to the reader, we can glean sufficient information to come to certain general conclusions with regard to the authorship of the pieces of news we have been reviewing.

As far as some of them are concerned, there is not the slightest difficulty in discovering why they were written and by whom. The origin and authorship of what we have dubbed personal news, of the information put in print by the government and by the spokesmen of sects and parties, and of the news set forth by aggrieved private persons in their own justification—all this is self-evident. For the rest, we shall have to look a little farther.

1. BALLAD-WRITERS

The ballad-writers should probably be regarded as a class apart, though they are by no means all of the same stamp. Some of them, such as Elderton and Deloney, we can almost call professionals. They were professionals in the sense that they regularly and frequently composed ballads, undoubtedly had the tricks of the trade at their command, and enjoyed a public reputation as ballad-writers. They were not professionals in the sense that they supported themselves by writing ballads, though perhaps they would have had the trade been sufficiently remunerative, and there can be no doubt that they wrote for pay, however meagre. It was men such as these who wrote most of the ballads on the more important kinds of public events—battles, executions of traitors, coronations—and such staples of the trade as "good-nights;" but, on the whole, there is scarcely a subject which they did not take up on occasion.

A great many ballads were doubtless written by amateur or semi-professional versifiers in the lower ranks of society. Some of them were drawn to the task by a slender talent for numbers and a more abundant ambition, or energy. Others were attracted by the subject rather than by the art; the ballad to them was a means of reaching the public. In the first group we should probably count the meanest panegyrists and the more artless commentators on public events of all sorts. To the second belong the moralists, the authors of ballads on miracles, prodigies, monstrous births, Catholic iniquities, and the like. Many of them were clergymen who would make even the ballad a thing of moral beauty; in expressing themselves in the ballad form, they were simply falling in with the mode, or making a grudging concession to it, while they kept their eye steadfastly on their main purpose, the improvement of the sons of Adam. Many ballads not written by clergymen or volunteer moralists were likewise tainted with morality, or at least with self-righteousness, for the moral flavor was as conventional in the sixteenth century as the unpractised orator's "Unaccustomed as I am to public speaking" or the preliminary formula of the writer of letters to the newspapers, "My attention has been called to an article in your journal," and sweetens ballads from authors of all kinds. Complementary to the clergyman-ballad-writers are the assiduous patriots who could not restrain themselves in the presence of a gracious public act of the queen's, a triumph of English valor, or a notable overthrow of the enemies of

[223]

the realm, and put their enthusiasm or their indignation into a proper new ballad.

The question arises also whether ballads were written to order, and, if so, by whom. Undoubtedly they were. The most certain instance that can be cited is a ballad on an apparition in the heavens in Germany, let us say. The news of this marvel reached England, we will assume, in the shape of a German book of news which fell into the hands of a London bookseller. Well aware of the taste for this sort of information, he prepared to put it on the market by having it translated. At the same time he was sensible of the opportunity for putting out a ballad on the same subject; indeed, he knew that if he didn't do so, somebody else might. He therefore took steps to prepare a ballad to go out into the world as a supplement to his book, as the numerous simultaneous entries of book and ballad clearly show. Where did he get his ballad? We cannot suppose for a moment that it was always procured in the same way, and there are at least half-a-dozen different kinds of ballad-writer by whom he may have had it composed. He may have written it himself; he may have had a journeyman or an apprentice in his shop with a knack of versifying; he may have employed the translator to furnish both the prose narrative and the ballad; he may have applied to a gifted friend—very possibly, in such a case as we have assumed, a poetically-inclined student of divinity or a holy clerk with the requisite enthusiasm for supernatural manifestations; he certainly numbered among his acquaintances a dozen or more ballad-authors whose compositions he had previously published and who would gladly rise to this new subject; and of course there were probably a number of needy hacks, journeymen of belles-lettres, notorious to all members of the publishing trade and at anybody's service for an extremely modest fee.

These ballad-writers, as a class, remain somewhat apart

[224]

from the authors of the prose news we have to deal with. Very likely some men worked in both groups, but most of them were probably attracted into one to the exclusion of the other. They not only used distinct techniques, but their minds, I fancy, also worked in somewhat different ways. Even the authors of edifying ballads on marvelous examples and the authors of the corresponding prose reports were, as a rule, not the same person, even though their ethical and theological points of view were much the same and even though I believe many of both kinds were of the clergy. Those who chose the ballad as the form of their meditations on such a theme must have been men of a more ingenious and fanciful turn of mind, with a taste— possibly a guilty and secret taste—for poetry (by your leave) and music; but the authors of prose homilies were born dialecticians and casuists, grim dogs who abhorred any compromise with worldly vanities. A similar difference can be detected, I think, between the authors of patriotic ballads and of patriotic news in prose. The former are distinguished by the same penchant for happy conceits and pleasant turns of thought; the latter are more literal-minded creatures, sober and legalistic, though their matter and motive are roughly the same. The authors of ballads on other subjects, however moral the burden of their song and however meagre their talent for pleasing, seldom forgot altogether that part of their business was to please; the prose-writers, as a rule, put their minds on exhorting or informing.

2. PROFESSIONAL AND QUASI-PROFESSIONAL NEWS-WRITERS

The nearest approach to the modern working journalist is to be found in the translators who worked for the publishers of our period. It seems possible that in translation a man could have found work steadily enough to make it his trade and presumably to live by it, or at least to make it a very important side-line. We know, for example, that Raphael Holinshed was regularly employed by the publisher Reginald Wolf as translator and editor, as was Foxe the martyrologist by John Day, and Gabriel Harvey, Barnaby Barnes, and Thomas Nash seem also to have had a similar connection with printers. In large publishing houses there may have been a member of the staff whose duties were editorial, including translation. It is even more likely, since most of the publishers of news were not the wealthier members of the craft, that certain men, known to the trade as proficient in languages, were employed by different publishers as the need arose. So many translations, some of them books of news, bear the names of Arthur Golding, Edward Grimestone, and Edward Aggas that, if we make an allowance for books they may have translated without acknowledgment and for books which have since been lost, we may suppose that they were almost continuously employed in this work. They are the only persons connected with the publishing of news on the side of authorship of whom we can safely assume that they may have earned a livelihood by their work.

Yet it is very likely that some of the anonymous books of news which we have reviewed were composed by hack-authors for pay. We know that needy scribblers existed in the Grub Street of those days and that they had no more scruples about the subjects on which they employed their pens than the hacks of any other era. The opportunities in news-writing, ballads excepted, were probably not very great, but such as they were they were doubtless welcome in proportion to the return foreseen. Surely men of as ready a wit as they would not have failed to see an opportunity for their pens in a royal entry into the city, the execution of a notable traitor, or a natural catastrophe coming within the range of their knowledge or observation.

[226]

Except for what we must attribute to moralists and patriots, men of this sort possibly wrote a large part of all the domestic news. Even what they had no personal knowledge of, such as floods, fires, and trials in the provinces, they could have written up from reports and letters or even from common rumor.

As far as a few of them are concerned, we have no doubt that they occasionally employed themselves in this kind of work: news written by Munday, Chettle, Thomas Brewer, Thomas Kyd, Thomas Middleton, Anthony Nixon, the younger Peacham, Dekker, for example, is perfectly well known, and makes us suspect that still more was produced by them and other literary Jacks-of-all-trades of their kind. Munday was possibly the most adaptable of those named: his prodigious efforts as reporter-extraordinary of the capture, trial, and execution of Father Campion and his lord mayor's pageants have already been mentioned; he has also been credited with *The Admirable Deliuerance of 266. Christians by Iohn Reynard Englishman from the captiuitie of the Turkes*,[1] and the translation of the story of a prolonged fast, *A True and admirable Historie, of a Mayden of Confolens*,[2] and of a book relating the marvelous history of Dom Sebastien, king of Portugal.[3] A somewhat different sort of journalist, and an earlier, was Thomas Churchyard, Gent., but nearly all his writings are topical or occasional. "My waking goodwil to the world," he says in the preface to his *Scourge for Rebels*,[4] "first, for the pleasuring of friends, and generally to please the multitude, keepes my pen alwaies occupied in suche matter as the time bringeth forth." Probably this is not a complete confession; we can hardly doubt

---

[1] Thomas Dawson, 1608.

[2] Iames Roberts, 1603.

[3] *The strangest aduenture that euer happened*, as above, p. 187.

[4] For Thomas Cadman, 1584.

that Churchyard hoped to make money by his writing. Most of the occurrences he wrote about either he or his friends had taken part in, but on one occasion he explains that he had got his information from two letters which he had seen at court.[5] It was not because they were unprepared for the work or because opportunities were lacking that hack-writers composed so little of all the news published; it was because the pay was smaller than in other branches of their trade.

Furthermore, besides paid writers outside the publishing trade, there may have been those inside it who took some part in the writing of the news. We have little evidence that the news which came to them was prepared by the publishers themselves, but we can say at least that they may have prepared it. A number of the printers and booksellers of our period are known to have had a hand in the writing, translating, or collecting of one or more books— Caxton, John Gough, Walter Smith, Robert Copland, Richard Grafton, John Awdely, Stephen Peele, Nicholas Bourman, Thomas Hacket, William Seres, Nicholas Ling, Henry Haslop, Edward Aggas, Thomas Nelson, Richard Serger, Henry Roberts, Thomas East, Richard Day, William Barley, Edward Blount. It would seem that sixteenth century publishers were, as a rule, men of some education, or even taste, and though most of the news was published by the meaner brethren of the mystery, the writing of it would never have demanded of them any but the lowest degree of literary skill. Besides, they may have had in their shops journeymen or apprentices with a command of the pen who could have done the more elementary kinds of literary work. Anthony Munday and Henry Chettle were both apprenticed to stationers in their youth; it was in the printing office that they felt the liter-

[5] *A plaine or moste true report of a daungerous seruice* . . . *for the takyng of Macklin.* . . . Ihon Perin, 1580.

[228]

ary vocation, and they may have done a little writing for their masters before they left the trade. It is a safe guess that there were other journeymen and apprentices in publishing offices who could do literary work of the more modest sort, including the translating and making up of books of news.

The publisher was probably more likely to collect, arrange, revise, and edit copy than to write a complete news-report *de novo*, and we should therefore assume that it was this kind of editorial work rather than original writing to which whatever talent there may have been in his shop was usually applied. It is not uncommon to find an address by the publisher to the reader, implying that the publication thus introduced was brought into being without the author's participation. Pirated editions, some translations, reissues, and books patched up from material of various origin were brought to the press in this way. Books of news were often fabricated out of miscellaneous matter. Suppose a document—the decree of a foreign king, or the confession *in extremis* of a condemned criminal —came into the publisher's hands and suppose it needed an introduction or brief recital of the circumstances as a setting. Why may not the publisher and his staff have sometimes provided this matter? It is equally likely that when he put several pieces together in a single book— translations, documents, reprints, and/or fresh material—, as was a not uncommon practice, or when he received advices in the form of private letters, narratives ill-digested or composed by awkward hands, he again performed the necessary editorial labors of cutting, piecing, correcting, and synthesizing himself. Even the small publisher would not always turn over to the compositor a piece of copy just as he received it, no matter how; sometimes he must surely have exercised his own wits to make the book he proposed to issue more attractive.

We have even a little direct evidence of this kind of editorial supervision. In 1588, during the excitement over the Armada, John Wolf printed in a book called *The Holy Bull, And Crusado of Rome* a few Latin verses which had appeared in a German book with Spanish sympathies printed at Cologne. With them he printed a number of "answers," also in Latin verse. This same matter was also printed (with slight alterations) in another book of Wolf's, *A true Discourse of the Armie which the King of Spaine caused to bee assembled*, where he must have inserted it because he felt it was pertinent and useful to round out the book's contents. An instance of a publisher's postponing to a second edition a diagram which the author had prepared for the first, "ob illiberalem chartæ, & turpe priuatum commodum," has recently been pointed out.[6] Perhaps the curious fact that almost precisely the same words of pious instruction appear in two broadsides describing monstrous pigs, published by different stationers within a year of each other, may be explained by supposing that the second publisher, finding himself in want of something to give his broadside the proper moral tone, appropriated the exhortation from his rival's. Robert Barker, in the preface to *His maiesties speach in this last Session of Parliament* (1605), says:

Hauing receiued (gentle reader) the copie of the Kings last Speach to the Parliament as neere to the life of his owne wordes, as they could bee gathered; And being about to commit them to the Presse, as I did his former, There is presently comen to my handes a discourse of this late intended most abhominable Treason against his Maiestie and the whole State. And because that a great part of his Maiesties Speach was grounded vpon that fearefull accident, whereof this Discourse doth make an ample declaration; I haue thought it would not bee vnpleasing vnto thee to ioyne them together in the Presse.

[6] F. S. Ferguson: *Times Literary Supplement*, 7 June 1928, p. 430.

As the discourse came to him from an official source (and perhaps the copy of the speech as well, despite his implying something else), he printed it just as he received it, but his editorial hand can probably be traced in other places besides the preface. The marginal notes may be his, for one thing, and at signature H4^v, at the end of Fawkes's signed confession, the following explanation is certainly his:

And in regard that before this discourse could be readie to goe to the Presse, *Thomas Winter*[,] being apprehended, and brought to the Tower, made a confession in substance agreeing with this former of *Fawkes*, onely larger in some circumstances: I haue thought good to insert the same likewise in this place, for the further cleering of the matter, and greater benefit of the Reader.

After this interpolated confession, the author of the discourse resumes with "But here let vs leaue *Fawkes* in a lodging fit for such a guest," and goes on to relate the events leading up to the trapping of Catesby, Percy, and Winter. This discourse, then, must have been written after Winter's capture but before his examination in the Tower, when he made the confession which Barker, as it seems, inserted where he thought it most appropriate while the book was going through the press.

On signature Aiij. of *Certaine aduertisements out of Ireland, concerning the losses . . . to the Spanish Nauie* we read:

After this vvas printed thus farre, as euery day bringeth more certaintie in particulars of the losse of the Spaniardes in Irelande, these reportes vvhich follovve came from Ireland, being the examinations of seuerall persons there taken and saued.

It is undoubtedly the printer who speaks thus, and why may he not have done whatever cutting, pasting, and rewriting was necessary, little as it probably was, to graft the new information, in the form of depositions, on the old? In the spring of 1608 Nathaniel Butter published a book of *Newes From Lough-foyle in Ireland*, an account of an out-

[231]

break of violence on the part of Sir Cahir O'Dogherty, the rebel. Some time later in the same year he published an amplified edition of this book entitled *Newes From Ireland . . . Newly imprinted and inlarged by further instructions.* This contains all of the older book except the last paragraph, and six or seven pages of new matter which,with the exception of a new concluding paragraph, is inserted in the latter part of the old text by a not too dexterous surgical operation. Whatever the origin of the first version, it is entirely possible that the enlarging of it was done by the publisher himself or by one of his assistants. Such a title as *A Briefe discourse of the merueylous victorie gotten by the King of Nauarre, against those of the holy League, . . . Whereunto is added as soone as it came to my hand since the first Impression, The true copie of a Letter sent by the King of Nauarre to his Secretary . . .*[7] suggests the publisher's acting as his own editor. Near the end of *The copie of a letter sent out of England to don Bernardin Mendoza*[7a] we find the following paragraph (signature F):

The Printer to the Reader.

Although it be well known, that neither the first writer of these Letters nowe by me printed, nor yet the Spaniard *Don Bernardin* to whome they are directed, had any desire to heare of any good successe to the state of England: as may appeare . . . in *Don Bernardin,* who was so impudent, or at least, so blindly rash, as to disperse in print, both in French, Italian, and Spanish, most false reports of a victorie had by the Spaniards . . . : yet whilest I was occupied in the printing hereof,a good time after the letters were sent into Fraunce, there came to this Citie certaine knowledge, to all our great comfort, of sundrie happie Accidents, to the diminution of our mortall enemies in their famous Fleete, that was driuen out of our seas about the last of Iuly . . . Wherfore I haue thought it not amisse to ioine the same to this Lettre of *Don Bernardin,* that he may beware, not to be so hastie of himselfe, nor yet to permit one *Capella,* who is his common sewer of reports, to write these false things for truthes.
The particularities wherof are these.

[7] Iohn Wolfe, 1587.
[7a] For Richard Field, 1588.

Then, without any space or change of type or printer's style, begin two and a half pages of reports from Scotland and Ireland. It seems almost certain that they were written by the same hand as the paragraph quoted.

If we are correct in supposing that the editorial hand of the publisher can be traced in the examples just cited, we still have hardly convicted him of playing a large part in the shaping of the news to the form in which it was printed, but we have established a probability that he did play some part. Furthermore, there can be little doubt that the arrangement, and wording of title-pages and the insertion of marginal topic-headings and linear sub-heads in books of news was, as a rule, of the publisher's doing, with the conventions of make-up to guide him. The title-pages were often extremely verbose, of course, and sometimes the sub-headings were copious and elaborate too. The following, *e.g.*, all printed in a book of fourteen leaves, suggest the sub-heads in a modern newspaper:

Certaine strange Accidents, happening by the late terrible Tempests of winde and weather.

There is yet a meanes to be made for reconcilement.

Seauen, or eight hundreth dead Carkases, some floating on the seas, betweene the coasts of Calice, & Newport in Flanders by occasion of late Tempests.

Many cast away euen before the towne of Yarmouth.

Many cast away neere the coast of Douer and Sandwich, and Way-borne Hope in Norfolke.

A Ship cast away comming from New-castle, and all the Passengers in it but the Maister.

A woman and a child taken vp drowned, with the womans nipple in the childs mouth.

Certaine hurts done at Great Chart in Kent, the Sunday after Christmas-day last, by the Tempest of Windes.

A prayer.[8]

[8] *The VVindie Yeare.* . . . For Arthur Iohnson, 1612.

[233]

Another kind of editorial or auctorial work which may sometimes have been done by the publisher and his staff is the writing up of notes and oral reports. There is no doubt that some news was taken out of the mouths of witnesses (possibly of others too, such as travelers who were merely telling what they had heard) willing to narrate their experiences, but unwilling or unable to write them out. News of fights at sea was sometimes gathered from returned sailors, and there is no reason why many other kinds of news could not have been carried to London in somebody's memory and there unloaded orally, and every probability that it was. Possibly most news from the provinces, of fires, floods, and such marvels as the whole countryside would be talking about, and even of murders, trials for witchcraft, and captures of highwaymen, was brought to London by travelers, and freely disgorged in taverns and at meeting places such as the Exchange and Paul's walk. The latter, the grand clearing-house of gossip and news of all sorts, was at the booksellers' very elbows; keeping shop there all day long, they must have been the best-informed men in England, willy nilly, and whether or not they were interested in publishing news. They would not only have been among the first to hear the latest rumors and reports, but they would also, with little trouble to themselves, have had many opportunities to listen to the accounts of visitors with news engraved on the tablets of their minds. Indeed, given this situation, it is hard to believe that something did not go on at the great meeting place of St. Paul's much like the work of a modern reporter covering a street accident (let us say), questioning witnesses and participants, comparing their stories, and constructing his own out of them. This sort of thing need not necessarily have been done by the publisher himself; a hack hungry for a subject or an amateur moralist impressed by the portentousness of the latest reports could

[234]

have done it too: but it is the kind of thing the publisher may occasionally have done. There is one book which was confessedly taken down from the recital of a traveler— *Strange and wonderfull things happened to Richard Hasleton . . . in his ten yeares trauailes in many forraine countries. Penned as he deliuered it from his own mouth.*[9] Unless we may assume that this hardy adventurer's mouth flowed with sanctimonious comment as well as "strange and wonderfull things," we must discount the implication of the title-page that the narrative was printed exactly as he related it.

All told, the part played by the publisher and his staff in the writing of news remains doubtful. The possibilities are large, but the evidence of actual authorship is much less. Though there is no reason why the publisher could not often have written his own news, and some probability that on occasion he did, from the evidence at hand we can conclude only that his part was chiefly editorial and supervisory, though that not infrequently was considerable.

3. Misrepresentation as an Incitement to the Reporting of News

To turn now from the part played in the writing of news by the only persons connected with the matter who can in any sense be called professionals to the much greater part played by amateurs, or at least non-professionals, we can reduce their motives in writing news, as explained by themselves, to just two. The first was to correct ill-founded rumors and maliciously false reports; the second was to delight and to benefit the reader.

Of these, the former is by all odds the more common. It would be a tedious task to enumerate all the books of news of our period which advertise themselves as correctives of

---

[9] For William Barley, 1595.

falsehoods; such a list would include many more than half of all the books which assert any motive at all. "I haue taken in hand this short discourse," says one, a narrative of the execution of two Catholic recusants, "cheefly to beat downe the vntrue reports of their fauourers and fellowe Traitours who secretly murmure that their death was only for Conscience sake."[10] "I haue thought it good," says another, an account of the assassination of William the Silent, "breefely and plainely to set downe the true circumstaunce thereof: and that for one speciall cause, which is, that considering the vntrue imaginations and fayned reportes, of this Princes death, now blased abroade . . . .: the trueth being layd open, and made manifest to all men, that then those reportes may be accounted fryuolous, and to be troden vnder foote."[11] The printer of an account of the coronation of Henry IV of France peremptorily admonishes the reader as follows:

Whatsoeuer other discourses of this argument that may peraduenture come to thy handes are false, counterfait, and rashly published, but this is true, perfect and written at leysure, with all order requisite. Thus much I thought good to giue thee to vnderstand, least otherwise, where thou seekest for trueth, thou mightest be abused with falsehood.[12]

The charge that false news is being spread confronts us so often, the correctives of it are so confident that it is inspired by disaffection, malice, and unscrupulousness, that we sometimes wonder whether anybody can be trusted. Without holding any brief whatever for the news-writers of our period, we may still suspect that in these accusations

---

[10] *The Life and end of Thomas Awfeeld . . . and Thomas Webley . . .* For Thomas Nelson, [1585].

[11] *The true report of the lamentable death, of VVilliam of Nassawe . . .* Middleborowgh: Derick van Respeawe, 1584.

[12] *The Order of Ceremonies obserued in the annointing and Coronation of . . . Henry the IIII. . . . .* Translated from the French by E[dward] A[ggas]. Sold by Iohn Flasket, [1594].

of willful lying so airily bandied about there must certainly have been a good deal of exaggeration. It was, like most others, a partial age, in which few minds were able to see the shades of gray between coal black and dead white. Everybody who did not enthusiastically believe that Queen Elizabeth was Gloriana, the compendium of all the womanly and royal virtues, could be nothing else but a perfidious intriguing traitor ready to encompass her assassination and to deliver the realm into the hands of the pope. It seems to have been not only common but usual and expected for the combatants in the political and theological arena to array themselves against each other in print and to challenge the adversary's account of what was happening round about them at the very moment. That the Protestants in France, for example, and their sympathizers abroad, should publish reports of the massacre of St. Bartholomew and that the Catholics should immediately answer them with narratives in which the same events take on a strangely altered complexion was surprising to no one, though it must have been confusing to the more simple-minded. "Bokes are extant on both parts," says, with just a trace of bewilderment, the translator of a report of these same occurrences, itself a bitter Protestant frontal attack. ". . . You must take it [the present book] as it is, onely for matter of reporte on the one parte, so farre to bind credit as it carieth euidence to furnish your vnderstandings."[13] A man of a different stamp was blunt Sir Thomas Baskerville, the English military leader, whose instinctive response to the aspersions cast upon him by a news-report of the enemy's is sufficiently explained by the title of the printed English counter check quarrelsome: *A libell of Spanish Lies: found at the Sacke of Cales, discoursing the fight in the West Indies*

[13] *A true and plaine report of the Furious outrages of Fraunce* . . . , as above, p. 179.

. . . and of the death of Sir Francis Drake. With an answere . . . by Henrie Sauile . . . And also an Approbation of this discourse, by Sir Thomas Baskeruile, then Generall of the English fleete . . .: Auowing the maintenance thereof, personally in Armes against Don Bernaldino, if he shall take exception to that which is heere set downe . . .[14] In the same way, Sir Robert Mansel, another naval commander, was moved to proclaim in print his willingness to defend his own version of the truth with his sword. Having served in an allied squadron of English and Dutch ships against the Spaniards, and finding that the reports of the engagement denied him the credit that was his due, he wrote an account of the exploit himself, published it, and dedicated it to the lord admiral in the following terms:

The sense which hereof I haue in the inwardest retraite of my soule, is the cause I haue thought my dutie both to you, and to the State not a little interessed, in a report very vulgar in many mens mouthes in the Citie, and by this time perhaps spred ouer the Realme. And confirmed by a Pamphlet printed, contayning a narration of the late seruice done vpon the Gallies: wherein no mention being made, neither of my selfe, nor of any of her Maiesties Shippes, nor of our nation, wee are all secretly touched with some note, either of negligence of the things committed to vs, (I specially) or of vnskilfulnes, or of want of courage: from the staines of all which it importeth me to cleere my selfe, . . . for mine owne sake, and our nations; . . . [and] for your Lordship.[15]

In short, the militant atmosphere of the books of news written by volunteer reporters and self-appointed guardians of the honor of their country and their faith, each of whom represents himself as an angel of light doing battle against the minions of darkness, is a reflection—exaggerated though we must certainly think it to be—of the spirit of

---

[14] Iohn Windet, 1596.

[15] *A true report of the seruice done vpon certaine Gallies passing through the Narrow Seas* . . . Sold by Iohn Newbery, 1602.

the times, of their disposition to take *au grand sérieux* differences of faith and opinion which, for better or for worse, we are less likely to maintain so intransigeantly to-day, of their more passionate attachment to allegiances in which our faith has been a little unsettled, of their pride, their ardor, their unquestioning devotion, and all those gallant sentiments of the heart which have since been somewhat disintegrated by the more inquiring spirit of these latter days.

There is no doubt, however, that before the end of our period this incessant contradiction of one news-report by the other had bred a rather general distrust of all "reports of truth" in print. This skepticism applied more particularly to the more preposterous kinds of news, such as miracles and supernatural wonders. "Beleeuing Reader," says the author of *Somewhat: vvritten by occasion of three sunnes seene at Tregnie:*[16] "You are saluted, by (I thinke) you know not whom: I would be sorrie you should: for a beggerly generation of mercenarie liers haue drawen an ineuitable suspition vpon the reporters of all truths in this kind." The author of *True and wonderfull*, the story of the Sussex dragon, as gross an imposture as cynicism or credulity ever practised, refers to the same suspicion in a more philosophical vein:

The iust rewarde of him that is accustomed to lie, is, not to be belieued when he speaketh the truth: so iust an occasion may sometimes bee imposed vpon the pamphleting pressers; and therefore, if we receiue the same rewarde, we cannot much blame our accusers, which often fals out either by our forward credulity to but-seeming true reports, or by false coppies translated from other languages, which (though we beget not) we foster, and our shame is little the lesse. But, passing by what's past, let not our present truth blush for any former falshood sake: the countrie is near vs, Sussex; the time present, August; the subiect, a Serpent; strange, yet now a neighbour to vs; and it were more than impudence to forge a lie so near home, that

16 As above, p. 146.

euery man might turn in our throates; belieue it, or reade it not, or reade it (doubting) for I belieue ere thou hast read this little all, thou wilt not doubt of one, but belieue there are many serpents in England.

But the authors of books of news of perfectly credible occurrences echo the same complaint, as, *e.g.*, the author or editor of *Lamentable newes out of Monmouthshire*, a report of floods,[17] who speaks of "the vsual vnfaithfullnes of men ordinarily in reporting of such accidents as these bee: whereby it often falleth out, that the relater of them reapeth much discredit." The stubbornness of doubting Thomases was responsible for the manifest anxiety of the authors of news-reports to furnish evidence conducive to belief. They are very particular to explain how well informed they are; they allude to gentlemen of worship and credit who know all they tell of to be true, just as one of Autolycus's ballads had "five justices' hands at it;" they bolster up their narratives with official-sounding documents, with affidavits, and with lists of witnesses—the more unlikely the news, the longer the list of witnesses ready to take their oath it is true. This skepticism seems to have infected even the worshipful Company of Stationers, for it is recorded that on 30 June 1593, when Thomas Newman and John Wynnyngton entered for their copy a report of a trial of witches in Huntingdonshire, the story was "Recommended for matter of truthe by master Judge Fenner vnder his handwrytinge shewed in a Court or assemblie holden this Daye," and the clerk providently added, "The note vnder master Justice Fenners hand is Layd vp in the wardens cupbord."[18]

We must also note that these allegations of error in other reports, if we take them at face value, imply a larger supply of printed news than we should assume on any other grounds. The adversary is always legion: "the

---

[17] As above, p. 206.
[18] Arber, II. 633.

manifold vntruths which are spred abroad," "many false copies," "many trifling Pamphlets" are typical of the phraseology nearly always used. We have a number of reasons for thinking more news was printed during our period than we now know of, and we have more explicit testimony than such statements as those just quoted. "The Bookebinders shops, and euery Printers presse are so cloyed and clogged with Bookes of these and such-like matters [i.e. "louing Songs, and amiable Sonnets," "famous mens actes done long agoe," and "things hapned in our dayes"], that they are good for nothing (as they say) but to make wastpaper," is one poetaster's complaint.[19]   On 29 December 1569 Henry Radeclyffe wrote to his brother, the Earl of Sussex, from London, "We haue euery daye seuerall newes, and sometyme contraryes, and yet all put out as true."[20] The translator of an account of a conversion to Protestantism in France, in 1616, remarked on this point as follows:

Many small Treatise and Pamphlets (that were daily thronged as it were to the Presse) doe giue hereof [i.e. of the troubles in France] a sufficient testimonie: so that wee might in a manner say (as it is in the first chapter of *Iob* often repeated) *Whiles hee was yet speaking, another came, and said*, &c.   While one booke of bad newes was yet a printing, another came and brought vs worse newes.[21]

But in spite of all such testimony, and of the natural willingness of a historian of journalism to make it out a more sumptuous banquet than anybody has ever supposed, we cannot accept the impression of as wide a dispersal of news in print as is given by these not too carefully calculated statements made in the heat of controversy.   The same excess of ardor which drove the authors of defensive news-reports to picture all their adversaries as limbs of Satan led them to multiply these limbs and their works

[19] *Elizabetha triumphans*, as above, p. 128.

[20] Wright: *Queen Elizabeth and her Times*, I. 346.

[21] *Newes from France: containing tvvo declarations of two new converts* . . . , as above, p. 187.

to a number never before imagined except by the demiurge who shaped the centipede.

4. NEWS-WRITING *CON AMORE*

But our volunteer reporters were not all stung to taking on them the task of writing news merely by the slanders and lies circulated, or about to be circulated, by the children of darkness. There are others who profess to have been drawn by a delight in the news they had possessed themselves of and an amiable desire to share it with others. Thus they resemble more closely the modern journalist, who, if he has any other interest in the news he collects and writes out than as potential bread and butter, views it as the making of a good story, as matter which will titillate the reader's curiosity. One says, "This haue I done both for thy comfort and information;"[22] another, "for that the thyng is so rare & notable that it shoulde not be kept from the posteritye;"[23] another, "because I know certaynly, that not a few, for their better satisfaction, are very desirous to vnderstand the truth thereof."[24] Sometimes the author alleges both this benevolent motive and the desire to correct false reports, as did John Proctor, the author of *The historie of Wyates rebellion:*[25]

> It hath been alowed . . . for a necessary policie in all ages . . . that the flagicious enterprises of the wicked . . . shuld by writing be committed to eternal memorye: partly that they of that age in whose tyme such thinges happened, mought . . . [behold] frõ what calamitie and extreme ruine, by what policie & wisedome their

[22] *A true report of the inditement . . . and Execution of Iohn VVeldon, William Hartley, and Robert Sutton. . . .* Richard Iones, 1588.

[23] *The Copy of a Letter Describing the wonderful woorke of God in deliuering a mayden . . . from an horrible kinde of torment and sicknes. . . .* By Iohn Fisher. Iohn Awdely, 23 March 1564.

[24] *The Late Commotion of certaine Papists in Herefordshire. . . .* For I[effry] Charlton & F[rancis] Burton, 1605.

[25] Robert Caly, 22 December 1554.

natiue coūtries were deliuered . . . : partly for a doctrine and a monition seruing bothe for the present & future tyme.

He goes on to explain that at first he had no intention of publishing his history.

But [he says] hearing the sundry tales thereof farre dissonaūt in the vtteraunce, & many of them as far wide frō truth, facioned from the speakers to aduaunce, or depraue as they fantased the parties: and vnderstādyng besides what notable infamie spronge of this rebelliō to the whole countre of Kent, & to euery mēbre of yᵉ same, where sundrie & many of them to mine owne knowledge shewed themselues most faythfull & worthy subiectes, . . . which either of hast or of purpose were omitted in a printed booke late sette furthe at Cāterbury: I thought these to be speciall cōsideratiōs, whereby I ought of duetie to my countrey to compyle and digest suche notes as I had gathered . . . and to publishe the same in this age and at this present, contrary to my first intent.

Some of these news-writers approach the self-appointed task with expansive enthusiasm. One says:

Albeit out of mine owne disposition . . . I haue beene euer a moste vnwilling Newes-sender: . . . from . . . this so strange though long wisht for, & most happy meeting of our King and his dearest brother, the King of *Denmark*, I was stirred vp to write you such particulars as eyther my selfe perticularly noted, or else I receiued from others, which were eye witnesses.[26]

And Daniel Powell, in recording the celebration held at Ludlow in honor of the creation of Prince Charles, can scarcely contain himself:

Myselfe (being not altogether an idle Actor, nor unwilling Spectator) was so rauished with the fullnesse of ioy, which I saw in the hearts of the people, as I wished my selfe then to bee transformed into the shape of the sweete Nightingale . . . that . . . I might eccho out to the eares of all men, the loyall affection of the British Nation to their Royall Prince.[27]

[26] *The king of Denmarkes vvelcome* . . . Edward Allde, 1606.
[27] *The loue of VVales to their soueraigne Prince* . . . Nicholas Okes, 1616.

Henry Goldwell justifies his publishing an account of the entertainment offered the French ambassadors in 1581 as an attempt to save a notable performance from oblivion:

Yet I considered vvith my selfe, better an ill reporter than a dumme speaker, better badly laid open then quite forgotten, & better Porredge then no repast? . . . Therfore sith no mā vvriteth at al of these vvorthies, nor no persō publisheth the exploits of these nobles, rather thē obliuion should diminish their merits, I haue attēpted the vvriting. And so nere as I could I haue made a collection both of their names, speaches, and the chiefest inuentions, vvhich as they bee, I present to your presence in name of a nevvse or noueltie.[28]

In William Patten's *Expedicion into Scotlāde of the . . . Duke of Somerset,*[29] we find an early allusion to the craving for news, which is what moved him to publish his history:

I more then half assure me, that (euen as I would be in case like my selfe) so is euery man desyrous too know of the maner and circū-staunces of thys our most valiāt victorie ouer our enemies, and pros-perous successe of the rest of our iourney. The bolder am I to make this general iudgement, partly, for that I am sumwhat by learning, but more by nature instruct[ed] to vnderstonde, yᵉ thursty desyer, that all our kynde hath to knowe. And then for that in euery cōpany, and at euery table (whear it hath bene my hap to be since my cum-mynge home) the hole communicaciō was in a manner nought els, but of this expedicion and warres in Scotland.

Even Samuel Daniel, though as a courtier he disdains the vulgarity of print, not over-graciously concedes to the curiosity of the public:

For so much as shewes and spectacles of this nature, are vsually registred, among the memorable acts of the time, . . . it is expected (according now of the custome) that I, beeing imployed in the busines, should publish a discription and forme of the late Mask . . . in regard to preserue the memorie thereof, and to satisfie their desires, who could haue no other notice, but by others report of what was done.[30]

[28] *A briefe declaratiō of the shews . . . performed before the Queenes Maiestie, & the French Ambassadours . . .* Robert VValdegraue, [1581].

[29] As above, p. 121.

[30] *The Order and Solemnitie of the Creation of . . . Prince Henrie. . . .* For Iohn Budge, 1610.

[244]

A peculiarly interesting testimony comes from the author of a narrative of the escape of four English sailors from the Turks by recapturing their ship and overpowering thirteen of the enemy:

Had *Iohn Cooke* beene some Collonell, Captaine, or Commander, or *William Ling*, some nauigating Lord, or *Dauid Iones* some gentleman of land and riches, or had *Robert Tuckey* beene one of fortunes minions, to haue had more money then wit, or more wealth then valour, oh what a triumphing had heere beene then, what rare Muses would haue toyld like Mules, to haue gallopt with their flattering encomiums, beyond the 32. points of the compasse, whilst these 4 rich caskets of homespun valour and courage, haue no pen to publish their deserued commendations, no inuention to emblazon their saltwater honour, but the poore lines and labours of a freshwater Poet.[31]

From such testimony it is evident that, even in an age of intense partisanship, when partisan and defensive motives account for the writing of much of the news, there was nevertheless some interest in news for its own sake, some curiosity about what was going on in the world which was free from the tutelage of political and religious allegiances, and a disposition in some news-writers to record the occurrences they had knowledge of merely because they were interesting to their contemporaries and would be enlightening to future generations. This is something like the historical spirit or the aim of the chronicler who records the events which happen in his own time more or less disinterestedly, with a certain detachment from the passions which they arouse in party-men, and with a more scrupulous respect for the truth, or at least for the whole truth, than the sectarian or bigoted historiographer, the pamphleteering zealot or proselytizer is likely to observe.

5. Participants and Witnesses as News-writers

A very great deal of the news of our period was written by eye-witnesses or actors in the events described. All

---

[31] *A relation Strange and true, of a ship of Bristol named the Jacob . . . . ,* as above, p. 134.

news, at all times, unless it is mere fancy, must go back ultimately to witnesses and participants, but in many books of news we have first-hand accounts. Some of them were written on the spot and some at leisure after the heat of the day was over; some were intended from the first for publication and some were brought into print by chance, or at least through none of the author's doing. But the fact that they were composed by witnesses, even if those witnesses were not always reliable observers or if they had not the best advantages in observing what they tell us of, gives them a certain authenticity, and it also enables us to understand, in a general way, who our news-writers, including many anonymous, really were.

The fact that many of these authors were witnesses and participants is self-evident: they tell us so themselves, as has often appeared already; they write in the first person; they speak of the part they played themselves in the story. The very fact that they were present at and bore a hand in what they narrate is the thing that moved them to reduce their observations to writing, as we have just seen. News of all kinds was brought to the public view by men of this sort. We should expect accounts of public occurrences such as royal entries into the city, public shows and pageants, executions at Tyburn, natural calamities by flood and fire to come from persons on hand at the time of occurrence who saw with their own eyes. Some reports of miracles, murders, and supernatural manifestations also came from the same source. Nearly all of the military news was also the work of witnesses. The war correspondents of those days were not writing men trained in Fleet Street or Park Row, but the soldiers themselves; and the greater part of the news from the front came back to England in the form of letters to friends. Sometimes, in spite of the writer's apologies for the uncouthness of a plain soldier's style and his protestations that nevertheless

he will do his best to satisfy his worshipful friend's impor-
tunities for news of the late good success, these narratives
are so fluently written as to excite our suspicions regarding
the authenticity of the warrior-author.   But there can be
little doubt that most of them go back ultimately to the
reports of a soldier in the army employed, even if there
intervened a certain amount of editing by the importunate
friend in London, who often took upon himself the responsibility of giving these narratives to the press, by the
publisher, or by a hired hack.   We must not forget that
this was a century of men accustomed to grasping the pen
as well as the sword, men like Gascoigne, Churchyard, and
Barnaby Rich—"*tam Marti quam Mercurio*," or, from our
point of view, "*tam Mercurio quam Marti*," in spite of the ex-
cuse of the writer of one book of news that "whoso[e]uer
followeth Mars taketh little acquantance of the Muses."[32]

In such a time as our period, when men were less hurried
than now, perhaps a little more curious and studious, and
when copious records were not easily available in print,
the habit of note-taking, especially among private gentlemen for their own information and entertainment, appears
to have been much more common than it is now.   We
meet it, during the sixteenth century, in several departments of thought and activity; it appears again in the
news of the time, for some of our authors refer to notes
made on the instant as the basis of their narratives.   An
account of a private gentleman's diligence in gathering
notes is given by the printer of *A true and plaine declaration
of the horrible Treasons, practised by William Parry*:[33]

When I had taken in hande, and beganne the printing of this
treatise . . . , a gentleman of good vnderstanding and learning,
came to me, and being made acquainted by mee with the former treatise, hee saide, that hee had by conference with diuers that were at

[32] *Newes from Brest.* . . . For Thomas Millington, 1594.
[33] As above, p. 54.

the araignement of this traytor, where also he himselfe was present, collected together the whole proceeding against him, and . . . hee had gathered into a shorte Treatise most manifest proofes of the horrible treason intended by the Traytor against her Maiestie.

This narrative, printed by C. B., *i.e.*, Barker, the queen's printer, probably is not the impartial account it pretends to be, but the material may still have been collected in this way, and even if it was not, the printer, in thus disguising its origin, surely did not draw upon his fancy, but merely described what was a usual practice. The notes of these amateur historians must have been the basis of the "imperfect reports" which news-writers so often complain of. There are several news-reports in the form of a journal or diary which was probably kept by the author from day to day throughout the experience or undertaking he is relating to us.[34]   In the preface to his *Expedicion into Scotlāde*, William Patten gives the following account of the collecting of the material for his history:

It pleased my very good lord, yᵉ erle of Warwyke, Lieutenaūt of the host (who thearby had pour to make officers) too make me one of the Iudges of the Marshalsey: as Master William Cycyl,[35] now master of the Requestes, . . . was the other: whearby we both, not beynge bounde soo straightly in daies of trauel, to ordre of marche: nor oother while, but when we sat in Courte, too any great affayres, had libertie to ride, to see things that wear doon, and leysure too note occurrences yᵗ came: The which thing . . . we booth dyd . . . Mar[r]y, since my cūming home indede, his gētilnes being such as too communicate his notes with me (I haue I cōfes) bene thearby, bothe muche a certeyned in many thinges I douted.   And sumwhat remembred of yᵗ, which els I mought hap to haue forgotten.

<hr/>

[34] See, *e.g.*, 1) *Ephemeris expeditionis Norreysij et Draki in Lusitaniam.* For Thomas Woodcocke, 1589. 2) *A Iournall, wherein is truely sette downe from day to day, what was doone* . . . *in both the Armies [in France]* . . . Iohn Wolfe, 1592. 3) *A true and large discourse of the voyage of the whole fleet of* . . . *London, to the East Indies.* . . . Sold by William Aspley, 1603. 4) *Algiers voyage in a iournall* . . . By I. B[utton]. [London?] 1621. 5) *A iournall or daily register of* . . . *the Siege of Berghen-vp-Zoome* . . . ., as above, p. 177.
[35] Queen Elizabeth's Lord Burghley.

Another author relates that, happening to be present in the Star-Chamber when some unexpectedly portentous proceedings took place, "I toke notes of the seuerall matters declared by the Lord Chancelour" and other officers of state.[36] His book, published by the royal printer, may also be something of a sham, but likewise, even if the author was not the chance witness he poses as, he would not have mentioned his taking notes had there been anything implausible about it. The author of the preface to *The most wonderfull and true storie, of a certaine Witch, named Alse Gooderige*[37] says that the book "was compiled by a priuate Christian & man of trade, who being with the boy [whom she had bewitched] almost in all his fits, did both take notes at the present of all that was doone and spoken." These notes were revised for publication by a person of greater learning.

The activity of many of these witnesses in collecting and writing their news closely resembles that of the modern reporter. We have even instances of what was possibly the work of a shorthand-writer. Several royal speeches, for example, some *ante mortem* statements of condemned prisoners on the scaffold, are said to have been "taken in writing," "gathered at the instant." We have already noticed several reports of conferences between incarcerated heretics and orthodox representatives of holy church, written by the disputants themselves. There is also plain testimony such as the following, from *A Breife and true report of the Proceedings of the Earle of Leycester:*[38]

Finding yet in my hands a briefe and true relation of his *Excellencies* honorable endeuours vpon her *Maiesties* . . . charges to relieue that Towne [of Sluys] (by me euen at that time committed to writing, when these matters were in Action, and my self present both at the

[36] *A true and Summarie reporte* . . . *of the Earle of Northumberlands Treasons* . . . C[hristopher] Barker, [1585].
[37] As above, p. 158.
[38] As above, p. 101.

Consultations and *Executions:*) I haue thought it my duetie . . . to Print and publish the same.

And from *The last terrible Tempestious windes and weather:*[39]

I my selfe am sure that the most part of what I write is true on mine owne knowledge, and the rest I haue gathered by relation from many husbandles widdowes, fatherlesse sonnes, and sonles fathers and mothers.

This is precisely the *modus operandi* of a modern reporter assigned to cover a similar catastrophe. The word *reporter* itself occurs not infrequently, but of course it has no technical significance and is a simple agent-noun meaning any one who makes a report of news.

6. SECRETARIES AND RECORDERS AS NEWS-WRITERS

Most of the reports of judicial proceedings, criminal trials, and the deliberations of organized bodies were probably composed by their own secretaries and clerks. This outgrowth of their duties is so natural that it neither surprises us nor calls for explanation. Many accounts of the sinister practices of witches were printed in the form of depositions and were doubtless derived from the records of the magistrate by whom the witches were examined or the minutes of the courts by which they were tried. Such a statement as the following probably means that the author was an official connected with the court in which the trial was held who took advantage of his privity to the evidence in the case to prepare an account of the matter; it can hardly be questioned, at any rate, that he had access to the records:

The orderly processe in [the witches'] examinations . . . I dilygently obseruing and considering their trecheries to be notable: vndertooke briefly to knit vp in a fewe leaues of paper, their manifold abuses.[40]

[39] Sold by Iohn Wright, 1613.
[40] *A true and iust Recorde of the . . . Examination . . . of all the Witches, taken at S. Oses . . .* By W. W. Thomas Dawson, 1582.

We find an undoubted instance of the work of a clerk of the court in *The wonderfull discouerie of witches in . . . Lancaster . . .*[41] This book was not only written by the clerk of the sessions but at the command of the judges of the circuit. "Wee found such apparent matters against them," they say in a statement over their names printed near the beginning of the book, "that we thought it necessarie to publish them to the World." After the clerk had done his work, one of the judges reviewed it and endorsed it, according to another statement printed in the book:

After he [the clerk] had taken great paines to finish it, I tooke vpon mee to reuise and correct it, that nothing might passe but matter of Fact, apparant against them by record. It is very little he hath inserted, and that necessarie . . . The whole proceedings and Euidence against them, I finde vpon examination carefully set forth, and truely reported, and iudge the worke fit and worthie to be published.

Edward Bromley.

Formal depositions are also found in two books published after the defeat of the Armada—one contains information taken from Spanish sailors captured in Ireland[42] and the other is the statement of a Spanish officer who fell into the hands of the Dutch.[43] A great many confessions of criminals which were, of course, taken down by judicial officers are found in the reports of the proceedings against traitors and other malefactors, but as a rule they do not make up the substance of the report, but are tacked on as a kind of appendix. Included in *A true relation . . . of that . . . murther . . . of Sir Iohn Tyndal*[44] is a copy of the examination of the murderer; the author says he "obtained leaue of his Honor" to print it. This permission, I imagine, was exceptional; as a rule, the law officers would

[41] For Iohn Barnes, 1613.
[42] *Certaine aduertisements out of Ireland,* as above, p. 128.
[43] *The Deposition of Don Diego Piementellj* . . . , as above, p. 128.
[44] John Beale, 1616.

[251]

not permit the verbatim publication of their records except under their own supervision or by their own people. But Sir John Tyndall was himself a judge who had been shot by a disgruntled litigant; the book seems to have been written by a friend of his, who was perhaps a lawyer of some standing, and was probably intended as a kind of justification of the murdered judge, so that, for these special reasons, "his Honor," who, by the way, was Sir Francis Bacon, the attorney-general, may have been glad to connive at an effort to clear the name of a professional colleague.

It seems likely that some of the accounts of the careers of murderers and other remarkable criminals were based on the evidence given at their trials, often with additions describing the inevitable execution such as any eye-witness could compose. It may be that these too are the handiwork of the clerk of the tribunal or of some other member of the lower ranks of the legal profession who, having been present at the hearings, conceived the idea of turning an honest penny by composing a biography of the prisoner for public consumption. Other narratives of criminal careers were undoubtedly written by another class of persons intimately connected with the punishment of criminals—their ghostly confessors. The clergyman who attended a criminal during his last days, who heard his confessions and repentance, who witnessed his behavior under the shadow of the scaffold, especially if impressed by the enormity of the malefactor's crimes or the edifying sincerity of his repentance, as most of these narrators seem to have been, might be very likely to set down the history of his entire lapse from grace from the information he had thus obtained. The clergyman would have the same motive to treat with a publisher that moved him to print his sermons, and possibly found material of this sort more readily marketable. One clear instance of this kind of news-writer is found. The Rev. Henry Goodcole, who, during the latter part of the reign of King James and for some time after the end of our period, acted as volunteer chaplain to the prisoners at Newgate, published several accounts of the lives and offenses of the evildoers whom he attended.[45] It was doubtless their pious embracing of the consolations of religion which interested him in these condemned wretches (although in one of his books he says that he has published it unwillingly and only at the importunity of others), and he himself regarded them as godly examples, which is not precisely the way in which all his readers regarded them. But he did not spoil his story, nevertheless; his books are narratives, and, indeed, his report of the trial of Elizabeth Sawyer, the witch of Edmonton, is delayed by only a very few pious asides.

7. PRIVATE CORRESPONDENTS

We have already seen scores of books entitled "The copy of a letter" or otherwise purporting to be copies of private correspondence. There is no doubt that a great many books of news originated in private letters and advices, most of them, indeed, being printed literatim, even if we occasionally suspect that the letter-form is a pleasant fiction invented by the author for his own purposes. Few, if any, of these letters were written to the publishers who put them in print, and how such private letters got into the publishers' hands is another question, which must be postponed for a little while; we are now concerned only with the way in which they came to be written.

This is not difficult to explain. News was spread in private letters long before printing was invented; it went right on being circulated in the same way after the printing press was introduced; it still is to-day. A distant

---

[45] 1) *A True Declaration of the happy Conuersion* . . . *of Francis Robinson* . . . Edw[ard] All-de, 1618. 2) *The wonderfull discouerie of Elizabeth Savvyer a Witch, late of Edmonton* . . . From VVilliam Butler, 1621.

correspondent, in the sixteenth century, could be relied upon to mention the news from his part of the world in almost every letter he wrote: if he knew it concerned a matter which his correspondent was interested in, or unlikely to have heard about in another way, he might give a very full account of it. Many men regularly corresponded with friends in distant parts for the sake of the news they could thereby obtain, sending news which they had heard in return. Great merchants and political magnificoes even hired agents to furnish them with news from strategic places. There are frequent references to the exchanging of news between friends, relatives, and patron and client in the books of news. One book begins, "Since my laste letters sēt vnto you, of the newes in these parties (Because I wyll kepe my fyrst promes, for enterchaūge of lettres);"[46] another writer says, "Sir, I thanke you for your Relation of *Ferrara;* and to make you paiment in the like commodities, I returne to you a true report of a fresh accident of State, happened here with vs;"[47] another, "*Good Sr.* according to the reciprocall contract between vs of Writing to one another, concerning such things as may pleasure either."[48] The news and gossip exchanged by John Chamberlain and Sir Dudley Carleton (reign of James I), for example, is well known and is regarded as an important historical source. At about the same time, the Rev. Joseph Mead, a fellow at Cambridge, sent regular letters to his friend Sir Martin Stutevile at Balham, Suffolk, made up of news which he had collected from other letters and from printed copies. Besides such regular correspondence, an enormous number of occasional and casual

[46] *A Copye of a Letter contayning certayne newes* . . . *of the Deuonshyre and Cornyshe rebelles.* See above, pp. 38, 54.

[47] *A Letter written out of England to an English Gentleman* . . . *at Padua* . . . See above, p. 54.

[48] *Tvvo letters or embassies* . . . *concerning the Troubles of Germany.* [Translated by W. Barlow of Amsterdam.] Amsterdam: 1620.

letters of news must have passed from place to place every year. We hear in many books of news that the writer was importuned by his friend for an account of what he was known to have seen or taken part in, thus:

> Sir (as you haue desired) I haue done all my endeauour to satisfie you with the truth of such noteworthy things, as in these parts happen; beeing recompenced by you with like for like from London, our naturall and beloued Citie.[49]

In *The Late Commotion of certaine Papists in Hereford-shire*,[50] we read of a request for news and also find copies of the letters of both correspondents. The first is a report of a speech of the lord chancellor in the Star-Chamber on the subject of the late commotion which the London correspondent, T. H.,. sends to a Herefordshire friend with a request for further particulars. This friend, E. R., replies, nine days later, enclosing "A true Relation of the late Commotion," and, later, sends another letter with more news, both of which are duly set forth. The whole collection, including a preface and "A necessary and godly prayer," was published by T. H. Some books of news which are not in the form of letters are represented as having been written by request. Thus Munday says, in his *Discouerie of Edmund Campion:*

> [Since the conviction of Campion] . . . there hath been cast abroad . . . such reports, Lybels, & trayterous speeches in the behalfe of the aforenamed [prisoners], bothe against me and the other of the witnesses. . .
> Wherefore, at the earnest intreatie of diuers, godlie and well disposed men, as also to discharge my selfe of the manifest vntruethes, . . . I haue beene so bolde, to discouer these Traitours, and their tretcherous practises, that it maye be seene and knowen, howe falselie and vntruelie they haue accused me.

---

[49] *Most true and more admirable newes, expressing the miraculous preseruation of a young Maiden of . . . . Glabbich . . . .* For Thomas Stirrop, 1597.

[50] As above, p. 242.

Likewise the author of *Elizabetha triumphans:*[51]

When it [= "my Pamphlet"] was (at the earnest request of one that might haue commaunded) both begun and finished very neere with-in the space of one whole moneth, I was afterwards three long moneths studying, whether it were better for me to burne it, or to giue it to the Presse . . . Then hauing intelligence of the commonnesse of Ballads, with Bookes to this purpose, I resolued my selfe to bestowe this my Pamphlet on the fire. But crabbed *Fortune* (who euer hinders willing enterprises) through the intreatie of diuers of my deerest friends, stayed my determinate purpose.

Such a statement as, "The order of the thing as I receiued the sāe I haue committed to paper,"[52] probably refers to information arrived in private letters, just as we have seen Churchyard making up a book on the strength of letters which he had been shown at court.[53] An account of a profitable privateering expedition was sent to London from "Dartmouth . . . , where I now remaine, about your affaires" by a business agent.[54] Some books of news which are not professedly copies of letters are nevertheless written in the first person and suggest that they originated in correspondence. An abundance of news must have existed in letters and private advices; it was necessary only to get it into the hands of the publishers to make books of news.

[51] As above, p. 128.

[52] *A Straunge and terrible Wunder wrought very late in the parish Church of Bongay* . . . , as above, p. 147.

[53] See above, p. 228.

[54] *The sea-mans Triumph* . . . , as above, p. 133.

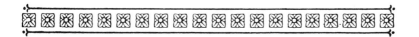

CHAPTER XI
NEWS-PUBLISHERS

TO GIVE a complete account of the methods by which the publishers of news collected it and placed it in the hands of the reader would be almost to write a history of the publishing trade during our period, a task before which a historian much better acquainted with early books and with more space than a chapter at his disposal might well blanch. It seems that many have blanched, too, for, while the publishing trade in our period has been carefully studied from the typographical point of view, very little information is available with regard to more prosaic matters, such as the publisher's business arrangements, the sources from which he procured the copy he printed, and the methods by which he distributed his wares. Such information is not easy to find, and we shall be able to put together only a very porous account of the publishing of news, in which the gaps are more conspicuous than the substance.

At the outset, it may be well to take a comprehensive view of the publishing trade in the sixteenth century which will give us bearings to steer by in our attempt to trace its activities. The Worshipful Company of Stationers, the trade in incorporated form, was composed of men who plied a number of different vocations. With some of these, such as bookbinding and paper-selling, we have no concern. The stationers' trade, *i.e.* the purveying of MS. books, paper, and other stationery wares, and the art of copying, existed before the introduction of printing, but the printers and sellers of printed books soon became the most important members of it. The earliest printers were, as a rule, publishers (*i.e.* men who ventured to bring out books), booksellers (vendors of books to buyers), and often bookbinders as well, but these various occupations gradually became more and more distinct and individual stationers pursued one to the exclusion of the others. By the end of the sixteenth century they were fairly well marked off one from the other.

The stationers whom we are concerned with can be separated into four, perhaps five, groups. First, there are the printers, the men who owned presses and actually produced books; in the reign of Elizabeth and that of James I, their number was comparatively small, for the government, in 1586, put a limit on the number of presses in the country, though, to be sure, this regulation was not always strictly observed. Most printers also published books—*i.e.* they accepted copy from authors, or otherwise obtained it, prepared it for the press if necessary, and floated the edition on the market. But as time went on, they tended more and more to the position of job printers, who took no initiative in the issuing of new books, but merely printed what they were hired to print. Most of them were no doubt booksellers as well; it seems unlikely that a printer could not have supplied a copy of a book he had printed himself, even if he was not the publisher, though he may not have dealt in other publications, and unless his printing establishment was strategically situated, his retail business may have been small.

The second class of stationers are the booksellers, the dealers in books at retail, the men who kept the shops at St. Paul's and the Exchange from which one actually purchased copies. These men were quite numerous, for their trade required less capital and perhaps less skill than the printer's. It also seems that tradesmen who were not members of the Stationers' Company, especially drapers, sometimes sold books at retail. The stock which the book-sellers traded in consisted of, first, their own books, the books they had published themselves, if any. But few, if any, could have dealt in their own publications exclusively; some are known to have published but few or none at all. We know that the custom of exchanging wares existed in the company, that one man would give another copies of a book he had issued for the equivalent value of copies of a book the second had issued, so that both books would be on sale in both shops—a system by which an indefinite stock of goods could be built up. But the booksellers who published no books must surely have bought their stock for cash, just as retail booksellers nowadays stock their shelves by purchase from book-publishers. Furthermore, it seems that retail booksellers were sometimes hired or deputed—on what terms we have no idea—to market an edition for the publisher. The publisher's part in such an enterprise was to secure the copy and to arrange to have it printed (or, if a printer, to print it himself); the retail bookseller's to place the printed copies in the hands of readers.

The activity of the bookseller as publisher was quite different from that as retail book-vendor, though many booksellers acted as both. Publisher is a term which, in the sixteenth century, did not necessarily apply to members of the trade; it referred rather to any one who brought the book into public view. The nomenclature of the trade made no distinction between a publisher of books and a retail book-merchant, though the difference between them was considerable and highly important. All publishers were, of course, booksellers as well,[1] but not all book-

---

[1] A few books, however, were published by their authors or sponsors. The first extensive publisher on record who was not a stationer, though he devised schemes for selling his books (lotteries and subscription plans), appears to be John Ogilby (1600–76).

sellers were publishers. It may be, however, that some men took a much greater interest in bringing new reading-matter to the public for its delight than in dealing out copies over the counter, and they may have left the latter operation chiefly to their confrères in the company. They were entrepreneurs rather than traders, and they resemble very closely the modern publisher of books in almost every way. These are the men we are chiefly interested in; they are the nurses of the public taste in books and have much to do with shaping it, and they play an important part in the growth of journalism. Among themselves, they tended to specialize, one man interesting himself in theology, another in belles-lettres, or law books, or school books, or ballads and other popular wares, or news.

In a complete catalog of the trade, we should have to distinguish one or more further classes of booksellers—the second-hand dealers, certainly, and possibly the whole-salers, whose chief business, or at any rate their specialty, was the distribution of books in large quantities—, but as the ensuing discussion has no bearing on their activities, we may pass over them. One further branch of the trade, however, which possibly did play an important rôle in bringing news to the public, remains to be mentioned. Certain stationers—some of whom kept their own shops and some did not—seem to have traded in manuscripts, without either producing them or publishing them. They rather acted as intermediary between the author or spon-sor of the manuscript and the publisher, much as present-day literary agents do. Most of them seem to have been the poorer members of the trade—freemen just out of their apprenticeship or journeymen in the employ of master-stationers—and one form which their operations took, the procuring of manuscripts over which the author had no control, is nowadays referred to as piracy. This kind of business could be carried on without any equipment or stock or capital whatsoever, and was probably the way in which a new-made freeman often began his career. We shall have to look further into this matter a little later.

1. Copy Offered to the Publisher

We must now try to answer the first question that arises: how did the news they published get into the publishers' hands? Part of the answer is easy: it was brought to them. Authors marketed their compositions in those days just as they do now; and a partisan apologist, having written an exposition of his point of view, naturally took it to a printer or publisher and often, no doubt, paid for the printing of it. This much is perfectly obvious.

It also seems that written news was brought to the publisher by volunteer go-betweens acting out of pure good nature. Their motives must have been very much like those of the volunteer news-writers we have noticed above, only here, instead of writing out a report of news, they merely carried it to the publisher. Having taken delight in the news themselves, they benevolently wished to share it with others. The publisher of *Iohn Huighen van Linschoten his Discours of Voyages . . .*[2] explains in his dedication:

About a Tweluemonth agoe, a learned Gentleman brought vnto mee the Voyages and Nauigation of *John Huyghen van Linschoten* into the *Indies*, written in the *Dutche* Tongue, which he wished might be translated into our Language, because hee thought it would be not onely delightfull, but also very commodious for our English Nation. Vpon this recommendation and opinion, I procured the Translation thereof accordingly, and so thought good to publish the same in Print to the ende it might bee made common and knowen to euerybody.

The sponsor of *A Summe of the Guisian Ambassage*,[3] who was also the translator, confides that

[2] Iohn Wolfe, [1598].
[3] As above, p. 177.

This little Pamphlet, (gentle Reader) . . . came vnto my hands by chaūce, perusing other bookes which were brought from Franckford . . . I thought good to publish the same to the view of the worlde, leauing the creadit thereof to the Reporter, that it may appeare both how cruell and bloodthirsty a generation these Papistes are . . . For as they haue in that noble Realme of *Fraunce*, and in other places shewed theyr malitious intents, so mynd they to do the like, it is to be feared in England.

Sometimes the sponsor acted against the wishes of the author:

[I] haue presumed to present vnto you a report of the late *Voyage into Spaine and Portingall*, sent vnto me almost 4. moneths sithence frō a Gentleman my verie nere friend employed in the same; . . . and because I haue often conferred with manie that were in the same Iourney, verie nere vpon euerie particular of his relation, and finde as much confirmed as I haue receiued, I presume to deliuer it vnto you for true and exact. Howbeit, forasmuch as it came vnto my hands with his earnest request to reserue it to my selfe, . . . the desire I haue to reconcile the contrarietie of opinions that be held of that action, & to make it known what honour the cause hath laid vpon our whole Nation, mooued me to publish the same.[4]

There are also instances in which the author sent his news to a friend with the request that it be put in print:

I will proceed to declare vnto you the succese of *D*[om] *Sebastian* King of Portugale, since his escape from the battell in Afrike: which I intreat your Lordship to cause to be imprinted, that all Princes may haue free knowledge of the historie.[5]

To his very friend Maister I. D.
. . . And least the same should be misreported, or the wicked suffred to wrest thinges, to abuse Gods Preachers,& for that the thyng is so rare & notable that it shoulde not be kept from the posteritye, I haue therfore sēt you the whole tru discourse thereof, . . . praying you to put the same in print.

[4] *A true Coppie of a Discourse written by a Gentleman, employed in the late Voyage of Spaine and Portingale*, as above, p. 122.
[5] Joseph Texere to Bishop ———, from Paris, 12 January 1602. *A Continuation of the . . . aduentures of Dom Sebastian King of Portugale*. For Iames Shaw, 1603.

From the City of Chester the .xv. of March. 1564. Your friend I. F.[6]

William Barley, the publisher of *Strange and wonderfull things happened to Richard Hasleton* . . . (1595), says in the dedication that "perusing my store of Papers and Writings of sundry mens labours, I chanced on this pamphlet," as if he had a large reservoir of copy to draw upon. As he would hardly have paid money for this brain-work if he left it to gather dust, it may have been presented to him by the author or other persons who thought it fit for publication. The following confidence imparted to "the Christian Reader" by Gerardus Gossenius, doctor in physic, the translator of a curious broadside published in 1586,[7] would also seem to indicate that a printer or bookseller might have all kinds of odds and ends of potential publications lying about in his shop:

When I was last busie with confuting of that pernitious booke of Iohn Enghibram (called the bluddy boke) through the murthers that haue beene committed by the Papistes among the Children of GOD, so found I at the Printers house, this Pamphlet printed in Dutch, and considering the matter, the person & the circumstances, I would not that the English nation, being novv (God be praysed) the most famous and renowmed, both for purity of Religion, and valiantnes in Cheualry, should be thereof depriued.

It is likely that a good deal of news was furnished the publishers in this way, especially news written by eye-witnesses and participants and intended primarily for their friends and correspondents. News of this kind was seldom hoarded by the recipient; on the contrary, he was much more likely to exhibit it proudly to his friends and acquaintances and sometimes, as we have seen, to go to the length of giving it to a publisher to be declared to the world in

[6] *The Copy of a Letter Describing the wonderful woorke of God* . . . , as above, p. 242.

[7] *The maner and order of proceeding against Christ* . . . *at Ierusalem* . . .

print. There are, of course, several ways in which a private letter could have come into a publisher's possession, but this is certainly one of them.

An interesting chain of facts leads us to think that there was another source in London from which news was sometimes supplied to the publishing trade—the French embassy. It is impossible to say that the ambassador sent round to the publishers copies of news which he received; on the contrary, they may have applied to him for it; but there is no doubt that he was the well-head from which it flowed. The following books, all published within a few years at the time of Henry IV's greatest success, are in one way or another connected with the ambassador, so that we can hardly doubt that he furnished their substance:

1) *The true discourse of the wonderfull victorie, obteined by Henrie the fourth . . . Compiled and sent hither* [to the ambassador?] *by one of the principall Officers of the Kings Maiestie.*[8]

2) *Sommaire discours au vray de ce qui est aduenu en l'armee du Roy . . . iusques au 15. de Septembre. Enuoyé par sa Maiesté a Monsieur de Beauuoir, . . . son Ambassadeur pres la . . . Roine d'Angleterre.*[9]

3) *The things which happened vpon the Prince of Parmas retire . . .* [10] Entered 8 December 1590 to Thomas Nelson "vnder th[e h]andes of the Frenche ambassadour."[11]

4) *The successe which fell out in the pursute of the Prince of Parma, together with a lettre of the Kinges to the marshall of Byron &c.* Entered 17 December 1590 to John Wolfe "vnder the Frenche ambassadour and bothe the wardens handes."[12]

5) *A iournall, or Briefe report of the late seruice in Britaigne . . . : aduertised by letters from the said Prince* [de Dombes] *to the Kings Ambassadour here resident with her Maiesty . . . Published, to*

---

[8] Also published in French. See above, p. 170.
[9] Also published in English. See above, p. 172.
[10] As above, p. 172.
[11] Arber, II. 568.
[12] *Ib.,* II. 569.

aunswere the slanderous bruites raised of late by some euill affected to that and other good actions . . . [13]

6) *Good newes from Fraunce. A true Discourse of the winning of sundry cheefe Townes . . . Published by Authoritie* [of the ambassador?].[14]

7) *The Copie of a Letter sent to Monsieur de Beauuoir Lord Embassador for the French king. vvherin is shewed the late attempt of a Iesuite who would haue killed the kings Maiestie with a knife.*[15]

We can scarcely call these books propaganda, though they may have been just as good. There is, however, little of the polemical in them; they are narratives of news. It is very good news indeed from the French king's point of view, and it was undoubtedly on that account that the ambassador permitted his private advices to be printed. The fact that these books seem to have been impartially distributed to a number of publishers suggests that the ambassador's reason for authorizing them was simply his pleasure in such a favorable turn in the king's fortunes and his willingness to have everybody know about it.

2. PROFESSIONAL PURVEYORS OF COPY

It is also probable that news was sometimes brought to the publishers, in the form of MSS. or foreign copies to be translated, by the literary agents mentioned above. We know little about the activity of these men, but there is no doubt of their existence, though we cannot say how many of them there were, or how large a trade they drove in copy. The best known is Thomas Thorp, who has been thoroughly investigated because he captured a MS. copy of Shakespeare's sonnets and had it published with an enigmatic dedication to a certain Mr. W. H., whom Sir Sidney Lee identifies as William Hall, another broker in

[13] For Iohn VVolfe, 1591. Licensed by the Privy Council (Arber, II. 588).
[14] For Thomas Nelson, sold by William Wright, [1591?].
[15] Sold by Iohn Flasket, 1594.

MSS. or literary agent.[16]   Men like Thorp are generally regarded as shady fellows, and there is no doubt that their methods of procuring MSS. which had passed out of the author's hands were probably none too scrupulous; but there are a number of entirely honorable ways as well by which they could have obtained matter for publication. If they were the dregs of the trade, as they are sometimes said to be, anything fit to print would have tempted them, and they certainly would not have turned up their noses at a marketable commodity such as a book of news, even though it promised a smaller reward than a book of sugared sonnets or a popular play.

The circulation of MS. copies gave men of this sort their opportunity to snatch the biggest prizes.   News-reports were sometimes interrupted in their circulation among the original proprietor's circle of friends and acquaintances and diverted into the channels of publication.   Sir Lewis Lewkenor's *Estate of English fugitiues vnder the king of Spaine* . . . came to be published in this way.   It is an account of the unhappy lot of the English Catholics in Flanders, who were barred from returning to England by their disloyalty and despised by the Spaniards on whose protection they were dependent.   It was first published in 1595 as *A discourse of the vsage of the English Fugitiues, by the Spaniard*[17] with the following preface:

The copie of a Letter sent out of the Low countries by a Gentleman entertained by the King of Spaine in pension: To a yong Gentleman his Kinsman in England.

My very good Cosin, vnderstanding as well by your Letters, as by the message lately done vnto me by the mouth of *A. T.* of the great longing and desire you haue to draw your self into these parts, & to imploy your selfe here in seruice of the Spanish king: & perceiuing also . . . there bee manye that are of your mind in that point . . .

[16] *Life of William Shakespeare*, appendix V.
[17] For Iohn Drawater.

I haue thought good for the particular loue which I beare . . .
towardes you, . . . but chiefely in respecte of the sincere, faythfull,
reuerent, and loyall fidelitye and regarde I haue to the person of our
. . . Soueraigne, . . . and to my natiue Countrie and Countrye-
men, to sette downe some notes . . . which . . . I haue gathered:
by which I hope I shall make manifest not onelye to you, but also
to all others . . . , if I maye haue the fauour to haue it published:
. . . how greatly you and they that desire to repaire hether . . .
in anye hope of good to be receiued from the sayde King, doo erre and
are deceiued.

An amended edition, under the title first mentioned above,
was issued by the same bookseller in the same year, with
the following address to the reader from the author
himself:

Being some fiue or sixe yeres since in those partes of Flanders,
which are subiect to the Spanish king, and seeing a miserable troupe
of my vnhappie countrimen . . . debarred from returne into
their countrie: and . . . daily ouerlooked with the proud eyes of
disdainfull Spaniards, and . . . knowing some of my good friendes
and acquaintance in England, possessed with the like humor . . . to
forsake their countrie and to settle themselues in the seruice and
dominions of the king of Spaine: I thought good to aduertise them of
. . . the small regard, distresse, pouertie, scorne, calamitie, &
affliction, befallen to such as had alreadie entred the course . . .
Hauing to that effect, written from thence priuatly to some of my
acquaintaunce, the coppies of my letters (contrarie to my intention)
were since my returne, by some of them giuen abrode, and lastly not
long since, a discourse printed in Paules Church-yarde, conteining
some parte of the substance thereof, but manye thinges that I had
written left out, and manye thinges inserted that I neuer me[a]nt,
and finally in the whole so falsified and chaunged, aswell in matter as
wordes, & ignorantly entermixed with fictions of the publisher, that
howsoeuer the vulgar sorte bee therewith pleased, those that are of
farther reach and insight, cannot but condemne it as a thing fabulous,
grossely handled and full of absurdities. Besides, the time and occasion to which that discourse was fitting, is now altogether past, and
therefore the same altogether impertinent. In regard of which and
other inconueniences, I thought it not vnfitte to publish the true
coppy of my owne letter, which though after so many yeares, cannot
but seeme stale . . . The former treatise (for though they are
suppressed, yet there are greate numbers of them extant) . . . was
by a fellow, that had stolne a coppy thereof, foysted to the print, in

[267]

hope of benefit, and now when the matter comes to examination, slipps his head out of the Coller and will not bee found.[18]

This is a clean-cut example of the publication of a book of news appropriated from copies circulating in MS., without the author's permission and in a form trumped up to make it look plausible. Another book published without the author's knowledge is *A true relation of such occurrences . . . as hath hapned in Virginia . . .*[19] It was brought to light by a certain I. H., who explains himself in his address to the reader as follows:

Happening vpon this relation by chance (as I take it, at the second or third hand) induced thereunto by diuers well wishers of the action, and none wishing better towards it then my selfe, so farre forth as my poore abilitie can or may stretch too, I thought good to publish it: but the Author being absent from the presse, it cannot be doubted but that some faults haue escaped in the printing, especially in the names of Countries, Townes, and People, which are somewhat strange vnto vs; but most of all, and which is the chiefe error, (for want of knowledge of the Writer) some of the bookes were printed vnder the name of *Thomas Watson,* by whose occasion I know not, vnlesse it were the ouer rashnesse, or mistaking of the workemen, but since hauing learned that the saide discourse was written by Captaine *Smith,* who is one of the Counsell there in *Virginia:* I thought good to make the like Apollogie, by shewing the true Author so farre as my selfe could learne.

---

[18] It is an interesting fact that both the unauthorized and the authorized editions were published by the same man. The book, however, was entered again by William Ponsonbye 26 August 1595 (Arber, III. 47); yet Drawater published a corrected and amended edition in 1596. On 26 September 1597 he assigned his rights to Ponsonby (*ib.*, III. 91). Two conjectures suggest themselves: either Drawater made his peace with the aggrieved author by putting the blame on a third person, *i.e.*, an intermediary who had procured the MS., the fellow who had slipped his head out of the collar, or Sir Lewis Lewkenor having applied to Ponsonby to bring out a correct edition, Drawater, with an undeniable title to the copy by having entered it in the register (*ib.*, II. 670), stood firm for his rights, succeeded in retaining the book, and later entered into a composition with Ponsonby on terms satisfactory to himself. These suppositions are, of course, not entirely irreconcilable.

[19] For Iohn Tappe, sold by W[illiam] W[elby], 1608.

Another account of the Virginia plantation, *The proceedings of those Colonies, since their first departure from England . . . ,*[20] was published by an admiring reader of the MS. in its circuit:

> This solid treatise, first was compiled by Richard Pots, since passing the hands of many to peruse, chancing into my hands (for that I know them honest men and can partly well witnesse their relations true) I could do no lesse in charity to the world then reveale; nor in conscience but approue. By the advice of many graue and vnderstanding gentlemen that haue pressed it to the presse, it was thought fit to publish it, rather in it[s] owne rude phrase than other waies.

But there has never been any doubt that MSS. were sometimes taken on the wing and published without the author's consent. What we are concerned with is the opportunity for literary brokers to carry on a trade in such captured wares.

Now, while a MS. written by an admired author was undoubtedly the most valuable prize a procurer of MSS. could carry off, a narrative of news was something likely to come within his reach more frequently. It was part of the bread of his trade, as a rich haul like Shakespeare's sonnets was the cake. When we recollect how much news was communicated in private letters and how many of these letters somehow got into print, can we doubt that some of them were picked up by somebody in the same way that errant MSS. were? And who was more likely to be alert to such opportunities than the stationers who made a living, or part of their living, by precisely this kind of snapping up of odd chances? Indeed, they could have done much more than merely lay hands on any written news which swam into their ken, though we have no evidence to prove that they did. If news-stories were sometimes written by returned soldiers and sailors and

[20] Published as the second part of *A map of Virginia* (Oxford: Joseph Barnes, 1612).

other witnesses, or composed out of their testimony, a dealer in copy may have officiated as literary midwife. If a Londoner received a book of news printed abroad which was suitable for issue in translation, a literary agent may have secured it from him and conveyed it to the publisher. These brokers could even have acted as intermediary between the author or sponsor and the publisher and made themselves useful to the former because of their familiarity with the mystery of stationer.[21] In short, there are half-a-dozen ways in which a stationer could have picked up a living by acting as broker-between in bringing copies of news to the press.

Thomas Thorp, an approved member of this auxiliary branch of the publishing trade, was involved in the publication of more than a dozen books of news, and if he came by them in the course of his scavenging of marketable copy (of some of them he was evidently the publisher as well), they would seem to indicate the wide range of the material which such a man picked up. Here is the list:

1) *A speach delivered, to the kings . . . maiestie in the name of the Sheriffes of London and Middlesex. By Maister Richard Martin of the Middle Temple.* Imprinted for Thomas Thorppe, and are to be sould by William Aspley, 1603.

2) *A true and large discourse of the voyage of the whole fleet . . . of the East Indian Marchants in London, to the East Indies.* For Thomas Thorpe, sold by William Aspley, 1603.

3) *A letter vvritten to . . . the East Indian marchants in London: containing the estate of the East Indian fleete with the names of the chiefe men of note dead in the voyage.* For Thomas Thorppe, sould by William Aspley, 1603.

4) *The preachers travels . . .* By John Cartwright. For Thomas Thorppe, sold by Walter Burre, 1611.

---

[21] The epitaph of Master William Peeter of Whipton near Exeter in the list below seems a very unpromising venture for a London publisher. Could Thorp have been employed by some of the late worthy's friends, or by an Exeter bookseller, to have this memorial put in print?

5) *The Odcombian Banquet . . .* By Thomas Coryat. For Thomas Thorp, 1611.

6) *A funerall Elegye in memory of the late virtuous master William Peeter of Whipton neere Exetour.* Entered to Thorp 13 February 1612 (Arber, III. 477).

7) *A congratulation to France, vpon the happy alliance with Spaine.* By F. de Menantel S. Denis. For T. Thorp, sold by W. Burre, 1612.

8) *A generall discourse of the Triumphe held in the listes royall at Parys in Aprill last for ioy of the kinges marriage with the Infant of Spayne &c.* Entered to Thorp 23 May 1612 (Arber, III. 486).

9) *A newe Mahomet lately sprange vp in Barbary who hath twyce defeated Mulley Sydan kinge of Marocco in battayle . . .* Ballad. Entered to Thorp 27 February 1613 (Arber, III. 516).

10) *The Eighth Wonder of the World, or Coriats Escape from his supposed drowning.* By John Taylor. 1613. Entered to Thorp 2 August (Arber, III. 530).

11) *A Famous Victorie, Atchiued in August last 1613. by the Christian Gallies of Sicilia, against the Turkes.* For Th: Thorp, 1613.

12) *The Charterhouse with the last vvill and Testament of Thomas Sutton Esquire.* For Thomas Thorp, 1614.

13) *A Proclamation given by the lords and States . . . against the slanders laid upon the Evangelicall and Reformed religion by the Arminians . . .* For T. T. and Richard Chambers, 1618. Entered to Thorp 23 October (Arber, III. 635).

14) *Barnevels Apology: or Holland Mysterie.* For Thomas Thorp, 1618.

This rather looks like the dredgings of a ready wit, willing to pick up any likely copy which he might hear of. True, there were a number of publishers who would issue almost anything they felt there was a sale for, but it is evident that Thorp's wares run in schools, as if every so often he opened up a new vein and tapped it for what it was worth while the chance availed. In 1603, he obtains access to some news from the East Indies (he may have got it by cultivating some of the governors of the company; indeed, it is not impossible that he induced them to employ him to see this news of their venture into print); in 1611

[271]

and 1613 he is taking advantage of Coryat's notoriety; in 1612 he has made connections with a French source; in 1613 it is the Mohammedan world;[22] in 1618, the Netherlands. All this is slender evidence on which to construct a picture of Thorp as a news-broker, but it does show that he was instrumental in bringing a certain amount of news to light, and that his part was that of discovery rather than publication, for most of these pieces seem to have been put on the market by other men.

It would further seem that other stationers who were undoubtedly active in the book trade sometimes participated in the launching of a book in another capacity than that of publisher. There are the Henry Robertses, father and son, both members of the company; their name appears in the registers about a dozen times between 1580 and 1613. One of them was an author, if not both. I know of no books certainly published by the elder Roberts and no address at which he (or his son) kept a shop, though he is known to have had at least one apprentice, very early in his career. Six books written by Henry Roberts, however, were published by other booksellers before the younger became a freeman of the company 18 August 1595. As late as 1616 a Henry Roberts was still writing.[23] The books entered by the Robertses were usually their own compositions, but occasionally other men's as well, e.g., Anthony Nixon's *Great Brittaines Generall Ioyes*,[24] which Henry Roberts entered 14 February 1613 (together with a ballad, author unspecified, on the

---

[22] A book on this subject had been published only a few weeks before. Two editions exist—1) *Late Newes out of Barbary* . . . and 2) *The New Prophetical King of Barbary* . . . (for Arthur Ionson, 1613). It was entered 27 January (Arber, III. 514).

[23] *A True Relation of a most worthy . . . fight . . . by two small Shippes of . . . London . . . against Sixe great Galles of Tunes.*

[24] For Henry Robertes, sold by T[homas] P[avier], 1613.

same subject).[25] Invariably, however, these books were published by or in association with other booksellers. We may therefore suspect that their business in the stationer's trade included dealing in MSS. and arranging for publication—their own MSS. first and foremost, but sometimes other men's as well.

There is not sufficient evidence to make out a similar case with regard to many other stationers, but there are a number of facts difficult to explain which the assumption that the procuring and placing of copy was a branch of the stationer's trade may partially clear up. Indeed, it is possible to contend that reports of news, because their interest evaporated more quickly than that of other kinds of copy and because they would pop up at any time in unexpected places, especially called for the services of a go-between. At any rate, in the records of many books of news we find the names of one or more stationers besides the minimum number of one (printer-publisher) or two (printer and publisher) required. How did these supernumerary stationers become concerned in the venture? Some of them were merely partners: thus we find three men had a part in bringing out *A Lamentable Discourse, vpon the paricide and bloudy assasination: committed on . . . Henry the Fourth* . . . in 1610—Windet, the printer, and Blount and Barret, the publishers. But Blount and Barret were doing business in partnership at this time, and the additional name is, therefore, not really supernumerary. But, for other books, other explanations suggest themselves, and some of these raise the possibility that the part of one of the allied stationers was merely the procuring of the copy.

Sometimes an extra stationer (in addition to the printer and publisher) was associated in the bringing out of a book in the capacity of retailer, as has been mentioned before.

[25] Arber, III. 515.

[273]

Thus we find that two books which John Windet published in 1594 were to be sold by Samuel Shorter and John Flasket respectively.[26] Windet had entered these books in the register and in 1611 he assigned them to William Stansby;[27] they were undoubtedly his property. His printing office on St. Paul's Wharf, Thames Street, probably was not visited by many book-buyers; he therefore arranged with Shorter and Flasket to sell the books at their shop at the great north door of St. Paul's. This sort of arrangement seems not to have been unusual; Windet frequently marketed his books in this way and so did other publishers. But such a combination might also have included a stationer whose interest in a book ceased after he had procured the copy and who had rather dispose of it to another for publication, or who preferred to let somebody else put up the capital for the publication of the book and was content with a broker's fee, or who had no shop of his own from which to sell books and was obliged to enlist another man's cooperation. We have just seen Thorp and Roberts, for one or another of these reasons, doing precisely this sort of business. We may also suspect that others, by choice or by necessity, gave the sale and distribution of books which they had been instrumental in bringing to the press to their colleagues.

For example, of the eight or ten pieces entered in the Stationers' register to John Kyd, only two are now known to exist in print, and these were both published in association with other men.[28] This stationer became a freeman in 1584, but there is no record of his having published anything before 1591, and he died before the spring of

[26] 1) *The French Kings Edict vpon the reducing of the Citie of Paris* . . . Iohn Windet, sold by Samuell Shorter, 1594. 2) *The order of Ceremonies obserued in the . . . Coronation of . . . Henry the IIII.* . . . , as above, p. 236.

[27] Arber, II. 647, III. 466.

[28] Hazlitt (IV. 6), however, mentions a book printed for John Kid, but I have never seen it and do not know where it is to be found.

1593. He is known chiefly from the entry of these few popular pieces; how most of them were published we do not know, for they have been lost. It is not known whether he kept a shop or worked for another stationer. In 1592 *The trueth of the most wicked . . . murthering of Iohn Brewen . . .* , a book attributed to Thomas Kyd, who is supposed to have been his brother, was printed for him, to be sold by Edward White, and *A most vvicked worke of a wretched Witch . . . ,* which had been entered to him,[29] was printed for William Barley. Here we see a third party entering into the bringing out of a book, very possibly in the capacity of furnisher of the copy. Likewise *The oration and declaration of Henrie IV . . .* was printed in 1590 for John Bowen, to be sold by Humphrey Lownes. It was entered as Bowen's copy.[30] All the books known to me with which Bowen's name is associated were published in conjunction with other men; it is not certain that he kept a shop of his own. Perhaps he was another stationer who picked up a few shillings when he could by procuring copy for publication and arranging with others to print it and sell it. Another book, *A true and perfecte description of a straunge monstar borne in . . . Rome . .* (an anti-Catholic tirade of French origin), was printed in 1590 by John Wolf for Walter Dight, to be sold by William Wright. This copy, however, was entered to Wright.[31] Nevertheless, it may be that Dight was the original mover of the enterprise, chiefly because it is hard to imagine what else he could have done to cause his name to appear in the imprint. Dight had been apprenticed to the printer Henry Middleton and had learned the printer's trade; a few years after 1590 we find him operating a press of his

[29] Arber, II. 607.

[30] *Ib.,* II. 559.

[31] As *The description of the holie leage both when yt was in his pride and also synce in his fall &c.* (Arber, II. 564).

own. But in 1590 he had been out of his articles only two years and he would seem to have had no press, or Wolf's services as printer would not have been called in. Perhaps he nevertheless wished to keep up his connection with the trade, looking forward to the day when he could procure a press of his own, by publishing this book which chance.had brought forward, and called on Wright, as an established bookseller, to help. In these and a number of other instances we find that there were more collaborators in the publication of a book than the printer and the seller; some of them were very likely the first owners of the copy whose part in the transaction was that of broker.

We also find that persons who cannot be traced in the records of the Stationers' Company and who probably were not stationers at all sometimes assisted in bringing out books. Some of them may have been tradesmen in other wares who, for reasons we cannot easily surmise, wanted to have books to sell in their shops. A more plausible explanation, however, seems to be that they acted as purveyors of the copy. It is not difficult to imagine that a stranger to the publishing trade, whether a member of another company or not, might occasionally come into possession of a piece of news that had not been published in England, that the idea might strike him that this intelligence, if printed, could be sold, and that he might enlist a printer and a bookseller in the enterprise of bringing it out, reserving a part of the profits to himself. Merchants trading with foreign countries, for example, would often have picked up books of news in foreign languages. As one instance, a book of news from Geneva was published in 1603 "for George Potter and Richard Canter, dwelling in the Popes Head Alley neare the Exchange."[32] Potter was a member of the Company of Stationers and

[32] *A perticuler and true narration of that great . . . deliuerance . . . of Geneua . . .*

he entered the book in the register on 27 January,[33] but there is no record of Canter, nor is there, apparently, any other record of Potter at the address in Pope's Head Alley. Could it be that Canter was a merchant in another trade who, having somehow come by this report, decided to publish it and enlisted Potter in the enterprise in order to obtain the assistance of an experienced stationer? A shopkeeper named Richard Lea is known to have had a part in the publishing of two books in 1615; there is no evidence to show that he was a stationer. He entered one of them in the register,[34] but the privilege of entry was not reserved exclusively to members of the company. It is a book called *The fall of man*, by Godfrey Goodman; apparently he published it in partnership with Thomas Man, for two issues are known, one "sold by Richard Lee" and the other "printed . . . for Thomas Man." He also had a part in the publication of a book of news from Germany; it was "printed by G[eorge] Eld for Richard Lea, and are to be sold at his shop . . . and by Edward Marchant."[35] Marchant was a member of the company. Perhaps Lea is another merchant who occasionally interested himself in the publication of a book. Nothing is known of a certain Ellis Bach except that in 1610 an edition of *The repentance of Jan Haren priest* . . . was printed by W[illiam] W[hite] to be sold by him at his shop. This book was entered on 2 July by Henry Rocket,[36] and another edition is recorded "printed for Henry Rockit and Nicholas Bourne." Apparently, then, Rocket and Bourne, who were both stationers, were the actual publishers; for that purpose they formed a temporary partnership (they had served their apprenticeship in the same shop). Bach may have been a shopkeeper who had been

[33] Arber, III. 225.
[34] *Ib.*, III. 578.
[35] *The lamentable Destruction of Mulheim* . . .
[36] Arber, III. 438.

[277]

instrumental in securing the foreign copies from which the book was translated and a second edition was printed off for him to dispose of. A different conjecture suggests itself to account for the name of Godfray Isaac, otherwise unknown, on the title-page of *Iohn Niccols Pilgrimage*, "printed by Thomas Dawson for Thomas Butter and Godfray Isaac." Knowing what we do about the composition of this piece of muckraking, we may hazard the guess that Isaac was a minion of Sir Owen Hopton or a trusted employé of some sort, that he was given Nichols's MS. with instructions to have it printed, that he enlisted the aid of Butter, who was an established bookseller and who entered the book in the register,[37] to launch the edition, and that his name was printed on the title-page in recognition of his part in the matter or, very possibly, because he had cannily stipulated for a share of the profits.

Another way in which a supernumerary stationer may have helped to bring out a book is suggested by the fact that a number of books entered in the registers by one man appeared without his name but as the publications of others. Quite a few copies entered as Edward Aggas's, for example, were actually published by other booksellers. Aggas practised bookselling in London for not less than thirty years, and undoubtedly published a number of books during that time, some of them, such as Mulcaster's verses on the death of Queen Elizabeth,[38] clearly work in which he had no part. But he was also very active in publishing news from abroad. Some of these translations he made himself; others, unacknowledged, may have been his work as well. Furthermore, he undoubtedly worked as translator for other publishers at the same time; for example, a number of books published and, if the imprint tells the complete story, procured by John Wolf were

[37] *Ib.*, II. 401.
[38] *In Mortem Serenissimæ Reginæ Elizabethæ.*

translated by Aggas.[39] But, in addition, some foreign books which he entered in the Stationers' registers, and which he therefore probably procured for publication in England, were issued in English by other booksellers without any notice of his participation on the title-page.[40] Sometimes, if not always, he made these translations himself. Perhaps, then, at least at certain times, Aggas gave his attention (aside, we should suppose, from keeping his shop) to importing books of foreign news and translating them, leaving the labor of floating the edition on the market to a confrère. A number of transfers of copyright are recorded in the registers; many more books entered to one man appeared with the imprint of another, just like those of Aggas cited above: all this trading suggests that sometimes the stationer who procured the copy could not, or did not care to, publish it, and therefore acted merely as broker.

Many similar instances could be cited of books brought to the public view with the assistance of more stationers than the minimum number required. Certainly they are not all to be explained in the same way, but among the various possible explanations, the existence of a trade in copy and of stationers who, usually or occasionally, preferred to deal in MS. rather than printed books is surely one. All the foregoing evidence is conclusive of only one thing— that sometimes other persons besides the author or his representative, if any, and the ostensible publisher had a hand in bringing copy to the market as printed books.

[39] 1) *Declaration set forth by the Frenche kinge, shewing his pleasure concerning the new troubles in his realme.* 1585. 2) *A Discourse vpon the present state of France,* as above, p. 178. 3) *Ordinances Set foorth by the King, for the rule . . . of his . . . men of warre.* 1591.

[40] 1) *A declaration exhibited to the French King, concerning the holy league.* For Thomas Cadman, 1587. See Arber, II. 471. 2) *A letter written by a French catholike gentleman to the maisters at Sorbonne . . .* [By Philippe de Mornay.] Iohn Wolfe, 1588. See Arber, II. 483. 3) *The Contre-League and answere to certaine letters sent to the maisters of Renes . . .* Iohn Wolfe, 1589. See Arber, II. 530.

3. COPY SOUGHT OUT BY THE PUBLISHER

The copy for the books which publishers issued that was not conveniently brought to them by persons interested in its publication they could have got in only one way—by going out and seeking for it. We have already seen that some news-reports were probably ordered by the publishers or provided by themselves. Furthermore, we should say, on antecedent probability, that on occasion they must surely have clamored for copy at the sources from which it could be expected, just as nowadays the latest channel swimmer, hammer murderer, or polar explorer is fairly besieged by the representatives of newspaper syndicates who will pay handsomely for the privilege of delegating an imaginative reporter to write the hero's memoirs in the first person. We feel sure, from the regularity with which certain publishers always offered the public an account of the latest murder and others provided an unfailing supply of news of the foreign wars, that they could not have come into possession of all this copy by chance; they must have made some arrangements to ensure their being provided with the material of their trade.

Furthermore, we find a little direct testimony to support this supposition. Tom Nash, in a characteristic passage in a letter written in 1596, mentions the eagerness of the publishers to get hold of copy sure to be popular at the moment:

For the printers there is sutch gaping amongst them for the coppy of my L[ord] of essex voyage & the ballet of the thre score & foure knights that though . . . Churchyarde [en]large his Chips, saying they were the very same w[ch] christ in [Car]penters hall is painted gathering vp as Ioseph his father [sta]nds hewing a peice of timber, and Mary his mother sitts [sp]inning by, yet wold not they giue for them the price of a [pr]oclamation out of date, or which is the contemptiblest summe [tha]t may bee . . . the price of [all] Harueys works bound vp togither.[41]

[41] *Works*, ed. McKerrow, V. 194.

How often and how far the publishers were willing to exert themselves to obtain copies of news it is impossible to say, but it is clear that they sometimes did so, and we think of many opportunities which may have spurred them to action. When we recall the clamor of the small printers in the latter part of the sixteenth century against the privileged patentees whose monopoly of nearly all the best work left them without enough work to keep their presses busy, we can scarcely believe that they did not occasionally bestir themselves to capture a report of news, one of the most numerous and accessible forms of matter fit for publication. If only they realized it, news could be found, on occasion, at sources which they could reach themselves—in the hands of their friends and acquaintances who corresponded with friends, relatives, and trade connections abroad, in the hands of court-recorders, jailers, clerks of the companies of merchant-adventurers trading abroad, in the pockets or the memories of one out of every three of the visitors who thronged in Paul's walk. In general they do not seem, as a matter of fact, to have been wide awake to their opportunities, but some of them, at least, could not have been altogether neglectful.

Another fact which makes us feel certain that the publishers did not always content themselves with the news which fell into their laps uninvited is the persistence and regularity with which certain of them followed up particular subjects. While Henry Gosson and Thomas Pavier lived, a murder was hardly complete without a ballad or two published by one or the other of these men; their murder pieces outnumber those of all the other members of the trade combined. John Trundle, in the reign of King James, was an industrious purveyor of incredible stories of supernatural marvels. John Bellamy published chiefly the kind of books which are nowadays prized as Americana, and William Welby, who seems, for a time, to have been

[283]

semi-official publisher to the Virginia Company, issued many more. Of all the news from France printed before 1600, half, roughly speaking, was published by four men—John Wolf (who published more than 60% of this half), Edward Aggas, William Wright, and Richard Field; the remaining half is distributed among more than forty. It could not have been by chance that so large a part of this news came into the hands of a small number of publishers; they must have taken steps to secure it. What these steps were we can only guess, but we can be sure they did not sit idle. We can even fancy certain publishers monopolizing particular incidents for themselves. Of the five ballads and one book entered in the register at the time of the murder of Robert Beech in 1594, Thomas Gosson or Thomas Millington had a hand in all but one: they entered two in partnership with Thomas Dawson, one jointly, and one each singly (even here they may have been acting for the firm).[46] John Trundle glorified the Overbury case in print almost single-handed.[47] It is a curious fact that Josias Parnell, a bookseller who, though he seems to have been in business for forty years, published only a few books, and next to no books of news at all, should have entered in one day two books and a ballad on Judith Phillips, a notorious confidence-woman,[48] as if he were determined to work that vein for all it was worth. Within a year of Queen Elizabeth's death, Thomas Pavier, in the face of the stiffest competition, had entered or published nine pieces in commemoration of her reign or in honor of King James.[49] Of

[46] Arber, II. 658–9.
[47] See above, p. 142 f.
[48] Arber, II. 672.
[49] 1) *Anglorum Lacrimæ* . . . Verses by Richard Johnson. 1603. 2) *The poores lamentation for the death of* . . . *Elizabeth* . . . 1603. 3) *King Iames his Welcome to London* . . . By I[ohn] F[enton]. 1603. 4) *A triumphant song of the Kinges coronation.* Entered 9 August 1603 (Arber, III. 244). 5) *Englands Wedding Garment* . . . In verse. 1603. 6) *A mournefull Dittie, entituled*

the thirty-five identified pieces concerning the Armada which are mentioned above,[50] John Wolf had a hand in twenty-one, a record which can be attributed only to his own energy. Furthermore, an entry of 13 October 1590—"Entred for his copie, The tables and mappes of the Spanierdes pretendid Invasion by Sea./ together with the discription thereof, by booke and otherwise. in all languages vnder the handes of the Archbishop of Canterbury, the lord Admirall, the lord Chamberlen of her maiesties house"[51]—suggests that Wolf actually obtained a monopoly for the publishing of the history of the Armada. Could it have been for services rendered at a time when the rest of the publishers showed symptoms of funk?

Furthermore, after the middle of the sixteenth century, we can be quite certain that some publishers specialized in the publication of news. There is no record before the end of our period of a man who published nothing but news, but there are a number who, primarily popular publishers, issued news-reports so profusely that they bulk very large in the total production of these men. The first extensive publisher of news on record is Richard Jones. Other men before him had done much. John Day, for example, had brought into the world a very interesting and valuable series of books of topical interest, as evidence, we should suppose, of his public spirit. William Seres and Henry Bynneman also supplied a good deal of news in their time, and a popular printer like John Allde poured from his press a steady stream of ballads and other ephemeral pieces, many of them topical. The name of Lucas

---

Elizabeths losse . . . Broadside. [1603.] 7) *The Royall entertainment into London of . . . King James* . . . Entered 21 March 1604 (Arber, III. 255). 8) *A newe songe of the triumphs of the Tilt before the kinge the 29 of March 1604.* Entered 28 March 1604 (*ib.*, III. 257). 9) *The kinges goinge to the parlament.* Ballad. Entered 28 March 1604 (*ib.*).

[50] See pp. 126–130.

[51] Arber, II. 564.

[285]

Harrison is conspicuous in the early lists of books of foreign news. But Jones, a prolific publisher of popular matter of all kinds for thirty-eight years, between 1564 and 1602, eclipsed all these. In a catalog of the kinds of news discussed in this treatise, he would be represented by about eighty recorded publications. Many of them were ballads, but he also issued two of Peele's encomiastic poems,[52] *The censure of a loyall subiect*,[53] and two works of Gascoigne,[54] as well as a number of curious verse-tracts less well known. The news which Jones published was almost all domestic, and therefore moral and patriotic. He overlooked none of the topics usually treated in news-reports, neither deformed swine nor the execution of traitors, blazing stars nor entertainments for the queen. Who would suppose that all this miscellaneous home news drifted into his shop by chance? Or that, if he sat in his house waiting for other men to bring him copy to publish, so much was offered him that he could refuse all but pieces with a popular appeal and yet publish so much? On the contrary, having been drawn into the métier of popular publisher because of a natural affinity for it or because he thought his best opportunity lay there, he surely took the initiative again and again to secure the kind of copy he was interested in publishing, by searching for it, by encouraging writers who had a taste for producing it, by ordering copy to be written for him.

The most extensive publisher of news before the reign of King James was unquestionably John Wolf, the self-styled Luther of the stationer's trade, a man of undoubted energy and force of character. Wolf was a prolific publisher of books of many kinds, and besides he printed

---

[52] 1) *An Eglogue Gratulatorie*, as above, p. 28. 2) *Polyhymnia*, as above, p. 18.
[53] As above, p. 119.
[54] 1) *The Princelye pleasures* . . . *at Kenelwoorth*, as above, p. 22. 2) *The Spoyle of Antwerpe*, as above, p. 188.

sometimes for other men; in 1583 he is reported to have had five presses, as many as the queen's printer himself, and there is no doubt that he was one of the busiest men in the trade. I have noticed about one hundred and fifty pieces entered or published by him, two-thirds of them translations from foreign books of news. Wolf was out of his apprenticeship about 1572; thereafter for several years he seems to have traveled on the continent and perhaps to have worked in printing shops in Italy. There is no record of him in London before 1579, but about that time he seems to have set up in business there, and he soon became notorious as the outspoken ringleader of the un-privileged printers in their fight on the monopoly of the patentees. In 1583, however, the authorities won him over to their side by making him considerable concessions, and—such is the frailty of our human nature—in a short time he was engaged in ferreting out the secret infringers of the sacred patents, his former associates. He printed in Latin, Italian, and French as well as English, and he is known to have sent some of his books to the continental book-fairs. As a matter of fact, it was not until the year of the Armada that Wolf began to publish news, and the total output mentioned above was piled up between that time and his death in 1601. Indeed, since he published almost nothing in the way of news before the summer of 1588 and then, as has already been noticed, put forth a heroic effort to furnish information and inspiration in print, it may have been this incident which opened his eyes to the opportunity that lay in publishing news and started him on the journalistic phase of his career. Several books on the Armada which he published were translated from foreign copies. At any rate, during the next three years, when events of the most exciting kind were hap-pening in France, he published translations of French news-reports in great numbers, and many more, from France, the Low Countries, and other parts of Europe, during the rest of the decade.

It is hardly questionable, in the face of this record, that Wolf obtained many of these books which he published in translation (and nobody knows how many more besides which he did not see fit to publish or which he did publish, but which we have no record of today) from a regular source of supply. That he was an energetic and able man is fairly clear; that he had connections on the continent can hardly be doubted: it is difficult to believe that he could have published so much news from foreign sources if he had not arranged for his friends or agents in continental cities to send him copies of such books of news of local origin as might interest English readers or in some similar way provided for a sufficient supply. If so, this arrangement is the nearest thing to a news-collecting organization we have so far met with.

The premier news-publisher of the first half of the seventeenth century was Nathaniel Butter, a tolerably well-known personage from the fact that his prosaic name and the novelty of such a news-publishing business as he and his partners conducted made him a frequent butt of the satirists of his time. The son of a bookseller, he was admitted to the freedom of the company early in 1604 and worked at his trade for the next sixty years. At first he published books of many kinds, including a number of books of news, more than half of them translations. In the autumn of 1622, furthermore, he became the leading spirit in the publication of the first English newspaper, though it would appear that he was not connected with it from the start and, for a while, he must have published a rival series. From this time forward, Butter devoted more and more of his attention to the publishing of news and assigned most of his copyrights to other books. In 1638 he and Nicholas Bourne obtained a royal patent giving them a monopoly of the publication of foreign news, but they had not long to profit by it, for in 1641 their news-book, although it pathetically pleaded that its news from abroad was "very fitting for this State to take notice of in this time of division and distraction,"[55] was overwhelmed by the competition of the flood of domestic periodicals which poured forth. Butter's name is found on some of these too, but he does not appear to have met with much success during the interregnum. He is said to have died poor in 1664.

The names of no fewer than six booksellers appear at various times on the title-page of the first English newspaper—Butter, Bourne, Thomas Archer, William Sheffard, Bartholemow Downes, Nathaniel Newbery—and they seem to have formed a kind of news-publishing syndicate. Some of them were associated in the publishing of news before 1622, Newbery and Archer, it would seem, as early as 1617. Bourne and Archer, who issued the earliest numbers of the periodical, jointly brought out several books of news about the same time and a little earlier. It is impossible to ascertain the relationships of the members of this syndicate. The connection may have been natural: Bourne and Archer served their apprenticeship in the same shop; Butter's widowed mother married a bookseller named John Newbery, but it is not known whether he was related to Nathaniel Newbery. But it is evident that they were all interested in publishing and selling news. That, jointly or severally, they had connections with continental sources of news is very probable; as far as their periodical is concerned, there is no doubt, for it frequently refers to the foreign letters, books, and copies by which it is advised and sometimes to the late arrival, or the non-arrival, of

---

[55] *Newes from forraigne parts for the last two weekes past* . . . For Nath: Butter, 5 March 1641.

expected information, as if a regular supply had been stipulated for.

When we compare the activity of the booksellers of our period with modern journalistic organization, they seem, on the whole, not fully alive to their opportunities and casual and feckless in their methods of procuring news. But it is evident, in at least a few men like those whose work has just been described, that some notion of journalism as a business opportunity not unlike that which newspaper publishers hold today, was beginning to dawn.

4. REJUVENATED NEWS

There is one more thing a publisher could do when news was scarce or troublesome to secure—*viz.*, he could publish an old story as the latest new thing. We have already noticed that some stories which originated as news enjoyed a long and honorable career in the press and that ballads on passing events sometimes survived long after the events had lost their bloom. But there was no fraud in reprinting matter of this sort, which was preserved for its undying interest and not for any pertinence to recent occurrences attributed to it. We do find, however, a few instances when deception was undoubtedly practised.

When a publisher prints a ballad of *The lamentation of George Strangwidge, who for the consentinge to the death of Mr. Page of Plimmoth suffered death at Bar[n] stable 1601,*[56] knowing, as he must have known, that the man had been executed eleven years ago, and had been duly honored at the time with sundry ballads, of one of which the present was evidently a reissue, he is attempting to deceive buyers and to give his broadside the added interest of contemporaneity. *The manner of the cruell outragious murther of William Storre . . .,* mentioned above as originally published in 1603, reappears in 1613 as the first of *Three*

[56] *Shirburn Ballads,* no. XXVI.

Bloodie Murders . . .[57] The text of the 1603 edition is
faithfully followed, even down to the testimonials of good
character, except that all tell-tale dates are omitted. The
book does not specifically say that the murder was committed in 1613 instead of 1603, but in the very first sentence the words "of late" give that impression, and the
other two bloody murders, which may really have been of
recent occurrence, are plainly dated. The account of the
troubling of Alexander Nyndge by an evil spirit mentioned
above[58] was reprinted more than forty years later as *A
true and fearefull vexation of one Alexander Nyndge: being
most horribly tormented with the Deuill, from the 20. day of
Ianuary, to the 23. of Iuly. At Lyeringswell in Suffocke.*[59]
This story was refurbished for its second course in the
lists: pronouns of the first person were changed to the
third, a prelude on fallen angels was added, and the details
of the demoniac's behavior were imaginatively expanded.
A still more extensive fraud was perpetrated in 1614 by
that busy miracle-monger and father of lies, John Trundle,
in a book called *A Miracle, of Miracles.* This consists of
three parts—an account of the possession by the devil of
a woman at Dichet in Somerset, a miraculous prophecy
by "a pore Countrey Maide . . . at Rostorfe, a mile
distant from Melwing, in Germanie," and a flood in
Lincolnshire. The flood was doubtless of recent occurrence
and the news of it Trundle had already given the world in
a separate book.[60] But the story of the miracle "which
lately happened at Dichet in Sommersetshire" is nothing
but the account of the experience of Mrs. Margaret Cooper,
published as far back as 1584.[61] In reissuing this yarn,
Trundle made the minimum number of alterations.

[57] N.p. See above, p. 99.
[58] P. 157.
[59] For W[alter] Burre, sold by Edvvard Wright, 1615.
[60] *Lamentable Newes out of Lincolne-shire* . . . 1614.
[61] See above, p. 157.

Where the preface to the 1584 issue alluded to other recent "strange examples," Trundle omitted one paragraph and inserted a puff of "the execution of God himselfe from his holy fire in heauen, on the wretched man and his wife, at *Holnhurst* in Hampshire: written by that worthy Minister maister *Hilliard*," *i.e.*, *Fire from Heauen*, described above,[62] which Trundle had published a few months back. For the beginning of the 1584, text "Vpon the nineth day of May last past Anno. 1584. There was a Yeoman," he substituted "Vpon the ninth day of Septemb. last past, there was a Yeoman;" he also omitted the last sentence and raised the words *God* and *Lord* to full capitals wherever they appeared. The list of witnesses he copied without alteration. The second narrative in the book, although it is definitely dated "the first of October last, 1613," is undoubtedly an old story too. *A true Report happened in Germany at Melwing by A mayd of 14 yeres old* was entered in the Stationers' register 18 August 1580,[63] and *A moste Strange and Rare example of a maide, happeninge at a Towne Called Rostorfe in Jermanie* on 22 November 1580.[64] The former entry probably refers to *A prophesie vttered by the daughter of an honest countrey man, called Adam Krause*,[65] and although I have never seen this book, I suspect it of being Trundle's source.

5. Prompt Publication

Now that we have explained as well as we can how news came into the publisher's hands, the next question to arise is what he did with it once he had got it. But it is unnecessary to repeat what is well known about the sale of books during the early history of printing; it will be possible

[62] P. 204.
[63] By William Wright (Arber, II. 375).
[64] By Edward White (*ib.*, II. 383).
[65] By Eyriak Schlichtenberger. For William Wright, 1580.

to take up only one point of peculiar interest in a discussion of printed news—the rapidity with which it was published.

Nowadays news is collected, relayed, printed, and distributed with vertiginous speed; a newspaper or a press association exults if it delivers a piece of news to its customers sooner than its rivals by only a few minutes; every managing editor's ideal is to have the news on the street the moment it happens, if not sooner. The news-collectors and publishers of the sixteenth century had none of the ingenious facilities which enable our newspapers to present the latest news to their readers with that impertinent promptitude they use, but it would seem that they were not unaware that news is a commodity which age withers and that they exerted themselves to give it to their readers as rapidly as they could. We have already seen that ballads on the burning of the Globe theater were in existence the day after the fire, and that after the earthquake of 1580 two ballads and three books were entered in the Stationers' register within forty-eight hours.[66] In his *Wonderfull discouerie of Elizabeth Sawyer*,[67] the Rev. Henry Goodcole speaks of "most base and false Ballets, which were sung at the time of our returning from the *Witches* execution." In other words, these ballads were being hawked in the streets before the fire which had burned the poor woman was quite cooled. It is hard to find unquestionable evidence of when books of news were offered for sale, but by comparing the date of occurrence with the date of entry in the registers, we can determine approximately how rapidly the issuance of the printed news was being pushed forward. It is true that there is no constant relationship between the date of entry and the date of actual appearance in the bookseller's shop; while most printed pieces seem to have been entered before they

[66] See above, pp. 163 f.
[67] As above, p. 253.

were published, some were undoubtedly entered afterwards. But it seems doubtful that, during the latter part of the reign of Queen Elizabeth, when the censorship was strict, a publisher would have had the printing of a book begun before he had authority for it unless he was quite sure the authorities could find nothing in it to take exception to. At the same time, we cannot assume that he always made his entry as soon as he received the licenser's *imprimatur;* he may have put off that formality for a few days, though he would have been pretty sure to claim the copy as his own before the book actually appeared on the market so that he was protected against the depredations of anybody who might reprint his publication. Nevertheless, when we notice that a book was entered two days after the event it relates, we may conclude that the publication of it was well under way and that it would be offered for sale with all possible despatch, in a few days more at the furthest. It should be remembered that the printing of a piece of news was not usually a considerable task: setting up and printing a broadside was a job that did not require more than a couple of days and, if necessary, could be rushed, and most books of news consisted of but four, eight, or twelve leaves.

The apogee of promptness, we should suppose, is the preparation of news ahead of time, and of this provident practice we find a number of examples. The event thus related before it had happened was, of course, necessarily predictable and inevitable. Queen Elizabeth's coronation day (17 November) was a favorite occasion for publishing vociferously loyal ballads, and a number of them were entered a few days in advance. In 1578 Christopher Barker entered his ballad so soon as 3 October,[68] and in 1587 Edward Hake's *Oration conteyning an Expostulation . . .*

[68] *A psalme or songe of praise and thankes gyvinge* . . . (Arber, II. 339).

with the Queens . . . Subiects . . . imprinted this
xvij. day of Nouember in the xxx yeere of the Queenes . . .
raigne was entered 30 October.[69] On 14 November 1588
John Wolf entered *A Joyfull ballad of the Roiall entrance of*
Quene Elizabeth into her cyty of London the   Day of novem-
ber . . .,[70] *i.e.,* not knowing exactly when the queen
would come to St. Paul's to give thanks for the victory,
he entered this ballad with a blank date so that he could
have it ready at the earliest possible moment after the
event. Books describing the execution of criminals were
sometimes prepared in advance too. *The Life, Appre-*
hension, Arraignement, and Execution of Charles Court-
ney . . . and Clement Slie . . .[71] was entered 13 March
1612,[72] although the execution did not take place till the next
day. *The araignment . . . of Arnold Cosbye, who . . .*
murdered the Lord Burke . . . the 14. day of . . .
Ianuary, and was executed the 27. of the same moneth.
1591.[73] was entered on the 25th.[74] More forehanded, but
less surprising, is Peele's *Farewell. Entituled to the . . .*
Generalls of our English forces . . .,[75] which was entered 23 February 1589,[76] although the expedition did not
sail until 18 April.

Ballads were probably easier to write, print, and sell
and more closely dependent upon the excitement of the
moment than prose books and we therefore find them
setting the best records for quick appearance. Some were
entered on the day of the event. Deloney's ballad on the
capture of "the great galleazzo" during the fight with the

---

[69] *Ib.,* II. 477.   Printed for Edward Aggas, 1587.
[70] *Ib.,* II. 506.
[71] For Edward Marchant, 1612.
[72] By John Busby and John Trundle (Arber, III. 479).
[73] For Edward White, 1591.
[74] Arber, II. 573.
[75] Sold by William Wright, 1589.
[76] Arber, II. 516.

[295]

Armada[77] was entered on 10 August;[78] as the events it describes happened between 31 July and 7 August, no time was lost, certainly, in bringing the news to London, in writing the verses, or in making ready to publish them. A ballad on the execution of eight of the Gunpowder plotters was entered on 31 January 1606,[79] the day of their execution, and another the next day.[80] There are a number of ballads which were entered one or two days after the event; indeed, we should almost say that two days was par for a ballad on an exciting incident sure of a warm welcome.

Though a little more time was probably required to prepare a book of news, books were also pushed with great haste. A book on the surrender of Kinsale was entered 22 January 1602;[81] the town had been given up on the 9th, and the news could hardly have reached London before the 22d. *A true report, of the Araignement and execution of . . . Euerard Haunce* was entered in the register 4 August 1581.[82] As has already been explained, this book is a corrective of another, *The Araignement, and Execution, of . . . Eueralde Ducket.*[83] Since Hance had been executed on 31 July, between that day and 4 August *The Araignement, and Execution* must have been published and the *True report* conceived and composed. Munday's *Breefe discourse of the taking of Edmund Campion*[84] and a

[77] As above, p. 127.

[78] Arber, II. 495.

[79] *Londons gladd tydinges Or A comfortable reporte of the Arraynement Condemnation and execution of Eight of the most principall Traitours that euer breathed Lyfe . . .* Entered to Edward Aldee (*ib.*, III. 312).

[80] *The Traytours Downfall Declaringe their Araignement condempcon and Execucons.* Entered to Thomas Pavier (*ib.*).

[81] *All the newes out of Ireland with the yeildinge vp of Chinsale &c.* Entered to Thomas Pavier & John Hardie (*ib.*, III. 200).

[82] *Ib.*, II. 399.

[83] See above, p. 103.

[84] As above, p. 102.

ballad on the same subject[85] were entered 24 July 1581,[86] two days after Campion was shut up in the Tower, and his *Breefe and true reporte, of the Execution*[87] on 31 May 1582,[88] the day after the last execution which it records. *A briefe Treatise. Discouering . . . the offences . . . of the late 14. Traitors . . . With the maner of the execution of eight of them*[89] was entered on the day of the execution,[90] as was Kyd's account of the murder of John Brewen.[91] Even the government, when it made public information about its own acts, seems to have used all possible despatch: *The true copie of a letter from the queenes maiestie, to the Lord Maior*[92] was entered three days after the proceedings it relates.[93] *A true and plaine declaration of the horrible Treasons, practised by William Parry,*[94] which includes "the maner of his . . . execution," was entered three days before he was executed[95] and would therefore seem to have been made ready in advance.

It is interesting to notice that foreign news was sometimes brought over with surprising rapidity. At first sight, it sometimes seems that the impossible was achieved, for we find that *The true coppie of a letter, written from the Leager by Arnham, the 27. day of Iuly [1591] . . .*[96] was entered in London on the 20th.[97] We must, however, take into account the fact that English dates at this

---

[85] *Master Campion the seditious Jesuit is welcome to London.* Entered by Richard Jones.

[86] Arber, II. 397.

[87] For William VVright, 1582.

[88] Arber, II. 412.

[89] As above, p. 136.

[90] 28 August 1588 (Arber, II. 497).

[91] As above, p. 275. See *ib.*, II. 614.

[92] As above, p. 45.

[93] 25 August 1586 (Arber, II. 455).

[94] C[hristopher] B[arker, 1585] (3 edd.).

[95] By Ralph Newberry 27 February 1585 (Arber, II. 440).

[96] For Andrew White, 1591.

[97] Arber, II. 590.

[297]

period were ten days slow on account of the obstinate refusal of the English to have anything to do with the popish way of counting time, and three days, therefore, had intervened between the writing of the letter and the entry. This is nevertheless very fast work, for the letter was translated from a Dutch book. But the English book is only five pages long and was printed at two impressions, so that both could have been worked off very rapidly Still more remarkable is *The Declaration of the Decree made by the Generall States . . . Dated the 15. of July, 1619 stilo nouo*,[98] which was entered 6 July[99] and would therefore appear to have been printed at the Hague, brought over to London, and entered all in one day. It seems, however, that 15 July must be a (deliberate?) mistake for 5 July and that eleven days is the interval instead of one—not a bad record, at that. Ten days to two weeks was apparently the shortest time for bringing news from the Netherlands to London, but this interval includes the time required to print the news in Dutch. *Newes from the Englishe armye out of Britanne the Thirde of June 1591 sent to a gente of accoumpte* was entered 5 June;[100] it was therefore entered either two days after it was received in London or twelve days after it was sent from the front. News from France took a little longer: *Remonstrances made by the Kings . . . ambassadour, vnto the French King*,[101] which includes a letter dated 26 July, was entered eighteen days later, 3 August.[102] An unusually complete account of bringing over news and issuing it in London is found on the title-page of a book printed 6 April 1573: *A true rehersall of the Honorable & Tryūphant Victory: which the defenders of the Trueth haue had againste . . . ye Albanists. Which*

[98] For Nathaniel Newbery, 1619.
[99] Arber, III. 651.
[100] By John Wolfe (*ib.*, II. 583).
[101] As above, p. 111.
[102] Arber, III. 571.

*came to passe . . . the xxv. daye of Marche. 1573. Trans-
lated out of Dutch into English, the thyrde day of Apryll:
the which Copy in Dutch, was Printed at Delft, the xxvij.
day of March laste paste.*[103] That is, the news of a battle
fought at Haarlem was for sale in London on the twelfth
succeeding day. In giving this complete record of the
origin of his news, was Jones pluming himself on such a
creditable record for promptitude?

Every book of news was not issued with as much speed as
those which have just been cited; good news, strange news,
and new news was always welcome in London even if not
quite fresh from the mint. Authors, publishers, and other
persons concerned in the matter could not, or would not,
always achieve the utmost promptness. But evidence
such as this seems to show that publishers did not fail to
appreciate the fact that news, like hotcakes, tastes best
right off the griddle.

The alertness which publishers seem often to have shown
in issuing printed news quickly was probably sharpened by
the competition of their rivals. Though the book trade in
the sixteenth century seems to have been a homogeneous
group of tradesmen who frequently coöperated with one
another, we can hardly doubt that a certain amount of
healthy competition existed. Except after an event of the
first magnitude had happened and books about it were
printed by the dozen, the records do not show much
duplication of prose reports, though some of the charges of
inaccuracy which we have already noticed were probably inspired by a desire to attract buyers away from com-
peting books, and we have seen one publisher roundly
denouncing the publications of all his rivals.[104] But
ballads issued simultaneously by different publishers on
the same subject frequently appear, sometimes in rather

[103] Richard Iones.
[104] See above, p. 236.

large numbers. Generally speaking, there could have been little to choose among them; one would serve the ballad-connoisseur's purpose just about as well as the next, and the first to be offered for sale, therefore, must have enjoyed a distinct advantage. Popular prose reports, especially murder books, were multiplied in the same way and likewise must have competed one with the other. By observing that the first piece of such a sort that was brought out skimmed the cream of the market, a publisher could hardly have failed to learn that, in topical publishing, promptness was a virtue that bestowed special rewards.

CHAPTER XII

THE IMMEDIATE FORERUNNERS OF THE
NEWSPAPER

1. SERIALS AND MISCELLANIES

THERE are just two great differences between the
scheme of the newspaper and that of the printed news
which we have been reviewing. In the first place, the
newspaper is a miscellany; it includes many kinds of news
from many places (and, in modern times, much other reading matter as well), though the so-called first English
newspaper was made up entirely of foreign news, and that
recorded very largely military campaigns and battles and
political maneuvers. The pieces of news published during
our period, on the other hand, are limited, as a rule, to a
single subject. In the second place, the newspaper is a
periodical; it consists of a series of parts appearing at
stated intervals and connected by uniformity (or continuity) of ownership, title, style of make-up, and (with allowance for the alterations attending upon human instability)
policy, and in its columns an incident extending over a
period of time is related in a sequence of daily (or weekly)
instalments. The first English newspaper only roughly
measures up to these specifications. Although it sometimes called itself the *Weekely Newes* and constantly spoke
of itself as a weekly collection, it appeared quite irregu-
larly. As far as our knowledge goes, the publishers managed to put out nearly fifty numbers a year, but sometimes
an interval of as much as two weeks separated two suc-

cessive issues, and again as little as two days.[1]   The title also varied from week to week and the names of the members of the syndicate of booksellers who published it appeared in the imprint in all sorts of combinations.   The printed news we have dealt with was, however, published occasionally, sporadically, without continuity.   Yet we find a few foreshadowings of these features during our period which, while they had no bearing whatsoever on the form of the first English newspaper, are interesting as dim anticipations of·what was to come.

There are a few instances of something like serial publication which are probably, however, not the genuine article.   For example, two complementary reports of a trial of witches of 1566 were entered separately in the Stationers' register; but they seem to have been published, though with distinct title-pages, as one book, for both are dated 13 August in the imprint.[2]   In two books reporting winter floods in the country in 1607 we find a closer approximation of serial publication; the second is an undoubted later addition, though it contains the complete text of the first as well.[3]   In *A Briefe discourse of the cruell dealings of the Spanyards, in . . . Gulick and Cleue,*[4] the publisher writes:

Also heere ought to stande the Letter of the Emperours Legate Carolus Sonderpuhill to the Admirant, but because the same is at large in our other booke (concerning this matter) we thinke needelesse to repeate the same heere againe.

[1] See no. 2 (of the second numbered series), 28 October 1623, and no. 3, 11 November; no. 6, 11 December 1623, and no. 7, 13 December.

[2] 1) *The Examination and Confession of certaine Wytches at Chensforde . . . the xxvi. daye of Iuly . . .* 2) *The second examination and Confession of mother Agnes Waterhouse . . . the xxvii. day of Iuly . . .* For Wyllyam Pickeringe, 13 August 1566.   See Arber, I. 328, 329.

[3] 1) *A true report of certaine wonderfull ouerflowings of Waters,* as above, p. 163. 2) *More strange Newes: Of wonderfull accidents hapning by the late ouerflowings of Waters . . .* For Edward White, [1607].

[4] Iohn Wolfe, 1599.

Our other book is *A briefe relation, of what is hapned since the last of August 1598* . . . ,[5] which was published about the same time.   The publisher seems to assume that the reader is familiar with the other book, as if they were complementary; if this remark had been intended as a mere puff, he might have mentioned the other book's title.

A few fragments of evidence which seem to imply serial publication can also be cited.   There are these entries of books in the Stationers' registers:

1) *The fift booke of the last troubles of Fraunce conteininge ye historie of the most memorable thinges happened Synce the death of henry the Third, of Fraunce, in the moneth of August 1589. vnto the siege of La Fere.*[6]

2) *Suite De l'inuentaire general De L'istoire de France.*[7]

3) *Calendarium Historicum or the first parte of Relacons of all the most notable occurrenses happened in Europe since the moneth of August 1601 till this presente August 1602.*[8]

Further parts of these series were not necessarily published in England.   Clearer evidence is found in two ballads entered by John White in September 1613—*The vntymely end of Master Page a vintener in London who was Murthered by a mayde servante of his house,* and *The second parte of the murder of master Page by his mayd and of her execucon by burninge in Smithfield for that fact .11. Septembris 1613.*   The latter is not the conventional second part of a ballad that was really a unit.   The former was entered on 8 September, before the execution had taken place; the second, which was entered on the day of the burning, apparently brought the history to its proper climax.[9]

---

[5] *Ib.*, 1599.

[6] Entered 7 November 1597 by Thomas Adams (Arber, III. 95).

[7] Entered 3 January 1600 by [William] Ponsonby (*ib.*, III. 153).   An earlier part was entered 7 November 1597 (*ib.*, III. 96).   There are copies of an edition printed by George Eld in 1607.

[8] Translated from the German by J. R.   Entered 6 August 1602 by James Shawe (*ib.*, III. 214).

[9] *Ib.*, III. 532.

Two other entries, in 1588 and 1589, plainly point to a continuous enterprise—*A booke in Frenche to be translated into Englishe, Intituled Premier Volume Du Recuell contenant les choses memorables advenues soubs la ligue, Qui s'est faicte et eleuee contra la Relegion Reformee pour l'abolir*,[10] and *The second Collection conteyning the history of the most notable thinges happened vnder the league.*[11] We might consider two books published in 1562 a series—*A declaration made by the Prynce of Conde, for to shewe the causes that haue constrained him to take vpon him the defence of the Kinges authoritie . . . ,* and *A seconde declaration of the Prince of Conde, To make knowen the causers of the troubles . . . in this Realme . . .*[12] Two books published by Thomas Pavier in 1601 definitely form a series—*Newes from Ostend, of, The Oppugnation, and fierce siege, made, by the Archeduke Albertus his Forces . . . ,* and *Further Newes of Ostend. Wherein is declared such accidents as haue happened since the former Edition . . .* The first was entered on 5 August,[13] and if the second is *The Journall or Register of the Daylie procedinges in and before Oste ende Synce the begynnynge of the siege* which Pavier entered on 9 September,[14] they were published about one month apart. As the former alludes to its being "Now newly imprinted; whereunto are added such other Newes and Accidents as haue lately hapned," these books may be part of a series of three, of which the first has been lost.

This evidence hardly implies a wide application of the idea of the serial publication of news, but shows that it was not altogether unappreciated before the foundation of the first newspaper.

The simplest form of miscellany—so simple as almost to

[10] Entered 19 September 1588 by John Wolf (*ib.*, II. 500).
[11] Entered 10 June 1589 by John Wolf (*ib.*, II. 523).
[12] For Edwarde Sutton, 1562.
[13] Arber, III. 190.
[14] *Ib.*, III. 191.

make the word a misnomer—is a book of several pieces of news of the same kind—two or three nearly simultaneous murders, miracles, or military operations in the same theater of war. Such books are not uncommon. In such a book, however, as *A True Recitall touching the cause of the death of Thomas Bales, a Seminarie Priest, who was hanged and quartered in Fleet-street on Ashwednesdaie . . . Wherevnto is adioyned . . . the death of Annis Bankyn, who vpon the next day following was burned in Saint Georges fields . . .*,[15] the connection between the two incidents is more casual, being only the accidental circumstance that both executions took place at the same time, for Bales was a traitor and Bankyn a murderess. Again, in *A True Report of the . . . condemnation, of a Popish Priest, named Robert Drewrie . . . Also the tryall and death of Humphrey Lloyd, for maliciouslie murdering one of the Guard . . .*,[16] a traitor's end and a murderer's are recounted in the same book, though this murderer turned out, on examination, to be a Catholic too.

In *A Discourse of The Queenes Maiesties entertainement in Suffolk and Norfolk . . . Wherevnto is adioyned a commendation of Sir Humfrey Gilberts ventrous iourney*,[17] the author's snatching at whatever opportunity was offered to publish his minor works in print will account for its miscellaneous make-up. There are a few other books of miscellaneous content—*A briefe relation, of what is hapned since the last of August 1598. by comming of the Spanish campe into the Dukedom of Cleue . . . Together with a Description of the VVhale of Berckhey . . . Also a Letter of the Emperour . . . The conspiracy of the three Bishops . . . The death of the Earle of Brooke . . . The list of the Souldiers leuied by the Protestant Princes of Germany;*[18]

---

[15] As above, p. 136.
[16] As above, p. 136.
[17] As above, p. 22.
[18] As above, p. 184.

[305]

The Protestants and Iesuites vp in Armes in Gulicke-land.
Also, A true and wonderfull relation of a Dutch maiden
. . . who . . . hath fasted . . . 14 yeares . . .;[19]
Newes out of Holland: Concerning Barnevelt and his fellow
Prisoners . . .: the Oration and Propositions made in
their behalfe . . . by the Ambassadors of the French King
. . . VVherevnto is adioyned a Discourse, wherein the
Duke D'Espernons revolt and pernicious deseignes are
truely displayed . . .[20]—but they are all translations, and,
as we shall soon see, the idea of collecting heterogeneous
parcels of news had been put in practice on the continent
long before the earliest of these books was printed.

Another approximation to the idea of the miscellany is
to be found in the chronicles of foreign history published
from the early years of the reign of Elizabeth. These
compilations are, of course, unified by their being devoted
to a particular war, or series of wars, or to a particular
country, or group of countries, but in their ranging, as
some of them do, over a century or more, and gathering
up a variety of information, they may be allowed something of the nature of the miscellany. A few titles will
show what they are:

1) *A discourse of the Ciuile warres and late troubles in Fraunce,*
drawn into Englishe by Geffray Fenton . . . [1568–70.][21]

2) *The Historie of Guicciardin, conteining the Warres of Italie and*
other partes . . . Reduced into English by Geoffrey Fenton.[22]

3) *A Tragicall Historie of the troubles and Ciuile warres of the lowe*
Countries . . . [1559–81.][23]

4) *The true history of the ciuill warres of France . . . from . . .*
1585 vntill . . . 1591.[24]

[19] As above, p. 147.
[20] As above, p. 175.
[21] For Lucas Harrison & George Bishop, [1570].
[22] For William Norton, 1579.
[23] By Theophile, D. L.; translated from the French by T[homas] S[tocker]. For Toby Smith, [1583] (2 edd.).
[24] By Antony Colynet. For Thomas Woodcock, 1591.

5) *The Mutable and wauering estate of France from . . . 1460, vntill . . . 1595 . . .* [25]

6) *A briefe cronicle, and perfect rehearsall of all the memorable actions hapned not onelie in the low-Countries, but also in Germanie, Italy, Fraunce, Spaine, England, Turkie, and other countries since . . . 1500 to . . . 1598.*[26]

But all these instances are interesting rather than important: the first English newspaper derived its form and its character from another source.

2. THE ANCESTRY OF THE NEWSPAPER

We have now arrived at the grand anticlimax of the early history of journalism in England—all the printed news discussed above had nothing to do, directly, with the origin or form of the first English newspaper. Indirectly it doubtless did much to prepare the way by creating a body of news-readers and, more importantly, by leading certain publishers into the purveying of news as a specialty of their trade. But the first English newspaper was almost entirely a translation of news-reports from abroad; its form was their form; and although its sources have not been traced, there is every likelihood that it also borrowed the idea of appearing weekly from the early weekly newspapers of the Netherlands and Germany. It was not a native growth; its ancestors were the same as those of the earliest continental periodicals.

In Germany the news-publishing trade flourished from the beginning of the sixteenth century; it was at least fifty years ahead of England. The peculiar political and social conditions in the states of the Empire encouraged it. There is evidence of a very active exchange of news in letters at the beginning of the era of printing. Many of

---

[25] Collected out of sundry, both Latine, Italian and French Historiographers. Thomas Creede, 1597.

[26] [John Wolf, 1598.]

these letters were private advices, just like the private letters which we have seen put in print in England. But many others were packets of news deliberately, energetically, and more or less regularly gathered by agents hired for the purpose by princes, diplomats, politicians, and merchant-barons. Eminent personages in England followed the same practice. Furthermore, in Germany, the public or semi-public newsletter-writer seems to have operated early in the sixteenth century. A scrivener or a bookseller with a taste for gossip or a postmaster to whom news was constantly borne on the four winds collected the latest intelligence every now and then and sent it by post to a list of clients. It was usually a small list of clients; news was never disseminated very widely by this method, though it is quite probable that each letter was read by dozens besides the client to whom it was addressed. I know of nothing of this sort in England before the parliamentary newsletters of 1628.[27] Most of the earliest printed news in Germany was derived from reports such as these.

It is a somewhat curious fact that the idea of gathering news from several sources in a single printed piece was so slow in taking hold in England; almost all the news we have examined above handles but one subject at a time. Even when we do find a book less strictly unified, it is usually made up of a recent occurrence and a set of historical parallels. Seldom do we find several distinct events reported in a single piece. In Germany, however, the idea of gathering recent news from miscellaneous sources into a budget seems to have been practised from the earliest times. It can be seen in early newsletters. There is an English printed book which, singularly enough, is a good example of private or semi-private news-gathering. It is called *Newes concernynge the general coūcell/ holden at*

[27] See Notestein & Relf: *Commons debates.*

Trydent by the Emperoure and the Germaynes with all the nobles of Hungarye/ Constantenople and Rome. Translated oute of Germayne into Englysh By Ihon Holibush. Anno. 1548.[28] The title is misleading; it is really a letter written from Augsburg where the imperial parliament was sitting and referring religious questions to the Council of Trent. It also includes news of a truce with the Turks, of a sea-fight, of a Hungarian nobleman possessed by a devil, and of half-a-dozen other recent happenings in various places. The author was a foreigner attending the emperor on business; from his mention of the "Byshoppe of Rome," we should suppose he was a Protestant. But whether or not he was an Englishman, and whether this book was translated from his original letter or from a German printed book we cannot say. This is the only printed example of its kind of informal news-gathering which I know of in England; by comparison, most of the printed letters mentioned above sound affected and self-conscious.

Early in the sixteenth century the Germans commenced collecting and printing recent news in budgets covering a year, a half-year, or a month. Such *Sammelzeitungen, Jahres-zeitungen,* and *Monats-Zeitungen*[29] go back at least to the second quarter of the century. These books are genuinely miscellaneous, but they are not serially continuous. I know of nothing of the same sort in England. About the time of the Armada, the semi-annual collections became especially numerous and important. A learned Catholic gentleman, Michael von Aitzing, in 1588, commenced writing a sober semi-annual chronicle which was published for sale at the Frankfurt fair and which therefore covered the six months' period between the current fair and the last. These compilations were called *Messre-*

---

[28] Thomas Raynalde, [1549].

[29] The German word *Zeitung,* which we nowadays translate as *newspaper,* in the sixteenth century meant no more than *tydings, relation.*

lationen (*Messe* = fair). Although they were not connected by identity of title or by numbering in series, they are the next thing to a semi-annual periodical. Much more significant for England was the series of Latin compilations begun in 1594 by a Frisian named Michael ab Isselt— *Mercurius Gallobelgicus: siue, rerum in Gallia & Belgio potissimum: Hispania quoque, Italia, Anglia, Germania, Polonia, vicinisque locis ab anno 1588 vsque ad Martium . . . 1594 gestarum, Nuncius.*[30] The first volume contained six years' news, but thenceforth continuations appeared semi-annually until 1635. After the author's death, the work was carried on by other men. Though professedly a collection of all news, this series, like the earliest English news-periodicals, made a specialty of the current wars. The name of Mercurius Gallobelgicus gave the series a unity lacking in the *Messrelationen*, and, in England at least, it seems to have caught the popular fancy. Dean Barlow quoted an anecdote from it in his sermon on the execution of Essex,[31] citing his source in a marginal note in precisely the same way he cited scriptural texts. Dr. Donne composed an epigram *To Mercurius Gallo-Belgicus*, accusing him of lying like a Greek. The name was the pattern of Mercurius Britannicus, the pseudonym employed in 1625–6 by the publishers of the first English newspaper. In the latter part of the seventeenth century, several newsbooks were dubbed with the same name, and Mercury as the title of a newspaper and the words *mercury* (for newsbook) and *mercury-woman* (for newsbook-seller) all come from the same ancestry. Mercurius Britannicus was, however, the invention of Bishop Joseph Hall, who adopted it as a pseudonym in publishing his *Mundus alter et idem* (1605?). In the original Latin,

[30] Coloniæ Agrippinæ [= Cologne]: Apud Godefridum Kempensem, 1594. Later volumes were published at Frankfurt.

[31] See above, p. 61.

Mercurius Gallobelgicus had a considerable circulation in England. A translation of one volume by Robert Boothe was also printed in 1614,[32] and another was entered in the Stationers' register 25 September 1619 by the master and the wardens for the Latin stock of the company.[33] Three other entries undoubtedly point to the translation of *Messrelationen* or possibly, as far as the last two are concerned, of *Mercurius Gallobelgicus* himself:

1) *Thoccurrences of Sixe monethes by way of discourse Concernynge French matters.* Entered 3 December 1589 by Edward Aggas (Arber, II. 536).

2) *Historicall Relacons or a true discription of all matters worthie memory in all Europe and other places adioyninge from the Moneth of Aprill vntill September 1602. Done by Andrew Strigell.* Entered 9 July 1603 by [Cuthbert] Burby (*ib.*, III. 241).

3) *Newes out of the Lowe cuntreies with a report of all thinges happened from the begynninge of this Last Summer till this present wynter betwene the States and the Archduke in Brabant and Friseland this yere 1605.* Entered 9 October 1605 by Thomas Pavier (*ib.*, III. 303).

3. CORANTOS

About the same time that the *Messrelationen* began to flourish, another kind of collection of news, not altogether unknown before, grew to an increased importance. This is a much shorter compilation, likewise bringing together news from many places, but covering a shorter period of time, usually unspecified, but seldom much longer than a week. These collections are the direct progenitor of the newspaper; they needed only to be issued periodically in a continuous series, identified by serial numbers or similarity of title, to become a newspaper. These collections, when the idea was taken up in England in 1621, were called *corantos*,

---

[32] A *relation of all matters passed, especially in France and the Low-Countries . . . Translated according to the Originall of Mercurius Gallo-Belgicus.* For William Welby, 1614.

[33] Arber, III. 657.

but I have not met this word in Germany, nor in the Netherlands until just a year or two before 1621 (though, of course, I am not well acquainted with the journalistic history of these countries). The earmarks of the coranto are a colorless, matter-of-fact tone, and the arrangement of the news under rubrics indicating the place and date of origin ("From Venice, the 13. of Ianuarie"). This arrangement under rubrics which are quite like the date-lines of modern newspapers is found in written newsletters early in the sixteenth century. The publication of news in this form was a journalistic enterprise; it was not carried on by polemical writers and it made no appeal, as a rule, to party or to patriotic feelings. Between 1590 and 1621 a number of corantos were published in translation in England as part of the annual grist of foreign news, as follows:

1) *News from Rome, Spain, Palermo, Geneuæ, and France. With the miserable state of the Citty of Paris, and the late yeelding vppe of sundrie Towns of great strength, vnto the King.*[34]

2) *Nevves Lately come on the last day of Februarie 1591. from diuers partes of France, Sauoy, and Tripoli in Soria.*[35]

3) *A true relation of the French Kinge his good successe, in winning from the Duke of Parma, his Fortes and Trenches, and slaieing 500. of his men . . . With other intelligences . . .*[36]

4) *Nevves from Rome, Venice, and Vienna . . .*[37]

[34] Translated from the French and the Italian. As above, p. 170. This news was probably selected from several sources for its palatability to a Protestant nation. The news from Rome relates the reception of an envoy from Henry IV of France by the pope, and tells how certain pasquils in picture were stuck up at Pasquil's post on that occasion and verses "by some fauourer of Christian Religion" were scattered abroad. Three pictures and three sets of verses are reproduced, and the account goes on to describe the pope's anger at this pleasantry.

[35] Truely translated out of the French and Italian Copies, as they were sent to right Honourable persons. Iohn Wolfe, 1591. There are none of the customary rubrics in this book, but otherwise it is quite in the manner of the coranto.

[36] Iohn Wolfe, 1592. The other intelligences may be a coranto drastically abridged. They emanate from various places—Provence, Aix, Muscovy, Germanie, *et c.*—in the usual way.

[37] For Thomas Gosson, 1595.

5) *Newes from diuers countries. As, From Spaine, Antwerpe, Collin, Venice, Rome, The Turke, and The prince Doria* . . . [38]

6) *A terrible deluge or ouerflowing in Roome, at their Christmasse last* . . . [39]

7) *A True Declaration of that which hapned since the enemies first comming to Bommell* . . . *vntil this present moneth of Iune, 1599. Wherevnto is annexed, some collections out of seuerall Letters from diuers places.*[40]

8) *Certen newes written towardes London from Italye Fraunce Hungarie and other places.*[41]

9) *A relation of all matters done in Bohemia, Austria, Poland, S[i]letia, France, &c that is worthy of relating, since the 2 of March 1618 [o.s.?] vntill the 4th of May 1619.*[42]

10) *A Most true Relation of the late Proceedings in Bohemia, Germany, and Hungaria.* . . . *As also the happie Arriuall of Sir Andrew Gray into Lusatia.* . . . [43]

11) *The certaine and true news, from all the parts of Germany and Poland, to this present 29. of October, 1621.*[44]

12) *The Present State of the Affaires betwixt the Emperor and King of Bohemia* . . . *Together With the Occurrents lately happened in the Armies of Generall Veere, the Princes of the Vnion, and Spinola.*[45]

---

[38] [Sold by William Barley,] 1597.

[39] Iohn Wolfe, 1599. This book was probably derived from one or more corantos. The news is narrated in the usual style; it appears under two rubrics— "From Rome the 25. of December 1598," "From Roome the 2. of Ianuary. 1599;" and it relates other occurrences besides the flood, a page and a half at the beginning being devoted to the religious ceremonies held during the Christmas season. Perhaps the reader was to infer that the calamity was a rebuke to idolatry, but there is no partisanship in the narrative.

[40] Printed according to the Dutch Copie, Printed at Amsterdam. Iohn Wolfe, 1599. Possibly the translation of a coranto: it is written in the usual style and, besides the news of the siege, consists of three letters from German cities.

[41] Part of an entry made 25 February 1602 by Matthew Law (Arber, III. 201).

[42] A book entered 1 June 1619 by Raphe Rounthwait (*ib.*, III. 649).

[43] Dort: 1620. This was probably compiled from several German newsbooks by some one whose object was to give notice of the progress of the Elector Palatine's fortunes.

[44] For B[artholemew] D[ownes], 1621.

[45] Translated out of the French, and High Dutch Coppies. [London? Edward Griffin?] 1620. This consists of a number of documents and what looks like a coranto.

[313]

4. THE SINGLE-SHEET CORANTOS, 1620–1

The corantos listed above appeared sporadically in England, and, although their originals have not been traced, it is improbable that they too were anything but occasional issues. By the year 1620, however, weekly periodicals had been evolved in Germany and the Netherlands, and the idea was bound to be communicated to other nations. It was in the Netherlands, at Amsterdam, that the earliest periodical of news in English, or something much more like a periodical than had ever been printed before, took its start. How and why news-sheets in English should suddenly appear in Amsterdam late in 1620 we can only guess, for very likely we have only a small part of the evidence before us, but that is exactly what seems to have happened. On 2 December 1620, at Amsterdam, George Veseler printed, "to be soulde by Petrus Keerius," a single-sheet in English, without a title, which bore on both sides a coranto-like collection of news from various parts of the continent. This is the first sign we have of the somewhat curious idea of publishing frequent batches of news in English in the Low Countries. On 23 December Veseler printed another sheet under the title of *Corrant out of Italy, Germany, &c.*, and he went on publishing similar corantos regularly, or at any rate frequently, at least until 18 September 1621. During the latter year, there is evidence that four other series were printed in the Netherlands, two at Amsterdam, and one each at the Hague and at Alkmaar. The last two "series" are represented by only one issue each and the total number of issues known is only twenty-five. They are fully described in an appendix.

The explanation of these developments is hidden from us, and will probably remain hidden until somebody investigates this chapter in printing history at Amsterdam. How the idea of publishing English corantos suggested itself to Amsterdam printers—to several of them almost simultaneously, it would appear—we can scarcely even guess. Veseler and Jonson had both previously commenced publishing precisely similar corantos in Dutch and the English issues were doubtless merely translations of these. Veseler also printed, in 1621, two books of news in English.[46] From this fact we may surmise that he had his eye on the English market or on the English population in the Low Countries and that the publication of these corantos was an extension of his own coranto-publishing business. But on such slight grounds all conjecture is futile.

The next step, it is clear, was the publication of the corantos in London.[47] This innovation appears to have been effected in the autumn of 1621, for six issues of a coranto printed at London for N. B. have been preserved.[48] The first is dated 24 September and the last 22 October. Curiously enough, the Amsterdam corantos cease shortly before this date: the last issue is Veseler's sheet for 18 September. From this fact it could be argued that the

---

[46] 1) *Certaine articles made by the French Kinge and the Duke d'Espernon.* 2) *A notable And wonderfull sea-fight, Betweene Two . . . Spanish shipps, And a Small . . . English shipp.*

[47] Mr. J. B. Williams ("The Earliest English Corantos," *Library*, 3d ser., IV. 437–40) argues that "an earlier series was in existence than those published . . . in 1621." But his evidence depends upon interpreting the word *coranto* to mean strictly a part of a periodical series, whereas I believe it has not been proved that the word means more than a budget of foreign news. When the Rev. Joseph Mead, whom Mr. Williams quotes, speaks of his corantos, he does not necessarily mean the numbers of a periodical series, though he was receiving copies of the Amsterdam corantos at that very time; by the same token and because we know he received news from the continent, he certainly does not necessarily mean corantos printed in London. When he speaks of Archer as his "corrantor," we are not justified in assuming that he means more than his publisher or seller of foreign news. See above, p. 69, for two books, not budgets of news and not parts of a periodical, which are entitled corantos. When the publishers of the first English newspaper wish to emphasize its periodicity, they speak of it as the weekly news, not as a coranto.

[48] See appendix, p. 328.

Amsterdam issues were printed for a London bookseller who transferred the printing of them to London in September, but, of course, we have no way of making sure that the issue of 18 September is the last that was printed at Amsterdam. The London corantos, moreover, resemble Jonson's and Clarke's rather than Veseler's; their title was *Corante, or, newes from Italy, Germany, Hungarie, Spaine and France. 1621*, with variations in the list of countries. Some of them are marked "Out of the Hie Dutch Coppy" and others "Out of the Low Dutch Coppy," so that they did not all depend upon an original printed at Amsterdam, though, to be sure, we know nothing about the Amsterdam printers' sources. Unfortunately, the initials of the London publisher could stand for either Nicholas Bourne or Nathaniel Butter, both active newsmongers. It was, however, more likely Bourne, because his name appears as publisher on the first English newspaper (the successor to this series of corantos) sooner than Butter's, and Butter, though he eventually became the leading member of the syndicate which carried on the enterprise, at first seems to have published a rival periodical (the second English newspaper, I suppose we shall have to call it).[49]

As a matter of fact, these six corantos have a very good claim to be called the first English newspaper; it is chiefly because they were not brought to light until 1912 that the title has been so often awarded to the series of newsbooks which began in the spring of 1622. Furthermore, it is plain that the series of newsbooks, the so-called first English newspaper, is the successor to the London corantos. The newsbooks differ from them in no way whatsoever except in that they were printed as quarto books instead of

[49] Some, however, prefer Butter. See G. F. Barwick: "Corantos," *Library*, 3d ser., IV. 113; Williams: *op. cit.* I can think of no better reason to suppose that N. B. was Butter than that, at this time, Bourne is usually found publishing in association with Archer, and Butter generally played a lone hand.

single-sheets. They tell the same kind of news, in the same style, under the same rubrics, and they come from the same source—Dutch and German copies (pieced out with private letters). If we could fill the gap between October and May, we could begin "the first English newspaper" in 1621. At any rate, it was published continously until 1632, then countermanded by order of the state, resumed in 1638, and swallowed up in the confusion attending the outbreak of the Civil War.

It appears, then, that the first English periodical of news was an imitation of a foreign fashion, imported whole. It did not grow out of the body of news which, in various forms, had previously been published, though the periodicals of news in Germany and the Netherlands had, of course, grown out of similar beginnings. We cannot say that the books of news of the sixteenth century and the first twenty-one of the seventeenth produced the first English newspaper, but only that they paved the way for it. They spread news broadcast and created an appetite for it among the people; they showed the publishers where an opportunity lay and incited them to publish more and more news and to improve their methods of issuing it. In time, they might have resolved themselves into a periodical series, but before they had reached that stage in their course, the periodical idea, full-grown, was impressed upon the minds of a group of publishers by the example of their neighbors.

The old custom of publishing news in separate batches was by no means abandoned in 1622; on the contrary, it persisted through the remainder of the seventeenth century. Except during the first few years of the Civil War, newspapers never had a fair chance until after the revolution of 1688. When the first newspaper was extinguished by the government in 1632, the publishers reverted to the older method of publishing semi-annual collections. During all this time there was plenty of opportunity for whatever scraps of news the licensers would allow. Domestic news was entirely imparted by the same means it had always been, sporadic books of news, until 1641, and frequently thereafter. Even today news is sometimes printed in the same forms that served the sixteenth century. The ballad was still popular in England in the nineteenth century; it has scarcely disappeared entirely even today. In Paris, in the summer of 1927, when the city was rocking with laughter over the *affaire Daudet*, a ballad on the escape of this redoubtable journalist from prison was sold in the streets. A few years ago, in the United States, during the trial of one of those bills of divorcement which providence sends among us to appease the greedy appetites of our popular newspapers, books were offered for sale on the newsstands which purported to give a full account of the testimony which was too unsavory for even the most sensational newspapers to print. If this history has a moral, it is perhaps that news, like love, will find a way.

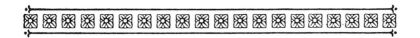

SUMMARY

IN THE history of the printing of news for public consumption during the period we have been reviewing, there is nothing to startle us or to upset any expectations we may have formed on the strength of our knowledge of the times. At the beginning of the last quarter of the fifteenth century, news awaited the introduction of the printing press into England; it was no upstart or novelty, but one of the oldest by-products of human intelligence. The printing press did nothing but carry it where it was wanted more cheaply, more copiously, more accurately, more quickly than it had been carried before. The usefulness of this invention in spreading information broadcast, in a form not subject to the vicissitudes which attended on the transmission of reports by word of mouth, was only gradually appreciated, but from the first some idea of this usefulness was grasped by persons and groups who, from interested motives, had need of reaching large sections of public opinion. In particular, the government itself found work for the new art in publishing to all parts of the nation information which it thought fit to be known and in justifying its courses to foreign princes; not later than 1520, we are sure, this use of the press was a part of the art of governing. Not far behind the anointed temporal powers were their adversaries, especially the opponents of their ecclesiastical policy, whose publicists and printers frequently found it a service to the cause to print information about public occurrences or to correct the reports of the enemy. Equally prompt to find a use for the printing press were the courtly poets, the authors of verses in honor of royal and noble patrons, who had no hesitation in giving their encomia to all the world, whose purpose was served all the better by doing so, and who thereby made known some information about the capital events in the lives of their masters.

After the accession of Queen Elizabeth in 1558, we find much more printed news than during the first half of the century and still more every new year. There are probably several reasons for the somewhat sudden increase in the number of pieces of news printed after the beginning of this golden age. Conditions in the printing trade account for a part of it: on the one hand, as the printing press became a more familiar instrument, it was more widely used for every purpose, and for new purposes, every year; on the other, the decline of the typographical art and the increase of the number of workmen seeking employment in the trade brought forth more and more trivial and ephemeral books. In the second place, the fact that the registers of the Company of Stationers commence at this time gives us a more nearly complete picture of the publishing of the succeeding years; at the same time, it is probably true that fewer books of the latter half of the century have been entirely lost, simply because there has been less time for them to get lost in. We know well enough that plenty of books printed after 1558 have not survived, what with the perishability of all man's handiwork, and, especially as far as books of news are concerned, the fact that printing of a momentary popularity was most likely to be read to tatters and, like present-day newspapers, to be cast aside when it had served its turn; there is every likelihood that an even smaller proportion of the books of news published before 1558 is known today. The entanglements of English political policy in the affairs of continental neighbors is another influence which brought more news to print in England, and probably the peace, the order, and the prosperity of the reign, which gave men the leisure and the security of mind to allow their curiosity free play, is another. Indeed, the very fact that the art of printing and the inquisitive spirit of the times had multiplied the literate population might be cited as one more. Finally, the temper of the nation—exuberant, venturesome, self-indulgent, proud, and fond of the curious as it was—ensured a reception for whatever news was put in print that could not have been expected in duller and straiter times.

At any rate, after the accession of Queen Elizabeth, we find not only a much greater abundance of the kinds of news that had previously been published, but also new varieties almost unknown before. The most important of these is the sensational and lurid reports of murders, miracles, monsters, and witches, written for the groundlings, which have been lumped in this discussion as popular news. The broadside ballad, which is a thing wholly aimed at the popular taste, and which, while it was likely to reflect in its artless way on any passing event, had a natural affinity for the wonderful, the extraordinary, and the shocking, must have existed in a rather robust state of health before the middle of the century, and the studious care with which an early printer like Wynkyn de Worde (*fl.* 1491–1535) catered to the popular taste makes us wonder that he did not print more news than he seems to have; yet the popular news published before the middle-point of the century is a mere trickle compared to the floodtide which flowed after it. Interesting as this news is to the present-day amateur of the curious for its own sake, its importance in this history lies in the fact that it brought news to people who had only a mild and puzzled interest in laborious accounts of diplomatic maneuvers and a faint appreciation of the studied conceits of courtly versifiers. The simple, jog-trot ballad restated events of

[321]

public moment and the virtues of national heroes in terms fit for their comprehension, shouting huzza at each new glory set in the crown of the English nation and opening the inexhaustible vials of its indignation on all traitors, enemies, and ill-wishers. But news of other and graver kinds was furnished in greater abundance at the same time—news from abroad, of which there was a really remarkable profusion, news of the discoveries and explorations of this adventurous century, news of affairs of state from disinterested sources, or, at any rate, from other sources than the government itself, news put forward as propaganda by mercantile interests and by the "favorers" of foreign powers, news of humbler persons and more commonplace occurrences.

This news was not published without some risk of danger to those concerned. for the government, eager as it often was to put information before the nation itself, watched others who did the same thing with a jealous eye. To publish news touching the state was a grave breach of a royal prerogative for which death was sometimes not too severe a punishment, and which always, according to the best official opinion, tended to disaffection and disorder. There were more ways in which a printed piece of news could offend ministers of the crown than even the wariest publisher could think of, so that the printing of news was constantly hampered and restricted by the official censorship and the fear of giving offense. We should surely have more news had not news of all kinds harbored so many dangerous possibilities and had the government been less swift to punish. It is largely in consequence of this fact that there is often a surprising unanimity of opinion in many news-reports about the ungratefulness and perversity of traitors lately hanged and quartered (let us say), that many reports of this kind are disappointingly vague about everything except that the traitor was the most

[322]

dangerous enemy to the queen drawing breath and that
he was undoubtedly drawn, hanged, and quartered, an
unrepentant Papist to the last, that much informing news
(usually accompanied by polemical thunder) was printed
secretly or in foreign parts, and that news-reports were
often put forth heavily swathed in moral or patriotic
sentiment so as to give the appearance of innocence.

Throughout this period, the publication of news depended partly, often entirely, on chance. News came to
the press more often of its own accord, on the wings of its
own urgency, than by the means which bring it to our
doorsteps today. There were no journalists in those
days whose ears were always cocked to hear its first
distant murmur, though there were writers, both hacks and
volunteers, and publishers who were usually ready to bestow some pains upon it when it drifted in their way. The
writing journalists of those days were not news-collectors,
but rather facile wits who applied themselves only to giving
to airy nothing, or information a little more substantial,
a local habitation and a name. The nearest counterpart
of the modern journalist is the sixteenth-century translator or compiler who spent a considerable fraction of his
time in translating and editing reports first printed in
foreign languages or the bookseller who, though usually
he never wrote a word of the news he published and at the
most could seldom have done more than the modern city
editor with his blue pencil, busied himself to find documents worth printing for the information they contained
and letters of news written to private persons. Most of
the collecting of news, in fact, was done by volunteers, by
anonymous witnesses and persons privy to the facts in
important occurrences who often had no idea that their
accounts would eventually be taken to the press. The
direct progenitor of the printed book of news is the private
letter of news. It was in these letters that news was

chiefly spread before the introduction of printing; it was in these letters that news was most abundantly collected for several centuries to come, until the newspaper-publishers perfected a system of their own for gathering news at its sources. A very large share of all the printed books of news mentioned in this treatise are confessedly copies of private letters, and many more were probably extracted from the same sources. Sometimes such letters were written by the agents of great nobles, ambitious statesmen, and merchant princes whose duties included the collection of news; sometimes they were written by friends and relatives to gratify the curiosity of their correspondents. Some of them were written spontaneously, without any thought of publication; others, more formal and decorous in style, were doubtless meant to be read by an audience of some extent, whether or not the writer was aware that they were destined to be printed. Indeed, it seems that when some one wished to offer information to the public, he would often write it out in the form of a letter to a real or imaginary friend. There is no evidence of any organization of the gathering of news except in the arrangements which we feel sure some publishers must have made, not later than 1590, to import books of news from the continent to be published in translation.

The publishers of news are the real heroes of this history, for it is they, rather than the writers, who are responsible for the fact that it is a history. After reviewing the evidence, we can hardly doubt that some of them were interested in news *per se*. They were interested in it, of course, as a commodity to sell, but, if that seems faint praise, what more could we say of such eminent journalists as John Walter or Mr. Ochs? They were not the publishers of tall historical folios or of the works of men of letters, but of anything that would interest a wide and not very discriminating circle of readers. Some of them

[324]

learned that news was something which falls into this category and applied themselves to supplying it, a few men almost to the exclusion of everything else. In doing so, they created an ever-widening audience, for the appetite for news grows by what it feeds on. Few of them, it would seem, were unusually capable men and they did not greatly improve their trade by collecting better news and publishing it in a more commodious form; but they stuck to their last, they did the best their somewhat unimaginative outlook indicated to them, and they did bring news to light in increasing quantity. If the publishers of the reign of King James had no conception of news, of the form best adapted to circulating it, or of the methods by which they might collect it except what the publishers of the first decade of Queen Elizabeth's reign had known, they had at least habituated the reading public, both high and low, to expecting it, and enjoying it, in much greater profusion.

Near the end of the reign of King James, the example given by the earliest newspapers of Germany and the Netherlands impressed itself on the minds of a group of London publishers with sufficient force to induce them to imitation. Thereupon the first English newspaper, so called in spite of the fact that it consisted of nothing but reports from the continent, took its start. The transition from the spasmodic series of reports from abroad published before 1622 by the booksellers who managed the first English newspaper and the less spasmodic, but not altogether regular, issues of the newspaper itself is easy and natural. At the start, it had nothing in common with what we understand by a newspaper to-day except the fact that it was a continuous enterprise: it never had a title by which every number was identified, and the idea of numbering the weekly issues in series did not suggest itself until the paper was six months old. It did not displace the occasional books of news in which Englishmen had been reading the current history of the world for a hundred and fifty years; it did not even exempt its own proprietors from the necessity of publishing occasional books as well. But it was a beginning, even though it was a beginning of which little came in the direct line—a beginning for which all the news reviewed in this history, likewise indirectly, had paved the way.

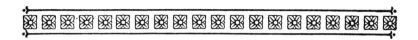

APPENDIX

The Single-sheet Corantos, 1620–1[1]

I. Amsterdam: printed by George Veseler (or Ioris Veseler or Veselde)

1) [No title.] *Imprinted at Amsterdam by George Veseler, A°. 1620. The 2. of Decemember.* And are to be soulde by Petrus Keerius, dvvelling in the Calverstreete, in the uncertaine time.

2) *Corrant out of Italy, Germany, &c.* [B. L. Same imprint.] *A°. 1620. The 23 of December.*

3) [Same title and imprint. B. L.] *1621. The 21 of Ianuari.*

4) *Courant out of Italy, Germany, &c.* [B. L. Same imprint.] *1621. The 31 of March.*

5) [Same title and imprint. B. L.] *1621. The 9 of April.*

6) *Courant Newes out of Italy, Germany, Bohemia, Poland; &c.* [B. L.] *Printed at Amsterdam,* By GEORGE VESELER. The 25. of MAY. [1621.]

7) CORANTE, OR, NEVVES FROM Italy and Germanie. *Printed in Amsterdam by* Ioris Veselde *the 20. of Iune* 1621.

8) [Same title and imprint as no. 6. B. L.] The 5. of IULY. [1621.]

9) [Same title and imprint. B. L.] The 9. of IULY. [1621.]

10) [Same title and imprint. B. L.] The 15. of IULY. [1621.]

11) Newes from the Low Countries, or a Courant out of Bohemia, Poland, Germanie, &c. Printed at Amsterdam by Ioris Veseler. August. 9. anno Dom. 1621.

12) *The Courant out of Italy and Germany, &c.* [B. L.] AT AMSTERDAM Printed by George Veseler. The 6. of Septembre. 1621.

13) [Same title and imprint. B. L.] The 12. of Septembre. 1621.

14) [Same title and imprint. B. L.] The 12. of Septembre. 1621.[2]

15) [Same title and imprint. B. L.] The 18 of Septembre. 1621.

II. Amsterdam: [Broer Jonson?]

1) COVRANTE, Or, Newes from Italy and Germany. Translated out of the Dutch Copie, and Printed at Amsterdam the 9. of Aprill, 1621.

---

[1] Seven of these corantos (Veseler 6, 7, [Jonson?] 1, 2, Jonson 1, 2, 3), hidden in MS. Harleian 389 at the British Museum, are, I believe, here described for the first time.

[2] A different and longer coranto, in part relating the same news as the preceding and, for the rest, new occurrences.

2) COVRANTE, Or, Newes from Italy and Germany, &c. Translated and taken out of the Letters come from these places aforesaid, and augmented with some newes from hence. Printed at Amsterdam this 22. of April. 1621.

III. Amsterdam: Broer Jonson

1) CORANTE, OR, NEVVES FROM Italy and Germanie. Printed in Amstelredam by Broer Ianson: dwelling on the new side, behinde Borchwa[ll] in the Siluer Can, by the Brewery, The 6. of Iune 1621.

2) CORANTE, OR, NEVVES FROM Italy, Germanie, Hungarie and Spaine. 1621. Printed at Amstelredam by Broer Ionson, dwelling on the new side behinde Borchwall in the siluer Can, by the Brewery, the 25. of June. 1621.

3) CORANTE, OR, NEVVES FROM Italy, Germanie, Hungarie, Spaine and France. 1621. [Same imprint.] the 3. of Iuly. 1621.

4) [Same title and imprint.] the 9. of Iuly. 1621.

5) CORANTE, OR, NEVVES FROM Italy, Germanie, Hungarie, Poland, Bohemia and France. 1621. Printed at Amstelredam by Broer Ionson, Corranter to his Excellencie, the 20. of Iuly.

6) CORANTE, OR, NEVVES FROM Italy, Germany, Hungaria, Bohemia, Spaine and Dutchland. 1621. Imprinted by *Broyer Iohnson* Corantere to his Excellency, the 2. of August. 1621.

IV. Alkmaar: M. H.

NEWES FROM THE LOW COVNTRIES. [B. L.] Printed at Altmore by M H, Iuly 29. 1621.

V. The Hague: Adrian Clarke

CORANTE, OR, NEVVES FROM Italy, Germany, Hungaria, Polonia, France, and Dutchland. 1621. [B. L.] Imprinted at the Hage by *Adrian Clarke*, the 10. of August. 1621.

VI. London: for N. B.

1) Corante, or, newes from Italy, Germany, Hungarie, Spaine and France. 1621. London Printed for N. B. September the 24. 1621. Out of the Hie Dutch Coppy printed at Franckford.

2) Corante, or weekely newes from Italy, Germany, Hungary, Poland, Bohemia, France and the Low Countreys. [B. L.] Printed at London for N. B. according to the Dutch copy, the 30. of Septemb. 1621.

3) Corant or vveekly nevves, from Italy, Germany, Hungaria, Polonia, Bohemia, France, and the Low-Countries. [B. L.] London Printed for N. B. October 2. 1621. Out of the Hie Dutch Coppy.

4) [Same title and imprint as no. 2. B. L.] the 6. of October. 1621.

5) [Same title as no. 3. B. L.] London Printed for N. B. October the 11. 1621. Out of the Low Dutch Coppy.

6) [Same title and imprint. B. L.] October the 22. 1621. Out of the High-Dutch Copy.

[328]

LIST OF WORKS CONSULTED

AND OF THE ABBREVIATIONS BY WHICH SOME OF THEM ARE REFERRED TO IN THE TEXT

Abbott (E. A.): Bacon and Essex. London, 1877.

Acts P. C. = Acts of the Privy Council of England. New series. Edited by John Roche Dasent *et al.* In progress (35 vols.). London, 1890–1927.

Albright (Evelyn M.): Dramatic publication in England, 1580–1640. N. Y., 1927.

Allen (William Cardinal): A briefe historie of the glorious martyrdom of twelve reverend priests. Edited by the Rev. J. H. Pollen, S. J. London, 1908.

Ames (Joseph): Typographical Antiquities; . . . augmented by William Herbert . . .; And now greatly enlarged . . . By the Rev. Thomas Frognall Dibdin. 4 vols. London, 1810.

Arber. = A transcript of the Registers of the Company of Stationers of London; 1554–1640 A.D. Edited by Edward Arber. 5 vols. London & Birmingham, 1875–94.

Bacon (Francis): The letters and life of Francis Bacon . . . collected . . . by James Spedding. 7 vols. London, 1861.

Barwick (George F.): Corantos. *Library*, 3d series, IV. 113 (A, il 1913).

Blades (William): The life and typography of William Caxton. 2 vols. London, 1861.

British Museum: Catalogue of books . . . printed in England, Scotland, and Ireland, and of books in English printed abroad, to the year 1640. 3 vols. London, 1884.

Bullen (George), ed.: Sex quam elegantissimæ epistolæ, printed by William Caxton in 1483. London, 1892.

C.S.P.D. = Calendar of state papers, domestic series, of the re,ₒn of Elizabeth, 1581–1590, preserved in Her Majesty's Public Record Office. Edited by Robert Lemon. London, 1865.

———: Calendar of state papers, domestic series, of the reign of James I. 1603–1610. 1619–1623. Edited by Mary Anne Everett Green. London, 1857, 1858.

C.H.E.L. = Cambridge History of English Literature. Edited by A. W. Ward & A. R. Waller. 14 vols. Cambridge, 1907–17.

Chappell (William): Popular music oᶠ the olden time. 2 vols. London, 1855–9.

Chappell (William) & Ebsworth (J. W.), edd.: The Roxburghe Ballads. 9 vols., 27 pts. London (Ballad Society), 1869–97.

Clark (Andrew), ed.: Shirburn Ballads 1585–1616. Oxford, 1907.

Collmann (Herbert L.), ed.: Ballads & broadsides . . . in the Library at Britwell Court Buckinghamshire. Oxford (privately printed), 1912.

D.N.B. = Dictionary of national biography. Edited by Leslie Stephen & Sidney Lee. 63 vols. N. Y., 1885–1900.

Deloney (Thomas): The Works of Thomas Deloney. Edited by Francis O. Mann. Oxford, 1912.

de Ricci (Seymour): A census of Caxtons. Bibliographical Society of London, Illustrated Monograph No. XV. London, 1909.

Duff (Edward Gordon): A century of the English book trade. [1457–1557.] London, 1905.

——: Fifteenth century English books. Bibliographical Society of London, Illustrated Monograph No. XVIII. London, 1917.

——: The Printers, Stationers and Bookbinders of Westminster and London from 1476 to 1535. Cambridge, 1906.

——: William Caxton. Chicago (Caxton Club), 1905.

—— *et al.*: Hand-lists of English printers, 1501–1556. London, 1895–1913.

Fairholt (Frederick W.): Lord Mayors' Pageants. Percy Society, vol. X. London, 1843–4.

Fincham (H. W.), ed.: Caoursin's Account of The Siege of Rhodes in 1480. Library Committee, Order of St. John of Jerusalem, Historical Pamphlet No. 2. London, 1926.

Firth (Charles H.): The ballad history of the reigns of Henry VII and Henry VIII. *Transactions of the Royal Historical Society*, 3d series, vol. II.

——: The ballad history of the Reigns of the later Tudors. *Ib.*, vol. III.

——: Ballad history of the Reign of James I. *Ib.*, vol. V.

——: Ballads and broadsides. *In* Shakespeare's England. 2 vols. Oxford, 1916.

——: Stuart tracts 1603–93. (Introduction.) Arber's English Garner, vol. 3. Westminster, 1903.

Gairdner (James), ed.: "The Spousells" of the Princess Mary, daughter of Henry VII, to Charles Prince of Castile. A.D. 1508. *Camden Miscellany*, vol. 9. London, 1895.

Gardiner (Samuel R.): History of England from the accession of James I. to the outbreak of the Civil War 1603–1642. 10 vols. London, 1883–4.

Gascoigne (George): Gascoigne's Princely pleasures, . . . presented before Queene Elizabeth at Kenilworth Castle in 1575. London, 1821.

Hales (J. W.) & Furnivall (F. J.), edd.: Bishop Percy's Folio Manuscript. 4 vols. London, 1867–8.

Hall (Arthur): An account of a quarrel between Arthur Hall and Melchisedek Mallorie. London, 1815.

Hart (W. H.): Index expurgatorius anglicanus. 5 pts. London, 1872–8.

Hawkes (Arthur J.): The Birchley Hall secret press. *Library*, 4th series, VII. 137 (September 1926).

Hazlitt (W. Carew): Hand-Book to the popular, poetical, and dramatic Literature of Great Britain, from the Invention of Printing to the Restoration. London, 1867.
————: Collections and notes 1867–76. London, 1876.
————: Second series of bibliographical collections and notes. London, 1882.
————: Third and final series of bibliographical collections and notes. London, 1887.
————: Supplements to the third and final series of bibliographical collections and notes. London, 1889.
————: Bibliographical Collections and Notes third and final series second supplement. London, 1892.
Historical Manuscripts Commission: Calendar of the manuscripts of the Most Hon. the Marquis of Salisbury. 14 pts. London, 1883–1923.
Ker (William P.): English literature medieval. N. Y.
Kingsford (Charles L.): English historical literature in the fifteenth century. Oxford, 1913.
Kleinpaul (Johannes): Die Fuggerzeitungen, 1568–1605. Abhandlung aus dem Institut für Zeitungskunde an der Universität Leipzig. Band 1, Heft 4. Leipzig, 1921.
Law (Thomas G.): Collected essays and reviews. Edinburgh, 1904.
Lemon (Robert): Catalogue of a collection of printed broadsides in the possession of the Society of Antiquaries. London, 1866.
Lilly (Joseph), ed.: A collection of 79 black letter ballads. London, 1867.
Lindsay (James L.), Earl of Crawford: A Bibliography of royal proclamations . . . 1485–1714, with an historical essay . . . by Robert Steele. 2 vols. (Bibliotheca Lindesiana. Catalogue of the printed books. Vol. 5–6.) Aberdeen, 1910.
McKerrow (Ronald B.): Booksellers, printers, and the stationers' trade. In Shakespeare's England. 2 vols. Oxford, 1916.
————: Printers' & Publishers' Devices in England & Scotland 1485–1640. Bibliographical Society of London, Illustrated Monograph No. XVI. London, 1913.
————, ed.: A dictionary of printers and booksellers . . . 1557–1640. London, 1910..
Minot (Laurence): The war ballads of Laurence Minot. Edited by Douglas C. Stedman. Dublin, 1917.
Morgan (J.), ed.: Phoenix Britannicus: Being a miscellaneous collection of Scarce and Curious tracts. London, 1732.
Nash (Thomas): The Works of Thomas Nashe. Edited by Ronald B. McKerrow. 5 vols. London, 1904–10.
Newdigate (Charles A.): Birchley—or St. Omers? Library, 4th series, VII. 303 (December 1926).
————: Notes on the seventeenth century printing press of the English college at Saint Omers. Ib., 3d series, X. 179, 223 (July, October 1919).
Nichols (John): The progresses and public processions of Queen Elizabeth. 3 vols. London, 1823.

[331]

Nichols (John): The progresses, processions, and magnificent festivities of King James the first. 4 vols. London, 1828.

Notestein (Wallace) & Relf (Frances H.), edd.: Commons debates for 1629. Research publications of the University of Minnesota. Studies in the Social Sciences Number 10. Minneapolis, 1921.

Park (Thomas), ed.: The Harleian miscellany. 10 vols. London, 1808–13.

Percy (Thomas), ed.: Reliques of Ancient English Poetry. Edited by Henry B. Wheatley. 3 vols. London, 1891.

Picot (É.) & Stein (H.), edd.: Recueil de pièces historiques imprimées sous le règne de Louis XI. Paris, 1923.

Plomer (Henry R.): A dictionary of the booksellers and printers who were at work . . . from 1641 to 1667. London, 1907.

Pollard (Albert F.): Tudor tracts 1532–88. (Introduction.) Arber's English Garner, vol. 2. Westminster, 1903.

Pollard (Alfred W.): Shakespeare's fight with the pirates and the problems of the transmission of his text. London, 1917.

Pollard (A. W.) & Redgrave (G. R.), edd.: A short-title catalogue of books printed in England, Scotland, & Ireland And of English Books Printed Abroad 1475–1640. London, 1926.

Read (Conyers): Mr. Secretary Walsingham and the policy of Queen Elizabeth. 3 vols. Oxford, 1925.

Reed (Arthur W.): Early Tudor drama. London, [1926].

Rollins (Hyder E.): An analytical index to the ballad-entries (1557–1709) in the registers of the Company of Stationers of London. *Studies in Philology,* XXI. 1 (January 1924).

———: The black-letter broadside ballad. *Publications of the Modern Language Association,* XXXIV. 258 (1919).

———: Notes on some English accounts of miraculous fasts. *Journal of American Folk-Lore,* XXXIV. 357 (1921).

———: Notes on the Shirburn Ballads. *Ib.,* XXX. 370 (1917).

———: William Elderton: Elizabethan actor and ballad-writer. *Studies in Philology,* XVII. 199 (1920).

———, ed.: Old English Ballads 1553–1625. Cambridge, 1920.

———: A Pepysian garland. Cambridge, 1922.

Salzmann (Louis F.): Original sources of English history. Cambridge, 1921.

[Say (C. E.):] Early English printed books in the University Library Cambridge (1475 to 1640). 4 vols. Cambridge, 1900–7.

Schottenloher (Karl): Flugblatt und Zeitung ein Wegweiser durch das gedruckte Tagesschrifttum. Bibliothek für Kunst- und Antiquitäten-Sammler, Band XXI. Berlin, 1922.

Scott (Walter), ed.: A collection of scarce and valuable tracts. Second edition. 13 vols. London, 1809.

Sheavyn (Phoebe): The Literary Profession in the Elizabethan Age. Manchester, 1909.

Shirburn Ballads. See Clark.

Sievers (Richard): Thomas Deloney, eine Studie über Balladen-litteratur der Shakspere-Zeit. *Palæstra* (Berlin), XXXVI (1904).

Simpson (Richard): Edmund Campion. London, 1867.

Skelton (John): The Earliest known Printed English Ballad. A ballade of the Scottysshe kynge. Edited by John Ashton. London, 1882.

Smith (John): Works. 1608–1631. Edited by Edward Arber. English Scholar's Library, no. 16. Birmingham, 1884.

Somers' *Tracts*. *See* Scott.

Stow (John): Annales, or, a general Chronicle of England. London, 1631.

Williams (Joseph B.), pseudonym: The earliest English corantos. *Library*, 3d series, IV. 437 (October 1913).

———: A history of English journalism to the foundation of the Gazette. London, 1908.

Wilson (F. P.): The plague in Shakespeare's London. Oxford, 1927.

Wright (Thomas), ed.: Queen Elizabeth and her Times, a series of original letters. 2 vols. London, 1838.

INDEX

In the alphabetical arrangement, titles are invariably entered according to the present-day spelling of the first word (articles, of course, neglected). Proper names are likewise entered according to the current spelling. After the name of a person, *A.* signifies that, on the pages following, citations of books &c. written, translated, or edited by that person will be found; *P.*, books &c. printed, published, or entered for publication. As a rule, these citations will be found in the footnotes. Entries from the Stationers' registers mentioned in the text are not indexed.

[335]

Bale, John, bp., 6; A.: 80.
Ballad concernynge the death of mr. Robart glover, A, 200.
Ballad intituled, A cold Pye for the Papistes, A [1570], 116.
Ballad intituled, A newe Well a daye, A [1570], 115.
Ballat intituled Northomberland newes, A [1570], 114.
Ballade of the scottysshe kynge, A [1513], 121, 195.
Ballad reioysinge the sodaine fall, A [1570], 115.
Ballads, 11, 31, 113, 118, 120 f., 129, 131, 135, 142 f., 146, 159, 188–203, 285, 294 f.; commenting on occurrences, 194 f., 198; conventionality of, 192; expressing personal opinions, 198–201; imperishability of, 201–3; lineage of, 189–91; popularity of, 191–3; relation of, to newsbooks, 196 f.; value of, as news, 193, 197; written to order, 224.
Ballad-writers, 17, 25, 31, 126, 143, 165, 191 f., 194 f., 222 ff.
Ballard, John, 119.
Bancroft, Richard, abp., 158, 195.
Bankes, Richard, P.: 135.
Bankyn, Agnes, 305.
Barenger, William, P.: 67.
Barker, Christopher, 38, 248 f.; P.: 37, 41, 44–6, 50, 54–8, 61, 67, 178, 294.
——, John, A.: 115, 154.
——, Robert, 53, 230 f.; P.: 37, 45, 48, 53–5.
Barley, William, 228, 263; P.: 27, 133, 149, 164 f., 175, 179, 235, 275, 313.
Barlow, W., A.: 254.
——, William, 61 f., 310; A.: 61.
Barnes, Barnaby, 226.
——, John, P.: 148, 183, 251.
——, Joseph, P.: 22, 24, 33, 99, 269.
——, Robert, D. D., 135.
Barnevelt displayed (1619), 179.
Barnevels Apology (1618), 179, 271.

Barrett, William, 273; P.: 157, 179.
Barrow, Henry, 79.
Bartlett, William, P.: 32, 126, 164.
Barton, Sir Andrew, 202.
Baskerville, Sir Thomas, 237 f.
Bate, Humphrey, P.: 133.
Battel of Birds . . . in Ireland, A [1622?], 130.
Bayles, Rev. Christopher (Thomas Bales), 136, 305.
Beale, John, P.: 251.
Beaton, David, abp., 80.
Beauvoir le Nocle, Jean de la Fin, seigneur de, 264 f.
Becon, Thomas, A.: 215.
Bedford, Francis Russell, earl of, 31 f.
——, Jasper Tudor, duke of, 30.
Beech, Robert, 141, 284.
Bell, Henry, P.: 215.
Bellamy, John, 283.
Belleforest, François de, A.: 88.
Bellet, Francis, P.: 92.
Berthelet, Thomas, P.: 42–3.
Best, George, A.: 281.
Bien Venu (1605), 27.
Bigges, Walter, A.: 122.
Bill, John, P.: 24, 37, 40, 45, 48, 98, 100.
Bills of mortality, 160–2.
Birch, William, A.: 18.
Birchensha, Ralph, A.: 131.
Bird, Roger, 166.
Biron, Charles de Gontaut, duc de, 125, 172, 175.
Bishop, George, P.: 78, 159, 179, 306.
Blackwall, William, P.: 146.
Blackwell, Rev. George, 48.
Blazyng Starre or burnyng Beacon, A (1580), 148.
Blessednes of Brytaine, The (1587), 18.
Blount, Edward, 228, 273; P.: 179.
Blower, Ralph, P.: 149, 164.
Bodrugan, Nicholas, A.: 59.
Body, John, 136.
Bohemica Iura Defensa (1620), 85.

Coranto (currant, courante), 70, 311 f., 315.
Courante of newes from the East India, A (1622), 69.
Corante, or nevves from Italy and Germanie (1621), 327 f.
Courant out of Italy and Germany, &c., The (1621), 327.
Corrant out of Italy, Germany, &c. (1620–1), 314, 327.
Coryat, Thomas, 271 f.
Cosby, Arnold, 295.
Cotton, Pierre, S. J., 95.
Courant Newes out of Italy, Germany, ... &c. (1621), 327.
Court trials, 46, 48, 53 f., 56, 60, 75, 77, 79, 156, 250 f.
Courtly poets, 13 ff., 140.
Courtney, Charles, 295.
Coverdale, Miles, bp., 77; A.: 77, 80.
Cowper, William, bp., A.: 216.
Cox, Francis, 100.
Craig, Sir Thomas, A.: 118.
Cranmer, Thomas, abp., 49, 76.
Credible reports from France and Flanders (1590), 171.
Creede, Thomas, P.: 151, 307.
Cresswell, Joseph, S. J., 91.
Criminals, 141–5, 193, 196, 252 f., 281, 284, 295.
Crompton, Richard, 57 f., 60, 88.
Cumberland, George Clifford, earl of, 128.

D., John, A.: 155.
D., R., A.: 183.
D., T., A.: 122.
Daniel, Samuel, 20, 24, 31, 140, 244.
Danter, John, P.: 148.
Daphnaida (1591), 31.
Darnley, Henry Stuart, baron, 118 f.
Darrell, Rev. John, 158 f.
Davies, John, of Hereford, 25; A.: 27, 142.

Davy, Sampson, A.: 116.
—— du Perron, Jacques, cardinal, 90, 92.
Dawson, Thomas, 284; P.: 102, 227, 250, 278.
Day, Angel, A.: 32.
——, John, 56, 226, 285; P.: 22, 49, 55, 57, 59, 77 f., 80, 116 f., 119, 131, 134, 173.
——, Richard, 228.
——, William, bp., 47; A.: 61.
De furoribus Gallicis (1573), 179.
De Iustitia Britannica (1584), 93.
De Maria Scotorum Regina ... Historia (1571), 119.
De Persecutione Anglicana, Epistola (1581), 91.
Deacon, Rev. John, A.: 159.
Declaration, conteyning the iust causes ... of this present warre, A (1542). 43.
Declaration exhibited to the French King, A (1587), 279.
Declaraciõ made at Poules Crosse ... by Alexander Seyton, The (1541), 98.
Declaration made by the Prynce of Conde, A (1562), 304.
Declaration made by the reformed churches of France, A (1621), 87.
Declaration of egregious Popish Impostures, A (1603), 48, 157.
Declaration of great troubles pretended against the Realme, A (1591), 37, 91 f.
Declaration of His Maiesties ... Pleasure ... in matter of Bountie, A (1611), 37.
Declaration of the causes, for the which, wee Frederick ... haue accepted of the crowne of Bohemia, A (1620), 84.
Declaration of the causes moouing the Queene ... to giue aide ... in the Lowe Countries, A (1585), 41, 44.
Declaration of the Causes moouing the Queenes Maiestie ... to ... send a Nauy to the Seas, A (1596), 44.

INDEX

Declaration of the causes, which mooued the chiefe commanders of the nauie, A (1589), 44.

Declaration of the Decree made by the Generall States, The (1619), 298.

Declaration of the demeanor . . . of . . . Raleigh, A (1618), 48.

Declaration of the fauourable dealing of her Maiesties Commissioners, A (1583), 55, 91.

Declaration of the lyfe and Death of Iohn Story, A (1571), 117.

Declaration of the Practises . . . by . . . Essex, A (1601), 48, 58.

Declaracyon of the procedynge of a conference, begon at Westminster, A [1559?], 47.

Declaration of the Quenes Maiestie: . . .Conteyning the causes which haue constrayned her to arme . . . her Subiectes, A [1562], 44.

Declaration of the recantation of Iohn Nichols, A (1581), 50.

Declaration of the Reformed Churches of France, The (1621), 87.

Declaration of the Sentence and deposition of Elizabeth, A (1588), 93.

Declaration of the true causes of the great troubles presupposed to be intended, A (1592), 92.

Declaration set forth by the Frenche kinge (1585), 279.

Declaration set forth by the protestants in France, A (1621), 86.

Declarations as well of the French king, as of the king of Nauarre, The (1589), 174.

Decree of the Court of Parliament at Paris, A (1615), 183.

Defence and true declaration of the thinges lately done in the lowe countrey, A (1571), 49.

Defence of the Catholyke cause, A (1602), 97.

Defence of the honour of Marie Quene of Scotlande, A (1569), 119.

Defence of the honorable execution of the Quene of Scots, A (1587), 120.

Dekker, Thomas, 23, 160, 227.

Delgadillo de Avellaneda, Bernaldino, 238.

Deloney, Thomas, 193, 222, 295; A.: 23, 127, 129.

Demoniacs, 157 f., 242, 291, 309.

Denham, Henry, P.: 164, 215.

Deposition of Don Diego Piementellj, The (1588), 128, 251.

Derby, Henry Stanley, earl of, 32 f., 77.

Derrick, John, A.: 131.

Der Straten, Derik van, P.: 80.

Discription of a monstrous Chylde, borne at Chychester, A (1562), 154.

Description of a monstrous pig . . . at Hamsted, The [1562], 155.

Discription of a rare or rather most monstrous fishe, The [1566], 152.

Discription of Nortons falcehood, A [1570], 115.

Description of the prosperitie . . . of the United Prouinces, A (1615), 180.

Des Diguieres, M., 86, 221.

Destruction and sacke cruelly committed by the Duke of Guyse, The [1562], 219.

Detection of that . . . Discours of Samuel Harshnet, A (1600), 158.

Detectioun of the duinges of Marie Quene of Scottes, Ane (1571), 56, 119, 177.

Determinations of the . . . vniuersities of Italy and Fraunce, The [1531], 42.

Dewes, Garrat, P.: 155.

Dialogue and complaint made vpon the siedge of Ostend, A (1602), 180.

Dialogicall Discourses of Spirits and Diuels (1601), 159.

Dight, Walter, 275 f.

Discourse and true recitall of . . . the victorie obtained by the French King, A (1590), 170.

Discourse concerninge the Spanishe fleete, A (1590), 129.

[343]

Floods, 162 f., 175, 181, 205 f., 210, 291, 302.
Fogny, Jean de, P.: 51.
Ford, John, 31; A.: 27.
Forme and shape of a monstrous Child, borne at Maydstone, The [1568], 155.
Fortunate Farewel to . . . Essex, The [1599], 131.
Fosbrooke, Nathaniel, P.: 24.
Fowler, John, 88; P.: 88.
Foxe, John, 78, 215, 226.
France, 44, 66, 68, 88, 90, 122, 124–6, 157, 168–80, 182–5, 187, 207, 219, 221, 236, 244, 248, 264 f., 271, 274, 279, 298, 303 f., 306 f., 311 f.
Franckton, John, P.: 131.
François I, king of France, 10, 27.
Franklin, James, 142 f.
Franklins Farewell to the World [1615?], 143.
Frederick, elector Palatine, king of Bohemia, 25 f., 72, 81, 83–5, 180, 186, 313.
French Kings Edict vpon the reducing of . . . Paris, The (1594), 274.
Friderici Nauseæ . . . Funebris Oratio (1536), 17.
Friendly Larum, or faythful warnynge, A [1570], 116.
Frendly farewel, which . . . Doctor Ridley . . . did write, A (1559), 77.
Frobisher, Sir Martin, 28.
Fulke, Dr. William, A.: 61.
Full declaration of the faith . . . of . . . Fredericke, . . . Elector Palatine, A (1614), 81.
Fuller, Nicholas, 75.
Fulwood, ——, 104.
Funerall elegie vpon the death of Henry, A (1613), 25.
Funeralles of King Edward the sixt, The (1560), 216–8.
Further Newes of Ostend (1601), 304.

G., M., A.: 33.
G., R., 56.

Gainsford, Thomas, A.: 131.
Game at Chesse, A, 98.
Gardiner, Stephen, bp., 6, 76.
Garnet, Henry, S. J., 53, 58, 136.
Garter, Bernard, A.: 28.
Gascoigne, George, 31, 188, 247; A.: 22, 286.
Gaufrydey, Lewis, 157.
Gaultier, Thomas, P.: 216.
Geneua. The forme of common praiers (1550), 80.
Gentile, Scipione, A.: 28.
Germany, 80, 126, 148, 150 f., 180 f., 220, 254, 277, 305, 307–14.
Gibson, William, A.: 115.
Gilbert, Sir Humphrey, 305.
——, Thomas, P.: 128.
Glemham, Edward, 133.
Gloucesters myte for the remembrance of Prince Henrie (1612), 24.
Glover, Robert, 200.
God doth blesse this realme for the receyving of straungers, 200.
Gods Handy-vvorke in vvonders (1615), 153.
Gods warning to his people of England (1607), 163.
Godlif, Francis, P.: 147, 155, 178.
Godly and Faythful Retractation . . . by Master Richard Smyth, A (1547), 98.
Godly ditty or prayer . . . for the preseruation of . . . our Queene, A [1569?], 114.
Godlie Dittie to be song for the preseruation of the . . . raigne, A (1586), 192.
Godly exhortation, by occasion of the late iudgement . . . at Parris-garden, A (1583), 204 f.
Golden Bull, The (1619), 186.
Golden Vanity, The, 203.
Golding, Arthur, 226; A.: 77, 164, 173, 179.
Goldwell, Henry, 244.
Gondomar, Diego Sarmiento de Acuña, count of, 72.

Good newes from Florence (1614), 187.
Good newes from Fraunce [1591?], 265.
Goodcole, Rev. Henry, 252, 293.
Goodman, Godfrey, bp., A.: 277.
"Good-nights," 144, 193, 196, 202.
Goodrich, Alice, 158.
Gordonius, Johannes, A.: 21.
Gossenius, Gerardus, M.D., 263.
Gosson, Henry, 283; P. 126, 131, 133 f.,
142 f., 146, 150, 165 f., 182, 197.
——, Thomas, 284; P.: 119, 312.
Gough, John, 105.
——, —— (stationer), 228; P.: 17, 27,
132, 215.
——, Sara, 105.
Governmental regulation, 7, 35 f., 48,
72 f., 107, 110, 112, 123, 168, 184, 213,
258, 288, 294, 317, 322.
Gowrie, John Ruthven, 3d earl, 20 f.
Grafton, Richard, 38, 54, 107, 228;
P.: 38, 43, 59, 80, 121.
*Grauissimæ . . . Italiæ, et Galliæ Aca-
demiarū censuræ* (1530), 42.
Gray, Sir Andrew, 313.
Great Brittaines Generall Ioyes (1613),
272.
Great Frost, The (1608), 165.
Greenwood, John, 79.
Greepe, Thomas, A.: 122.
Gregory XIII, pope, 128, 177.
Gresham, Edward, A.: 146.
Grey de Wilton, Arthur, 14th baron,
28, 131.
*Grieuances of the Owners and Masters
of shipping, The* [1621], 66.
Griffin, Edward, P.: 118, 313.
Griffith, William, P.: 77, 114 f., 154, 163.
Grimestone, Edward, 226; A.: 179.
Gubbins, Thomas, P.: 60, 127 f.
Guicciardini, Francesco, A.: 306.
Guise, François, duc de, 178, 219.
——, Henri I, duc de, 175, 177-9.
Gunpowder plot, 53, 117 f., 202, 296.
Gustavus II Adolphus, king of Sweden,
197.

H., M., P.: 328.
H., T., A.: 179.
Hacket, Thomas, 228; P.: 122.
——, William, 49 f., 117.
Hake, Edward, A.: 294.
Hales, Sir James, 76.
Hall, Arthur, 101.
——, Joseph, bp., 19, 310.
——, Rowland, P.: 80.
——, William, 265.
Hance, Rev. Everard, 103 f.
Harding, Rev. Thomas, 116.
Hardy, John, P.: 131, 163.
Haren, Rev. Jan, 277.
Harrison, James, A.: 59.
——, John, P.: 21.
——, Rev. John, 85.
——, Lucas, 286; P.: 80, 114 f., 179, 306.
H[arrison], Robert, A.: 126.
Harsnet, Samuel, abp., 158 f., A.: 48.
Hart, Andrew, P.: 24 f., 48.
Hartley, Rev. William, 136.
Hartwell, Abraham, A.: 159.
Harvey, Gabriel, 161, 226, 280.
Hasleton, Richard, 235.
Haslop, Henry, 228; A.: 122.
Hatton, Sir Christopher, 281.
Hawes, Edward, A.: 118.
——, Stephen, A.: 16.
Hawkins, Sir John, 28.
Hazardous journeys, 166.
Hearne, ——, 135.
*Hellish and horribble Councell, prac-
tised . . . by the Iesuites, The* (1610),
178.
Helme, John, P.: 25, 126.
Henri II, king of France, 108.
—— III, king of France, 170, 173 f.,
279, 303.
—— IV, king of Navarre and of
France, 45, 92, 94 f., 124-6, 149,
169-72, 174-6, 178 f., 184, 232, 236,
264 f., 274, 279, 312.
*Henrici octaui . . . ad Carolum Cesa-
rem . . . epistola* (1538), 42.

Henry V, king of England, 3.
—— VI, king of England, 14.
—— VII, king of England, 16, 23, 39, 68.
—— VIII, king of England, 10, 16, 23, 27, 37, 41–3, 80, 132, 167.
——, prince of Wales, 20 f., 24 f.
Henson, Francis, P.: 187.
Her maiesties most Princelie answere (1601), 55.
Hercusanus, Joannes, A.: 28, 120.
Here Begynneth The Iustes of the Moneth of Maye [1507], 140.
Hereafter ensue the trewe encountre . . . betwene Englāde and Scotlande [1513], 121.
Heroyk Life and Deplorable Death of . . . Henry the fourth, The (1612), 179.
Herring, Francis, M.D., 118.
Heywood, John, A.: 59.
——, Thomas, A.: 25.
Hilliard, Rev. John, 204, 292.
His maiesties declaration, Touching his proceedings in the . . . Parliament (1622), 40.
His Majesties speach in the Starre-Chamber (1616), 45.
His maiesties Speach in the Upper House (1621), 45.
His maiesties speach in this last Session (1605), 54, 230 f.
His majesties speech to both the Houses (1607), 53.
Hispanus Reformatus (1621), 98.
Histoire de la mort que . . . Campion . . . ont souffert, L' (1582), 96, 102.
Historie of Guicciardin, The (1579), 306.
Historie of Wyates rebellion, The (1554), 116, 242.
Hittchell, John, 204.
Hoc presenti libello . . . Cōtinentur . . . cerimonie & triūphi (1508), 23.
Hodgets, John, P.: 29.
Holibush, John, A.: 309.
Holinshed, Raphael, 226.

Holland, Compton, P.: 142.
——, Henry, P.: 152, 186.
Hollanders Declaration of the affaires of the East Indies, The (1622), 69.
Holy Bull, And Crusado of Rome, The (1588), 128, 230.
Honour of the Garter, The [1593?], 28.
Honour Triumphant (1606), 27.
Honorable actions of . . . Gleinham, The (1591), 133.
Honorable Entertainement . . . at Elue-tham, The (1591), 141.
Honourable Victorie obtained by Graue Maurice, The (1597), 197.
Hooper, John, bp., 77.
Hopton, Sir Owen, 51, 278.
Hoskins, Anthony, S. J., A.: 95.
Hotman, François, A.: 179.
How, William, P.: 116.
Howard, Lady Douglas, 31.
Hughes, Thomas, 22.
Humble, George, P.: 147.
Humble petition of the communaltie, The [1588?], 75.
Hume, David, A.: 25.
Humphrey, Laurence, A.: 22.
Hunsdon, George Carey, 2d baron, 89.
Hunt, Joseph, P.: 165.
Hurault, Michel, A.: 178
Hurlestone, Randall, A.: 215.
Hutton, Luke, 142, 202.

I Iohn Penry doo heare . . . set doune . . . my faith [1593], 79.
Illus[t]rissimi ac potentissimi regis . . . angliæ sententia (1537), 42.
Illustrissimi Principis Henrici Iusta (1613), 25.
Image of Irelande, The (1581), 131.
In effigiem Mariæ Reginæ, . . . Reg. matris (1603), 21.
In Henricum Fridericum . . . Lachrymæ (1612), 24.
In Mortem Serenissimæ Reginæ (1603), 278.

[358]

Vineyard (ship), 134.
Vision or dreame contayning the whole State of the Netherland warres, A (1615), 180.
Vox Populi, or Newes from Spayne (1620), 72, 177.
Vray discourse de la victoire . . . par . . . Henry 4., Le [1590], 170.

W., I., P.: 148.
W., R., A.: 134.
W., W., A.: 250.
Waldegrave, Robert, 107; P.: 20, 32, 80, 215, 244.
Walker, John, A.: 159.
Walkley, Thomas, P.: 146.
Walley, Henry, P.: 210.
——, Robert, P.: 28, 120, 134.
Walsh, John, 156.
Walsingham, Sir Francis, 59.
Ward, Roger, P.: 122.
——, Captain ——, 142.
Warnyng for Englande, A (1555), 71, 177.
Warning to the wise, A (1580), 164.
Waterhouse, Agnes, 302.
Waters, George, P.: 84 f.
Waterson, Simon, P.: 131.
Watkins, Richard, P.: 114.
Watson, Thomas, 31.
Wayland, John, P.: 108.
Webley, Thomas, 136.
Webster, John, A.: 25.
Wedderburn, David, A.: 25.
Weepe with Ioy (1603), 19.
Welby, William, 283; P.: 25, 27, 81, 163, 268, 311.
Weldon (*vere* Hewett), Rev. John, 136.
Wentworth, Thomas, baron, 117.
Westmoreland, Charles Neville, 6th earl of, 114.
Weston, Richard, 142 f.
——, William, S. J., 48.
Whetstone, George, A.: 31, 119.
Whitchurch, Edward, P.: 80.

White, Andrew, P.: 124, 133, 172, 297.
——, Edward, P.: 19, 23, 30, 77, 96, 103, 113, 120, 122, 126 f., 129, 135, 148, 150 f., 156, 163 f., 166 f., 171, 193, 275, 292, 295.
——, John, P.: 142, 303.
——, Sarah, P.: 25.
——, William, P.: 152, 277.
Whitgift, John, abp., 79.
Wilcox, Rev. Thomas, 212.
Wilkinson, William, 51.
William, prince of Orange, 173, 175, 179.
Williams, Sir Roger, 124.
Wilson, Robert, P.: 109.
Windet, John, 161, 273 f.; P.: 18, 118, 120, 162, 187, 238.
VVindie Yeare, The (1612), 165, 233.
Winning of Cales, The (1596), 193.
Winnington, John, 240.
Witchcraft, 48, 156 ff., 240, 250 f., 253, 275, 302.
Wither, George, 25.
Witnesses, 152, 155, 158, 240.
Wolf, John, 161, 230, 275 f., 278 f., 284–8; P.: 18, 28, 31 f., 55, 122, 126–9, 141, 146, 152, 158 f., 170–2, 179 f., 184 f., 187, 221, 248, 261, 265, 279, 295, 298, 302, 304, 307, 312 f.
Wolfe, Reginald, 226; P.: 31, 43 f., 98, 121.
Wonder woorth the reading, A (1617), 155.
Wonderfull Battell of Starelings, The (1622), 130.
Wonderfull discouerie of Elizabeth Sawyer, The (1621), 253, 293.
Wonderfull discouerie of witches in . . . Lancaster, The (1613), 251.
Wonderfull news of the death of Paule the .iii. [1552], 216.
VVonderfull yeare, The (1603), 160.
VVonders of this windie winter, The (1613), 165.